Mystery Women:
An Encyclopedia of
Leading Women Characters
in Mystery Fiction

Vol. III (1990-1999)

Part 2: M-Z & Index

Colleen Barnett

Poisoned Pen Press

Copyright ©2003 by Colleen Barnett

10 9 8 7 6 5 4 3 2 1

Library of Congress Catalog Card Number: 2001086357

ISBN: 1-59058-049-4

Poisoned Pen Press
6962 E. First Ave. Ste 103
Scottsdale, AZ 85251
www.poisonedpenpress.com
info@poisonedpenpress.com

Printed in the United States of America

Marti MacAlister

Author: Eleanor Taylor Bland

African-American policewoman Marti MacAlister found life in Chicago unbearable after her husband Johnny's death was termed a suicide by the Department. She transferred to nearby Lincoln Prairie, hoping to leave behind gambling, prostitution, drug dealing, and murder, but they had preceded her. Marti was tall and imposing, with four commendations from her ten years on the Chicago Police Department. Her children, Theo, initially aged nine, and Joanna, almost fifteen, put down roots in Lincoln Prairie. The family shared a house with a divorced teacher and her daughter. Paramedic Ben Walker became Marti's friend through work and his role as Theo's scoutmaster. Marti and her partner Vik Jessenovik, who had grown up in Lincoln Prairie, shared an office with vice cops Slim and Cowboy, bypassing racial and gender tensions.

In *Dead Time* (St. Martin, 1992), two children overheard a murder. The next morning schizophrenic Lauretta Dorsey, a former Navy therapist, was found dead. Vik and Marti, knowing that the children had been in the vicinity, had to locate them before the killer did.

Slow Burn (St. Martin, 1993) handed Vik and Marti a heavy caseload: arson at a clinic; the death of a young African-American man and the search for his sister; the killing of an impoverished elderly woman in a nearby apartment; and the reappearance of a pimp who preyed on teenage girls. The subplots were skillfully blended, and pragmatically addressed the racial problems that Marti and her family encountered.

Gone Quiet (St. Martin, 1994) began slowly with the death of Henry Hamilton, an elderly church deacon, but mounted in horror as Marti and Vik uncovered the chaos this old man had brought into the lives around him. A short-term substitute supervisor tested the partners, but Vik had the political connections needed to clear the case without interference.

The anniversary of her husband Johnny's death created tension for Marti and the children in *Done Wrong* (St. Martin, 1995). Her memories and anger intensified when the deaths of two of Johnny's fellow police officers confirmed her feeling that Johnny, a good cop, had been punished for his honesty.

Keep Still (St. Martin, 1996) found Marti awakening to the possibility that there might be another love in her life. Ben had become more than a family friend. Two major homicide cases (the death of an old woman who fell down her basement stairs and the drowning of a motel manager in the facility's pool) fused.

Marti and Vik were preoccupied with the murder of a young woman in *See No Evil* (St. Martin, 1998) and in helping the Vice Squad identify a Halloween flasher. Perhaps that was why she failed to notice signs of an intruder in her own home. Ghosts and a cat played roles in alerting Marti to death and danger.

The realization that discrimination had permeated the criminal justice system during the Sixties came home to Vik and Marti as they investigated the murder of an elderly member of a prominent family in *Tell No Tales* (St. Martin, 1999). Both were on edge: Marti was making the transition to married life and an expanded family; Vik was dealing with his wife's illness and a coexamination of the men who had shaped his youth.

In contrast to their own families where obstacles were overcome by love, Marti and Vik encountered dysfunctional relationships leading to arson, fraud, bombing and murder in *Scream in Silence* (St. Martin, 2000). A badly abused elderly woman had a son with an unreasoning hatred for anyone who offended him. A spoiled young man killed women for the pleasure he derived. A woman scarred by a teenage experience was unable to lead a normal life. These strands were woven into a blend of cozy and police procedural.

Relationships between mothers and their daughters dominated the narrative strains in *Whispers in the Dark* (St. Martin, 2001). Marti and Vik saw no way to solve the mystery surrounding the single arm found in a forested area until they connected the incident to body parts discovered as long as twenty years ago. They were drawn into the Lincoln Prairie artistic community, which may have included the killer as well as the victims. Sharon, Marti's closest friend since childhood, had been secretive about "Mr. Wonderful," the new man in her life. Neither Sharon's dying mother nor her neglected daughter Lisa were aware of the direction this relationship was taking.

Author Eleanor Taylor Bland did an excellent job of melding current social issues into tense narratives set in a Midwestern community.

Next book in this series: *Windy City Dying* (2002)

Devon MacDonald

Author: Nancy Baker Jacobs

Devon MacDonald, a thirty-three year old red-blonde, switched from schoolteacher to private investigator at a time of personal crisis. Her husband Noel disappeared shortly after their only child had been killed in a traffic accident. Devon, unable to return to a classroom filled with children near in age to her deceased son, searched for a new career. She settled into a partnership with ailing but avuncular detective Sam Sherman. Devon, the child of older parents, always felt unwanted, confirming her stance on abortion in favor of "wanted" children.

Devon had a child-related case in *The Turquoise Tattoo* (Putnam, 1991). A Jewish doctor, whose child needed a bone-marrow transplant, hired her to find children whom he parented through a medical school sperm bank. When a child was found, the legal father would not consider involvement. After he was poisoned, the doctor became a suspect.

Noel, whom Devon had not divorced, sought a reconciliation in *A Slash of Scarlet* (Putnam, 1992), but she was hesitant. She was searching for Brentwood Peters, a charming con man who had bilked several local women out of their savings. Devon went undercover as a potential victim, setting up an isolated confrontation that ended in murder.

In *The Silver Scalpel* (Putnam, 1993), Devon searched for a pregnant teenager at a time when St. Cloud, Minnesota was divided into Pro-Life and Pro-Choice supporters. Violence caused a fire at the Women's Medical Center, killing two occupants, but it was greed, not religion, that motivated the arson.

Devon's cases arose out of contemporary social problems, and tackled controversial issues.

Maggie MacGowen

Author: Wendy Hornsby

Margot Eugenie Duchamps MacGowen, had settled for "Maggie." She was 5' 7" tall, and had her nose redone because it had a bump. The daughter of a college professor, she had worked as a news anchor, then as a Los Angeles documentary filmmaker. She had met and married Scott, when he visited her parents to offer condolences for the death of her brother Marc in Vietnam. Maggie's sister Emily had responded to Marc's death by rebellion, conspiring to bomb a university building, thereby causing the death of a graduate student. In reparation, Emily became a doctor and dedicated her life to charitable work. After Maggie's divorce, she settled for shared custody of their daughter, Casey and received ownership of the family home in San Francisco. She shared it with an ugly dog, named Bowser.

As *Telling Lies* (Dutton, 1992) began, Maggie responded to Emily's call, but arrived too late to save her from a savage attack causing brain damage. The attack occurred at the time when Aleda Weston, a coparticipant in the bombing, had surrendered to the police after 22 years in hiding. The investigation, centering on the current lives of the ex-rebels, was compelling. Maggie developed a relationship with twice-divorced police detective Mike Flint.

In *Midnight Baby* (Dutton, 1993), Maggie worked with Guido Patrini on a film about children and their mothers, contrasting the neglected with the overindulged. She met fourteen-year-old Pisces who survived on the street by the Badger game, and worked with Sly, a nine-year-old thief and blackmailer. This exposed her to a world where children were sold for sex or inheritances, even by their own parents.

Mike Flint was anticipating retirement as *Bad Intent* (Dutton, 1994) opened. For all the intensity of their relationship, Maggie was a career woman unwilling to make a long-term commitment. In an atmosphere of racial politics, Mike had been accused of manufacturing evidence that sent an African-American man to prison. Maggie's interest in clearing Mike's name influenced the documentary film that she and Guido Patrini were producing, creating tensions between them.

Maggie tackled a major project under the auspices of a television network in *77th Street Requiem* (Dutton, 1995), reviewing the killing of a police officer, who had been a close personal friend of Mike. Her conflict of interest and her resentment of network pressure added to her concern. Evidence indicated that the killing of officer Roy Frady was connected to the Symbionese Liberation Army (SLA), Patty Hearst, and possible police involvement.

Maggie's life was in personal disarray as *A Hard Light* (Dutton, 1997) began. Her daughter, Casey, still a teenager, was considering a transfer to a Boston dance school. Mike Flint, burned out as a detective and revolted by a current case where teenagers tortured a young man, wanted to retire. A substantial offer had been made for the home that Maggie and Scott had occupied in San Francisco. She could use the money. Scott, now married and practicing law in Denver, was desperate to purchase the house. Into this confusion came a mystery from the past. Vietnamese refugees, employees of a museum, had assisted in the transfer of valuable artifacts to prevent them from being confiscated by the Communist regime. Some of those items were turning up for sale; and there were rumors of smuggled gold. Maggie turned her attention to the refugees. She would juxtapose their story with Mike's case on the teenagers in her next documentary. A complex, well-plotted story.

Maggie could be fearless and ruthless, loving but ambitious and successful, if not always likeable. The series had an explicit sexual flavor.

Kathryn Mackay

Author: Christine McGuire

Kathryn Mackay, a petite young divorcee, held her own in a courtroom. After Kathryn's father died, she had been raised by her mother and a strict stepfather in Kansas City, Missouri. The strictness provoked rebellion and, but for a kindly public defender, Kathryn might have ended up as a law-breaker instead of an attorney. In tribute to her mentor, Kathryn went from law school to the public defender's office. Embittered by the system, she transferred to the district attorney's office. Her marriage to fellow attorney Jack Hallam ended in divorce. His subsequent death was hard on their daughter Emma. She and Emma lived in Santa Rita, northern California.

As *Until Proven Guilty* (Pocket Books, 1993) began, the district attorney's office investigated sadistic killings by a man who courted attention, sending puzzles to the police. The media took advantage of leaks at headquarters to provide the notoriety the killer desired. Slowly the list of suspects was narrowed, although the killer fought back. The narrative contained considerable explicit brutality.

During *Until Justice Is Done* (Pocket, 1994), the police department and district attorney's office suffered from burnout. The extensive crimes, the legal loopholes, and the revolving door limited their capacity to deal with new cases. Witnesses feared to testify. Kathryn's former husband had been shot down in a courtroom. Emma panicked every time she was separated from her mother. Someone was taking the law in his hands killing rapists who evaded conviction. Kathryn had more than her reputation on the line.

As *Until Death Do Us Part* (Pocket, 1997) began, the primary investigator for the prosecution lost his arm when a package intended for the defense table exploded. His replacement, Dave Granz, had become very close to Kathryn and to Emma since Jack's death. Emma's special need for Kathryn's attention at this time had to compete with her mother's heavy caseload. It included: the prosecution of an HIV carrier who continued to have sex with women, an investigation as to the source of the bomb, and a series of deaths of men found in bondage situations killed by incendiary devices placed on their bodies. The narrative was interspersed with vignettes about "Angel," the serial killer. Dave and Kathryn put it all together, but not before another tragedy took place.

What was initially construed as a house fire in *Until the Bough Breaks* (Pocket, 1998) was declared murder/arson by Medical Examiner Morgan Nelson. Attorney Lawrence Lancaster was already dead when the fire broke out. Finding the culprit was only the first step. Anna Lawrence, his wife, based her defense on the battered woman's syndrome. Kathryn's focus was distracted by rape charges against her lover, investigator Dave Granz.

The sudden death of Kathryn's boss, District Attorney Hal Benton in *Until We Meet Again* (Pocket, 1999) led to her appointment as acting district attorney. Her efforts to solve the mysterious deaths of young Hispanic girls were sabotaged by a rival for that promotion. Her investigation of possible sexual abuses at a county medical facility brought her personal and professional lives into conflict again. The man who currently met her needs was Dr. Robert Simmons, director of the facility where the abuses occurred. She did not need a second betrayal.

Although she had been elected as district attorney of Santa Rita County by *Until The Day They Die* (Pocket, 2001), Kathryn did not concentrate on the conventional administrative and public roles of the office. She assumed personal responsibility for the highly publicized cases of infant kidnapping, working the crime scenes with her former lover, Dave Granz now in the Sheriff's department. She was still obsessed with locating Dr. Robert Simmons.

These were raw, terse narratives. Kathryn came across as rather unstable to hold high office.

Next books in this series: *Until the Final Verdict* (2002); *Until Judgment Day* (2003)

Joanna Mackenzie
Author: Margaret Duffy

Her work as an English police officer had given Joanna Mackenzie valuable experience. When terminated, she put her hard-earned skills to good use as a private investigator. Her cases occasionally brought her into contact with her former lover, Chief Inspector James Carrick. There were problems in the workplace. She was irked with her partner Lance Tyler. He co-opted the glamorous overseas assignments, relegating her to lost dogs and petty theft.

In *Dressed to Kill* (St. Martin, 1994), Joanna's probe of missing yard shrubs segued into the murder of an unpopular client and the theft of a valuable church reliquary. Both Carrick and Joanna were at risk of serious injury as they followed the intertwined trails of their cases. He wanted to resume their relationship, but she was deterred by the awareness of how much she physically resembled his deceased wife.

Carrick's career was at risk in *Prospect of Death* (St. Martin, 1996) when he was discovered in a wrecked car with an elevated alcohol blood content. He had spent the earlier evening with fellow Scots, celebrating the birthday of Robert Burns. Joanna enlisted the help of Patrick Gilliard (see Volume 2, Ingrid Langley Gilliard), a character from another series by author Margaret Duffy, to prove that Carrick was being framed to cover up a murder.

The relationship between Joanna and James Carrick was in a precarious state as *Music in the Blood* (Piatkus, 1997) began. His wife Kathleen was dead. Still, the affair he had with Joanna while she served as his sergeant had led to an official reprimand for him and a forced resignation by Joanna. Further estrangement arose when Carrick became over-involved with opera star Kimberley Devlin. Devlin had been buried alive after a hit-and-run accident. Carrick's interest in her attacker became part of a large-scale investigation by MI5. Patrick Gilliard and Joanna, who was now his employee, went undercover at a Scottish castle to end the smuggling of criminals into the United Kingdom.

Joanna and James Carrick were married as *A Fine Target* (Piatkus, 1998) began. She was out of town taking university courses when Carrick was notified that an abandoned car belonging to Patrick Gilliard had been found. It was not Patrick's body that lay nearby but that of his brother, Larry. Both Patrick and his wife Ingrid were the target of killers, remnants of a police unit that had gone beyond its authority. Patrick had killed their leader, but an associate sought revenge. The narrative ended with the rogue cops overcome by Carrick, Gilliard and his equally unscrupulous confederates. Neither Ingrid nor Joanna had any role in the action.

Good character development, intriguing plots from an established author.

Next book in this series: *A Hanging Matter* (2002)

Kate MacLean

Author: Noreen Gilpatrick

Kate MacLean had left the San Francisco Police department under a cloud. Unsure whether or not she was meant to be a police officer, she worked as a waitress in a variety of locations, then applied at the Eastside Police Department outside Seattle. She was assigned to paperwork until Sam Morrison took her on as his partner.

Because she was first on the scene during *Final Design* (Mysterious Press, 1993), Kate had primary responsibility for investigating the death of Catherine Fletcher, a partner in a struggling graphic arts business. Insurance coverage made the surviving partners suspect, but Kate probed Catherine's personal relationships: the husband whom she reamed in the divorce settlement, the daughter and grandson she ignored for years, the second husband who had been replaced by a lover. When two more members of the firm died of poison and the survivor was imprisoned, Kate persisted until she found the killer.

Although Kate and her partner, Sam Morrison, had become intimate, as *Shadow of Death* (Mysterious, 1995) opened, he gave his marriage another chance. For Sam that meant a transfer to the duty desk, and no ongoing contacts with Kate. This left her to deal alone with a major murder investigation. The corpse of a pregnant student from a highly structured religious school was found in a nearby forest. The administration of the school and church were indignant that any guilt might be attached to a member of their staff, but cooperated when a second murder occurred.

Kate bucked the system that, in turn, denied her adequate support, not an ideal situation for a female officer.

Annie MacPherson

Author: Janet L. Smith

After her parents' divorce, Annie MacPherson lived initially with her mother, who was married to a Hollywood producer. At fifteen, she joined her father in Seattle. A redheaded Phi Beta Kappa, Annie earned a magna cum laude degree in English before entering law school. After graduation she worked five years in the prosecutor's office, then turned to private practice.

Annie served as the power of attorney for Dorothy Lymon in *Sea of Troubles* (Ballantine, 1990). After her former husband died, Dorothy had inherited a plush resort in the nearby San Juan Islands. Annie was sent to arrange its sale. When a guest disappeared, the potential purchaser threatened to sue. Annie solved the disappearance and subsequent murder, not only to protect her client, but because she was attracted to the prime suspect, adventurer David Courtney.

Back in Seattle, Annie protected her interests when, in *Practice to Deceive* (Fawcett Columbine, 1992), she and her partner were absorbed by the firm in which her father had practiced. The death of a confidential secretary alerted Annie to the reason for her recruitment.

Loyalty to a former college friend motivated Annie to visit winemaking country in *A Vintage Murder* (Fawcett, 1994). Taylor North's friendship had once been important to Annie, but after a misunderstanding, they parted without resolving their problems. When Taylor's abusive husband was murdered at a winery gala, she was the obvious suspect. The second most likely suspect was an attractive wine maker, who had been Taylor's lover, and became Annie's, but greed was the motive behind the killing.

An underrated series, deserving of more notice.

Royce Madison

Author: Kieran York

Royce Madison had found acceptance in her hometown, Timber City, Colorado (population: 3,000). Her deceased father, Grady had been a popular Timber County sheriff. Her mother, Molly, ran the local bakery, Molly's Kitchen. The Madison family was among the early pioneers in the area. After three years in the Denver Police Department, Royce moved back home and was hired by her father's replacement to serve as a deputy. Because of strained feelings between Molly and Royce, she stayed at her grandmother Dora's rural home. Her closest friends in town were Gwen Ives and Nadine Atwell, honorary aunts who co-owned the local newspaper. They had a lesbian relationship, which made them supportive of Royce's orientation.

During *Timber City Masks* (Third Side Press, 1993), Gwen and Nadine were not supportive of Royce's affair with supercilious teacher Valeria Driscoll. Valeria spent much of her leisure time with wealthy heiress Trish Chandler-Sumner, preferring to keep her relationship with Royce sub rosa. Trish's murder brought Royce into conflict with the current sheriff, Yancy Sumner. Sumner's indolent brother Luther was Trish's widower and poised to inherit a fortune. Yancy provided Luther with an alibi and diverted the investigation to a young Native American, Ray Tierra-Blanca. Once involved in her own probe of Trish's death, Royce found clues to the murder of her father.

By *Crystal Mountain Veils* (Third Side, 1995), Royce had turned her attention to Hertha White, the new veterinarian, but that too posed a problem. Royce had been named acting sheriff, but was opposed in a forthcoming election. Her rival was backed by a right wing coalition that did not favor a woman sheriff, particularly one with a lesbian lover. Royce's big case was the murder of a vitriolic reporter, Sandra Holt. Holt had come to Crystal, where movie star Godiva was shooting a film. Costar Tyler McDermott was the son of a judge and of a leader of the right wing coalition. In solving these cases, Royce earned the respect of the men who served under her.

Lt. Gianna "Anna" Maglione

Author: Penny Mickelbury

Twenty years in the Washington D.C. police department had earned Gianna Maglione the leadership of the Hate Crimes Unit. She and her lesbian lover, African-American newspaper reporter Mimi Patterson, shared professional interests in the community, but from widely different perspectives. Gianna was tall with mahogany hair and hazel eyes. Her sexual orientation was not so much a problem in her job as was her tendency to ignore administrative tasks in favor of fieldwork.

The personal relationship between Gianna and Mimi was complicated by their professional responsibilities. In *Keeping Secrets* (Naiad, 1994), Gianna was determined to suppress information about a serial killer in order to protect her investigation. Mimi insisted on the right of the public to know and the need to inform potential victims. After the third victim, a pattern emerged. The killer targeted gay married men who continued to have homosexual affairs.

During *Night Songs* (Naiad, 1995), Gianna convinced her supervisors that the Hate Crimes Unit should handle crimes against prostitutes. The "Daniel Boone Killings" consisted of knives thrown from passing cars. Her task was more difficult because of the high profile suspects.

Magdalena "Maggie" Maguire

Author: Kate Bryan, pseudonym for Ellen Recknor

Maggie Maguire was a private investigator, a novel occupation for a female in the last quarter of the Nineteenth Century. The job utilized the substantial list of skills that she had developed in her peripatetic young life. When Maggie was two her mother died and her care was left to her father, "General" Custis Maguire. He was a huckster who ran a traveling circus in the Western states. Maggie received a grounding in classical education from the General who had attended an unnamed university. Over the course of thirteen years she had also learned jujitsu, knife throwing, marksmanship, card tricks, animal training, roping and riding, wire walking, tumbling and juggling. Her most unusual skill, which came in handy, was mesmerism (hypnosis).

Her ability as a contortionist made her valuable to her father as a shill when he sold his patent medicines. This unconventional education came to an end when the "General" realized that Maggie's increased physical maturity had attracted the attention of male members of his troupe. At age fifteen she was sent to Miss Sophia Beckmyer's Academy for Young Ladies of Good Breeding and Refinement. Given her ethnic heritage of Irish, English, Scotch, Dutch, French, Spanish, Portuguese and Mandan Indian, her "good breeding" may have fallen short. Her propensity for wild and explosive pranks eliminated any claims of refinement.

When the "General" died leaving Maggie without financial security, both she and Miss Sophia were happy to end her schooling. Given the small amount of money she had available, Maggie went to Chicago where she applied for work at the Pinkerton Detective Agency. Her tenure there ended when she quit, disappointed at the low level assignments she was given and appalled at the excessive use of force when the Pinkertons raided Jesse James' family home. She moved to San Francisco, recruited her somewhat older cousin Grady Maguire (out of jail), and set up M. Maguire & Co, Discreet Inquiries. She achieved some success over eight years, including regular work from Quincy Applegate of Western Mutual Specialties.

Puritanical, but crooked, timber baron Horace Hogg had willed a fortune to his missing daughter Harriet. At his death, Quincy Applegate hired Maggie to find the young woman in *Murder at Bent Elbow* (Berkley, 1998). There were conditions for the inheritance, Harriet was to present herself as a virginal, sober and stable young woman. This might not come easy for a child who had been abducted by Indians at the age of six, and only returned to society as a young woman. Maggie hesitated to take the case until she met the secondary beneficiary, Ralph Scaggs. When she found Harriet (now known as Hattie), a dirty drunken whore in Bent Elbow, Maggie contended with those who sought to learn Hattie's secrets and then kill her.

A Record of Death (Berkley, 1998) was more than faintly reminiscent of Agatha Christie's *And Then There Was None*. Oh, the guests invited to a free vacation on Cutthroat Island were not all murderers. Each guest had been invited by a person or group he or she was unwilling to offend. Their host, Sam Warden, made known to the group via an Edison "talking machine" that he was intent on revenge. Maggie and Grady were among the invitees.

Maggie could refuse Quincy Applegate nothing, so, in *Murder on the Barbary Coast* (Berkley, 1999), she went undercover as Magdalena Obermyer to the Children of Golgotha. Brother Ascension, an ex-convict, who induced his followers to bequeath him money, masterminded the cult. Grady, Otto Obermyer, and Quincy set up a scam to counter the con man before another person died suddenly.

These were romps into history with a dauntless heroine. Flaws may be found, but it is better to just enjoy.

Trish Maguire
Author: Natasha Cooper, pseudonym for Daphne Wright

Trish Maguire, an English barrister and Queen's Counsel, had a caseload focused on children. As an expert in this field, she spent spare time writing a treatise on the subject. Trish was programmed to burnout due to her need for success, and her emotional ties to the children whose cases she handled. She had no long-term relationship with a man, but has had serial short-term affairs. The question of how to prevent the abuse and neglect of children oppressed her because all of the solutions suggested (abortion, sterilization, and state intervention) had been ineffective or failed to meet the criteria of personal freedom that Trish espoused. Pondering these alternatives had slowed down her work on the book.

In *Creeping Ivy* (Simon & Schuster, 1998), Charlotte, the four-year-old daughter of Trish's cousin Antonia, disappeared. The police focused on the child's nanny (Nicky); on Antonia's lover (Robert Hithe), and on Antonia's former husband (Ben) who never believed Charlotte was his child. Trish had to move carefully because her innocent interest in the child had been manipulated by Antonia to add her to the suspect list. Antonia's character was explored to explain her part in the child's disappearance and eventual return.

Kara Huggate, a friend and a caring social worker was brutally assaulted and murdered shortly before she was to testify in Trish's case as *Fault Line* (Simon & Schuster, 1999) began. Perhaps Trish's involvement might have stopped then had not another client, Blair Collons, insisted that his firing and Kara's murder were motivated by their investigation of corruption in local government. The narrative also introduced Chief Inspector William Femur, his lesbian assistant "Cally" Lyalt, and cocky young constable Steve Owler. George Henton, the solicitor who was Trish's lover, quarreled with her because she refused to even meet her long absent father. George returned when Trish needed him.

Trish was not acting as a barrister when she involved herself in the reinvestigation of Deb Gibbert's conviction for murder during *Prey to All* (Simon & Schuster, 2000) She was providing legal advice to her friend Anna Grayling's television documentary on the case. Deb had been convicted of killing her contentious invalid father. Her primary supporter, Member of Parliament Malcolm Chaze, was subsequently murdered. Trish concentrated on Deb's troubled family and the possibility that the doctor who testified against her might have been prejudiced. To some degree, Trish's sympathy for Deb was based on similarities in their lives. Both had difficult relationships with their fathers. Trish's father, Paddy Maguire, had recently reinserted himself in her life. Trish's relationship with George had reached the point where they talked about having a child together.

Next book in this series: *Out of the Dark* (2002)

Sgt. Kathleen Mallory

Author: Carol O'Connell

Kathleen Mallory's origins were obscure, but they had been painful and surfaced in her dreams. She resisted delving into them as was recommended by the police psychologist. She had been rescued from the streets as a child of ten or eleven by New York City Detective Lou Markowitz, and cherished by his wife, Helen, as if she were their own. She joined the police force, reaching the rank of sergeant and earning distinction for her work with computers. Lou did not want Kathleen on the streets. He was unsure how much she had been marked by the experiences of her early life. Helen had sent Kathleen to parochial schools but she preferred Judaism. Neither faith made any deep impression on her, although she had a strong need for structure. She found it in computers and the Special Crimes Unit. She permitted almost no one to use her first name. She was "Mallory." She was interested in her appearance, but her apartment was sterile, organized to the point of obsessiveness.

During *Mallory's Oracle* (Putnam, 1994), Lou Markowitz was killed in an "unfashionable" neighborhood, investigating serial crimes against wealthy older women. Lou's replacement, Lt. Jack Coffey believed that Mallory was too emotionally involved to be effective, so he placed her on compassionate leave. This did not deter her from following the case, finding the killer, but escaping death only with the help of her eccentric friend, Charles Butler.

While still recuperating, Mallory was sent to a death in a public park in which the victim had initially been identified as "Mallory" in *The Man Who Cast Two Shadows* (Putnam, 1995). Following the trail of a jacket she had donated to charity, Mallory discovered the victim's identity, and moved into a posh residential hotel where the killer was one of several suspects. She maintained her partnership with Charles, investigating a young boy who might have paranormal powers, but who might also be a vicious killer. Her psychological limitations made Mallory unappreciative of Charles' fierce love.

Killing Critics (Putnam, 1996) placed Mallory in the Manhattan art world, following a trail first made by Markowitz. There had to be connections between the deaths of young dancer Aubry Gilette a decade before and that of artist Dean Starr. Starr had been stabbed in the presence of witnesses, who assumed his corpse was performance art. Hampered by bureaucratic and political interference, Mallory used religion, the Mafia, and those who loved her to determine whether the recent deaths were motivated by revenge or a fear of disclosure. The narrative left the reader uncertain as to Mallory's future.

When Mallory appearred in *Stone Angel* (Putnam, 1997) a.k.a. *Flight of the Stone Angel*, she was in Dayborn, Mississippi, the town where a mob had stoned her mother, Dr. Cassandra Shelley. Mallory did not need to know why, only who. She did not welcome the appearance of Charles Butler, who followed her there, or Sgt. Riker, who hoped to keep her from murder. Within hours after she arrived, Babe Laurie had been killed with a rock, and Sheriff Tom Jessop had placed Mallory under arrest. He and others of his clan had been part of the murderous mob from which Mallory had fled as a child. Charles persisted through lies, confusion, and violence that left the community in shambles, and Mallory still unhealed.

On her return to duty in *Shell Game* (Putnam, 1999) Mallory met a killer as cold, joyless, and intelligent as she. The death of a second rate magician when a complex illusion misfired, introduced her to other more practiced magicians. The group had a history, stretching back to their experiences in the Second World War, which had deeply affected their lives. The narrative was complex to the point of confusion, unsustained by emotional content. Readers who had hoped for some redemptive quality in Mallory after she resolved her childhood recollections, may be disappointed. Charles must be equally crippled to persist in a similar expectation.

It may not be possible to like Mallory, but it is difficult to forget her once encountered. A stunning series.

Next book in this series: *Crime School* (2002); *Dead Famous* (2003)

Wanda Mallory

Author: Valerie Frankel

Wanda Mallory was a redheaded New York City private investigator, who had been a researcher for a pornographic magazine. She was 5' 7", in her late twenties, usually dressed in Hanes T-shirts and jeans, but only occasionally wearing underwear of any brand. A Dartmouth graduate, she "fondled" her gun (named "Mame"). Her lover and assistant, photographer Alex Beaudine may have been attracted by her frequently mentioned mammary glands.

In *A Deadline for Murder* (Pocket, 1991), although hired by publisher Belle Beatrice to shadow her lover, Wanda was quickly dismissed as the bearer of bad news. Belle was strangled a short time later, and the police believed that Wanda either committed the crime or knew the killer.

In *Murder on Wheels* (Pocket, 1992), Alex and Wanda split when head biker Storm Bismark hired her to recover money he owed loan shark "Saint" Nick Vespucci. The investigation was punctuated by brutality, booze, and blither.

In *Prime Time for Murder* (Pocket, 1994), Wanda was hired to protect Sabrina Delorean, mistress of ceremonies for a television dating game. Sabrina survived the show, but a bullet that may have been intended for her killed a male contestant.

During *A Body to Die For* (Pocket, 1995), Wanda, while trailing her lover Max, met Jack Watson, a former pro tennis player who hired her to investigate Amaleth, his wealthy wife. When Amaleth's lover was murdered, Jack was arrested. Wanda frequented the athletic club run by Amaleth seeking another suspect. She ended up in the hospital, but with a wedding ring and a valuable formula to provide for her future. The pace was frenetic. The characters were eccentric, but not always appealing.

Hannah Malloy

Author: Annie Griffin, pseudonym for Sally Chapman

Although Hannah Malloy and her sister Kiki Goldstein were featured as partners in the series, Hannah emerged as the dominant character. Over the narratives, Kiki was more passive—a not too bright plump little woman who at sixty still thought of herself as a femme fatale. She rarely thought of anyone else, in fact. She was constantly in pursuit of a man, eligible or ineligible, interested or almost unaware of her. Part of Hannah's involvement in cases came through protecting Kiki. She was a codependent in her tolerance for Kiki's outlandish attire, her schemes to get male attention, and her self-centered reactions to tragedy. Both sisters had been married twice; both had lovers outside of marriage. Physically Hannah was tall, slim, and, when she chose to be, strikingly attractive. Like Kiki, a dyed blonde, she tinted her hair auburn.

Hannah was traditional only in comparison to Kiki. She was one year older, and had been employed as an executive secretary to the head of a major corporation. Still, she had been a hippie and protestor in the Sixties and had a wild side that emerged on occasion. In retirement she devoted time to her poetry, her garden (particularly roses) and to volunteer work (principally with cancer patients). She had been a cancer victim, undergone a double mastectomy, and for a considerable period of time avoided intimacy with males. Following the mastectomy, Hannah chose not to have reconstructive surgery, but found an alternative that satisfied her. There had been a third sister, who died leaving behind a daughter, Lauren. Lauren, an accountant, was as virginal and naïve as Kiki was sexually aggressive.

As the series began, Kiki was living with Hannah in her home in Hill Creek, California where both had grown up. The women shared the use of Kiki's elegant 1992 Cadillac convertible. Sylvia Plath, a pet Vietnamese pig, and Teresa E. Eliot, a dog, completed the household. The sisters had an agreement that whatever their sexual adventures might be, none would be carried out within the confines of their shared home. Both women were members of the Hill Creek Rose Club, and frequented the Book Stop Coffee House and Ellie's Lady Nail's emporium. The best gossip came from the latter.

Hill Creek was near San Francisco but had developed its own character. Most of the residents were wealthy, educated, and absorbed in whatever was currently popular as to variants in style, food tastes, personal development, and political attitudes. Naomi, neighbor and local psychic who communicated messages from a long deceased Native American, Red Moon, was a good friend and frequent accomplice. John Perez, a retired chief of police from a nearby city, became Hannah's friend, then lover. He finally accepted her need for danger and was there when she got into trouble.

As *A Very Eligible Corpse* (Berkley, 1998) began, Hannah was bored by her everyday life. She had her garden, the pets, her twice-a-month poem in the local paper and the volunteer work but they did not add up to much in the way of excitement. Thanks to Kiki, she soon had more stimulation than she wanted. Dour Arnold Lempke vowed to expose the Church of Revelations where his daugher Lisa was a member. When both Arnold and Reverend Swanson, the director of the church, were murdered, Kiki was arrested. She proved to be resilient while incarcerated—losing weight, exercising, and making friends with her hooker cellmate. Hannah was determined to prove Kiki's innocence. For the first time in years, Hannah felt a sense of purpose.

Matters of the heart were significant in *Date with the Perfect Dead Man* (Berkley, 1999). Kiki pursued screen director Frederick Casey when he attended the Hill Creek Film Festival, only to find him dead in bed. Lauren, the niece who had been sedately dating Detective Larry Morgan, fell madly in love with Casey's actor son, Brad. Even Hannah was affected. In Perez's absence, she enjoyed the admiration of Casey's partner, Hinkley

Bowden. Hannah was certain that the wrong person had been arrested for Casey's death and that of his assistant Angie. Some of what she learned was painful.

Geraldine Markham, retired botany teacher, had been a mentor to Hannah. In *Love and the Single Corpse* (Berkley, 2000), Geraldine and five members of her 1955 botany class met at the tree they had planted that year. Aware that Geraldine was ill, Hannah agreed to meet with her soon to discuss a problem. Not only was Geraldine murdered in her hospital bed, but Mendoza, her hired killer, lay stabbed to death in the room. Against all advice, Hannah sought the person who had hired Mendoza. She discovered a Geraldine she had never known existed in the process. The narrative continued Griffin's use of two murders with separate killers. Hannah's treatment of the second killer was more sympathetic in each instance.

Hannah's determination to prevent Signatech, a software producer, from moving into Hill Creek motivated her to run for mayor in *Tall, Dead, and Handsome* (Berkley 2001). The subsequent demise of her two rivals for the position raised Hannah to the level of murder suspect, causing her to be ostracized within her social circle. The victim, as in prior narratives, had been the object of one of Kiki's love fantasies. Author Annie Griffin's seemingly deliberate failure to make clear the last name for a character was annoying.

An interesting series, but hopefully the next narrative will have a suspect outside of Kiki's intimate acquaintances. Hannah was an interesting character; Kiki never developed.

Griffin, writing as Sally Chapman, is also the author of the Julie Blake series.

Munch Mancini

Author: Barbara Seranella

This series (set in California in the 1970s) presented Munch Mancini as a tiny auto mechanic with an incredible history. Munch's mother had been a hippie vagrant who died when Munch was nine. Most of their life together had been spent in communes. Her putative father, "Flower George" Mancini, was not only abusive but tried to pimp Munch. This proved to be more than she could handle so she shot him, but not mortally, and took off. Over the years, Munch had supported herself anyway she could, including prostitution. She discovered that working as an auto mechanic was safer in the long run. Her real name, Miranda, just didn't fit. She had begun her drug and alcohol abuse in her preteens. Munch loved machinery and was attracted to bikers, but was rejected by "Satan's Pride" because of her addictions.

In *No Human Involved* (St. Martin, 1997), Munch set out to learn who had killed Flower George. Mace St. John, an experienced detective, believed Munch was innocent of the crime. He was able to prove that George had already been dead when Munch took a shot at him. This did not clear Munch's record by any means. She had been arrested no less than thirteen times for assorted crimes under different names. She had been made pregnant by Sleaze Garillo, but aborted the child, leaving her infertile.

Now living in Venice Beach, California, Munch was walking the straight line as *No Offense Intended* (HarperCollins, 1999) began. She was under a suspended sentence with three years probation hanging over her head. One of the conditions was that she stay away from felons, but it wasn't easy. Jon "Sleaze" Garillo sought Munch's help for his infant daughter before he was killed. Munch's risk taking sent her back into an unsavory atmosphere. Equal attention was paid to the painstaking police work of Det. "Jigsaw" Blackstone who competed with FBI agents in solving Garillo's murder. Now Munch had another reason to stay straight, a child who needed a mother.

Munch remembered those who helped her kick her drug addiction. In *Unwanted Company* (HarperCollins, 2000), she reached out to help teenage friend Ellen Summers. Recently released from prison, Ellen needed a job and a place to stay. Her potential employment as a driver for Munch's limousine service turned into a disaster.

Within a short period of time during *Unfinished Business* (HarperCollins, 2001) Munch learned of the death and mutilation of Diane Bergman and the rape of Robin Davies. Both women had their cars serviced at the station where Munch had recently been promoted to department manager. Mace St. John, a detective who seriously tested Munch's current relationship with Garret Dimond, drew her into the investigation. However when she began to question a possible connection between the incidents and the station, Asia, her adopted daughter, was threatened. Never one to back away from a challenge, Munch persisted but it was twice as hard as she had anticipated.

Next books in this series: *No Man Standing* (2002); *Unpaid Dues* (2003).

Dr. Calista "Cal" Marley

Author: Bill Pomidor

Cal Marley and her husband, Plato, left medical school with ambitions as high as their student loans. They purchased a huge rundown house and delapidated furniture. Their household included an aging Australian shepherd dog (Foley) and a cat (Dante). Plato, who had attended Siegel, the Cleveland area medical school, had a large number of geriatric patients in his general practice office. Cal, a Chicago native with a degree from more prestigious Northwestern University Medical School, was a forensic pathologist and deputy coroner. Both held teaching positions at Seigel Medical College. She was a tiny blonde whose painstaking work made her intolerant of any less competent approach to medicine.

During *Murder by Prescription* (Signet, 1995), the couple spent their first wedding anniversary at a geriatric conference at which Plato was a presenter. The stay at Chippewa Creek Lodge was also an opportunity for Plato and other professionals to confer on a proposed textbook. When two members of the group died from ostensibly natural causes, Cal insisted on autopsies, researching combinations of drugs that might mask murder.

The Anatomy of Murder (Signet, 1996) found Cal and Plato tutoring failure-prone medical students in anatomy. All Cal had in mind was helping the students, but their cadaver was a university researcher whose death may have been too convenient.

By *Skeletons in the Closet* (Signet, 1997), Cal had become assistant professor of anatomy at Siegel Medical College, deputy coroner, and was on staff at Riverside General, where Plato was the primary physician in geriatrics. The discovery of a skeleton in the excavations for an addition to the College harkened back to similar corpses attributed to the Kingsbury Killer, who had never been identified. Cal investigated discrepancies in the skeleton collection of the college. There were nine more skeletons than there should have been. The death of a medical researcher at an award dinner connected to the most recent skeleton. Both Cal and Plato had a professional interest in tracing the skeletons to patients who had died prematurely.

Cal had been an important witness in the trial of mentally ill Jimmy Dubrowski, convicted as the Westside Strangler. Riverside Hospital's top managers were drafted into a survival bonding experience in *Ten Little Medicine Men* (Signet, 1998). The isolated setting provided a splendid opportunity for a killer to begin a campaign of revenge. Long hours with little personal time had become weariness for both Cal and Plato. They needed to make changes in their lives.

In *Mind Over Murder* (Signet, 1998), Jimmy Dubrowski escaped, leaving Cal vulnerable. She and Plato thought they would never be safe until Jimmy was returned to prison. Fortunately for Jimmy, they found another solution. That problem solved, Cal had a special Christmas gift for Plato.

Catchy and interesting at paperback prices.

Cat Marsala

Author: Barbara D'Amato

The titles, *Hardball, Hard Tack, Hard Luck, Hard Women* sounded clipped, competent, and explosive. Chicago reporter, Cat Marsala, who was short and stocky with dark hair and eyes derived from her Italian heritage, met those expectations. Still single in her early thirties, she worked freelance in a city with strong newspapers. She juggled on going relationships with two "steady" beaus: John Banks, an establishment type stockbroker who was there when she needed him, and Mike Murphy, a stereotypical alcoholic reporter who needed her. Cat had a parrot named "Long John Silver." Her brother Teddy had been convicted and sent to prison because of his drug activities.

It was a chance to interview drug legalization activist Louise Sugarman that enticed Cat to a sherry party in *Hardball* (Scribners, 1990). While she was sitting next to Louise, a bomb exploded killing the activist and leaving Cat partially amnesiac.

A cruise on a Lake Michigan sailboat hosted by a socially prominent Chicago family, Cat's assignment in *Hard Tack* (Scribners, 1991), sounded promising. She did not enjoy the internal tensions that surfaced in the close confines of the boat. When an obnoxious fellow guest had his throat slit, Cat sought the submerged motive for murder.

A trip downtown with her mom put Cat on a murder scene in *Hard Luck* (Scribners, 1992). The victim, a lottery executive whom she had planned to interview, dropped on her unexpectedly from an upper story window. Cat's employment prospects improved after media attention.

She was commissioned to produce a television segment on hookers in *Hard Women* (Scribners, 1993). Anxious to score on this one, Cat immersed herself in the milieu of prostitution. Her empathy so impressed Sandra Love, a high-class escort service employee, that when she was savagely beaten, she came to Cat for refuge. Sandra ended up dead, but she left a trail of HIV infected men behind.

In *Hard Case* (Scribners, 1994), Cat investigated a university hospital trauma center, spending five days in the midst of surgeons, nurses, and administrators who were trying to save lives, and one who was a killer. Dr. Sam Davidian, the trauma surgeon and a suspect in the death of the unit administrator, offered Cat a third choice. Mike Murphy was still fighting alcohol. John Banks was still boring.

Cat appeared more vulnerable during *Hard Christmas* (Scribners, 1995). Tired of murder and mayhem, she chose a "soft" assignment, tracing the growth, sale, and use of Christmas trees. The De Graafs of western Michigan wanted to keep the family tree farm, even though it was a marginal operation, or did they? Was there among the group someone who would kill to capitalize on the value of the land for development? Cat's special feeling for thirteen-year-old Nell made her reluctant to pry into the family's secrets, but she could not be silent once she learned the truth.

In *Hard Bargain* (Scribners, 1997), Cat responded to an emergency call from old friend Chicago Chief of Detectives Harold McCoo. She investigated a questionable shooting by police officer Shelly Daniels. Daniels had taken a domestic violence call to the home of her sister Marie that resulted in the death of her abusive brother-in-law, also a police officer. McCoo's handling of the case and leaks about the investigation from within his squad damaged his reputation at a time when top officials were jockeying for appointment to replace the current police superintendent. Careful review of the evidence by Cat saved Daniel's job and McCoo's reputation.

Cat had barely presented a visiting Dalmatian with a meaty bone in *Hard Evidence* (Scribners, 1999) when her dinner guest (and lover) Dr. Sam Davidian identified the bone as human. The most prestigious supermarket in Chicago asked Cat to identify the victim and the killer before their reputation went down the drain. The background of the setting was well researched but may be more than the readers want to know about meat departments.

Author Barbara D'Amato integrated the mystery in *Hard Road* (Scribners, 2001) into the Oz series by author Frank Baum, who had been a friend of her father. Cat's brother Barry, the director of an Oz Festival at Chicago's Grant Park, was suspected of murder partly because of Cat's testimony. Loyalty was important to the Marsala family. Cat had to find the killer or be ostracized.

D'Amato did remarkable research on the background of her narratives. This was an excellent series set in the Midwest.

Jennifer Marsh

Author: Judy Fitzwater

Jennifer Marsh's desire to be published verged on fanaticism. It was more than financial success that she needed. Her deceased parents had left her a trust fund that paid the rent. She had attended college but remained in her hometown. She and her partner Dee Dee Ivers ran a small but profitable catering business in Macon, Georgia. Dee Dee handled the meat dishes because Jennifer was a vegetarian. Her specialty was vegetable bouquets. The nine unpublished mystery novels on her closet shelf were a constant prod to her dissatisfaction. She was not alone in her ambition. She regularly attended a writer's critique group, most members of which were still waiting for publication. Others included: Teri, an African-American who wrote suspense novels; April, married and pregnant again who did children's books; Leigh Ann, who favored romance in her life and her fiction; and Monique, an older woman who had published once and only once. All took part in her investigations.

What made Jennifer even wackier was the way that she expressed her desire to have a child. She had already named this unconceived being, Jaimie, and carried on conversations with her/him. For the time being she settled for Muffy, her adopted greyhound. Her long time romance with investigative reporter Sam Culpepper was chaste to the point where it must have been difficult for him.

It was unreal to believe that Jennifer was willing to die in *Dying to Get Published* (Fawcett Crest, 1998). On the other hand she gave consideration to killing literary agent Penney Richmond. Plan A was to do so while leaving a trail that would draw police attention, but having an alibi that would prove her innocence. Plan B was needed when she ended up in jail for a murder she had not committed. Her potential alibi, attractive reporter Sam Culpepper was willing to help solve the murder.

Emma Walker had been a friend in need to Jennifer, but, in *Dying to Get Even* (Fawcett, 1999), Jennifer seemed unlikely to return the favor. She had come upon a dazed Emma at the site of her former husband Edgar's murder, holding the weapon in her hand. Raised Baptist, Jennifer could not lie on the witness stand when called by the prosecution. Gathering her critique group together, she hoped to make amends for her testimony by finding the real killer.

Obviously babies were important to Jennifer. In *Dying for a Clue* (Fawcett, 1999), she had two touches with reality. First, her experience in tagging along with sleazy private investigator Johnny Seeman could be dangerous. On their first outing he was shot and a nurse murdered. Second, she learned how deep was the bond between parent and child, for an adopted child as well as a birth child. The imaginary Jaimie was hard to stomach.

Jennifer knew that graduates attended class reunions primarily to gloat over their achievements—family, career, and financial success—so why would she attend one in *Dying to Remember* (Fawcett, 2000)? Leigh Ann, her pal from the critique group, did not want to go alone to the Riverside High School All Classes Reunion and had registered them both. A letter from Danny, her senior prom date, tipped the balance. Others had their own agendas for attending: to relieve guilt, to prove innocence, to resurrect the bones of a missing classmate. Jennifer had a strange ally in investigating Danny's death; his wife, Sheena, her worst enemy in high school.

In *Dying to be Murdered* (Fawcett, 2001), Jennifer had to be talked into accepting $1,000 to spend a week at the home of Mary Bedford Ashton. Mary was convinced that she would be killed. Jennifer's job was to chronicle the events in the Ashton mansion so that the murderer would be identified and prosecuted. A bloody bedroom and a missing corpse ended Jennifer's stay, but not her sense of duty.

The last two in the series showed considerable improvement. They presented Jennifer more favorably and had better plotting.

Next book in this series: *Dying to Get Her Man* (2002)

Dorothy Martin

Author: Jeanne M. Dams

Dorothy Martin, a recent widow, had left southern Indiana to settle in England, a move that she and her husband Frank had planned before his death. They had been retired teachers. Dorothy purchased a rundown Seventeenth Century gatehouse in Sherebury, an English cathedral town. She knew she would need time and money to bring the home up to her standards, but Dorothy enjoyed the challenge. Now she had time to read old friends—Agatha Christie, Ngaio Marsh, Dorothy L. Sayers, and new ones Ellis Peters and Charlotte MacLeod. Her friendly manner and distinctive hats drew attention among the locals, and encouraged friendships with neighbors.

One contact, that with Chief Constable Alan Nesbitt, came about during *The Body in the Transept* (Walker, 1995). Dorothy tripped over a corpse in the Cathedral. The death of unpopular Canon Billings was no accident. Dorothy methodically listed her suspects, followed a few red herrings, but eventually confronted a killer with a literary motive.

Alan saw Dorothy on a decorous level; although, in *Trouble in the Town Hall* (Walker, 1996), he made it clear that marriage was on his mind. Murder was on Dorothy's. She and cleaning woman Ada Finch had discovered the corpse of an unknown young man in the controversial Town Hall. The preservationists wanted the building repaired through local contributions. A major murder suspect wanted to renovate it as a mall. Because Alan was preoccupied with a royal visit, Dorothy took the murder investigation on herself.

Holy Terror in the Hebrides (Walker, 1997) a.k.a. *Death in Fingal's Cave* was a disappointment. Dorothy's "vacation" on Iona (an island off the coast of Scotland) forced her into contact with a group of squabbling religious advocates. When the least popular member of the lot fell to his death from the rocks in Fingal's Cave, Dorothy looked at his companions for a killer. Without Alan in support and isolated by a severe storm, she allowed her imagination to run rampant. When he rejoined her, Alan set Dorothy's mind at ease and made her an acceptable proposal.

Her intervention in murder investigations had provided stimulation in Dorothy's life. During *Malice in Miniature* (Walker, 1998), she was unable to restrain herself when her friend Ada's son Bob was accused, first of theft, then of murder. Even after Bob was exonerated, Dorothy persisted, sifting among other possible suspects until there was only one remaining. Alan had been offered a prestigious appointment at Bramshill Police Staff College. Awed by the social demands that would be made upon her as his wife, Dorothy withheld her approval of the move.

During *The Victim in Victoria Station* (Walker, 1999), while Alan was in Zimbabwe for a conference, Dorothy totally ignored police procedure. Upset when there was no mention of a death she had observed while riding the train, she enlisted friends to determine who the victim had been and why he had been murdered.

Who would kill kindly biologist Kevin Cassidy, formerly a professor at Randolph University where Dorothy's deceased husband Frank had worked? Cassidy had suspected that he was in danger, so, in *Killing Cassidy* (Walker, 2000), he arranged a $5,000 bequest to Dorothy, conditioned on her return to Hillsburg in the United States to collect the money. The letter accompanying the check revealed Cassidy's suspicions. Without status and treated with hostility by local police and suspects alike, Dorothy and Alan came to believe that there were grounds for Cassidy's fears. When Dorothy had been despondent about a miscarriage, Cassidy had spurred her back into activities. She owed him justice.

Like many criminal investigators in retirement, Alan never forgot the case, which he had failed to solve. In *To Perish in Penzance* (Walker, 2001),

Dorothy convinced Alan to vacation on the Cornish coast where, thirty years before, a young blonde woman had died of a drug overdose. Within days, Dorothy and Alan were helping the local police with the death of another young woman. Not only was Alexis Adams found in the same cave as the prior victim, but she was also her daughter. Alan found the local police cooperative. Dorothy, as always, took a strong role in questioning suspects and possible witnesses, using her intuition to good advantage.

Cozy and low key.

Next book in this series: *Sins Out of School* (2003)

Saz (Sarah) Martin

Author: Stella Duffy

Saz Martin, who had been raised in Kent, now lived in south London where she shared a relationship with Dr. Molly Steele (of Asian and Scottish parentage). Her parents accepted her lesbian orientation. They retained some hope that it was a temporary phase or that Saz would "settle down." Her sister Cassie had a more conventional life, the wife of Tony and mother of four children. Professionally, Saz was a private investigator. It remained to be seen how professional she was.

Calendar Girl (Serpent's Tail, 1994) was a disjointed narrative, almost experimental in its presentation, particularly when Maggie Simpson, a comedian who was embroiled in a lesbian affair, carried the narration. Meanwhile, Saz was hired by John, a heterosexual male who, although married, had an asexual relationship with a woman whom he had met regularly until she disappeared. John had loaned the mystery woman a sizeable amount of money. This was a case worth investigating. It took Saz to New York City where she worked undercover (very little) at the Calendar Girl Casino.

As *Wavewalker* (Serpent's Tail, 1996) opened, Saz received a recent picture of Dr. Max North and his heiress/sculptor wife Caron, an older picture of Max, plus twenty £50 notes. A subsequent phone call from an unidentified woman told Saz to investigate Max, who had merchandised a system of group therapy in England. Max, an American from a prosperous background, had a conventional medical and psychiatric education, but there was a substantial gap in his resume and personal history. Saz's client, for very personal reasons, wanted Saz to explore that time period. After her investigation, Saz wondered if her client were as dangerous as Max.

Beneath the Blonde (Serpent's Tail, 1997) first explored an earlier time spent together by two young girls, one of whom obsessed about the relationship when the other moved away. The second focus was on the current stalking of singer Siobhan Forrester. Two members of the musical group, *Beneath the Blonde*, were murdered before Saz, who had been hired to guard Siobhan, uncovered the events that haunted the group. It had seemed a wonderful opportunity for Saz to recover from the trauma and burns incurred in a prior case, but instead the case tested her sexually, emotionally and physically. She returned to Molly with secrets she could never reveal.

The decision to have a child involved intricate planning. Saz's egg would be fertilized by sperm from Chris Marquand, a gay friend. Molly, who had better health insurance, would be inseminated and bear the child. In *Fresh Flesh* (Serpent's Tail, 1999), there were unforeseen results. Chris' interest in finding his own birth parents had been put on hold when his adopted father was alive. Now, a father-to-be, he asked Saz to research the matter. Her investigation unearthed a conspiracy to sell infants. The children, now adults, had differing reactions to the disclosures. For one, there was a rage that he vented on Saz.

The narratives included explicit lesbian sexual passages.

Kate Martinelli a.k.a. K.C.

Author: Laurie R. King

Although Katerina Cecilia (K.C. or Casey), then Kate Martinelli, was raised in an Italian-Catholic family no parents or siblings appeared in the narratives. Her sexual orientation was only hinted at in *A Grave Talent* (St. Martin's 1993) where her lover, Lee, was not initially described as a female. Lee, a therapist, had been a teaching assistant at the University of California-Berkeley when Kate was a student. Until they met, Kate had considered herself heterosexual. Lee took part in an investigation of child murders by Kate and her crusty supervisor, Al Hawkin. The climax left Lee handicapped and Kate traumatized by her "outing" as a lesbian San Francisco police officer.

Kate spent a year behind a desk after the incident but was ready to return to work in *To Play the Fool* (St. Martin, 1995). In this context, the "fool" was not an irresponsible individual, but one who had detached himself to play the role of the jester. Brother Erasmus, a suspect in the killing of a street person, was such a man: difficult to find, even more difficult to understand. Kate sought the reason for his Biblical quotations and three-track life before she could induce him to testify against the killer.

On medical leave, Kate provided childcare for Jules, Al's twelve-year-old stepdaughter while he was on his honeymoon in *With Child* (St. Martin, 1996). Part of Kate's plan was to visit Lee, who had ended her "smothering" relationship with Kate. En route, Kate was disabled by a headache. She awoke the next morning to find Jules missing in an area terrorized by a serial killer, but he wrote the police stating she was not one of his victims. Lee and Kate worked together to find Jules and erase suspicion that Kate had killed the girl.

The anger, not only by females who had been physically and/or sexually abused by men, but also by those who empathized with them, burst into violence during *Night Work* (Bantam, 2000). Kate, who was generally sympathetic but not to the level of vigilantism, investigated the murders of males who had abused women and girls. Her involvement went beyond the professional level when her friend, lesbian minister Roz Hall fanned the women's rage to flames. Lee and Kate were considering parenthood, hopefully a girl baby.

Her publication through mainstream St. Martin's and Bantam plus an Edgar Award, can be seen as recognition both of author Laurie R. King's writing and of more general acceptance of the sub-genre. What distinguished Kate from many other lesbian sleuths was the low-level treatment of physical intimacy.

Caroline Masters

Author: Richard North Patterson

Caroline Masters, a tall dark American woman in her forties, who was estranged from her family, made minor appearances in two early books by author Richard North Patterson. During *Degree of Guilt* (Knopf, 1992), she presided over the murder trial of Mary Carelli, a prominent television reporter. Christopher Paget, father of her son, Carlos, had defended Carelli.

Paget, by then in love with his unhappily married assistant, Terri Peralta, became the murder suspect in *Eyes of a Child* (Knopf, 1994) when Terri's husband was killed. He chose Caroline, then in private practice, to defend him. Politics had influenced the district attorney's decision to prosecute.

The focus changed in *The Final Judgment* (Knopf, 1995) when Caroline became the primary character. She had a traumatic childhood during which she saw her unfaithful mother's fatal crash and suffered from the domineering control of her father. Depressed by the loss of her lover, Caroline left everything connected to her family in New England. She went to law school in California, eventually becoming a candidate for the U.S. Supreme Court. At that moment, her professional life had to be put on hold. Her niece Brett, who had a special claim on Caroline, was on trial for murder.

The tension in *Protect and Defend* (Knopf, 2000) arose from Republican control of the Senate and the recent election of a young Democratic president. The stage for conflict was set by (1) new legislation requiring the consent of one parent for an abortion of a minor when the fetus was viable; (2) the litigation brought by a fifteen-year-old daughter of pro-life parents seeking to have that law declared unconstitutional; and (3) a vacancy on the Supreme Court that could affect the outcome of that case. President Kilcannon nominated Caroline Masters, then an appellate court justice. He and Chad Palmer, chairman of the Senate Judiciary Committee, had to deal with a woman's right to an abortion within their own families or relationships. Caroline's past was up for scrutiny, exposing an action taken many years before that affected her life and the lives of others in her family. The narrative explored the personal and political impact of a question that divided the country. Like the prior appearances, this was a gripping narrative with well-developed characters and a dramatic conclusion.

Molly Masters

Author: Leslie O'Kane

Molly and Jim Masters were married when the series began, but separated temporarily due to his transfer to the Philippine Islands. By the time Jim applied for transfer back to the United States, Molly and their two children were occupying her parent's home in upper New York State. It had been seventeen years since Molly had been in the Albany suburb of Carlton, and she had mixed feelings. She was able to continue her work, designing personalized greetings to be sent via fax machine, while caring for Karen (age seven) and sensitive Nathan (only five). The Masters family had previously lived in Boulder, Colorado where Molly had established "Customers for Friendly Fax," and where she felt more integrated into the community.

Molly's return to Carlton in *Death and Faxes* (St. Martin, 1996) brought reminiscences of her prickly relationship with teacher Phoebe Kravett, whom Molly had unfairly criticized in the school newspaper. Mrs. Kravett, seemingly holding no grudge, had designated Molly as the administrator of a trust to fund scholarships for local students. Burdened with guilt, Molly had to make certain that one of her classmates had not murdered Phoebe.

Jim, Molly and the children remained in Carlton during *Just the Fax, Ma'am* (St. Martin, 1996). The philandering husband of a high school classmate entered Molly's cartoon in a contest sponsored by a pornographic magazine. When the husband died, Molly, feeling a need to strengthen her local reputation, risked life and limb to find his killer.

The Cold Hard Fax (Fawcett, 1998) placed Molly in the basement, as she witnessed the murder of the previous owner of her home through a small window. The victim, Helen Raleigh, had been digging in the Masters' yard. That was surprising. When Molly dug into Helen's past, she was even more surprised.

Molly's plans for a working vacation in the Denver area during *The Fax of Life* (Fawcett, 1999) went awry. The resort rented for her workshop was rundown. The participants' dislike for one another culminated in a murder. Evidence pointed to Molly as the killer, although she had no motive. Molly continued to risk her life although her children were still young.

As a parent, Molly took an interest in the local schools during *The School Board Murders* (Fawcett, 2000). As a daughter, she was even more concerned about accusations that her father Charlie Peterson was unfit to serve on the local school board. When his primary accuser was murdered, the problem escalated. Her husband Jim and Sgt. Tommy Newton were bypassed again when Molly risked her life to clear her father's name.

Molly's life was heavily focused on the schools again in *When the Fax Lady Sings* (Fawcett, 2001). She took part in a PTA fundraiser, appearing as one of seven clowns in a skit. Someone wearing a clown suit murdered the director of the production during the dress rehearsal. Even with a closed pool of suspects, Molly couldn't leave this one for the police to solve. Her business, faxable greeting cards, was not doing well. She needed to find a job that would keep her busy. The locals were referring to her as "Typhoid Molly."

Witty, but warm; loaded with red herrings and technicalities, but with credible killers. Molly was less credible; making tremendous demands on her husband's patience, risking her children's welfare; a loose cannon.

Next book in this series: *Death of a PTA Goddess* (2002)

Angela Matelli

Author: Wendi Lee

Angela Matelli grew up in a large family that needed all the help it could get. Her dad had abandoned them. Thanks to a hard working mother, Angela entered college, and then left Boston to join the Marine Corps where she served in the military police. While in the Corps, Angie drove for Colonel

Ev Morrow until their awareness of mutual attraction caused him to transfer her rather than incur the jealousy of his unstable wife, Earlene. After six years service, she returned to the Boston area, going into business as a solo private investigator. Angela invested her savings in an apartment building, partly occupied by family members.

She was *The Good Daughter* (St. Martin, 1994). An early client, Tom Grady, had been a partner of Angela's uncle, a police officer. He worried about his daughter's relationship with ex-convict Brian Scanlan, and well he might. Brian was connected to ILAP (International League for Advancement of Peace), an organization tied to IRA terrorism. Angela was in personal danger because she continued her investigation after Grady was killed. Angela utilized their common Marine Corps background to enlist the support of Detective Lee Randolph.

In *Missing Eden* (St. Martin, 1996), Ev Morrow, now stationed in California, needed Angie to find his daughter taken by Earlene to Boston. Angie found where Eden had been living but she had disappeared. The ravaged body of her best friend had been found on the seashore. Angie resisted her feelings for Morrow, but she could not abandon his child.

Deadbeat (St. Martin, 1999) had an interesting plot: the theft of credit cards; then, their expansion to new accounts on which major expenditures were made. Thanks to her widespread contacts, Angie traced one member of the gang who was killed shortly thereafter. She worked with the police department, but Angie had to save her own life with aikido. A heavy dose of the Matelli clan.

There was never a choice when Al, Angela's brother with Mafia connections, disappeared in *He Who Dies* (St. Martin, 2000). Family came first with Angela, even without her mother urging her to find Al. Finding Al became a problem when (1) they found his friend Eddie dead in Al's condo; (2) the police considered Al the most likely killer; and (3) most seriously, the Mafia found him first. Al had decided to go "straight" to preserve his marriage. The Mafia reacted very negatively. Angela called upon her network of cops, reporters, computer experts, and family members to help.

Angela was an interesting character, independent for her own needs but overburdened with the problems of her sisters. She had potential for further development.

Next book in this series: *Habeus Campus* (2002)

Nell (Mary) Matthews

Author: Eve K. Sandstrom

Nell Matthews' lack of trust in men traced back to her childhood. Her parents divorce, her father's disappearance, and her mother's death had scarred her. She might have understood her dad's need to leave, but not his failure to return when her mother died. Fortunately she had kindly grandparents who provided for her needs. College romances, even with the academic whom she referred to only as "Professor Tenure," never reached the level of commitment. Nell became the daytime "violence beat" reporter (police, sheriff's office, and fire department) for the Grantham, Oklahoma *Gazette*. She shared a house with her gay landlord Rocky Rutledge, graduate student Martha Henry, and nursery school teacher Brenda.

Nell and police officer Mike Svenson met in *The Violence Beat* (Onyx, 1997). Dan, the son of Irish Svenson, the deceased Grantham police chief, had returned to his hometown after reaching the rank of senior detective in the Chicago Police Department. People were skeptical of this decision as he had to start all over as a police officer, but his experience and skills were put to good use as head of the negotiating team. Mike rescued Nell and a small child in a hostage situation. Their subsequent romance had to survive a serious conflict of interest. The hostage taker had been murdered, leaving behind suspicions of Irish's murder. Nell balanced her responsibility to the *Gazette* against a need to help Mike clear his father's name.

By *The Homicide Report* (Onyx, 1998), Mike and Nell were nearing the end of a six-month period, after which they agreed to marry or end their relationship. That seemed less important when the death of unpopular *Gazette* copy editor Martina Gilroy had personal ramifications for Nell far beyond the crime itself. Martina had hinted that she was aware of information about Nell's family, particularly her father, Alan. The search for Martina's killer brought about a tender reunion, and the fear that it might not last.

In *The Smoking Gun* (Signet, 2000), Mike Svenson, now Nell's unofficial fiancé, killed the man who attacked Patsy Raymond, the director of the Grantham Women's Shelter. Mike, a skilled hostage negotiator, had a profound sense of failure. Not only had the attacker been the son of the most powerful woman in the Grantham area, but within twenty-four hours a second death occurred. This was not Nell's beat, but she could not leave the case alone.

Eve K. Sandstrom is a competent author. Nell is an interesting sleuth. A tad too many coincidences.

Dr. Lauren Maxwell

Author: Elizabeth Quinn

After the death of her veterinarian husband Max in a plane crash, Lauren Maxwell lived with her son Jake, daughter Jessie, and Nina Alexeyev who had been Max's partner. Although Nina was a lesbian, there was nothing but friendship between the two women. Both missed Max. Lauren, a Ph.D. in biology from the State University of New York-Buffalo, had moved to Alaska because of Max. She remained there as an investigator for the Wild America Society. Her previous experience had been with the Alaska Fish and Game Commission.

Out in the wilderness in *Murder Most Grizzly* (Pocket, 1993), Lauren came upon the ravaged corpse of her friend, Roland Taft, a solitary man who had devoted his life to the study of the grizzly bear. Dismayed with the official theory that Roland had been carrying a gun when attacked by a bear, Lauren solicited the help of Belle Doyon, a traditional Athabascan. Together they sought the ties between Taft's death and hunting parties, an angry father, and a vengeful government official.

Belle Doyon was shot but not killed in *A Wolf in Death's Clothing* (Pocket, 1995), possibly because of her opposition to expanded oil leases. Lauren, concerned with her son Jake's behavior, arranged for him to help the Indians gather fish and game for the winter. She remained nearby to monitor latent hostility by recent white settlers against the natives. Lauren's awareness of Athabascan mythology and tradition enabled her to distinguish between the need for scientific research and the right of the tribe to honor its dead.

Lauren met an attractive Russian botanist in *Lamb to the Slaughter* (Pocket, 1996) when she served as a guide for scientists meeting in Denali Park. Konstantin Zorich worked with Lauren to discover why murder was necessary to disrupt a scientific review.

Federal legislation authorizing the capture of orca whales for scientific research aroused environmentalists in *Killer Whale* (Pocket, 1997). The murder of Sam Larrabee, nephew of Lauren's best friend Vanessa, followed by the explosion of a fisherman's boat united Lauren, Vanessa, and biologist Owen Stuart against the whale hunters. Her two goals, to prevent the capture of the orcas and identify the killer, clashed in a thrilling conclusion.

Excellent series at paperback prices.

Dr. Haley McAlister

Author: Janice Kiecolt-Glaser

Haley McAlister, at forty, had a comfortable professional life as a clinical psychologist and college professor in Houston, Texas. Her personal life was shattered when Ian, the man with whom she had shared the prior eight years, died in a car accident. She referred to herself as a "widow" so perhaps they had been married, although she did not share his name. Haley had a prior short marriage when she was twenty-two.

Personal tragedy was not new to Haley. Her mother had died after the birth of her younger brother. Within a year, Haley had been diagnosed with leukemia. Although she recovered, she spent the years from age thirteen to fifteen in virtual seclusion. Even when she returned to school, she sensed reluctance on the part of her schoolmates to become close. Her personal isolation had given her sensitivity to the unspoken messages that people conveyed by their posture, facial expressions, and what they said. She turned this and her Ph.D. in psychology into a specialty; i.e. lie detection.

Unfortunately her experiences had made her less, not more sympathetic with the people she treated. She avoided individual therapy, preferring to work with groups. She exercised regularly, running and swimming at a health club. She lived in suburban Piney Point Village. Like many female sleuths she had an antique car: a 1960 Corvette convertible, which she treasured. Considering the risks she took, Haley was wise to have Pavlov, an impressive Great Dane, as a regular companion.

The death of graduate student Alicia Erbe in *Detecting Lies* (Avon, 1997) reinforced Haley's reluctance to give individual therapy. Alicia had requested the special attention while a member of a therapy group. The police and Haley's colleagues perceived her death as suicide—not a happy result for a treating professional. A lawsuit by Alicia's previously neglectful parents was a real possibility. It didn't help that Alicia's body had been found in a car parked outside Haley's office building. For subtle reasons Haley became convinced that Alicia had been murdered. To protect herself, she investigated Alicia's associates at the college.

Haley had seen Kitty Evanston very briefly as a possible test subject for memory loss after surgery. As *Unconscious Truths* (Avon, 1998) began, Kitty withdrew from the test group, planning to go to a different hospital for a second surgery. She was convinced that she had been under anaesthetized during a prior operation, causing her great pain and subsequent nightmares. Kitty's death occurred just as Haley began work on the renewal of a National Institute of Health grant to the Anesthesiology Department. Her interview with staff revealed a hostile work environment, exacerbated by nasty pranks. When the suspected prankster was murdered, Haley connected his death to Kitty's. She had no trouble in identifying liars from among the suspects. There were several.

Cassidy McCabe

Author: Alex Matthews

Cassidy McCabe was willing to take on almost any task. That was not necessarily a virtue in a social work trained therapist. A tiny divorcee in her thirties, Cassidy had a solo practice conducted from her home in Oak Park, Illinois. She had a stray cat (Starshine) for a companion, but allowed her house and yard to deteriorate. Although Cassidy advised others as to their personal crises, she had never recovered from her father's abandonment when she was five or from the end of her marriage to an unfaithful man. On at least one occasion, her reach so exceeded her grasp as to endanger her client. Cassidy's solo practice denied her the professional support of peers.

Cassidy was comfortable in tolerant and diverse Oak Park, which bordered on a tough Chicago area. In *Secret's Shadow* (Intrigue Press, 1996), she was stunned to learn that a client, Ryan Hollister, whom she had been treating for two years, had killed himself. Not only was the family threatening to sue, but Cassidy became convinced that Ryan had been murdered. Although Cassidy became romantically involved with Ryan's half-brother, Zach, a newspaper reporter, she still kept in touch with her feckless former husband.

During *Satan's Silence* (Intrigue, 1997), Cassidy not only shared a client's problems with Zach who used the material as the starting point for an investigative report, but went beyond her professional skill level. Based on information gained during this session, Cassidy uncovered serious child abuse and sacrifice.

Vendetta's Victim (Intrigue, 1998) alerted Cassidy to a man who preyed upon vulnerable women, introducing himself at funerals, and then seducing them into medically risky relationships. Her mother, never a resource, became a problem when she planned to marry a man whose children warned Cassidy that he was abusive.

Her responsibility as a citizen did not weigh heavily on Cassidy in *Wanton's Web* (Intrigue, 1999). She abetted Zach in the concealment of a crime, the murder of the woman who bore his son seventeen years before. Proving that Zach was innocent of the crime took longer. Her sense that

Zach's social background was superior to her own often seemed unduly important.

There was something for everyone in *Cat's Claw* (Intrigue, 2000). Zach, by now married to Cassidy was having problems separating himself from an undercover role. Cassidy's neighbors were murder victims and cat killers. Toss in an eccentric but lovable grandmother and an emotionally needy stepson. Unfortunately the ingredients were not a comfortable mix.

Never before *Death's Domain* (Intrigue, 2001) had Cassidy's personal and professional lives been so conflicted. A series of events (publication of her obituary, references to a regrettable incident in her past, and threats) consumed her life. Certain that the taunter was both dangerous and vengeful, Zach and Cassidy coexamined her past to avert a second tragedy. Zach too had problems, coping with Bryce, his recently discovered son. This may be the best of the series.

The narratives used italics at times to express Cassidy's inner thoughts. The plotting improved in the later books.

Next book in this series: *Wedding's Widow* (2003)

Christina McCall

Author: William Bernhardt

Ben Kincaid was the dominant character in the legal series in which Christina McCall made regular supporting appearances. Ben was a former government attorney who went into private practice in Oklahoma City. In *Primary Justice* (Ballantine, 1991), Kincaid was eagerly recruited by the large law firm in which Christina, a divorcee in her thirties, worked as a paralegal. She was as out of place in the money grasping, status conscious firm as was Ben. He was distinguished by his idealism; Christina by her strawberry colored hair, unconventional dress and inappropriate use of French phrases. She eagerly assisted Ben in burglary, and when his success forced him out of the firm, she quit her job.

In *Blind Justice* (Ballantine, 1992), Christina was employed by another large firm, while Ben opened his own struggling office. Her arrest for the murder of a reputed drug dealer put her in jail and Ben in conflict with the judicial system and the FBI.

During *Deadly Justice* (Ballantine, 1993), Ben tried corporate law. Christina served as his legal aide. She and his private office staff saw him as betraying his ideals for advancement. Eventually Christina and Ben's former brother-in-law police Lt. Mike Morelli saved Ben from himself and his unscrupulous legal associates.

Christina was so appalled at Ben's defense of a white supremacist in *Perfect Justice* (Ballantine, 1994) that she declined to work with him. He and other members of his staff successfully proved that his client was the dupe of a sinister organization and the victim of a vengeful woman.

Except for benefiting from a fashion update by Ben's mother, Christina played no significant role in *Cruel Justice* (Ballantine, 1996). Ben had accepted what seemed to be a hopeless case when he agreed to defend a developmentally disabled African-American youth in a murder case. Reminiscent of the better Perry Masons, he synthesized the information gained during interviews into a brilliant cross-examination that exposed the real killer.

In *Naked Justice* (Ballantine, 1997), a novel that included overtones of the O.J. Simpson trial, Ben defended Wallace Barrett, a former football star (now the first African-American mayor of Tulsa) who was accused of murdering his wife and two small children. Ben, currently caring for, and learning to care about, his eighteen-month-old nephew, needed a productive case. Christina had informed him that they were not making expenses. Ben came to believe that Barrett, whom he knew slightly as a parent at day care, was incapable of killing his children, and successfully defended him. Christina made Ben aware of a tricky highway curve that saved his life when he was stalked by an enemy from the past, but otherwise only served as emotional support.

By *Extreme Justice* (Ballantine, 1998), Ben had given up the practice of law and work on his book, turning to music to make a precarious living. When a precariously balanced corpse "dropped in" on his combo's opening night, the police department targeted Earl, the proprietor of the jazz "Emporium" and a past friend of the victim. Ben put his lawyer hat back on and enlisted the support of his former associates, including Christine, to help Earl. It was more comfortable than he had expected.

Ben barely remembered George Zakin, the environmental activist whom he had successfully defended in a murder trial six years before. In *Dark Justice* (Ballantine, 1999), their paths crossed again. Ben, on a book signing tour in a small Washington state town, learned that Zakin was charged with murder again. Although Ben sympathized with the environmental group involved, he deplored their violence. Christine and other staff members were summoned to help.

Ben was fatigued by a prior case, but not too tired to see Cecily Elkins in *Silent Justice* (Ballantine, 2000). Cecily's son had been one of eleven victims of leukemia caused by industrial pollution. Ben put his firm at financial risk to file a class action suit against Blaylock Corporation, the polluter that would be represented by the firm for whom Ben had previously worked. Mike Morelli had a case that ran parallel to Ben's, the murder of an executive at Blaylock, followed by other brutal killings with the same modus operandi. The cases eventually fused, along with information that a half-dozen fishing buddies were fighting over ill-gotten gains. Christine, now going to law school, remained at Ben's side cheering him on when he was ready to quit and sharing his danger.

The characteristics that Christina treasured about Ben were his downfall in *Murder One* (Ballantine, 2001): his devotion to his client, his belief in confidentiality, and his vulnerability to a woman who manipulated him. She stood by helplessly as his legal assistant until the point when he was arrested for murder, jailed, and treated very badly. By that time, she had graduated from law school with a distinguished record. She not only represented Ben as his attorney but also cooperated with him as he identified the real killer without compromising his ethics.

Christina added color and realism to Kincaid, but took a long time to develop as a character. She began as a Della Street clone, but her decision to go to law school moved her up a notch. As an attorney, she may hit the big time. The narratives usually began with a mysterious prologue, and ended with an unexpected revelation, after the more obvious solution was announced. Above average legal thrillers.

Next books in this series: *Criminal Intent* (2002); *Death Row* (2003)

Emily "Blue" McCarron

Author: Abigail Padgett

Blue McCarron had been raised Episcopalian, as would be appropriate since her father was an Episcopalian priest. As an adult she was unaffiliated with a church and considered eccentric by many. She was vegetarian, but that did not mean being different in California. Her mother, Betsy had died in a car accident when Blue and her twin brother were thirteen. A close family friend, Carter Upchurch, Blue's godmother, had assumed a maternal role in her life. Her brother David moved from juvenile delinquency to armed robbery and was sentenced to a Missouri prison. His redemption by a church visitor had led to a reconciliation between Blue and David.

Blue had become a computer whiz as a subjunct to her practice as a social psychologist at the Ph.D. level but rarely used the title, "Dr." Her doctoral dissertation *Ape* in which she made comparisons on the gender characteristics of apes and human had been published. As a social psychologist, her work was in predicting trends and advising businesses, rather than in clinical work so she did not need a client accessible office.

Blue's decision to purchase a vacant desert motel where she lived and had her office was based on the end of a relationship. The old motel went cheaply because there was no water on the premises. Misha, her lesbian lover, had left without explanation. As a result, Blue resigned her teaching position at San Gabriel University, although she continued to teach young girls at a juvenile detention center. Her subsequent African-American lover, Roxie Bouchie, a forensic psychiatrist, maintained a home in nearby San Diego.

It was time for Blue to cut off the crippling depression after Misha's disappearance. In *Blue* (Mysterious Press, 1998), she agreed to assist in the defense of Muffin Crandall, a sixty-one-year-old widow who was held for trial in the murder of a drug dealer whom she said had invaded her home. What distinguished these revelations was that the corpse had been stored in a freezer for five years until a power failure made its presence obvious. Blue arranged to have Roxie Bouchie evaluate Muffin's mental stability, but before any defensive strategy could be developed, Muffin was poisoned in the jail infirmary. At that point Blue thought it was over and planned to concentrate on locating Misha, but it had just begun. The ensuing struggle involved two of the most important people in Blue's life.

As *The Last Blue Plate Special* (Mysterious Press, 2001) began, Blue was designing polls for political candidate Kate Van Der Elst. A fundraiser was disrupted by the news that California State Assemblywoman Dixie Ross had died of a stroke. Blue and Roxie thought it strange that another female California State Senator had died in a similar incident only two weeks before. Evidence mounted that a serial killer was targeting women who had achieved success in occupations previously dominated by men. In Blue's personal life, she was forced to make a painful decision.

Author Abigail Padgett is also the author of the "Bo" Bradley series. (See page 79.)

Dr. Gail McCarthy

Author: Laura Crum

In spite of the fact that her parents died before she entered college, Gail McCarthy never gave up her dream of becoming a veterinarian. She worked at other jobs until she graduated from the University of California-Davis with her D.V.M. Her job at the Santa Cruz Equine Practice returned Gail to her hometown. In addition to her elderly and ill-humored Australian Cattle Dog (Blue), she had rescued a gelded quarter horse (Gunner) from euthanasia, and adopted an injured tabby cat. Fiercely independent and living in a small cabin, Gail had never married although she had a relationship with an older man, Lonny Peterson. She was a tall, dark-haired woman in her thirties, who enjoyed winter sports.

In *Cutter* (St. Martin, 1994), the investigating officer considered the death of cutting horse trainer Casey Brooks on a well-schooled mount to be an accident, but Gail was unconvinced. Casey had been harsh in his criticism of other trainers and owners, and his death occurred shortly after horses in his care had been poisoned. Her method of detection was to ask questions until the threatened killer retaliated.

Gail stumbled on two corpses in *Hoofprints* (St. Martin, 1996). After she found the murdered bodies of Cindy and Ed Whitney, Gail barely missed death at the hands of a sniper and was threatened by a hired killer. Only a chance encounter put her in a position to end her fears and expose a treacherous friend.

A training session at Lake Tahoe gave Gail a chance to ski while earning education credits as *Roughstock* (St. Martin, 1997) began. Her former vet school roommate, Joanna Lund, was diverted by the attentions of thrice divorced Jack Hollister. Jack's murder placed suspicion on Joanna and sent Gail on the trail of his three ex-wives and others who would benefit from his death.

In *Roped* (St. Martin, 1998), rancher Glen Bennett was plagued by accidents (some deadly), but he refused to bring in law enforcement. His daughter, Lisa, a high school friend of Gail's, was frantic, aware that the incidents were escalating and that some member of her family was probably involved. On a personal level, Gail moved to a larger place, but not with Lonny who had finally filed for divorce.

Just before Gail took off on a long awaited solo trip into the mountains in *Slickrock* (St. Martin, 1999), she discovered the dying Bill Evans, a veterinarian who did not want to live. Something in that encounter made Gail sense danger. As she traversed the hills and meadows with her horses and dog, meeting other groups of campers, she was cautious. Whom of the other riders could she trust? A redheaded stranger seemed her best bet, and her future. Lovely descriptions of the terrain.

The relationship with Lonny had ended by *Breakaway* (St. Martin, 2001). Whatever had been there for either of them was not strong enough to keep Lonny from moving away or to cause Gail to go with him. She was aware that, even with a partnership in the veterinary practice and the home she had carefully constructed, she was depressed. Intellectually, she knew that the early death of her parents and the struggle for her career had developed a need for independence that limited her personal future. Nicole Devereaux, an expatriate artist, whose horse had been sexually abused by a

human male, fascinated her. Nicole refused to involve the police, but Gail wondered if the crimes might escalate.

The primary plot was interspersed with warm, fuzzy James Herriott-like tales that horse lovers will enjoy.

Next book in this series: *Hayburner* (2003)

Lara McClintoch

Author: Lyn Hamilton

Lara McClintoch had made a business out of her knowledge of antiques. She and husband Clive Swain had been partners in a shop located in the Yorkville area of Toronto. The collapse of their marriage ended cooperation between them. Clive opened up a nearby store. Lara continued with a series of business partners (most recently Sarah Greenhalgh) and lovers (Lucas May who remained a friend after their affair ended). Clive's second wife Celeste, had sufficient resources to indulge him in a business without immediate prospects for success. Lara's shop cat, Diesel, lasted through many of the changes. Lara had been raised in a middle class Presbyterian home, she now inclined towards an earth mother concept of life, like that which existed in Malta centuries before and still lingered.

A cryptic message from Lara's old friend, Dr. Hernan Castillo Rivas sent her to Merida, Mexico in *The Xibalba Murders* (Berkley, 1997). Within days his corpse was found in the museum where he had formerly served as director. Fortunately Lara had good friends in Merida where she had spent part of her early years. With their aid she was able to overcome those who conspired to sell indigenous artifacts to foreign dealers. Among her newer friends was one whose loyalty she came to doubt. On Lara's return she purchased an interest in the antique shop, which she had sold to settle her divorce from Clive.

Martin Galea, a prominent Toronto architect with whom Lara had briefly considered an affair, sought her out in *The Maltese Goddess* (Berkley, 1998). He wanted someone to prepare his Maltese home for an important meeting. Considering that he made many purchases at her shop and that the trip would be something of a vacation, she agreed. When the newly purchased furniture arrived in Malta, an unfamiliar chest contained Galea's body. Attractive Sgt. Robert Luczka of the RCMP, who was assigned to work with the Maltese police, assisted Lara in preventing an assassination. Bad news waited on her return to Toronto.

The Moche Warrior (Berkley, 1999) was set in the coastal region of Peru where a pre-Incan treasure brought together smugglers, archeologists, and killers. Lara joined them incognito to save her business and her reputation. She had purchased at an auction a box of Peruvian antiquities that included the warrior, an ear ornament. Subsequently her shop had been robbed and a corpse left behind. Sgt. Rob Luczka, RCMP, had a conflict of interest: his responsibility as a police officer and his growing affection for Lara.

Lara accompanied her friend Alex Stewart to Ireland to claim an inheritance in *The Celtic Riddle* (Berkley, 2000). The decedent had left behind a dwindling fortune, a squabbling family and a vengeful enemy. A hidden treasure meant to restore the family solidarity was to be located through clues left by the testator. Lara and her friends raced a killer and almost lost.

Clive had a great idea, an antiques and archeology tour to Tunisia with Lara in charge as *The African Quest* (Berkley, 2001) began. Of the more than a dozen applicants who signed up, there were several with hidden agendas: revenge, blackmail, and destruction of an enterprise. Lara was without her usual resources as she sought the connections between a Fourth Century treasure ship sunk off the Tunisian coastline and the murderous incidents that were plaguing her tour group. The historical sub-text described the treachery on board the treasure ship and a young boy who lived to denounce the traitor.

Next books in this series: *The Etruscan Chimera* (2002); *The Thai Amulet* (2003)

Shirley McClintock
Author: B. J. Oliphant, pseudonym for Sherri Tepper a.k.a. A. J. Orde

Even though she was officially retired and twice widowed, Shirley McClintock would scoff at senior citizen discounts. Ms. McClintock (she used her family name, not that of either husband) had left a responsible position in the federal government to return to her family's Colorado ranch. With the help of foreman J.Q. (John Quentin), Shirley ran a herd of pedigreed Belted Galloways.

Life had not always been that simple. A drunken driver had killed her son, Sal. Son Marty disappeared in the Amazon jungle; after which her first husband died of grief and heart problems. A second shorter marriage was ended by cancer. She and J.Q. shared a physical relationship, but marriage was not in their plans. Shirley was physically robust at 6' 2"; the only sign of aging, her graying hair. Her politics were diverse. She was adamantly pro-choice and intolerant of fundamentalist religions, but contemptuous of "knee jerk" liberals, particularly ACLU members. She promoted the responsibilities of minorities, including the primacy of the English language. However vehement Shirley could be on ideology, on a personal level, she championed the underdog and the vulnerable.

During *Dead in the Scrub* (Fawcett, 1990), a deer trail led Shirley first to a skeleton, then onto the personal affairs of an unhappy family and their fundamentalist church.

By *The Unexpected Corpse* (Fawcett, 1990), Shirley and J.Q. had added twelve-year-old Allison to the household as a foster child. Shirley was an only child, but she had an extended family of cousins, aunts, and uncles. A series of murders, bequests, and thefts of historic silver forced her to act as executor and sleuth.

Shirley's first husband had bequeathed her property in the District of Columbia, necessitating a trip to make financial arrangements. On her return in *Deservedly Dead* (Fawcett, 1992) she was aghast at the changes. Land speculator Eleazar Azoli had not only damaged the environment but also created ill feeling among other residents. Shirley solved Azoli's murder and Allison's personal problem, but could not restore her sense of belonging.

Death and the Delinquent (Fawcett, 1993) took Allison, Shirley, and J.Q. to New Mexico where an unhappy child created havoc, ending in her death. In identifying the killer, Shirley realized her need for a fresh start. The change was not that simple. Colorado had been the McClintock home for four generations.

Even after six months as the proprietor of a New Mexico guest ranch in *Death Served Up Cold* (Fawcett, 1994) Shirley was unsettled. She was having a problem with memory lapses. On the advice of Xanthippe Minging, a teacher who had joined the menage to tutor Allison, she discontinued a medication for insomnia to which she had become addicted. Shirley needed all her faculties. Not only had a guest been murdered, but Allison's relatives schemed to get custody of the child for mercenary reasons. Shirley's solution to the murder was intriguing, but distasteful.

A Ceremonial Death (Fawcett, 1996) was overloaded with Shirley's opinions on schools, the legal system, and families. Allison was having difficulty integrating into the local school, hassled by a jealous classmate who resented her achievements. When Allison discovered her rival's corpse, she was not a serious suspect, but Shirley connected the death with another recent murder. She found the local sheriff totally incompetent so set to work to find the killer. Instead, the killer found her.

Renting cottages to guests was not without its dangers. Shirley suffered from destructive children, demanding mothers of the bride, and free-spending honeymooners in *Here's to the Newly Dead* (Fawcett, 1997).

She needed all of her self control when there was a possibility that her son Marty might still be alive after sixteen years.

This was one tough lady who ran roughshod over opposition.

Dr. Anna McColl

Author: Penny Kline

Anna McColl was a clinical psychologist who worked in a group practice in Bristol, England. She had never married but had serial affairs. She could have used a little help for her obsessive-compulsive behaviors.

As *Dying to Help* (Macmillan, 1993) began, Anna's lover, David, had returned to his former wife Iris. Her evenings and weekends were lonely but there were challenging cases at the office. She was planning a research project on "frequent attendees" (hypochondriacs or those perceived as such). Young Jenny Weir had been referred by her general practitioner because of her continued visits. Another client asked Anna to exonerate her brother from a charge of murder. The two cases merged in a credible narrative with a rambling introspective style.

Readers may need access to a diagnostic codebook to enjoy *Feeling Bad* (Macmillan, 1994). Anna dealt with anxiety neurosis, incest, sibling rivalry, homosexuality, and sexless marriages. It all began when Luke Jesty, still burdened with guilt because of sister's death six years before, fell apart. He had been present when Paula Redfern was catapulted into traffic and killed. Anna needed more information about both Luke and Paula to verify that she had not misdiagnosed his condition. She was diverted by an emotional response to a suspect.

Anna's plans for a two-week vacation had to be cancelled in *A Crushing Blow* (Macmillan, 1995). She used the time to help Geraldine Haran with her agoraphobia. During her visits to the Haran home, Anna became aware of Geraldine's interactions with her husband, her son and those relatives who occupied the other portion of the duplex. As her concern for Geraldine progressed, Anna probed into the death of a lonely widower who was murdered in a nearby forest. The narrative was marred by excessive red herrings and tag ends.

Social scientist Maggie Hazeldean had scheduled an appointment to meet with Anna. In *Turning Nasty* (Macmillan, 1995), she died before the consult could take place. Bill, Maggie's estranged husband, and their son Ian could not put closure to her death until they knew who had killed her. Among the suspects were not only associates of Maggie but also clients of

Anna, so she shared the family's need to know. By now Anna had her Ph.D. and was Dr. Anna McColl. Again, there were many diversions into subplots.

Sally Luckham, aged twelve, had narrowly escaped abduction at the hands of a woman as she walked home from school. She was referred to Anna to get a coherent description of the incident and the person involved. During *Ending in Tears* (Macmillan, 1997), persons who were suspects in the death of Tom Luckham, Sally's recently deceased father contacted Anna. She realized that she might know more than the killer wanted her to. On the more positive side, Anna found that Professor Owen Hughes' absence for an exchange program in Australia was a relief. Inspector Howard Fry was her new admirer. The narrative began well, but was overpopulated.

Karen McDade

Author: Emer Gillespie

With no intent to minimize the trauma of rape, it can be said that Karen McDade might have taken steps on her own behalf. Jack, her lover at the time, had become increasingly possessive and jealous. His interpretation of her innocent encounter with a male friend drove him into a frenzy that culminated in rape. She received no encouragement from the London police who said that, given their past sexual history, it would be her word against his. Nevertheless she declined to follow up on suggestions of counseling. She drew back from all but the closest friends and declined to join a group where she could share her sense of betrayal. Instead she moved to a different home address where she slept during the day. She worked as a film editor during the night hours, sequestered in a third floor room at her office at Finest Cut.

Karen's mother had been killed in a car accident when she was eleven. Her father never recovered from the loss, and they both feared intimacy. She had no brothers or sisters. Her constant companion was Job, a huge Bouvier des Flandres, who accompanied her everywhere that the law and her boss allowed. Lacking family resources, she overwhelmed her good friends John and Sarah. Sarah and Karen had been friends since they met as students at the North London Polytechnic. Her father thought college a waste. Sarah had chosen marriage and a family. Karen had decided that she would never have children, fearing that she would harm them by dying. Sarah's husband John had helped Karen when her career was at a standstill by suggesting that she take a course in film editing. Even with her handicaps Karen was successful in her work for Finest Cut, an independent production company.

Her most recent project had been a series on women from a variety of different backgrounds and nationalities done for Nordic Communications. Her work was well appreciated by her boss, Bob Wilkes.

Given that chaotic a life, Karen's discovery of a young woman's body in the alley near the offices in *Virtual Stranger* (Headline, 1998) accentuated her fears. Had Jack located her? Was he the man who had plagued her with sexually taunting on the phone? Three years and four months had passed since the rape, but it was always fresh in her mind. She finally recognized that the victim, young Katie Sewell had appeared in an independent film made by Rob Benson that she had edited. Was the killer someone she knew or worked with?

Karen took a leave of absence from Finest Cut during *Five Dead Men* (Headline, 1999) to work with Rob Benson on a documentary. Their film focused on a civic renovation project. The confluence of death on the construction site and Karen's reconnection with estranged members of her family had a devastating impact on her. Rob, waiting patiently for her to recognize his feelings, and faithful dog Job shared in the repercussions from betrayal and death.

Nuala Anne McGrail

Author: Andrew M. Greeley

Nuala McGrail could not possibly be as lovely, as bright, and as engaging as narrator Dermot Coyne described her. Author Andrew M. Greeley was prone to exaggerations. She was the child of low-income parents in the Gaelic speaking section of western Ireland who won a scholarship to Trinity College in Dublin.

At nineteen she was close to graduation but lacked the funds to continue. In *Irish Gold* (Forge, 1994), Coyne visited Ireland to research his grandparents' involvement in the battle for Irish independence from 1917 to 1924. Dermot had been devoted to Nell Pat, his grandmother, and believed that her journals would explain why his grandparents left Ireland in 1920 and never returned. A chance encounter with Nuala in a student pub provided Dermot with a translator and an object for adoration. The translations were a potential danger to English authorities and their Irish allies. Nuala's youth and innocence kept Dermot from taking advantage of her, although she was deeply in love with him.

The terrain changed in *Irish Lace* (Forge, 1996) and the blend of a past conspiracy with the present was more labored. Nuala's degree entitled her to a Morrison visa and a job as an accountant at a prominent Chicago firm. Chicago and its environs were the home of the Coyne family, which took Nuala to its heart. She became preoccupied with emanations from an area formerly used as a Civil War prison camp. Nuala's stay in Chicago was jeopardized by her contact with Irish revolutionaries who frequented the pub where she sang. Nuala and Dermot set the date for their wedding.

The McGrail and Coyne clans gathered for the event in *Irish Whiskey* (Forge, 1998). When Nuala and Dermot visited a local cemetery, she had another of her intuitive flashes; the grave of James "Sweet Rolls" Sullivan, a bootlegger who rivaled Al Capone, was empty. This information came in handy when Nuala needed leverage. A former friend charged Dermot with stock manipulations. It took Cindy Hurley (his attorney/sister) and Nuala, to prove his innocence. Interference with wedding plans by Nuala's pompous older brother didn't help, but it padded out a weak narrative.

Greeley continued his mix of Irish mysticism and history in *Irish Mist* (Forge, 1999), exploring the assassination of Kevin O'Higgins who had brought stability to Ireland after Michael Collins' death. En route to a Dublin charity concert, Nuala had a "spell" which involved her and Dermot in ancient tragedies and current duplicity.

Poor Dermot. In *Irish Eyes* (Forge, 2000), he realized that baby daughter, Nelliecoyne, had inherited her mother's "fey" (the ability to see into the past or future). Screams from the child as they visited the family cottage on Lake Michigan sent Nuala and Dermot into a voyage of discovery. Although distracted by the antics and death of an ambitious music critic, they connected a one hundred-year-old shipwreck to a lost treasure. An engrossing view of Chicago Irish in the 1890s.

Nuala and Dermot visited western Ireland in the present, and in the past during *Irish Love* (Forge, 2001). They now owned an ample bungalow near the Connemara coast. Within weeks of their occupancy there were bombings, and shots were fired. Nuala and Dermot immersed themselves in the journal left behind by a Chicago reporter describing the vicious destruction of a local family during the 1880s. They learned about the local feuds that scapegoated a man and the incompetent and unjust English police, court system, and politics that allowed innocent men to go to the gallows. Nuala and Dermot uncovered a greedy plot to destroy the local community. When she came to Ireland, Nuala had been suffering from post-partum depression that forced her to put her career on hold. Her experiences, although stressful, and the time spent with her parents restored her balance. She sang again.

You don't have to be Irish to enjoy the series, but it helps.

Next book in this series: *Irish Stew!* (2002)

Annie McGrogan

Author: Gillian B. Farrell

Annie McGrogan, a New York City actress, spent her "at leisure" hours as a part-time private investigator. She was a slender redhead with serious aspirations, having studied under such legitimate drama teachers as Geraldine Page and Jeff Corey. Her ability to disguise herself on stage or at work was an asset. As she detected, she absorbed impressions to use in her stage and screen portrayals. Annie had ended her ten-year marriage for a handsome lover, who then dumped her.

In *Alibi for an Actress* (Pocket, 1992), Annie maintained a platonic relationship with her partner, Sonny Gandolpho. They were assigned to guard television soap actress Lucinda Merrill, but became her alibi when her unfaithful husband was murdered. Annie's personal life merged with her professional responsibilities in a taut narrative.

During *Murder and a Muse* (Pocket, 1994), she explored the nature of relationships, while researching her part in a new movie by unconventional director, Alan De Lucca. Until he was murdered, Annie had been drawn to De Lucca. She had invested her professional skills in the movie, and needed the pragmatic Sonny to help her return to reality.

Imaginative premise. Do not expect realism.

Madison McGuire

Author: Amanda Kyle Williams

Lesbian sleuths are frequently portrayed as police officers or private investigators. Madison McGuire offered an interesting alternative, espionage agent. The reluctance of government security forces to employ homosexuals was acknowledged in the series. Madison, whose mother died when she was five years old, spent her adolescence in England where her father, who worked for the CIA, had been stationed. Professionally, she preferred to work alone, but had allies within the espionage trade who came to her assistance on occasion, including Max Rudger, an ex-IRA agent.

Madison had been forced to resign from the CIA during *Club Twelve* (Naiad, 1990). Her lover, Elicia planned to use Madison's car to get groceries. As she entered the vehicle, another car drove by. She was fatally shot. From that point on, Madison had a goal, the destruction of an international conspiracy for world domination. She demanded the support of the CIA or threatened to carry on alone. She was unprepared for the betrayal of an old friend.

Although Madison had lost her security clearance, she was recalled in *The Providence File* (Naiad, 1991) to infiltrate the Palestinian Liberation Army, presenting herself as a renegade CIA agent. Her current lover resented her return to duty.

In *A Singular Spy* (Naiad, 1992), Madison was employed as a trainer at the Clandestine Entry Program Center until a disloyal CIA employee was murdered in Geneva. The agency sent McGuire with a handpicked team to uncover other moles, considering the task force expendable.

The Spy in Question (Naiad, 1993) provided Madison with a new interest, singer Dani Stone, and a new assignment for the CIA. A small American unit was sent into Peru to destroy drug production sites. Madison was to contact a populist leader willing to fight the Senderos, betrayers of the peasants they had promised to liberate. Surprisingly naive after two decades of government employment, Madison was shocked at the duplicity of the political system. She and others, who were concerned about the integrity of the Agency, disregarded their orders.

The books provided interesting plots and did not limit themselves to lesbian or feminist issues.

Judith Grover McMonigle (Flynn)

Author: Mary Daheim

Judith Grover was a tall gray haired, ex-librarian and widow. She had married Dan McMonigle on the rebound. He might not have realized that he was second choice, but something was bothering Dan because he ate himself to death. With son Mike off to college, Judith remodeled the spacious Seattle family home into a bed and breakfast, adding her querulous mother, Gertrude, to the household. Gertrude became an overworked gag that detracted from Daheim's otherwise light touch.

In *Just Desserts* (Avon, 1991), former opera star Oriana Bustamanti commandeered the entire establishment while her home was being fumigated. Her husband Otto had been expected to make a major announcement as to his estate plans at a family dinner. The planned entertainer, a fortuneteller, was poisoned during tea and cream puffs. Anxious to protect her reputation, Judith solved the murder, which meant spending time with Lt. Joe Flynn, who had jilted her twenty years before.

Judith and her cousin, Renie (Serena) Jones vacationed in Canada during *Fowl Prey* (Avon, 1991). They connected with the reunion of producer Max Rothsides' original theatrical team. The death of a street peddler and his parakeet stimulated Judith and Renie to play detective with long distance help from Joe Flynn.

Judith's active Catholicism was evident in *Holy Terrors* (Avon, 1992) when she catered the parish post-egg roll repast. The death of volunteer Sandy Frizzell cancelled the meal, but the revelation of Sandy's gender was even more of a shock. Flynn, freed of his marriage, was ready to try again with Judith.

Their long delayed honeymoon occurred as *Dune to Death* (Avon, 1993) began but Joe suffered a disabling injury. Unwilling to postpone her honeymoon again, Judith invited Renie to join her at the cottage while Joe languished in the local hospital. Judith and Renie had a dead landlady to test their skills.

In *Bantam of the Opera* (Avon, 1993), while Joe was in New Orleans for a conference, Judith provided "bed and breakfast" for an egotistical opera star and his retinue. A dose of poison finished the tenor, but did not alter Judith's propensity for high-risk investigations.

When Judith and Renie visited the family cottage to bury Dan's ashes in *A Fit of Tempera* (Avon, 1994) they became acquainted with artist Riley Tobias. Before Tobias was murdered, he gave Judith a landscape, touching off a search for a parent, a painting, and an obvious killer.

Judith and Renie agreed to cater the family birthday party for "Uncle Boo" in *Major Vices* (Avon, 1995), knowing that they would earn little appreciation. Boo's death in the locked room of an isolated family home put Judith in a quandary. Joe was out of town, and his rival, Det. Buck Doerflinger was handling the case. Judith proceeded as usual. She hid clues, tampered with evidence, and found the killer.

In *Murder, My Suite* (Avon, 1995), Judith (now Judith Grover McMonigle Flynn) recovered from the disastrous visit of gossip columnist Dagmar Chatsworth and her entourage at the bed and breakfast. She and Renie headed for a free week at a Canadian ski resort. Her neighbors were Chatsworth et al who had brought their problems with them. Murder ensued, but the narrative diverted to scenic descriptions, Judith's unwarranted jealousy of her husband's contacts in an investigation, and mother jokes.

The foursome, Judith, Renie and their spouses, journeyed to England in *Auntie Mayhem* (Avon, 1996). While the men fished in Scotland, the wives visited a magnificent but undercapitalized manor home. The potential heirs to the estate were considering making it into a "bed and breakfast" facility, but ninety-four year old Aunt "Pet" had to die first. Her death set Judith and Renie to detecting. Fortunately, their husbands arrived in time to rescue them.

Nutty As a Fruitcake (Avon, 1996) was set during the Christmas holidays, when Judith's exuberant, even excessive, celebration clashed with Joe's negative memories of Christmases past. The death of neighbor Enid Goodrich did not spoil Judith's enthusiasm, but the arrest of Enid's long-suffering husband George did. Many people had a motive for disposing of Enid. Judith intended to exonerate George. There was a handy network of Bed and Breakfast facility owners who assisted one another in crisis times.

In *September Mourn* (Avon, 1997), Judith and Renie traveled to isolated Chavez island to substitute for ex-high school classmate Jeanne Barber in running her three cabin hostelry. An obnoxious guest died shortly after Renie had cracked a plate over his head. Judith looked among the permanent residents of the island for others with motives to kill the victim, and found more than she needed. Her intrusive questions were tolerated by the suspects to an unrealistic degree.

Her son Michael's wedding created a crisis for Judith. Was this the time to tell him about his father? The time to talk never came during *Wed and Buried* (Avon, 1998). Judith witnessed a "bride's" murder on an adjacent hotel rooftop during the reception. Patient Joe agreed to check. A corpse did show up the next day, but it was the groom's. Judith's insistence on carrying on a parallel investigation in a case with no friend or relative involved got no support from Renie and created problems for Joe.

Judith decided to end her catering services. In *Snow Place to Die* (Avon, 1998), she accepted a final assignment to accommodate Cousin Renie. She would provide an evening meal for the management staff of a telephone company holding their annual retreat at an isolated lodge. The winter weather made it impossible for Judith and Renie to leave as the corpses increased and the suspects dwindled. Agatha Christie would be pleased.

It may take special skills to keep track of the cops and criminals (with assorted aliases) who filled Judith's bed and breakfast in *Legs Benedict* (Avon, 1999). The narrative was heavily seasoned with coincidences and sweetened by personal pathos. Those who were regular fans of the series knew what to expect and would enjoy.

Daheim pulled out all the stops in *Creeps Suzette* (Avon, 2000). Judith and Renie were persuaded to investigate murderous attempts on the life of rich, reclusive dowager Leota Burgess. Creepers (the family home) and the family lineage were well populated by ghosts and evidence of miscegenation, murder and suicide, mental instability, infidelity and racial prejudice. Murders spanning sixty years were solved but only with the help of Detective Edwina Jefferson and newly licensed private investigator Joe Flynn.

Renie and Judith were booked for orthopedic surgery at Good News Hospital during *Suture Self* (Morrow, 2001). They occupied their recovery time by investigating the deaths of three other patients. All three had recovered well from surgery, only to die unexpectedly. Renie's complaints against the food and medication became tiresome. Judith not only solved the crimes but also assisted in the parallel case on which Joe was working.

Characters in the *Bed and Breakfast* books were reminiscent of past television series; e.g. Judith's mother resembled Sophie, the wisecracking, ill-humored senior citizen on *The Golden Girls.* Judith played Lucy Ricardo to cousin Renie as Ethel Mertz. By #17, the series moved up to hardcover. Some may prefer the Emma Lord series also by Daheim.

Next books in this series: *Silver Scream* (2002); *Hoakus Croakus* (2003)

Kathy McNeely

Author: Louis Charbonneau

A less likely category for female sleuths has been scientists, except for the recently popular pathologists and longtime favorite archaeologists. Kathy was a Ph.D. level zoologist studying the impact of oil spills on Antarctic birds.

She kept warm with a handsome archeologist adventurer during *The Ice* (Fine, 1991). Kathy had rescued birds earlier when the *SS Kowloon* oil spill contaminated the area. Her more recent assignment, funded by the National Science Foundation, was to predict the spill's long-term impact by tabulating the survivors. The U.S. team headed by marine biologist Dr. Carl Jeffers accommodated a Russian expedition, a film company, and American business interests seeking precious minerals. The prize was valuable enough to incite murder.

Kathy's reputation preceded her so that, although her technical skills were unassailable, scientist Jason Cobb wondered whether she was a prima donna in *White Harvest* (Fine, 1994). She rescued him from death, and worked with an Eskimo hunter and an undercover agent to fight the human predators who ravaged the walrus herds.

An interesting diversion from the private investigators, housewives, and policewomen.

Camilla McPhee

Author: Mary Jane Maffini

Camilla McPhee, who had not recovered from the death of her lover Paul, had two resources: her extended family and Justice for Victims, the non-profit agency she founded to represent the victims of crimes. At age thirty-two she considered herself the ugly duckling, short, dark and stocky, as compared with her three sophisticated, tall, slim blonde sisters. Camilla had been the "caboose" in the family, a birth, which her mother did not survive. Her father Donald, principal at St. Jim's high school, was well known in the community. Her sisters had married well, although Alexa was widowed. They worked at finding an appropriate spouse for Camilla. The McPhee family had its roots in Nova Scotia, but had settled happily in Ottawa, the national capitol of Canada.

Initially Camilla had practiced criminal law. Her dismay at the limited attention paid to the victims of crime led her to establish Justice for Victims, which she ran from a cluttered office. Her father, who had a proclivity for rescuing the children and grandchildren of friends, induced her to hire young Alvin Ferguson. Once Camilla got beyond the annoyance of Alvin's presence (he played rock music on his radio) and his appearance, she found him to be capable and loyal. There was some relief in sending him off on research projects so she could complete the necessary paperwork on her desk. She had achieved some success with Justice for Victims, partly because she had a highly developed network of friends in the police department, the Royal Canadian Mounted Police, the legal profession, and social services groups.

Camilla had known Robin Findlay since kindergarten, too well to believe that she would kill vitriolic columnist Mitzi Brochu in *Speak Ill of the Dead* (RendezVous Press, Toronto, 1999). The police, notably Sgt. Conn McCracken, considered the fact that Robin was discovered at the scene of the crime with bloody hands to be significant evidence. Mitzi had targeted dozens of prominent persons in her columns, usually female, and generally those who carried more weight than Mitzi considered acceptable. Camilla rallied her resources, including an attractive man who reawakened feelings dormant since Paul's death.

Everyone wanted serial abuser Ralph Benning put away for a long time during *The Icing on the Corpse* (RendezVous, 2001). Someone did something about it and murdered him. The police turned their attention to his former wife until she too was found dead; then, to Camilla's client, Lindsay Grace who had testified against him. They finally arrested social activist Elaine Ekstein who enjoyed the attention. With help from Alvin Ferguson and her elderly neighbor Violet Parnell, Camilla targeted the killer in time to attend her sister Alexa's marriage to Det. Sgt. Conn McCracken.

Add author Jane Maffini to the list of engaging female mystery novelists from Canada.

Next book in this series: *Little Boy Blues* (2002)

Sutton McPhee

Author: Brenda English

Sutton McPhee was deeply attached to her younger sister, Cara. Sutton had been twenty-five, living away from the family home in Hilton, Georgia and Cara, nineteen and in college, when their parents had been killed in a traffic accident. The sisters were very different. After her parents died, Cara quit college to return to Hilton where she immersed herself in church work. Sutton used her journalism degree to work her way up from a small Georgia newspaper to a larger one in Tallahassee. It was there that she met, married, and divorced Jack Brooks, a city planner whose rigidity she found intolerable. After Sutton moved on to a better job as the education reporter with the Washington News, Cara was lonely. She moved to the D.C. area to be closer to Sutton. They did not share a home. Sutton had a condo in Alexandria, drove an ancient Volkswagen Beetle, and studied yoga. Cara lived near her job as secretary for the Bread of Life Church in West Springfield, Virginia until her death. Sutton had few close relationships after Cara's death until she met Noah Lansing and his young son, David. Before Noah, she had enjoyed sex without requiring any commitment.

In her professional life, Sutton had developed a network of personal resources in the police department, which proved valuable when she could not obtain information through regular channels. The best of these was police public information officer, Bill Russell.

Cara's murder in a parking lot adjacent to an ATM was initially assumed to be a random killing in *Corruption of Faith* (Berkley, 1997). Although the police continued to think so, Sutton unearthed evidence that Cara had been unhappy and disappointed with people whom she had trusted. Sutton took advantage of her position on the newspaper, motivated by a need for revenge against those who had found Cara too dangerous to live. She feared she might be fired, but was promoted to police reporter.

Two cases—the rape and murder of a senatorial aide and the murder of the well-respected wife of a county supervisor—merged in *Corruption of Power* (Berkley, 1998). Sutton's "hard headed" pursuit of information led to a conflict with attractive detective Noah Lansing. Lansing had painful memories of damage caused by a young reporter, setting up a hostile impression of Sutton. When Sutton and Lansing cooperated, they became so attracted to one another that she had to worry about a conflict of interest.

Sutton was more than a reporter in *Corruption of Justice* (Berkley, 1999). She had investigated the deaths of police officer Dan Magruder and foundation director Robert Coleman. Now she was the witness who could tie the cases together. She jousted with Noah Lansing (whom she loved) and with rival *News* reporter, Sy Berkowitz (whom she detested). Sutton's need for independence made it difficult to accept protection from others. Perhaps she feared she might come to relish it; at least, she realized it was a facet of Lansing's love for her.

Portia McTeague

Authors: Faye Sultan and Teresa Kennedy

As the series began, Portia McTeague was in her forties, working in Charlotte, North Carolina as a forensic psychologist, but available for court appointed roles in adjacent states. She usually acted for the defense, but in the second narrative voluntarily sought to be on the investigative team as a profiler. Her origins were in small town Mississippi where she received little attention from her alcoholic father or her social climbing mother. There had been no siblings. A cousin had raped her when she was eleven. He pimped her to his friends, getting her cooperation through drugs. A second rape took place while she was in college. When she became pregnant, her parents gave her $10,000 and sent her off on her own. The child presumably was given up for adoption.

Portia later adopted Alice (at age six) at the request of the girl's mother. Alice became the center of Portia's personal life. She had parlayed the $10,000 from her parents into a Ph.D. in psychology, but she still needed help. Dr. Sophie Stransky, her therapist, continued to see Portia after retirement. Portia was claustrophobic, had no sense of direction, read while driving on superhighways, and hated cats. Portia's other support was attorney Declan Dylan, bound to a wheelchair by a car accident. He was a rich widower who cared very deeply for Portia. On the more positive side, Portia volunteered time to work at Charlotte's Help Line.

Portia was already feeling burnout when she let Dylan convince her to serve as an expert witness for defendant Jimmy Wier in *Over the Line* (Doubleday, 1998). The question was not whether Jimmy had killed two elderly women while delivering groceries. Dylan wanted a verdict of not guilty by reason of insanity or at least a life sentence, rather than legal execution. Portia felt personal pain as she delved into the childhood abuse suffered by Jimmy. The pressure broke down some of her own defenses, allowing her to face her past.

Portia's decision to phase out her forensic work for criminal defendants and concentrate on a clinical practice in *Help Line* (Doubleday, 1999) did not provide the expected peace of mind. She was, in fact, bored with the more humdrum aspects of her work. Her affair with private investigator Alan Simpson and her personal and therapeutic relationship with Dr. Stransky were disrupted by Portia's venture into profiling. She allied herself with law enforcement on a serial murders case, unaware that she had been led into danger and, even worse, had endangered a friend.

She was a troubled woman, seeking to solve other people's problems, while personally addicted to danger and darkness.

Jayne Meadows

Author: Steve Allen

Steve Allen and Jayne Meadows may have had a more egalitarian marriage than most Hollywood couples, but Jayne was a supporting player in Steve's mystery series. She is a real person, born to American missionaries in China, who developed a comfortable reputation as an actress and television comedienne. Her sister, Audrey, was best remembered for her work as Jackie Gleason's wisecracking wife in *The Honeymooner* skits. A brother, Edward, became a corporate attorney. Jayne married Steve, then divorced with children, and they had a son. She was tall, redheaded, and witty, confrontive with those who annoyed her, but sympathetic and maternal with the vulnerable.

During *The Talk Show Murders* (Delacorte, 1982), in which a crude rock star was killed during the Toni Tonielle show and *Murder on the Glitter Box* (Zebra, 1989) wherein Steve substituted as host of a major television show, only to have a guest poisoned on stage, references were made to Jayne, but she never appeared.

Murder in Manhattan (Zebra, 1990) brought the Allens to New York City, where Steve had a small part in a film, the cast of which was embroiled in arguments and affairs. While Jayne shopped till she dropped, Steve survived a ship explosion, a cold swim, and a helicopter rescue.

As *Murder in Vegas* (Zebra, 1992) began, the Allens interrupted a vacation so Steve could assist old friend, Bobby Hamilton, in presenting a Vegas show. Jayne befriended Bobby's promiscuous daughter, while Steve defended him on a murder charge.

The Murder Game (Zebra, 1993) brought the Allens back for a reprise of a game show on which Jayne had appeared during the Seventies. Several suspicious deaths occurred to members of the original cast making Jayne very uncomfortable, and sending them out to sea with a corpse.

The Allens were invited on the maiden voyage of *Atlantica*, a fabulous ocean liner in *Murder on the Atlantic* (Zebra, 1995). Steve's only responsibility was to perform one evening, but he involved himself in the family troubles of the ship owner and the deaths of his heirs.

Wake Up to Murder (Kensington, 1996) reunited the Allens with Cat Lawrence, whom they had befriended as a young girl. Needing a replacement for her coanchor on a morning talk show, Cat recruited Steve. Jayne traced suspects when a series of accidents ended with murder, but her talents were underutilized.

In *Die Laughing* (Kensington, 1998), the Allens discovered a corpse while attending a funeral, not the one expected to be in the coffin. Allen repeated plotting that he had used in an earlier book to explain whether or not comic Benny Hartman was really dead.

Considering Allen's verbal wit and breadth of knowledge, his mysteries were a disappointment. There could have been more of Jayne's acerbic touches; less of Steve's personal philosophy and name-dropping.

Possible other: *Murder in Hollywood* (1988) was not available for review.

Elizabeth "Tenny" Mendoza

Author: Melanie McAllester

Few people called Tenny Mendoza "Elizabeth." The nickname "Tenny" was a backhanded tribute to her tenaciousness. She held a graduate degree, but chose employment as a police officer in Bayview, a California town. Her family, four siblings and her parents, was supportive of her career choice and her sexual orientation. Tenny described herself as one-half African-American and one-half Mexican. She had been successful as a homicide investigator in Bayview but was chosen by her captain to work on a three-person team investigating the serial rapes of lesbians. The rapes were taking place in two different California jurisdictions.

In *The Lessons* (Spinsters, 1994), Tenny worked with lesbian patrol officer Ashley Johnson and prejudiced sexual assault officer Steve Carson. The police procedural aspects of the narrative were matched by the gradual development of a good working relationship among the three detectives. Each learned a lesson, but not the ones the rapist was trying to teach.

The local police force was ready to write off young Kelsey Sabatos' abduction as a domestic dispute in *The Search* (Naiad, 1996) on the premise that her father had taken the child from his former wife and her lesbian lover. Carter, Kelsey's mother, and Tenny, her former lover disagreed. The ties between Tenny and Carter, and between Tenny and Kelsey were so powerful that she quit her job, traveled to Chicago, then Brazil to bring Kelsey home. In so doing, she uncovered a child-selling ring.

Dr. Anne Menlo

Author: Maxine O'Callaghan

Petite child psychologist Anne Menlo practiced in the Phoenix/Scottsdale area where she shared a suite with two other Ph.D. professionals, Andrew Braemer and Cynthia Lynde. She chose to live in a more isolated area near Cave Creek. Detective Bern Pagett had shared her home for a while, moving towards marriage, but it never happened. He continued to visit, staying over several nights a week, but they were no longer on the wedding track.

Commitment was difficult for Anne, a matter she frequently discussed with Rosemary Biederman, who had been her advisor in the Ph.D. program at Arizona State University. Multiple sclerosis had diminished Rosemary's professional career but she always made time for Anne. Anne had relied upon Rosemary during her college years when she failed to recognize that a child under her care was being sexually abused. After Nicki Craig killed herself at age ten, Anne's sense of guilt never totally left her. She volunteered regularly at a child abuse center.

Unlike Bern, Anne relished the outdoors. Her one and a half-acre property included a natural basin where wildlife came to drink the water. She rode her mountain bike up and down the hills for exercise. Anne's parents lived in San Diego but they did not figure in the narrative; nor did her brother Kevin. Bern had convinced Anne to be on call for the Phoenix police department in cases where children needed immediate care. Given her tendency to become personally involved, this may have been a mistake.

During *Shadow of the Child* (Jove, 1996), Anne not only found it difficult to work on a case managed by Bern, but she found herself drawn to three-year-old Danny Lewis. The boy had been kidnapped and then discovered by the police in a home where a woman had been murdered. Initially mute, Danny responded to Anne. She was determined to protect him, even from Bern's questions. Bern suffered both physical and emotional damage from their experience. They also acquired a badly mistreated half

Doberman, half Black Labrador dog named Duke who only gradually allowed himself to be cared for.

In *Only in the Ashes* (Jove, 1997), the only way that Kathleen Graley could cope with the death of her young daughter was to know how and why Rachel had died. With some misgivings, Anne agreed to investigate. The fire that consumed the house in which the child's body had been found was determined to be arson. Bern was assigned the case. In a parallel situation, Anne sought the mother of an "abandoned" girl, Chrissie. Both struck an emotional chord in her: the mother grieving for Rachel, the child, seeking her mother. An engrossing read. Readers who enjoy her might try O'Callaghan's earlier series featuring Delilah West (Volume 2).

Ophelia O. Meredith

Author: Tanya Jones

At age thirty-two, Ophelia O. Meredith had a number of significant achievements. She was a solicitor in the firm of Snodsworth, Parrish, Ranger located in Rambleton, Yorkshire, England. She had a happy marriage to Malachi, owner of a computer consulting business called Wet Nose Solutions, a reference to their three Labrador Retrievers. She was expecting her sixth child, all of whom had been named after Popes due to the Catholic faith she and Malachi practiced. Even daughter, Joan, could claim a papal designation, although with a cloud over it. The boys had such cumbersome names as: Pius, Innocent, Urban, Hygenus, and Adeodata (called Dodie), sure to make them the subject of ridicule on the school playground. The dogs were also gifted with unusual names: Digabyte (Gigi), Megabyte (Meg), and Reredorter (Rea). To house this motley group, Ophelia and Malachi had recently purchased a rundown property, Moorwind Farm. He had difficulty in planning and carrying out income producing employment.

Faced with the loss of employment in *Ophelia O. and the Mortgage Bandits* (Headline, 1995), she did not hesitate to hide the corpse of her new employer. She needed money to redeem the family's abducted Black Labrador, more money than she could obtain as an attorney, so she reluctantly pursued a circular Ponzi scheme. Fortunately for her peace of mind, extraneous events, an enterprising secretary and the brighter than expected Meredith children saved her from further felonies (and sins).

As *Ophelia O. and the Antenatal Mysteries* (Headline, 1995) began, Ophelia had limited time for other activities; just surviving was an effort. However, she and her friend Polly aborted a legal scam designed to bilk the medical profession. At the conclusion, she produced and Malachi delivered a second daughter. Fortunately, Malachi's business had become successful.

The religious orientation was treated with humor, rather than ridicule, for a change.

Laura Michaels

Author: John Miles, pseudonym for John Bickham

Aspiring social worker Laura Michaels was a dark-haired divorcee with a nine-year-old daughter. While completing her graduate degree, she worked part-time at Timberdale Retirement Center.

Her personal life improved in *A Permanent Retirement* (Walker, 1992) when she met Deputy Sheriff Aaron Lassiter during his investigation of an apparent suicide by a Timberdale resident. Laura's suspicion that the death might be a homicide was incited by obsessive mystery fan/resident Maude Thuringer. Maude was one of several minor characters whose peculiarities became routine: Judge Emil Young, whose ponderous speech slowed down the dialogue; Still Bill Mills, whose "malapropisms" suggested he should have a brain scan; and Ken Keen, who suffered from memory loss and an overabundance of male hormones.

The notably inefficient administrator at Timberdale hired a professional acting group to entertain the residents with a mystery weekend in *Murder in Retirement* (Walker, 1994). The death of obnoxious impresario, J. Turner Redwine, provided Laura and Aaron with too many suspects, but she persevered even with amnesia brought on by a blow on her head.

The regulars reappeared in *A Most Deadly Retirement* (Walker, 1995) during which mysterious lights, attacks on residents, and the apparent suicide of a possible suspect kept them busy. Administrator Judith Epperman avoided responsibility; Maude Thuringer played Jane Marple; and social director Francie Blake vamped investigator Aaron Lassiter while Laura probed the record of a man who had killed before and was willing to kill again.

Limited character development over the series.

Maris Middleton

Author: Kaye Davis

The name was a clue. Her father had wanted a son, to be named for his two favorite baseball players, Roger Maris and Mickey Mantle. She was stuck with Maris Mantle Middleton. Her sister was tabbed Landry Middleton, but settled for Lana and a conventional marriage. Maris' sexual orientation had been accepted by her family, but posed problems when Mary Ann, her lover of ten years, was diagnosed with terminal cancer. Her employer, the Texas Department of Public Safety, did not have a policy that allowed compassionate leave for non-marital partners. Maris chose to leave the agency where she had worked as a forensic chemist. After Mary Ann's death, she cashed in her pension benefits and an insurance policy to fund her own business as an "independent crime scene specialist." Although she had excellent contacts with law enforcement agencies and enough referrals to keep busy, Maris was depressed and drinking heavily as the series began. Her only comfort was Earnhardt, her border collie, named after Dale Earnhardt, the NASCAR racer.

Maris was still mourning Mary Ann when she met FBI agent Lauren O'Conner in *Devil's Leg Crossing* (Naiad, 1997). Lauren had taken a leave of absence from her Chicago office to investigate the disappearance of her niece, Karin. Karin, who lived in a small Texas town, had been spending time with dubious characters. There was also suspicion that she might have been the victim of sexual abuse by a family member. Dissatisfied with the local police investigation, Lauren sought out Maris whom she had met briefly in the past. The two women developed a personal relationship, but the results of their probe had tragic consequences.

By *Possessions* (Naiad, 1998), Lauren had transferred to the Dallas FBI office. Maris, who had working relationships with both the Texas Rangers and local sheriff's departments, was hired to do the lab work on a grisly murder in Pierce County. A package sent to her home contained a single black dress shoe and a menacing message that tied the recent death to a series of killings. Gradually Maris and Lauren, together with local law enforcement, developed a profile: a male, connected to police work, who hated lesbians. He sought out victims who wore red fingernail polish and black dress shoes; then, abducted, mutilated and killed them. As they came closer to his identity, the killer targeted Maris.

When retired sheriff Nelda "Sherf" Archer was brutally beaten to death in *Until the End* (Naiad, 1998), Maris and her friend Gayle Blessing were determined to find the killer. Current sheriff Odell Wilbarger had good intentions, but both women brought special skills to the investigation. They believed that the motive for Sherf's death originated in a bank robbery during the 1940s, the loot from which had never been found. Besides capturing the killer and recovering the missing treasure, Maris proved the innocence of a young driver accused of vehicular homicide.

Author Kaye Davis had the technical background to provide credibility to the narratives. She offered more than some readers would want to know about mutilations, sexual activity, and serial killers.

Brenda Midnight

Author: Barbara Jaye Wilson

A small town girl from Belup Creek, Brenda Midnight moved to New York, settling finally in a Greenwich Village neighborhood. She married and divorced four times. A job with Needleson Brothers (hatmaking materials) led her to launch her own business. She put her artistic skills to work as a milliner, not a seller of headwear, but a designer and creator of original hats. Her shop was called Midnight Millinery, and was distinguished because she was unwilling to make exact copies of any hat. Her customers could be assured that they would not encounter another woman wearing the same hat. She advertised her product by wearing hats on almost every occasion. Her other constant fashion accessory was a five-pound Yorkshire terrier, named Jackhammer.

Whatever Brenda's last name had been in Belup Creek, she chose not to use it in New York. Noting a sign on the premises, which included the word "Midnight," she appropriated it for her last name. She struggled to make a living in her shop on West Fourth Street. Brenda was active in a neighborhood association that met at Pete's Café. She was a vegetarian who controlled her "risks" by neither flying nor eating meat. Initially she was so straitened by finances that she slept under her cutting table. This persisted until she was bequeathed a studio apartment. Brenda was a tiny woman but in good physical condition and fearless. She had good and loyal friends who created an ensemble approach to the series.

Carla Haley inveigled Brenda into doing the headpieces for the high society wedding of attorney Ashley Millard in *Death Brims Over* (Avon, 1997). Carla, who had designed the gowns, was found dead shortly after Brenda was robbed of the headgear by a mysterious "Lady in Pink." Brenda rallied her friends: television actor Johnny Verlane, computer expert Chuck Riley, and self-retired artist Elizabeth Franklin Perry. Plan A was to infiltrate the law office where Ashley worked. They had to improvise. There was no Plan B.

The first step to enjoying *Accessory to Murder* (Avon, 1998) was accepting that there was a good reason for moving Buddy Needleson's corpse from his business premises to the exterior of the morgue. Once done, the reader can enjoy the machinations of Brenda and her friends after they realized that (1) Buddy had been murdered, (2) they had interfered with a potential police investigation, and (3) that Johnny Verlane's agent Lemmy Crenshaw was the first choice of the police for killer.

Death Flips Its Lid (Avon, 1998) was a convoluted narrative during which ex-husband Nado P. Sharpe visited Brenda because he quarreled with his new wife. Against her better judgment, Brenda allowed him to escort her to Johnny Verlane's going away party. Johnny's *Tod Trueman, Urban Detective* show had been a success. Brenda left early. Nado stayed behind only to become witness to a murder. Typically, he panicked, fled from the scene, and stole a police car. Coincidentally the victim was a romantic rival of another of Brenda's good friends. More coincidentally there was an influx of former friends from Belup Creek. Brenda had to get involved. As usual she rallied her more dependable friends to find the real killer.

Chuck Riley, the reclusive computer genius who facilitated many of Brenda's investigations saved her life in *Capped Off* (Avon, 1999). It all began when she waited in an outer room at Castleberry's Department Store to show her line of hats to well-respected buyer Doreen Sands. Why would she get involved when Sands' corpse was discovered in her office? Probably because someone planted a gun in Brenda's purse where her detective friends, Turner and McKinley, found it.

The pain of having mistaken a real kidnapping of her friend Dweena (formerly Edward) for a ruse to entice her to a surprise birthday party in *A Hatful of Homicide* (Avon, 2000) was mingled with guilt. Once Dweena was freed, she wheedled Brenda into trying to retrieve the $50,000 ransom she had paid. Not that it was Dweena's money or Brenda's. That was part of the problem. Another problem was Dweena's sidelines; i.e. what she referred to as her "diplomatic vehicle relocation project" (she boosted cars of diplomats) and SOB (Save Our Brothels), an effort to halt the demolition of older buildings in the neighborhood. When murder was done, everybody lied, even the corpse.

Credibility took a vacation in *Murder and the Mad Hatter* (Avon, 2001) when Brenda agreed to marry sleazy talent agent Lemmy Crenshaw. Never mind that she loved television actor Johnny Verlane or that Lemmy tricked her into the arrangement. Somewhere under the froth of a stolen bra collection, a fictional plan to resuscitate New York City, time travel romances, and the loss of a lucky fountain pen, there was a murder.

Interesting side characters, but plotting weakened by the multiplicity of issues.

Francesca Miles

Author: Melissa Chan, pseudonym for Jocelynne Scott

Francesca Miles was both a private investigator and film critic in Melbourne, Australia. She lived with Luana Joyschild Adams, her lesbian lover. An earlier marriage to Tony Sanford had failed. Francesca was a strong feminist; still, she worked well with Joe Barnaby, Inspector of New South Wales Police Department. They had met when Francesca marched against Australia's involvement in the Vietnam War and he policed the crowd. She was allowed to take part in interviews he conducted when they shared an interest in the case. She preferred to serve clients, who were involved with feminist causes, even though they didn't always pay well. Her second job and her great interest was the movies.

Based upon their friendship, Inspector Joe Barnaby made Francesca an integral part of his investigation in *Too Rich* (Spinifex Press, Australia, 1991). She was allowed to accompany him to the penthouse where unfaithful businessman Daniel Gleixner lived with his mistress. He had died under suspicious circumstances, which pitted his wife Rose against the mistress, Elizabeth. Francesca was included in the interviews with family members, two of whom subsequently died. She did not share her version of the case with Joe Barnaby, only with the killer.

One after another, Melbourne community leaders were being murdered during *Guilt* (Artemis Press, Melbourne, 1993). Luana, Francesca's lover was the estranged daughter of Gordon Burton Adams, the first victim. When Barnaby came from South Wales to see if a murder in his jurisdiction was connected, he included Francesca in his investigation. Patterns emerged but Francesca and Joe interpreted them differently. For different reasons both opted for a simple solution.

Other book in this series: *One Too Many* (Artemis, 1993) unavailable for review.

Lydia Miller

Author: Eleanor Hyde

Although her roots and her family were still in Ohio, Lydia Miller had become a New Yorker. She turned her clothes sense and experience as a model into a well paying job on *Gazelle*, a fashion magazine. A tall blonde, she reflected elegance and control.

However, as *In Murder We Trust* (Fawcett, 1995) began, her equanimity had been overwhelmed by Manhattan's heat. She had declined an invitation from Adam Auerbach, a wealthy twice-divorced man, to visit his place in the Hamptons; then, changed her mind when the electricity failed. She was surprised to find Adam dead when she arrived; even more surprised to learn that she had inherited a substantial bequest. It was no surprise that she became the prime suspect for cantankerous detective Barolini. Fortunately Kramer, his assistant, not only trusted Lydia but also shared her love for John Steinbeck. Lydia was active in the investigation, but put herself into serious danger by concealing information.

Disillusioned by the backbiting in the design field, Lydia tendered her resignation at *Gazelle*; then agreed to take a sabbatical, as *Animal Instincts* (Fawcett, 1996) began. Her experience, coupled with volunteer work at an animal shelter alerted her to extravagant claims for a "youth" product and a thriving trade in stolen pets. A confusing narrative.

Robin Miller

Author: Jaye Maiman

Robin Miller was a romance writer, then a private investigator in New York, but was still searching for her place in life. She was distrustful of firearms because they had caused the death of her sister. Yet, she had killed in self-defense. Her father never spoke to Robin after her sister's death, and died before they could be reconciled. Her sexual relationships had been difficult. Two of her lovers were killed. She desired women, but was uncomfortable with that realization. Robin studied the disciplines of Tae Kwon Do, but existed primarily on junk food.

In *I Left My Heart* (Naiad, 1991), the death of Robin's lover, Mary Oswald, an investigative reporter, might have been caused by anaphylactic shock, suicide, or murder. Knowing Mary's care with medications, Robin believed it had been murder. Mary had been Robin's lover when they both worked in New York. They had parted when Robin was experiencing a difficult time with her father's death after their long estrangement. Before she finished her investigation, Robin realized that she had never known the real Mary. Robin's career as romance writer Laurel Carter went into eclipse when she was "outed" as a lesbian during the investigation of Mary's death.

By *Crazy for Loving* (Naiad, 1992), Robin worked in Tony Serra's detective agency. When David Ross, the errant husband whom Robin was trailing, was murdered, Tony pulled Robin off the case. A twelve-year-old

African-American boy was arrested for the killing, a solution unacceptable to Robin.

In *Under My Skin* (Naiad, 1993), a vacation provided little relief. While visiting friends in the Poconos, Robin's flashbacks to an unhappy childhood were interrupted when a potential client was murdered.

Robin's relationship with television chef K. T. Belleflower faltered during *Someone to Watch* (Naiad, 1995). A primary murder suspect, Lurlene, had been K. T.'s childhood friend. There were others with a motive to kill, necessitating serious risk taking behavior by Robin.

Baby, It's Cold (Naiad, 1996) placed Robin in a difficult situation. She had been seeing Phyllis for several weeks when Michael, the son of Phyllis and her gay former husband, was kidnapped. Robin agreed to investigate without contacting the police. The narrative explored the hunger of some gays and lesbians to have children. K. T. Belleflower returned.

San Francisco police detective Tom Ryan, who had worked with Robin at the time of Mary Oswell's death, had been a good friend, even a surrogate father. In *Old Black Magic* (Naiad, 1997), when she and K. T. Belleflower visited New Orleans, Robin became aware of a murder, closely resembling the death of Tom's estranged wife years before. At first, Tom discouraged Robin's involvement, but agreed to have his former police partner, Theobald Sweeney, now a private investigator, contact her. Sweeney was a crude and bitter man, but he wanted justice for Tom Ryan and would kill to get it.

K. T.'s pregnancy was terminated by a miscarriage. She and Robin planned another artificial impregnation. Sex was not only explicit but integrated into the text.

Kate Millholland

Author: Gini Hartzmark

Katharine Anne Prescott Millholland had a pedigree longer than her name. Her wealthy Chicago area family had sent her to North Shore Country Day, Bryn Mawr, and the University of Chicago Law School. Yet life had not been kind. Her brief marriage to Russell Dubrinski, disapproved of by her family, had ended when he died of brain cancer. Kate was not close to her parents—a father addicted to alcohol, and a mother who valued her social position and reputation before her children. Her brother, Teddy had committed suicide. Kate's decision to practice law was acceptable because she practiced Mergers and Acquisitions in Callahan Ross, a corporate firm. With little personal life, Kate became so obsessed by her work that her clothes were selected by her secretary or through a personal shopper. She gobbled M & Ms in times of stress.

In *Principal Defense* (Ivy, 1992), corporate raider Edgar Eichel threatened Azor, a major client of Callahan Ross. The matter became personal when the teenage ward of the Azor CEO, Stephen Azorini, was found dead. The Azorini family was connected with the Mafia, so Kate had to tread carefully as she uncovered evidence of sexual and financial misconduct. Even when injured and amnesiac, Kate fought to save Azor and its attractive CEO with the help of investigator Elliott Abelman.

Kate had become a partner in Callahan, Ross by *Final Option* (Ivy, 1994). That did not protect her from suspicion of murder when she found a major client dead in his wrecked vehicle. Kate searched for missing files to defend the corporation from federal charges, going to great lengths to save herself from a too humble killer.

In *Bitter Business* (Fawcett Columbine, 1995), Kate dealt with the business affairs of the contentious Cavanaugh family, in which she found parallels to her own. Not only was there a possibility that Jack Cavanaugh's irresponsible younger daughter would sell her shares in the closely held family corporation, but someone killed his reasonable older daughter, leaving the body for Kate to discover. Lover Steve Azorini wanted a live-in relationship, but found competition from Elliott Abelman.

Fatal Reaction (Ivy, 1998) was set in a background of international finance and biochemical experimentation, but Millholland mastered these complex fields. When a key player in the negotiations was murdered, Steve called on Kate to find the killer and thereby save his corporation from financial ruin. She did so with help from Elliott Abelman and her mother, Astrid. Kate's relationship with Azorini was seriously weakened.

In a somewhat lighter vein during *Rough Track* (Ivy, 1999), Kate was diverted from representation of sleazy twin restaurateurs who wanted an IPO (initial public offering) by the plight of her best friend, Chrissy Rendell. Jeff, Chrissy's husband, was suspected of murdering his father, the owner of a Milwaukee, Wisconsin football franchise. Her secretary Cheryl, Elliott, and a beefy football player helped Kate survive. Meantime, she moved beyond her affair with Azorini.

The Prescott-Milholland families had been major supporters of the Prescott Memorial Hospital where Kate's roommate Claudia held a fellowship during *Dead Certain* (Fawcett, 2000). When the Board of Trustees voted to sell the hospital to a profit-making corporation (HCC), Kate and her mother Astrid were horrified. Prescott Memorial had a significant patient population from the underprivileged, who would no longer be served by the change. A series of post-operative deaths at the hospital complicated the struggle to keep the facility independent and endangered first Claudia's job, then her life.

An interesting combination of love and business.

Tori Miracle

Author: Valerie S. Malmont

Her early years as the daughter of an American diplomat had provided Tori Miracle with extensive travel and an elegant lifestyle. Her world crashed when her younger brother Billy, whom she was supposed to be watching, wandered off and died from a snake bite while they were in Thailand. After Billy's death, Tori's mother became an alcoholic. Her institutional costs were not covered by health insurance. Tori's father consoled himself with a younger woman and his work. Tori, a college graduate, had some success with a book. However when she lost her job as a crime reporter, she barely had enough money to subsidize her mother's care, pay her rent, and feed two cats (Fred and Noel). A tiny woman in her mid-thirties, her personal life was equally dismal; e.g. a fiancé who dumped her because she had spent too much time working on the book.

As *Death Pays the Rose Rent* (Simon & Schuster, 1994) began, Tori visited Alice-Ann, her college roommate, now married to Richard, a wealthy publisher living in Lickin Creek, Pennsylvania. Richard, as a descendant of the town founder, annually received a single rose as a tribute from the community in a well-attended festival. Tori's arrival with the cats did not help the deteriorating relationship between Alice Ann and the unfaithful Richard. He had recently embarked on a money-raising scheme, the details of which he had not shared. Richard was found dead and Alice-Ann was among the suspects. Lickin Creek had a history, which included real estate fraud, an invention by Thomas Edison, Civil War history, and underground tunnels. Lots of action but the tunnels were better connected than the plot. Tori had not been totally accepted in Lickin Creek; too well traveled, an accomplished linguist, and a published author.

Lickin Creek might be a small town, but in *Death, Lies, and Apple Pies* (Simon & Schuster, 1997) it was overpopulated with characters. Tori returned to the area to continue her relationship with Garnet Gochenauer, the chief of police. Garnet's widowed sister, Greta who had moved in with him, was a leader in the opposition to a local nuclear waste depot. Underemployed and unemployed men and women wanted jobs. Landowners who would benefit supported the project. Motives for two unexplained deaths multiplied. Tori's life was threatened on several occasions before the killer disclosed himself.

Tori adjusted to the changes in her life during *Death, Guns, and Sticky Buns* (Dell, 2000). Police Chief Garnet Gochenauer must have misunderstood her intentions because he took leave to advise the Costa Rican police. Her full-time position at the *Chronicle* drew her into a reenactment of a Civil War execution sponsored by Lickin Creek College for Women. The firing squad's ammunition had been tampered with causing the death of former congressman Mack Macmillan. Tori's reputation as a harbinger of disaster motivated her to discover who had substituted real bullets for the blank wads. Her courage and sense of humor made it possible to survive her own depression at the need for a breast biopsy.

Health did not seem to be a problem for Tori in *Death, Snow, and Mistletoe* (Dell, 2000). She had mixed feelings about the news that her father was to marry the much younger woman who was bearing his child. She was affected, as were all the citizens of Lickin Creek, by the disappearance of five-year-old Kevin Poffenberger while roaming the woods with older cousins. The discovery of a skeleton revived memories of another five-year-old boy who had disappeared thirty-seven years before. The news left one woman heavy with guilt; another, burning for revenge.

Intricate plots and interesting, but eccentric, characterizations.

Next book in this series: *Death, Bones, and Stately Homes* (2003)

Meredith "Merry" Mitchell
Author: Ann Granger, pseudonym for Ann Hulme

Merry Mitchell was a convent educated British career diplomat who, by age thirty-five, had been stationed in a variety of foreign countries. Tall, slim, and hazel-eyed with brown hair, she had served with dedication and competence, earning the respect of her colleagues.

In *Say It with Poison* (St. Martin, 1991), Merry returned to England to attend the wedding of Sara, the child of cousin Eve and Mike, the man whom Merry had loved. Mike's death had never been satisfactorily explained until Merry, with the assistance of Chief Inspector Alan Markby, solved two murders.

Merry accepted a post in London, commuting from Markby's territory in *A Season for Murder* (St. Martin, 1992). She approached the affair with Alan cautiously, unwilling to limit her independence. He sought her help in the investigation of a tragic hunting death that might have been murder.

During *Cold in the Earth* (St. Martin, 1993), Merry rented a London apartment but housesat in Bamford during her vacation. Markby was unhappy with the continued development of his hometown by real estate brokers. The tensions in the community increased when a bulldozer uncovered a corpse. As an outsider, Merry offered Markby a different perspective of the suspects, many of whom he had known from childhood.

In *Murder Among Us* (St. Martin, 1993), Alan and Merry were invited to the grand opening of a posh restaurant and inn. Their evening out was interrupted by a chase after a nude protestor who led pursuers to a corpse.

Merry, who would not live with Alan, but would be desolate if he were out of her life, had a change of heart in *Where Old Bones Lie* (St. Martin, 1994). She purchased a small cottage in Bamford. She spent her vacation helping her archeologist friend Ursula Gratton, who suspected her former lover of killing his wife. Old and new disappearances vied with hippies and skeletons for attention.

Fixing up her new home preoccupied Merry for the first half of *A Fine Place for Death* (St. Martin, 1995), while Alan and his temporary assistant, Sgt. Helen Turner, investigated the death of a young hooker. However, Merry became heavily involved when a second teenager, who had sought her help, was brutally murdered. Operating independently and against Alan's advice, she worked with an elderly retiree to find more than one killer.

Even during their spare time, Merry and Alan could not escape murder. In *Flowers for His Funeral* (St. Martin, 1995), wealthy Alex Constantine died in their presence from a "thorn" prick at a flower show. Merry was shocked to learn that the grieving widow was Alan's former wife, Rachel, and irritated to find that he was expected to provide support and counsel. The Secret Service became very interested in the case because Constantine had a prior identity in Lebanon. That did not keep Alan and Merry out of the investigation. This was a carefully plotted narrative with an unusual ending. Markby accepted a promotion that would require a transfer.

Actually, as *Candle for a Corpse* (St. Martin, 1996) began, Markby worked at the regional office, but continued to make his home in Bamford. When gravediggers found bones that should not be there, and proof of an undetected murder surfaced, Alan took responsibility for the case. Merry was in the neighborhood when the bones were discovered, knew many of the suspects, and made it her business to know them better, even peering through their windows. Fortunately Alan kept on the trail, and was available when the killer added Merry to his hit list.

A Touch of Mortality (Headline, 1996) concentrated on Alan's role because police procedure was the key to the killer in what seemed to be a neighborhood feud. Merry's friendship with a victim aided in the solution.

Merry and Alan were determined to avoid controversy on their vacation in Parsloe St. John, but, as *A Word After Dying* (St. Martin, 1998) evolved, they found it impossible. Initially Alan agreed to take part in the investigation of the death of elderly recluse Olivia Smeaton. Merry was appalled that Alan coveted the Smeaton house as a retirement home. The community, rife with rumors of Satanism, made it clear that Alan and Merry were not welcome.

Alan made the deductions to solve the murders in *Call the Dead Again* (St. Martin, 1999), but the characterizations that will remain in the reader's mind were of the females: (1) Merry, unable to commit to Alan; (2) Kate, the hidden daughter of a prominent attorney who became a catalyst for disaster; and (3) Carla, the attorney's wife, overwhelmed by a sense of betrayal.

Hugh Franklin remarried too soon after the death of his wife in *Beneath These Stones* (Headline, 1999). Too soon, because neither he nor Sonia realized how miserable she would be in an isolated farmhouse. After a bitter quarrel, Sonia left one evening. The next day, her corpse was found. Hugh's daughter, Tammy, had vital information that would solve the case and absolve her father of suspicion. Merry and Alan discerned the truth about Tammy and Sonia.

Death in its many forms, including murder and wartime service had diminished the Oakley family. By 1999, as *Shades of Murder* (Headline, 2000) began, two elderly sisters were believed to be the end of the line. As they considered selling the rundown manse, another possible heir threatened their precarious position. Friends, including Merry and Alan, rallied to protect the spinsters from Jan who claimed to be a cousin. His death by arsenic poisoning threatened the sale of the property and the status of the sisters. In the conclusion, Merry decided to sell her Bamford house and to seek a place where both she and Alan could live...as a married couple.

The series contained above average writing. Merry was an independent heroine who had a significant role. Some of Granger's female characters were more memorable than admirable.

Next book in this series: *A Restless Evil* (2002)

Michelle "Mitch" Mitchell

Author: Doug Allyn

Michelle "Mitch" Mitchell placed a high value on her independence. As a motherless teenager, she had refused to consider an abortion when she became pregnant and ran away from her father's home. She bore a son, Corey, and supported him without the help of the man she believed to be his father. While working as a diver for Exxon Oil on the Texas Gulf, Mitch (as she preferred to be called) earned a degree in marine biology. Her commitment to a career ended her engagement to a man who wanted her to lead a more conventional life. When her father died, after years of estrangement with only minor exchanges through the mail, she was surprised to inherit his bar/grill/diving facility on Lake Huron. Corey, then in the middle grades, did not return to Michigan with his mother, but continued his education in Texas.

When she returned to Huron Harbor, her intention was to sell out as soon as it could be arranged. However, as *Icewater Mansions* (St. Martin, 1995) opened, entranced by her sense of the lake and out of sheer stubbornness, she turned down an offer to purchase and began to renovate the "Crow's Nest." New complexities entered her life when doubts arose as to whether her father had died a natural death. Then the man whom she believed to be Corey's grandfather sought custody of the boy.

By *Black Water* (St. Martin, 1996), Mitch had placed Corey in boarding school and made a commitment to Huron Harbor. Her skill as a deep-water diver drew her into the disappearance of Jimmy Calderon who came to town searching for a father he had never known. His brother, Ray, believed that Jimmy had been murdered and would not leave Huron Harbor until he found the killer. Always an outsider herself, Mitch and her friend, Sheriff Charlie Bauer, became Ray's allies.

Mitch wanted her son Corey to live with her, but, during *A Dance in Deep Water* (St. Martin, 1997), the parent-child relationship was tense. As Mitch learned about her own mother's family, she grappled with her hatred for the father who wronged his wife and child. She and Corey grew closer. Along the way, she dove deep into a flooded mine to determine whether or not her father was a killer.

Allyn's narratives were concerned with family relationships, particularly the emotional ties between children and parents.

Tess Monaghan

Author: Laura Lippman

Theresa Esther Weinstein Monaghan, better known as Tess, worked as a reporter on the *Baltimore Star* until it collapsed. There being an overabundance of unemployed reporters in Baltimore, she chose another profession, private investigator. Tess had lots of connections in the city. The Monaghans and Weinsteins were well represented in government circles. Her dad was a city liquor inspector; her mother, a secretary for the National Security Agency; Uncle Donald was in state government. Aunt Kitty Monaghan, who owned a Fells Point bookstore, offered the upstairs for an office/apartment. Tess, who had attended nearby Washington College where she was on the crew, still rowed for exercise. She was a tall brown-haired woman, fiercely independent, trying to survive without a steady source of income. Her lover at the time the series began was Jonathan Ross, a reporter on the *Baltimore Beacon & Light*.

In *Baltimore Blues* (Avon, 1997), a simple assignment trailing attorney Ava Hill for her fiancé, Daryl Paxton produced evidence that Ava had been spending time with senior attorney Michael Abramowitz at O'Neal, O'Connor, and O'Neill. Abramowitz's murder after a fracas with Paxton focused suspicion on him. Tess and her rowing coach, paraplegic attorney Tyner Grey had more than one mystery to solve. Who had killed Abramowitz? Who had paid him to cover up another murder? Tess' sense that she had achieved some form of justice was tempered by the fact that someone died in the process.

Tyner offered Tess a full-time position as investigator for his law office with the understanding that she would earn enough hours to qualify for a license. In *Charm City* (Avon, 1997), she investigated staff at the local newspaper to determine who had authorized the reinsertion of an investigative report. Management had ordered the material withdrawn until there was further verification of fraud involving the purchase of a National League basketball franchise. The intended purchaser, "Wink" Wynkowski, committed suicide after the story was printed. Bar-owner "Uncle" Spike Orrick, a shirttail relative who was brutally beaten in what might have been a robbery, had left his greyhound Esskay in Tess' keeping. The blending of these two incidents resulted in an engaging narrative in which management rivalries, spousal abuse, cruelty to animals, and fraudulent reporting played parts. The romance that had developed between Tess and "Crow," a guitar player who made it big in the music business, faltered, but Tess kept the dog.

By *Butchers Hill* (Avon, 1998), Tyner had forced Tess to go it alone, so she was operating out of Aunt Kitty's upstairs. Two new cases came in the same day. Luther Beale had been sent to prison after killing one of a group of foster children who had terrorized his neighborhood. Released after serving his sentence, he wanted to make amends to the surviving children. Unfortunately, as Tess located the children they were murdered. In the second case, "Mary Brown" hired Tess to find her half-sister, missing for thirteen years. Gradually Tess discovered the identity of her client and her reason for employing Tess.

Texas was foreign to Tess, but in *In Big Trouble* (Avon, 1999), that was where her concern for Crow took her. Inklings that he was in big trouble forged an alliance between Tess and Crow's parents. They hired her to find their missing son. The search led Tess to two recently deceased ex-convicts, and then connected with a twenty-one-year-old tragedy that still motivated murder. The plotting and characterizations were excellent.

In *The Sugar House* (Morrow, 2000), tracing a Jane Doe victim had begun as a favor for Tess' dad, Patrick. It did not end there. Ruthie Dembrow wanted one thing: the name of the young victim for whose death her brother had been sent to prison. He had been knifed shortly after his arrival. The trail of "Jane Doe" was still there to be followed from an unhappy home to an institution for young rich and vulnerable bulimics. The facility was still functioning, although its financial procedures were suspect. The search ended with favors too: one by Patrick could cost his job; another, that Tess could accept graciously. She had continued to live above Aunt Kitty's bookstore but Kitty and Tyner Gray were very much in love, and three was a crowd.

A client for whom she refused to provide services during *In a Strange City* (Morrow, 2001) enticed Tess and Crow to be present on January 19th when an anonymous figure annually visited the grave of Edgar Allan Poe. Two visitors appeared that night; one was murdered, but not necessarily by the other. Clues and messages deposited at Tess' home drew her deeper into Poe's life and its relevance to Baltimore history. The destructive nature of those for whom "collecting" became an obsession was a significant factor in the narrative. At this time, Tess lived in her new home. Crow was a frequent visitor. She was still working for Al Keyes agency in order to earn the necessary training for an independent investigator's license.

The Baltimore background was authentic and colorful. The characters and plotting are way above average for paperback originals. Don't miss them, and any future books in the series.

Next book in this series: *The Last Place* (2002)

Hester Latterly Monk

Author: Anne Perry

See: Hester Latterly, page 372.

Adele Monsarrat

Author: Echo Heron

Adele Monsarrat was dedicated to nursing. She had become a fixture at Ward 8 of Ellis Hospital in Marin County near San Francisco. The ward in general, and Adele in particular, had a reputation for wackiness that was well earned. She was a tall, slim, dark-haired woman in her thirties who insinuated herself into murder investigations. Like the hospital administration, the police tolerated her because she had valuable skills.

From childhood Adele had been fascinated by police work. She had discovered the bodies of a neighbor woman and her child as a youngster and was instrumental in the arrest of the killer husband. During high school she worked for a security business, learning to pick locks and disarm alarm systems. She graduated from high school at sixteen. During her nurses training at the University of California, Adele also studied drama. Over the years, she collected a closet full of costumes, which she used undercover with wigs and make-up.

She was a vegetarian, but addicted to peanut butter, potato chips, and popcorn. She avoided alcohol and had no interest in drugs. Frequent mention was made of her "crazy woman" laugh. Given the descriptions of her days at Ward 8, maybe she needed to be a little crazy to survive. Although she had been raised Catholic by her widowed librarian mother, Adele considered herself one-half agnostic and one-half atheist. If she worshipped anything, it was nature. She saw a lot of it because she religiously ran eight to twelve miles each morning.

Adele's early marriage to Vietnam veteran Gavin Wozniac ended in divorce. He had taken off for a period of years justifying her petition to terminate the marriage. On his return, they eventually established a civilized friendship. He married again, this time to someone more tolerant of his idiosyncrasies. She did not. During their marriage, Gavin had taught her some martial arts skills and how to handle a gun. For support, she relied on her close friendship with fellow nurse Cynthia O'Neil, on the non-human companionship of Nelson, her vegetarian Black Labrador, and eventually on her feelings for Detective Tim Rittman. When none of these were available, she relied on help from imaginary friends, including some well-known fictional detectives. Adele drove a 1978 Pontiac station wagon named the Beast, tolerating its frequent bad moods. She was less tolerant of HMOs and the pressure they placed on hospital administration to replace nursing staff with cheaper, untrained workers.

Readers should be warned not to read *Pulse* (Ivy, 1998) if they are contemplating surgery. The patients on Adele's ward were very sick. Many of her fellow workers were in bad shape—mentally ill, and promiscuous to an alarming degree. They were dying off more quickly than the patients, and these were not natural deaths. The narrative, which contained many vignettes concerning hospital care, could have used editing.

Ward 8 had barely recovered from a serial killer scare when, in *Panic* (Ivy, 1998), it was overwhelmed by mysterious deaths seemingly from a viral disease. The initial patient was Iris Hersh, the daughter of a doctor, but she may have infected her nurse, Cynthia O'Neil. Adele put the rest of her life on hold as she fought to save Cynthia while investigating the Hersh family during her rare off work hours.

Adele bonded with the amnesiac patient she dubbed "Mathilde" in *Paradox* (Ivy, 1998). The young woman had been discovered badly burned at the scene of a car accident. Inside the vehicle was the corpse of a young child. Detective Tim Rittman, who had achieved status close to that of a coprotagonist although he had not become Adele's lover, believed that Mathilde was complicit in a series of murders. Adele disagreed, risking both their lives to prove him wrong.

During *Fatal Diagnosis* (Ballantine, 2000), Adele's work environment was unpleasant because the nursing staff was overburdened and administration sought budget cuts by replacing senior staff with new hires. Adele's devotion to her patients might have assisted in their recovery but it made her a prime target for dismissal. She and fellow nurses Cynthia O'Neill and Wanda Percy were alerted to the possibility that patients who had prior surgeries in Europe were potential murder victims. Adele needed the combat expertise that she had learned from her Green Beret ex-husband and help from Cynthia and Tim Ritmann to survive the enemies she acquired while investigating a scheme, which threatened not only individuals but also communities.

The narratives included intricate plotting and focused on serial killers, and the frenzied atmosphere of Ward 8. They provided flashes of wacky humor.

Lane Montana

Author: Kay Hooper

Lane Montana, a licensed private investigator in Atlanta, advertised her skills as a "finder of lost objects." She claimed an "instinct," although when tested at Duke University for Extra Sensory Perception, she flunked. Lane survived financially through inherited investments. She was a small, green-eyed dark haired woman in her early thirties, who shared her Atlanta loft with a Siamese cat, "Choo." Lane was very close to her artist brother, Jason. Her widowed mother's multiple marriages may account for Lane's single state.

In *Crime of Passion* (Avon, 1991), Jeffrey Townsend failed to identify the object he wanted found during the message he left on Lane's answering machine. When she arrived at his home, he was dead. Police considered her presence in the electronically secure Townsend home, her delay in contacting them, and the erasure of Townsend's message to be suspicious. That seemed reasonable, but Lt. Trey Fortier not only believed Lane but tainted evidence, and then shared access to department records and facilities with her. Their affair created a definite conflict of interest.

House of Cards (Avon, 1991) focused on the new relatives acquired when Lane's mother married Englishman Adam Rowland. During a stay at the ancestral home, Larry, the innocuous appearing insurance executive married to Aunt Emily Buford, was murdered. Lane knew there was a killer in her family tree, but had to identify the right person.

Britt Montero

Author: Edna Buchanan, a well-known Miami reporter

Britt Montero mirrored the reporter that author Buchanan was in reality: tireless, ambitious, intolerant of police brutality, and stimulated by her work. Britt was a blond, green-eyed Cuban/American whose father had been executed by the Castro government. Her mother worked as manager of an "upscale fashion house." Their relationship was strained, because after Britt's father died, her mother farmed her out to assorted relatives in Florida. Britt survived two years at Northwestern University in Evanston, Illinois, but transferred to a warmer climate to graduate. Aged forty, as the series began, she was a crime reporter for the *Miami Daily News*. Britt, who considered television reporters unnecessarily intrusive, prided herself on being a print journalist. She not only carried a gun, but supported handgun ownership. She had never married, sharing her home with a cat, Billy Boots.

In *Contents Under Pressure* (Hyperion, 1992), Britt's sources at the police department dried up when asked questions about the death of D. Wayne Hudson, a former football player, who had fled when pursued by night shift police. Hudson's wife asked Britt to search beyond the obvious reason for the pursuit. Attractive Sgt. Ken McDonald was willing to help so long as it did not jeopardize his job.

Miami, It's Murder (Hyperion, 1994) began with Britt depressed by the end of her relationship with McDonald. The narrative blended two story lines: (a) the suspicion of retired detective Dan Flood that gubernatorial candidate Eric Fielding had committed a murder 22 years before; and (b) a series of murders, seemingly executions of criminals who had escaped justice through technicalities.

By *Suitable for Framing* (Hyperion, 1995), Britt, comfortable with her status at the *Daily News*, had no qualms about helping a novice reporter. She realized that she was being undermined in time to save her reputation. She was less fortunate in helping Howie, a young African-American drawn into crime by his friends, and betrayed by the juvenile justice and social services systems.

Britt had resolved to stay out of Cuban politics, but in *Act of Betrayal* (Hyperion, 1996), she had no choice. She was focused on a pattern of missing boys. The *Daily News* wanted her insider status, as the daughter of hero Tony Montero, for a series on Cubans in Miami. Juan Carlos Reyes, a powerful candidate for leadership in Cuba after the anticipated demise of Castro, and Jorge Bravo, a struggling patriot who no longer accommodated American goals, both sought Tony's journal, which identified a traitor. Britt's daytime activities were still exciting, but her nights were haunted by dreams of the man she had killed.

In *Margin of Error* (Hyperion, 1997), Britt's editor offered her a "plush assignment," sharing her workdays with charismatic movie actor, Lance Westfell as he prepared for a role as a reporter in a film set in Miami. The world of make-believe left Britt confused as to who were the victims, who, the villains in an over blown narrative. Not up to Buchanan's standards.

Britt, although exposed to crime and criminals, believed that environment, not genetics could cause individuals to be evil. This conviction did not survive in *Garden of Evil* (Avon, 1999). She ignored the need of an older woman and misjudged her own ability to cope with a killer. She became aware of a destructive family trait that could well be carried on by a child yet unborn. This was a character building experience for Britt.

Deception by a son, cruelty by one husband, and a lack of trust by another all entered into the tragic resolution of Kaitlin Jordan's death in *You*

Only Die Twice (Morrow, 2001). R. J. Jordan had been convicted of his wife Kaitlin's death in 1991. After multiple appeals had failed, he was due to be executed. When Kaitlin's body washed upon on a Miami Beach shore, Jordan won his freedom, but the casualties had only begun. Britt wanted to know where Kathleen had been during the years after she disappeared and why she returned to Florida just before R. J. was to die. Terrific plotting.

Britt would be unbelievable, if it were not that Edna Buchanan is too. Next book in this series: *The Ice Maiden* (2002)

Kellie Montgomery

Author: Valerie Wilcox

Sailing Puget Sound off Seattle was more than a hobby for Kellie Montgomery. It filled her life after her husband Wendell died. Harbormaster Bert Foster, who had formerly been married to Kellie's sister, found her a job at the sailing school, Sound Sailing, maintained at the exclusive Larstad's Marina. Against her daughter Cassie's wishes, Kellie sold the family home and used the proceeds to purchase the forty-foot-sloop *Second Wind* on which she made her home. She had taught in the Seattle school system for fifteen years, but at age forty wanted something different. Cassie, who had been adopted by Kellie and Wendell, was attending school out East so the sloop offered all the space Kellie needed. She may have been insensitive as to how vulnerable Cassie felt losing her beloved father and the home she grew up in. A peripatetic cat named Pan-Pan joined Kellie's crew.

Kellie was part of an extended family, dominated by her older sister Donna. Donna's power arose not only from her formidable personality but from her role as trustee of a fund created when their parents were killed in a car accident. Besides Donna, Kellie had another sister and three brothers. Their parents had enjoyed a close marriage. Mom, a Mormon, had descended from Brigham Young. She and Kellie's dad, an Irish Catholic, had raised their family in Maine. Kellie and Wendell were the first of the family to move to Seattle; followed by Donna and Bert.

Even with her job as manager of the sailing school, there must have been a void in Kellie's life. To the dismay of Detective Allen Kingston she was drawn to murder investigations. On one occasion that occurred before the events in the first narrative, she had "assisted the police." That only increased her passion for snooping.

While sailing, Kellie had noted a drifting yacht and called the Marina for a rescue as *Sins of Silence* (Berkley, 1998) began. She recognized the victims when she prematurely boarded the ship: Donald Moyer, the attorney who processed Cassie's adoption and his wife Miranda. Kellie's motive for aggressively seeking their killer was based on concern that the potential purchasers of Larstad's Marina might blame Bert Foster for poor security measures. That convinced her, but not Kingston. When Cassie returned on vacation, determined to find her birth parents, Kellie had another reason to want to know more about Donald and Miranda Moyer.

Things held dear by Kellie were endangered in *Sins of Betrayal* (Berkley, 1999). Detective Allen Kingston had not been in touch. Was it because his new partner was a tall blonde? Her favorite sister, Kate was drinking heavily. Was she ill? The management of Larstad's Marina was considering punitive measures against the owners who lived on board their boats. This could mean Kellie would have to move the *Second Wind* elsewhere. Juggling all this, Kellie tracked down a pair of aging lovers whose marriage might make them targets for murder.

The narratives read well, and expressed a deep love for sailing and for the Seattle area. As to Kellie, Tracy Lord would call her "yar."

Claire Montrose

Author: April Henry

A sparse childhood and lonely teenage years had contributed to Claire Montrose's personality. Her unwed mother spent a large amount of time watching television after she was awarded disability payments for a fall incurred while shopping at a Portland grocery store. Her sister Jean did not finish high school, but went to beauty school and was working at a mortuary at the time of the series. Claire's high school years had been grim. Her after school hours were spent working at a pizza parlor, using her wages not for personal needs but to pay family bills. This experience caused her to live sparsely and avoid debt. Her first full time job was with the Oregon Department of Transportation Special Plate Department. As a hobby she collected names of cute license plates. She was a single woman in her early thirties, tall with red gold hair.

As *Circles of Confusion* (Harper Paperbacks, 1999) began, Claire's bland existence was electrified by an inheritance from Aunt Cady, a spinster who had served in the Women's Army Corps in Germany during World War II. Among Aunt Cady's meager possessions were a diary and a small but intriguing painting. Spurred on by dissatisfaction with her current life, Claire flew to New York City for an appraisal. Naïve but not stupid, she shared her story with two attractive men who differed as to the authenticity of the painting: a Vermeer (very rare), a Van Meegeren (excellent fake), or a more amateur effort. It was worth killing for. A well-done art story.

Dante Bonner, one of the experts whom Claire had consulted in New York City, wanted to remain a part of her life. In *Square in the Face* (Avon, 2000), they shared a long distance romance. Each was emotionally attached to their home locale. Claire had no confidence in marriage based on her family's experience. Her mother and sister both had children outside of marriage. One of her grandmothers had married five times. Claire's heart melted when she learned that her friend Lori's three-year-old son had been stricken with leukemia and needed a bone marrow transplant. The best potential donor was a daughter that Lori had given up for adoption. Lori thought the best person to find that child was Claire.

Claire vacillated about attending her twentieth high school reunions but, in *The Heart Shaped Box* (HarperCollins, 2001), she decided to go. She lived in Portland, so could easily drive to nearby Minor, Oregon. Some of her classmates seemed unchanged. Cindy Weaver, former prom queen and head cheerleader, was still vivacious and hungry for attention. Others had exceeded early expectations: Richard Crane, the shy but intelligent year-book photographer, had become a software multi-millionaire. Sawyer Fairchild, then a student teacher, was a rising politician. When Cindy was murdered during the first night party, Claire defended the innocence of Logan West who had spent most of the intervening years fighting schizo-phrenia. Museum curator Dante Bonner escorted Claire to the event and served as her Watson.

An excellent series, still in paperback.

Dr. Jean Montrose

Author: C. F. (Francis) Roe

Jean Montrose was the doctor that rural Scottish (and American) commu-nities long for—a compassionate general practitioner dedicated to her patients. Her marriage to Steven, owner of the local glass works, occasion-ally suffered from her lack of attention. Their daughters, Lisbie and Fiona, reluctantly accepted additional home responsibilities and the absence of their mother at critical moments, but paid a price. Jean's work at autopsies established a working partnership with Chief Inspector Douglas Niven.

In *A Nasty Bit of Murder* (Signet, 1992) a.k.a. *The Lumsden Baby* (Headline, 1990), she was uncomfortable with the crib death of an epileptic infant and the subsequent death of his aristocratic but alcoholic father. Her probe into their deaths was interspersed with glimpses of a rural practice, reminiscent of James Herriott's veterinary series.

During *A Fiery Hint of Murder* (Signet, 1993) a.k.a. *Death by Fire* (Headline, 1990)), local superstition and modern lasers vied for the responsibility for arson and death by incineration. Jean's absorption led to a brush with infidelity and a failure to notice Lisbie's alcoholism.

In *A Classy Touch of Murder* (Signet, 1993) a.k.a. *Bad Blood* (Headline, 1991), the Montrose family drove through the placid countryside, only to discover a wrecked car whose driver had been shot. The deceased had been engaged to marry the beautiful daughter of the Earl of Strathalmond. Both the victim and his politically ambitious brother were less than admirable. Jean made Doug Niven aware than the real killer would never pay for her crime.

A Bonny Case of Murder (Signet, 1994) a.k.a. *Deadly Partnership* (Headline, 1991) focused on the tangled lives of two couples: entrepreneur Donald Tarland and his psychologist wife, Teresa, and local restaurateurs Bob and Louise Fraser. The murders of Frasers' flirtatious daughter Caroline and Tarland's partner, Mac MacFayden, led Doug Niven and Jean to uncover the cold calculating plot to use Caroline's death for financial advantage.

A Torrid Piece of Murder (Signet, 1994) a.k.a. *Fatal Fever* (Headline, 1992) centered on Dr. Derek Sutherland, who failed both as an anesthesiologist and as a father; on parents, whose ambitions for their child led to callous disregard for others; and on a haunted cleric who tried to protect a boy from a vengeful killer.

In *A Relative Cause of Murder* (Signet, 1995) a.k.a. *A Death in the Family* (Headline, 1993), seductive Moira Dagleish used men for gratification. Her politically powerful uncle used his office to enhance his career. Moira's death targeted other men in her life, leaving the one man who dominated it for Jean to discover.

Doug Niven could not ignore Jean as a suspect in *Hidden Cause of Murder* (Signet, 1996). The growing antipathy between her and Diane Taggart, her new partner, was known to the community, and was exacerbated by Taggart's charges against Jean to the Medical Board. When Jean was cleared, she did not share her knowledge of a second killer, allowing private justice to deal with the matter.

The death of abusive bully Robertson Kelso after surgery in *A Tangled Knot of Murder* (Signet, 1996) produced several suspects. The primary was surgeon Hugh Kirkwell who had reason to hate his patient. As in many prior narratives, Jean kept Inspector Douglas Niven from making a serious error.

Readers are cautioned that, except for the last two narratives, the American and English editions have different titles. These were cozy, reader friendly books, and a buy at paperback prices.

Abigail Moon

Author: Marjorie Eccles

The British based series was an ensemble, with Sgt. Abigail Moon as a contributing member. Widowed Inspector Gil Mayo was the series protagonist. Over a period of time Abigail became his preferred professional partner, but his personal relationship was with Sgt. Alex Jones. Abigail had a life of her own, a small place with a garden for puttering, and an on-going affair with Ben Appleyard, editor of the local newspaper. The series based on Mayo included several books during the 1980s before Abigail was introduced.

Abigail joined Mayo's team in *The Company She Kept* (St. Martin, 1996). She acted as his assistant when he connected a recent murder to a death fourteen years before. The earlier victim was a woman whom no one missed but no one forgot. Abigail had a short-term affair with a man in her unit who returned to his wife and a seriously ill son.

Mayo was available for significant interviews, but Abigail, now an inspector, was in charge of the murder investigation in *An Accidental Shroud* (St. Martin, 1997). The violent death of an antique jewelry dealer involved a fascinating array of suspects connected by birth, complicity, and greed.

Two seemingly unrelated crimes, the death of an out-of-town businessman and that of a young girl delivering newspapers divided the resources of Gil Mayo's unit in *A Species of Revenge* (St. Martin, 1998). Only as the evidence was gathered did they collectively realize how closely the crimes were entwined. Abigail's personal life played no part in the narrative. Her interviewing skills contributed to the success of the investigation.

In *A Death of Distinction* (St. Martin, 1998), Alex Jones, burned out and physically damaged, resigned from the police force. She joined her sister in an interior decorating business. Abigail could not consider such an alternative. Her career was too important. Gil and Abigail investigated the murder of a recently retired prison administrator.

Ben's decision to leave Lavenstock left Abigail emotionally adrift in *Killing Me Softly* (St. Martin, 1999). Soon she was too busy to focus on her own needs. Drugs were pouring into the area. Initially there were no connections to the death of an unfaithful husband. The two lines of enquiry met as the narrative developed. Women were disappearing from the community, one of whom was desperately in need of help. Early portions of the books described the potential victims, the killers, and suspects.

The Superintendent's Daughter (St. Martin, 1999) gave Abigail her opportunity to head the investigation into Kat Conolly's death. Gil had been taken off the case because of Kat's close friendship with his missing daughter, Julie. Still the emphasis of the story was on Kat: her devotion to her womanizing father, the mystery of her parentage, the men she loved and left, and the man she wanted but could not have. Structurally the narrative moved back and forth among characters at a mildly confusing rate.

A Sunset Touch (Constable, 2000) had an intricate plot revolving around the descendants of Jerzy, a Free Polish airman during World War II, and his English lover. Abigail was assigned to the death of Stefan Kaminski. He had encouraged Jerzy's son Tadeusz to come to Lavenstock. A fire in which Kaminski perished was at first believed to have caused the death of Tadeusz's children. When Jerzy escaped Poland, he had brought along a valuable painting. Inspector Martin Kite, was simultaneously investigating an attack on Cecily Haldane, wife of the local vicar. The rivalry between the two detectives was subordinate to the mystery of a wartime romance, the search for a smuggled work of art, and the interplay between Jerzy's and Cecily's children. Ben Appleyard, the roving reporter, had returned from the East and sought to reestablish his relationship with Abigail.

Abigail's request for promotion to Detective Chief Inspector would entail a transfer. In *Untimely Graves* (Constable, 2001), the Lavenstock police department was under pressure from higher authorities to solve three murders: those of a young athlete, an unidentified woman, and the bursar of prestigious Lavenstock College. Breakthroughs came when the "mystery woman" was identified and a relationship established between her and the bursar.

Author Marjorie Eccles' supporting characters—the victims, their families, the suspects, and the criminals—were well drawn. Eccles packaged more plotting, character building, and nuances into a 200 plus page book than some others do in twice the volume.

Phyllida Moon

Author: Eileen Dewhurst

At age thirty-eight, Phyllida Moon had resigned herself to a midlevel career as an actress in English repertory theatre. It had not met the goals she set when she trained at RADA (Royal Academy of Dramatic Arts). Then, neither had her marriage to Gerald, who was incapable of fidelity. Gerald, the stage manager for the company, went too far when he dallied with a cast member. Phyllida's loyalty to the Independent Theatre Company had been based partly on her affection for the prior producer. When ill health forced him to resign, he was replaced by Wayne Cryer who had no respect for Phyllida's work. At the point of quitting before she was fired, Phyllida had a generous offer to work in a forthcoming television serial.

As *Now You See Her* (Severn House, 1995) began, she decided to stay on in Seaminster, the town in which the company was currently playing. She let Gerald know that he was no longer a part of her life. The television series in which she would be cast as a female detective would not begin production for several months. Phyllida decided to seek employment as a private investigator with Peter Piper's agency to gather background. She accomplished this by role playing, setting herself up in various guises to gain information about possible incest, the mysterious death of a young student, and a teacher who took advantage of his students.

Phyllida took on two distinct personas in *The Verdict on Winter* (Severn House, 1996)—one as a daily domestic, the other as a receptionist in an art gallery. In both cases she was observing the behavior of art expert, David Lester. Lester's widowed sister, who shared his home, attributed the changes in David to anonymous letters implying that he was selling a forged painting. When David was murdered, he was blamed for possible art fraud at his gallery. Phyllida's powers of observation enabled her to discover a different motive for David's death.

The police department's lack of interest in the simultaneous disappearance of Carol Hargreaves and Maggie Trenchard sent their husbands to Peter Piper's agency in *Roundabout* (Severn House, 1998). When the women's bodies were discovered, Chief Superintendent Kendricks accepted help from the ubiquitous, "Mary Bowden" (the name by which Phyllida was known to the Seaminster Police). She had some concern about her need to submerge herself in these false identities. At some point, she reexamined who Phyllida Moon was.

After a successful two months in London performing in *A Policeman's Lot*, Phyllida found herself eager to return to Seaminster and her multifaceted job with Peter's agency. As *Double Act* (Severn House, 2000) began, he had a major assignment ready for her. She was to audition for a local dramatic society in order to observe a young man who might have fallen in with drug dealers. Phyllida watched the interactions among members of the theatre group. The deaths of a major contributor, writer/producer Henry Hutton, provided more than enough drama.

Phyllida's unexpected gallbladder surgery disrupted her plans to seek out attractive Dr. Jack Pusey who had relocated to Edinburgh as *Closing Stages* (Severn House, 2001) began. However it suited the needs of

Detective Chief Inspector Kendrick who wanted an undercover agent in Stansfield Manor to look for evidence that dementia patients were being euthanized. During her recuperation, Phyllida became familiar (in one case very familiar) with members of the staff and other patients. She returned later as a health care worker. The narrative was interspersed with the dilemma of a medically oriented family watching a loved one succumb to Alzheimer's.

No Love Lost (Severn House, 2001) exposed the dangers of unrequited love and jealous love. Peter Piper's Detective Agency had been hired by both parties in a marriage, each suspicious that the other had been unfaithful. When the wife was savagely murdered, Phyllida's input was made available to the police.

Much was made of Phyllida's mousy unprepossessing appearance as compared to the roles she played. She coveted the self-possession and allure that she portrayed when being someone else.

Next book in this series: *Easeful Death* (2002)

Teodora "Teddy" Morelli

Author: Linda French

It could have been worse, Teddy Morelli had sisters named Delizia; Tomasina, and Elizabetta and brothers, Raffaele, Carlo, and just plain Joseph, Jr. Joseph senior had met his wife, referred to in the series as "Marmee," in Italy where she performed Shakespeare for tourists on street corners. He had been an engineer, a designer of cockpits for Boeing Aeronautics. Joseph, Sr. had died; Marmee still played an important role in her children's lives.

Teddy was tiny, a former gymnast, now a history professor at Rainwater University in Bellingham, Washington. She had a Ph.D. with a specialty in Western American History. Her sister Tomasina a.k.a. Tabor was a female professional wrestler. Dr. Aurie Scholl, a fellow professor at the University, had discarded Teddy for what seemed to be a better marriage. When it ended in divorce, he wanted a second chance. Since he had used some of her original material in a professional publication without giving her credit, Teddy was hesitant. Teddy's current project was researching Chinook, the jargon, as distinguished from the language, used by the white traders and Native American hunters and fishers along the Pacific Coast.

Talking Rain (Avon, 1998) opened in Vancouver, British Columbia. Teddy had traveled there to watch Tabor fight. She was the villainess in her competitions. Tabor was gay, a fact she unsuccessfully tried to hide from

Marmee. Tabor was more comfortable never acknowledging her orientation to her mother. Tabor had a devoted male suitor, a wrestler named "Steamboat" Stevens who was also aware of Tabor's sexual preferences, but loved her anyway. Tabor had been sharing a home in the Bellingham area with Margaret Zimmerman, an author of children's books. When they returned from Vancouver, Margaret was dead. The sisters were whirled into a succession of wild events: treasure hunting, embezzlement and burglary. Another suspicious death was blamed on Teddy. A little knowledge of Chinook helped.

Teddy had never been a big fan of her sister Daisy's husband, botanist Leo Faber. In *Coffee To Die For* (Avon, 1998), she was impressed by his genetically altered mocha coffee. When Leo was murdered, there was a mad rush to find the greenhouse where he had been growing his R-19 beans. Some of the seekers didn't care "beans" about coffee. Leo had a sideline in marijuana. Teddy, pulling a reluctant Aurie Scholl along, was determined to get there first, even if it killed her.

Alert always to her need for tenure at Rainwater State University, Teddy paid her dues in *Steeped in Murder* (Avon, 1999). She escorted potential donor, Sally Pickett-Patchett, around the area, but drew the line at embellishing the reputation of Sally's ancestor, General George Pickett. When Ira Dedmarsh, chairman of the history department, was murdered, Teddy cooperated with the police and provided living quarters for Dedmarsh's attractive replacement. Fortunately the Pickett-Patchetts were not only Civil War buffs, but also rock and rollers.

Cordelia Morgan

Author: Bett Reece Johnson

Cordelia Morgan was a hired gun, trained by The Company to kill. For a dozen years this had been her life. As the series began she was burned out. She had been angry since childhood. Her mother had finally left her abusive husband, going to what seemed to be a refuge, a female village in New Harmony, North Dakota. The place was destroyed in a massacre, which the FBI either sanctioned or covered up. Cordelia's mother, Rachael, had died in the flames.

She returned to her father, a man involved in horses and gambling. Through him she met Psichari Pasonombre, who mentored her into working for The Company. He became her surrogate father, although she later feared his wrath when she walked off the job. Cordelia had not explained her reasons. She was fleeing from Simon Cruz, the man with whom she had lived for two years. He was also involved with The Company. She had stolen information to protect the reclusive feminist author, Anna Lee Stone. She did this aware that Stone's controversial book might have triggered the New Harmony massacre in which Rachael died, but that it had also given Rachael the courage to flee from a brutal husband.

Psichari knew that Cordelia had already exceeded the usual length of service with The Company. He had given her one more assignment in *The Woman Who Knew Too Much* (Cleis Press, 1998). He sent her to investigate the suspicious death of a raunchy old reclusive in New Mexico. Under an assumed persona, Cordelia joined the environmental protest group to which the victim belonged. They were resisting efforts to transfer water rights, a transfer that might increase pollution. Cordelia's sympathy for this group and her growing affection for Anna Lee Stone put her at odds with The Company. A product (plasterone) might alleviate impotence in males, but a side effect would be increased physical abuse of their sexual partners. Chemicals from the process might be present in local waters. Simon Cruz, head of The Company's Sangre de Christo laboratory, covered up evidence of the danger.

Cordelia was in flight when, in *The Woman Who Rode to the Moon* (Cleis, 1999) she agreed to help Claire James, a friend of her mother. Claire's alienated daughter Camilla had been found hanging in a barn at El Gato, an enclosed Colorado community that Claire had begun. Under a false identity, Cordelia moved into El Gato where she crossed paths with J. S. Symkin ("Sym"). Both Cordelia and Sym were aware that there was evil at El Gato. It appeared in the greed of a land developer, but more seriously in the brutality and sexual excesses of two men. Sym was vulnerable. Cordelia was vengeful. At the end, Cordelia was on the run again.

Johnson's prose, particularly as it related to settings, was exceptional. Next book in this series: *The Woman Who Found Grace* (2003)

Taylor Morgan

Author: Megan Mallory Rust

Taylor Morgan's life had been focused on airplanes since her father taught her to fly his Cessna 185. Flying is a way of life in Alaska because of the scarcity of highways. She worked as a pilot of Tundra Air Charter in Bethel, but eventually found that boring. A new job as pilot for LifeLine Air Ambulance offered more challenges. She settled into a remote cabin on the outskirts of Anchorage, which required a four-wheel drive vehicle in the winter—her choice, a Suzuki Sidekick. Her lover, pilot Steve Derossett, who also worked with LifeLine, spent much of his time at the cabin, but

Taylor was often alone. She had decided against having a pet because her schedule was so uncertain. She was obsessed with planes and thought best just sitting in a cockpit. On occasion, she ignored regulations to transport passengers in need of immediate help.

There was a loneliness to being the only female pilot at LifeLine, so in *Dead Stick* (Berkley, 1998), Taylor welcomed new employee Erica Wolveton. When Taylor conducted Erica's check flight, she was impressed with her cool demeanor and technical skills. She grieved when Erica was among five persons killed in a plane crash. The NTSB (National Transportation Safety Board) representative made a preliminary decision that Erica, the copilot, had panicked and caused the crash when the pilot had a heart attack. Taylor had noted several anomalies at the scene of the crash that convinced her that someone had tampered with the aircraft.

Out of gratitude to her former employer, Tundra Air Charter, Taylor used vacation time to help them out during *Red Line* (Berkley, 1999). This entailed leaving Anchorage and her lover Steve behind, and going to Bethel on the edge of the tundra. The Yukon-Kuskokwin Delta contained small, isolated, and impoverished villages, most of which prohibited alcohol. A few flights involving serious injuries convinced Taylor that someone was smuggling liquor via planes. What profit would there be in such a venture? At least enough to kill for.

The murder of an experienced Lear jet pilot left LifeLine short of trained staff in *Coffin Corner* (Berkley, 2000). Taylor and Steve ignored the Anchorage police in the investigation of Carter Masterson's death. Instead, they focused on reasons why fellow pilots might have killed him. Lear jet pilots were the cream of the crop, and they knew it. Taylor wondered if murder could be motivated by the desire for professional advancement. She was dying to fly a Lear herself.

Little of Taylor's background, appearance, or interests (beyond the need to fly) emerged in the narratives, but the technical details and descriptive material were excellent.

Ruthie Kantor Morris

Author: Renee B. Horowitz

When the series began, Ruthie Kantor Morris was a widow in her fifties. There had been no children in her marriage to Bob, although she had endured three miscarriages. Her work as a pharmacist sustained her. She had helped out at her dad's drug store as a teenager and earned a degree in pharmacy. By that time family owned drug stores had become passé. She was employed by a pharmacy in a Food Go supermarket in Scottsdale, supervising a younger professional and a technician. While at the university, Ruthie had been deeply in love with fellow student Michael Loring. Her parents placed heavy pressure on Ruthie to end the romance because Michael was not Jewish. In deference to their wishes, she did so. Her marriage to Bob had been a happy one, but she never forgot Michael. She had an excellent job, and owned a home with a swimming pool large enough to swim laps, but she was lonely.

Ruthie was meticulous in her pharmacy work so was concerned during *Rx for Murder* (Avon, 1997) when Harry Slater, a favorite customer, died from a drug reaction. Betsy, Harry's much younger wife, and waitress Denise Seaford, who had an eye on Harry, were both suspects. This caused a conflict of interest for Ruthie when she learned that Betsy was Michael Loring's daughter. His presence reawakened her feelings, but even he might be a suspect.

Exacting and cautious as Ruthie might be, she was accused of substituting the wrong medication in *Deadly Rx* (Avon, 1997). Young Amy Brookman needed pain medication, antibiotics, and Methergine to control bleeding after a miscarriage. When she died, the medication in her blood stream was Coumadin (a blood thinner). Amy's parents planned to sue both Ruthie and Food Go for negligence. Ruthie could lose her license, taking away the primary focus in her life. Her friends Denise Seaford and Michael Loring rallied to help her. Unfortunately Michael seemed interested in another woman.

May Morrison

Author: Nancy Star

The entertainment scene has always been popular in mysteries e.g. the theater-based novels of Ngaio Marsh during the Golden Age. The focus currently has been on movies and television. May Morrison, a divorcee with two daughters, was employed as a New York City television talk show producer. Part of her job was to keep the volatile Paula Wind (of *Paula Live*) under control. Todd, May's former husband, was now comfortably married to a tissue paper heiress. May had a tough schedule, with childcare being an ever-present problem. Her own mother Shirley lived in Florida, and had no desire to lend a hand.

During *Up Next* (Pocket, 1998), there was a touch of the *Murphy Brown* ensemble. May had Pete Jackson repairing her house to provide comic relief. James Barnett, producer of a rival talk show, fell 39 floors down to the sidewalk from his apartment while a killer watched from above. The possibility of suicide seemed even less likely when two more television personalities died shortly thereafter. Even though Detective Paul O'Donnell was personally attracted to May, he could not eliminate her as a suspect. Eventually she seemed more likely to be the next victim.

May planned an episode on alternative medications for *Paula Live*. In *Now This* (Pocket, 1999), her perspective was changed by a series of mysterious deaths. The victims had been unrelated except by attendance at a luxurious spa or through friendship with May's friend and neighbor, Stacey. Although May had ignored Paul O'Donnell's advice and offer of a gun, she did accept a more appropriate gift, an engagement ring.

Kate Mulcay

Author: Celestine Sibley

Katy Kincaid, later to become Kate Mulcay, appeared in a single mystery in the Fifties, *The Malignant Heart* (Doubleday 1958), as a "damsel in distress" newspaper reporter. She was a dauntless redheaded heroine who risked danger to learn which of her fellow reporters had killed the women's editor and an elderly reporter. Police Lieutenant Benjamin Mulcay, who was to become Katy's husband, came to her rescue.

In the current series, Kate was widowed. During the marriage, Ben had discussed his cases with Kate. After his death, Kate left Atlanta for a rural log cabin, bringing along her pet cat and dog. She remained active as a stringer for big city newspapers. Although independent, she did not see herself as a militant feminist, preferring to judge people by other standards than gender.

In *Ah, Sweet Mystery* (HarperCollins, 1991), Kate would not believe that her elderly neighbor Miss Willie Wilcox killed her stepson Garney, even after she confessed. She proved otherwise. There were interesting touches, such as when a Georgia grande dame showed them "how it's done" at a Nelson Eddy-Jeanette MacDonald festival.

In *Straight As an Arrow* (HarperCollins, 1992), Kate vacationed on Ila Island off the West Florida coast. Her host and hostess, permanent residents, suspected that the increased murders and dangerous attacks on the island were connected to the struggle between environmentalists and developers.

Kate wanted full-time work in *Dire Happenings at Scratch Ankle* (HarperCollins, 1993) and was assigned to the Georgia political beat. She was interested in the transition from "good old boy" representatives to blow-dry legislators. What seemed at first to be a generous effort to restore

Native American lands to Georgia ended in the disappearance and death of a state representative. The ending was downbeat, unusual for the series.

Kate appeared to be too wise and worldly to be duped by a young reporter (à la *All About Eve*), as depicted in *A Plague of Kinfolks* (Harper-Collins, 1995). It was also difficult to believe that even Southern hospitality would allow her to become the victim of such sleazy relatives as the Texan cousins who appropriated her home. These situations formed the background for Kate's investigation into a neighbor's death.

Spider in the Sink (HarperCollins, 1997) was episodic, showing Kate as a soft touch who reached out to everyone who sought her help. She would have plucked a spider out of the sink rather than kill it. Yet when a charming new minister paid court to Kate, she was unable to give him the benefit of the doubt. This narrative portrayed Kate as in her late forties, younger than before. An older Lady Bountiful, Iris Moon, was killed shortly after installing two street persons in her guesthouse. The police assumed the "guests" had killed her, but Kate went beyond the easy answer.

Author Celestine Sibley was an excellent writer with skills honed as a reporter. Her narratives moved with style and grace.

Lorelei Muldoon

Author: Wenda Wardell Morrone

It was a wonder that Lorelei Muldoon had developed any social skills at all. She was the daughter of Professor Hank Muldoon, a theoretical scientist in the field of mathematics and computers. He was an undemonstrative father with tunnel vision. Lorelei inherited a somewhat lower level of mathematical and theoretical expertise. It was sufficient for her to establish her own fledgling New York City company, which aided corporations in protecting their computer systems from hackers. On her staff (in fact half of her staff) she had a young computer whiz Rudy Persich. Lorelei had identified Rudy as the hacker who diverted $50,000 from his father's business accounts to subsidize his purchases of sports memorabilia. That was one way to get parental attention. Rudy's court requirement of public service was carried out through his teaching at the COBOL school, where unemployed adults received training to make them competent for jobs.

Lorelei realized very quickly that her trip to Senator Fred "Bandit" Coleman's isolated cabin in *No Time for an Everyday Woman* (St. Martin, 1997) was a mistake. A mistake that Bandit paid for with his life and put Lorelei at risk. There were hidden agendas, and personal relationships that pushed the narrative from intricate into confusing. Lorelei was on the run most of the time, but when she settled down to the spreadsheets, she saw the pattern that led to murder. The numbers went out of her head when a reckless mountain man got to her body, but they settled for a spectacular short-term relationship.

In *The Year 2000 Killers* (St. Martin, 1999), Rudy had developed a device that would minimize the problems of Y2K systems that interacted with those that were damaged. He was unaware that, when he shared his Y2K bridge disk with the COBOL students, he was triggering a disaster. Terrorists killed Rudy, kidnapped Lorelei, and manipulated a ten-year-old computer whiz to carry out a massive transfer of foreign assets. Hank, Lorelei's father joined her and a hard-edged Y2K government team to foil this scheme. Although blinded by personal considerations, Hank succeeded in doing so. This was a tense narrative, hard to put down.

Clare Cliveley Murdoch

Author: Ann Crowleigh, pseudonym for
Barbara Cummings and JoAnn Power

See: Clare and Miranda Cliveley, page 131.

Kate Murray

Author: Peg Tyre

Kate Murray was a crime reporter, who had worked her way up from copy girl to researcher, and finally reporter on the *New York Daily Herald*. A tiny woman with dark hair and brown eyes, she was single and on the rebound from an affair as *Strangers in the Night* (Crown, 1994) began. Work was not going well. After mishandling a big story because of her naïve trust in a mother's description of her son, she had been placed on six months probation. The murder of African-American nurse Margaret Severing on her doorstep offered Kate a chance to redeem herself. Dominick, a young drug addict who had witnessed the crime, contacted Kate, but she considered him a crank caller. John Finn, the detective assigned to the case, was fighting his own depression, and his unresolved attraction to Kate.

Kate left the *Daily Herald* when an unacceptable new owner took over during *In the Midnight Hour* (Crown, 1995), finding work on a local television station. Finn, who had succumbed to alcohol, was reassigned to a narcotics squad, which he realized was "on the take." He and Kate reconnected conveniently when she prevented his "buddies" from learning that he was taping their conversations. A one-nighter left Kate pregnant, causing her to consider an abortion. She risked her job on Channel 7 to direct police squads to a major drug delivery. Finn, once aware that he was to be a father, cleared his name and gave up alcohol.

Jordan Myles

Author: Martina Navratilova and Liz Nickles

An injury incurred while mountain climbing forced Jordan Myles to abandon a promising career as a professional tennis player. Encouraged by sports doctor Gus Laidlaw to find related work as a physical therapist, Jordan entered college and earned a degree. She became associated with the Desert Springs Sports Science Clinic near Palm Springs California, in partnership with Gus Laidlaw and Bill Stokes, a former Olympic marathon runner. Her relationship with Gus, a divorced man, had become more personal. Her own short marriage to sportscaster Tim Tulley ended when she was injured. Jordan had many friends on the circuit, and was welcomed and respected in her new role, but missed the excitement of being a performer. Her constant companion, except when she went to England, was a Jack Russell terrier, "A. M." named after Alice Marble, the U.S. tennis champion of a past generation.

Her lifestyle kept Jordan on the road, dressed for comfort not for style, eating vegetarian whenever possible, and occasionally behind on her paperwork. In the old days, there had been a manager to pay bills, make reservations, and remind her of appointments. The physical therapy work was supplemented by television opportunities as a color commentator at major tennis tournaments and on an interview series.

The Total Zone (Villard, 1994) found Jordan at Madison Square Garden to attend an award ceremony for Marissa Storrs, a lesbian tennis legend who had been a friend to her. She was summoned back to Desert Springs to care for Audrey Armat, a promising newcomer whose parents controlled her personal and professional lives. Jordan realized that Audrey's problems were more than physical, but played no part in her disappearance. Fearing bad publicity for the Sports Clinic, Jordan worked with disheveled but competent Noel Fisher ("The Fish") to find her. Although they failed to rescue Audrey, they discovered who had killed another top tennis contender and what made it necessary for Audrey to flee her family.

In *Breaking Point* (Villard, 1996), Jordan was welcomed by the professional staff and invited to a soiree at the Global Sports greenhouse across from Roland Garros where the French Open was held. When Catherine Richie, a computer expert who may have used her skills illegally, crashed through the building's glass ceiling to her death, Jordan was too late to resuscitate her. It was not too late to trace a killer. Jordan and one-time competitor Kelly Kendall played doubles as investigators, and won.

The rapport between Gus and Jordan had been intermittent at best, but in *Killer Instinct* (Villard, 1997), there was a serious rupture. Although he assured her that they had a great future together, that future was not to be with the Sports Clinic. Under the influence of commercial magnate Trent Byers, Gus envisioned a line of herbal products to enhance performances of both professional and amateur athletes. He wanted Jordan to tout "Duration" on her television show. Her reluctance infuriated him, but she was concerned about a series of unfortunate mishaps to tennis players. Fortunately the "Fish" was available to lend a hand.

Alice Nestleton

Author: Lydia Adamson, pseudonym for Frank King

It wasn't necessary for a reader to like cats and theatre to enjoy Alice Nestleton, but it helped. She had been raised in rural Minnesota by her grandmother, and then trained at the prestigious Guthrie Theatre in Minneapolis. Alice was very selective about her theatre roles. As she explained, perhaps too frequently, she was only interested in the avant-garde. This contributed to her limited finances but provided her with ample time to solve mysteries. She now lived in New York City, but Alice traveled if the part was right. Physically she was tall, very thin, with blonde hair going gray. Since her divorce, there had been temporary liaisons, but the man who most consistently figured in her life was Anthony Basilio, a struggling theatrical designer. Tony had always loved Alice, even though he married someone else. Her feeling for him was based on loneliness.

In *A Cat in the Manger* (Signet, 1990), cat-sitting brought about Alice's discovery of Harry Starobin's body. When his wife learned that seventy-nine-year-old Harry had led a secret life, she hired Alice to find his killer.

A Cat of a Different Color (Signet, 1991) found Alice teaching an acting course at the New School for Social Research. An unusual breed of cat, presented to her by a student, led Alice into a murder investigation, in which she needed Basilio's help and his recollections of road shows.

During *A Cat in Wolf's Clothing* (Signet, 1991), a New York Police Department special unit hired Alice at $300 a day to help them solve seventeen murders tied together by an abandoned mouse and a disappearing cat.

Barbara Roman was the nicest friend Alice ever had. In *A Cat By Any Other Name* (Signet, 1992), Alice refused to believe that Barbara had jumped out of a window during a meeting of her garden club. Initially no one agreed. When Tim, Barbara's roaming husband, was killed, the police took a second look. This was the pick of the litter in an otherwise routine series.

During a performance of the *Nutcracker Ballet* at Lincoln Center in *A Cat in the Wings* (Signet, 1992), former ballerina Lucia Maury was arrested for the murder of principal dancer Peter Dobrynin, missing for three years. Alice and Lucia had been roommates. Her family hired Alice to investigate.

Devastating reviews of her latest theatrical role inclined Alice to take time off in *A Cat With a Fiddle* (Signet, 1993). She delivered a cat to violinist Beth Stimson in rural Massachusetts. Beth was convening with other members of the Riverside String Quartet at the Covington Center for the Arts. The death of concert pianist Will Gryder was considered the act of a juvenile burglar, but not by Alice.

Alice took advantage of Tony's absence during *A Cat in a Glass House* (Signet, 1993) for a torrid affair with an ambitious young Eurasian detective. While enjoying a Chinese dinner, Alice witnessed a murder that made no sense until she traced a kitchen cat and foreign medications for male impotency.

She needed a vacation by *A Cat With No Regrets* (Signet, 1994), so a role in a film to be made in rural France seemed promising. The death of the primary backer within minutes of their landing put a crimp in the production. Alice's harebrained scheme to smoke out a killer by risking fire in a hospital was unprincipled.

Who better than Alice to investigate the death of a veterinarian in *A Cat on the Cutting Edge* (Signet, 1994)? The murderer's trail led through a cat shelter foundation to the secrets of a Bohemian group that included poetess Edna St. Vincent Millay.

What do actresses do when they are "at leisure"? Anything they can, so in *A Cat on a Winning Streak* (Signet, 1995) Alice performed in an Atlantic City Casino. She did not anticipate the murder of a woman whose cat brought her such luck that she was banned from the casinos.

Her niece, Alison Chevigny, convinced Alice to pose for negligee ads in *A Cat in Fine Style* (Signet, 1995) exposing her to the world of advertising and the murder of their host. Cats played a part, but more important was the breach between Tony and Alice. His attraction to a young make-up artist made him a suspect in her death.

In *A Cat Under the Mistletoe* (Dutton, 1996), "Roberta," a neurotic cat in Alice's care, needed psychological treatment, but when Alice visited the therapist's office, she found her dead. Aaron Stoner, a detective whom

Alice was seeing regularly, recalled a similar murder ten years before. There had to be a connection. Somewhere among the therapist's clients was a killer.

Aaron Stoner became more important in Alice's life when her affair with Tony ended during *A Cat in a Chorus Line* (Signet, 1996). The blow-up came after she and Tony witnessed the murder of old friend John Cerise. The killer confessed, but Alice could not end it there. She had to know why an elderly composer left his money to his cats, and how Cerise had earned two million dollars. Tony's accusation that Alice had abandoned the theatre to dwell upon cats and detection could not be easily dismissed.

Alice was depressed by her breakup with Tony and the lack of opportunities in the theatre as *A Cat on a Beach Blanket* (Dutton, 1997) began. A chance to housesit in the Hamptons offered her solitude, which she enjoyed for a very short period of time. Her need for companionship drew her into the community of the wealthy New Yorkers who had purchased oceanfront property, and were tearing down the shacks of fishermen. While attending a poetry reading, Alice became acquainted with members of an artistic group, one of whom was blown up before the afternoon ended. Alice's insistence on investigating the murder and then, in an admission of failure, entertaining the suspects, may have led to a second death.

In *A Cat on Jingle Bell Rock* (Dutton, 1997), Alice was very much at leisure, when old friend Jack Rugow invited her out for a drink. Jack, the producer and director of a repertory company, was concerned about funds for Sustenance House, which provided services for the poor. Jack had come to depend on an anonymous annual donation, but this year none had been received. Alice discovered the donor too late. He was dead and so was Will Holland, another member of the Sustenance House Board of Directors. Were there cats in the narrative? Of course, a pair of Siamese who led Alice to information about comfort pets, theft, and the cause of the donor's defection and death.

A Cat on Stage Left (Dutton, 1998) was the sixteenth in a series that was showing signs of wear. Mary Singer would pay $2,500 if Alice would care for her cat, but as Singer exited the car, her chauffeur shot her and left. Who was the heavily disguised chauffeur and who had occupied the backseat of the car? The cat carrier contained a stuffed feline, not a real animal, but Alice waited a long time to check the stuffing. With the help of Sam Tully, writer of a television private investigator series, Alice researched the play that tied the suspects together, and the suicide that led to murder.

In *A Cat of One's Own* (Dutton, 1999), Jake, a cat with the skills of Willie Sutton, escaped. Later its owner, a friend of Alice, was murdered. Alice had succeeded in finding the distinctive cat. Now she had to find a killer. The plot had major holes, but then reality was not a high priority in this series.

A Cat With the Blues (Signet, 2000) found Alice becoming quirkier. Her search for the killer of fellow actor Elias Almodovar and for a cat kidnapper lacked authenticity. Her flashes of intuitive thinking were erratic. The quick trip love affair was contrived.

The axiom that "no good deed goes unpunished" held true in *A Cat With No Clue* (Signet, 2001). An anniversary gift from Alice to a married couple led to a triple homicide. Her pals initially helped in the possible connection to a prior child abduction, but grew tired of Alice's theorizing.

Next books in this series: *A Cat Named Brat* (2002); *A Cat on the Bus* (2002)

Jane Nichols

Author: Maureen Tan

Jane Nichols was a survivor, but it wasn't getting any easier. As a child, she had been present when her parents were assassinated in Greece. Jane's dad had been in the diplomatic service. Her mother seemingly was a charming hostess and helpmate. Jane had been in the car with her parents when they were ambushed and murdered. Her grandfather raised her, then passed her along to his friend "Mac," Douglas MacDonald, who recruited her into England's MI5 (Internal Security). While posing as an Irish stewardess, Jane survived an attempt to kill her only because her lover Brian intervened, causing his death. Five years later, a bloody incident in Belfast where she was undercover with the I.R.A., left her so burned out that she could no longer function professionally. She had worked with partner John Wiggins, steely, dispassionate, and deadly.

Fortunately she had inherited money and the income from her second occupation, as the author of a mystery series, featuring P.I. Andrew Jax. Jane used the name "Max Murdoch" as her literary pseudonym, and her literary agent, Dora Hollingsworth, handled her business affairs.

When Dora arranged for Jane to attend a writer's conference in Atlanta, Georgia in *AKA Jane* (Mysterious Press, 1998), Jane saw a picture in the newspaper that forced her to return to espionage, the face of Jim O'Neill, the man who had ordered her death and caused Brian's. MI-5 made it impossible for her to carry out her own vengeance, but offered her support and supplies to bring O'Neill to justice. Jane, struggling to maintain an identity of her own, juggled her feelings for the new man in her life, and her need to erase guilt from the past.

The losses in Jane's life had made her leery of commitments. In *Run Jane Run* (Mysterious Press, 1999), she left her comfortable existence and her lover, police chief Alex Callaghan, behind in Savannah, Georgia, to take a new assignment. MacDonald sent Jane and John Wiggins to rescue Hugh, the dissolute nephew of a prominent Member of Parliament, Sir William Winthrup. Hugh was being held hostage at a family estate in Scotland. Jane had flashbacks after meeting members of the Winthrup family, a sense that Sir William may have played an important role in her life.

Terrific books. Never let up on the tension.

Alix Nicholson

Author: Sharon Gilligan

The gift of a camera had made photography an important part of Alix Nicholson's life and a second source of income. A native of Southern Missouri, Alix's home life had been unhappy. Her mother died of cancer when Alix was twelve. The tension between her and her stepmother Ellen led to truancy and rebellion. Her career as a Missouri high school teacher was disrupted when two female students misused cameras and photographic equipment to take nude photos. The fact that she was a lesbian made that incident more serious. Although she did not lose her teaching certificate, she was fired. After the termination, she expanded her photography career and worked as a substitute teacher in the Dubuque, Iowa school system.

At age forty, Alix was a tall blonde woman who dressed casually. The longest relationship in her experience ended because her lover did not approve of Ann's selection for an assistant. Brian, a former student, eventually died of AIDS.

It was for Brian as much as the potential for a documentary that Alix went to Washington, D.C. in *Danger in High Places* (Rising Tide Press, 1993) for a ceremony celebrating the AIDS quilt. Contention as to how government money should be divided between AIDS research and research focusing on cancer in women caused nurse Sandra Hastings to disrupt the rally. When Sandra was murdered, Alix's pictures of the rally uncovered the killer, proving the innocence of a lesbian Congresswoman.

Danger! Cross Currents (Rising Tide, 1994) harkened back to Alix's years as a high school teacher. An opportunity to teach a course in photography at a California college reunited her with Leah Claire. Leah had been accused of murdering her lesbian lover, a woman whose greed and indiscretions had earned her multiple enemies.

Dr. Deirdre "Didi" Nightingale
Author: Lydia Adamson, pseudonym for Frank King

Deirdre "Didi" Nightingale must be taken with a grain of salt. She was a licensed veterinarian who returned from a year's service in India to a local practice in Duchess County, New York. Didi lived on an inherited estate with four resident servants who were paid no wages. Two of the servants, Charlie, who served as her veterinary assistant while promoting his own remedies, and the cook, Mrs. Tunney, were elderly. The situation with the other two, Abigail in her early twenties and Trent Tucker, at nineteen, was less credible.

A diminutive brunette with pale green eyes, Didi was single, and scarred by a bitter ending to her relationship with a professor at the University of Pennsylvania veterinary college. Both of her parents were dead—her mother more recently. Didi accepted a role as head of the household.

Didi had always looked upon Dick Obey as her best booster, so his death in *Dr. Nightingale Comes Home* (Signet, 1994) was not only a surprise, but also a personal loss. She could not believe that Obey, drunk or sober, could have died from an attack by stray dogs. Didi's probe uncovered a Dick Obey that she had never known, and startling information about her household and her recently deceased mother.

Perhaps because of her experience with elephants in India, or because she had always loved the circus, in *Dr. Nightingale Rides the Elephant* (Signet, 1994) Didi served as veterinarian for Dalton's Big Top during their stay in Duchess County. Didi could not prevent the tragic death of a performer and a subsequent suicide, but she successfully treated mysterious illnesses in the menagerie. Almost too late, Didi brought a fatal connection to the attention of the authorities.

Through the death of a friend, Didi learned about the old style German Shepherds raised by the monks of Alsatian House in *Dr. Nightingale Goes to the Dogs* (Signet, 1995). Elderly recluse Mary Hyndman had a Shepherd pup that disappeared when she died. Mary purportedly had left money to the monks. Taking Abigail with her, Didi checked out the monastery, its specialized training, and the method by which dogs were allotted to prospective owners. Her presence triggered a death for which Abigail was a suspect.

In *Dr. Nightingale Goes the Distance* (Signet, 1995), the suicide of a distinguished veterinarian and an injury to a horse he was tending forced Didi to deal with her unresolved feelings for Dr. Drew Pelletier, the college professor with whom she had a short affair. Was he an unscrupulous scientist, a killer, or merely a philanderer?

Didi took advantage of an opportunity to commune with nature in *Dr. Nightingale Enters the Bear Cave* (Signet, 1996). She joined a scientific expedition into the Catskill Mountain Forest Preserve. The area was presumed to be isolated but the group met with murder, treachery, and a monster bear.

She considered pigs to be highly intelligent animals, but they brought nothing but trouble to Didi in *Dr. Nightingale Chases Three Pigs* (Signet, 1996). She was suspected of killing a wealthy pig farmer whom she barely knew, because love letters addressed to her were found in his possession. Police Officer Allie Voegler balanced his unrequited love for Didi against the evidence, but he joined her probe into illicit activities on the pig farm.

Didi's presence at the Blessing of the Animals in *Dr. Nightingale Rides to the Hounds* (Signet, 1997) made her a witness to the assassination of reclusive John Brietland. He had made enemies when the family factory had closed, putting locals out of work. It was not clear that Brietland was the intended victim or whether or not the killer had been a "hired gun." Another suspicious death had taken place at the same site seven years earlier. Didi and Allie worked out their personal relationship while muddling through to an unsatisfactory conclusion.

Dr. Nightingale Meets Puss in Boots (Signet, 1997) took Didi's household to New York City where Abigail was hired to sing at a nightclub. Her employer was shot when he took the stage to make the introduction. Although Abigail, Trent, Charlie and Mrs. Tunney returned home, Didi stayed on, visiting a former veterinary school classmate whose clientele included killers by proxy.

In *Dr. Nightingale Races the Outlaw Colt* (Signet, 1998), Allie was unable to handle the death of his friend and fellow police office, Wynton Chung. After he was suspended from his job, he depended on Didi to investigate a series of murders dramatized by a mysterious colt. Their relationship survived but Allie's professional record was seriously damaged.

1999 was not a good year for Didi. Business was slow. She was concerned about paying her bills and maintaining her staff. *Dr. Nightingale Traps the Missing Lynx* (Signet, 1999) had an incredible plot. The death of a television weatherman was tenuously connected to the uncovering of a pre-Civil War Underground Railroad station.

Didi faced a dilemma in *Dr. Nightingale Seeks Greener Pastures* (Signet, 2000). The farm animal business in her area was diminishing. It became necessary for her to develop skills in other veterinary specialties. With that in mind, she attended a conference in Atlantic City. The murder of a conference speaker was tied to the deaths of persons involved in horse racing and gambling. Friend Rose Vigdor and former beau Allie Voegler made unwise choices that damaged their ties to Didi. The ongoing saga of Charlie's moneymaking schemes did nothing to help.

The murder of best friend Rose Vigdor six months after she left Hillbrook was incomprehensible to Didi during *Dr. Nightingale Follows a Canine Clue* (Signet, 2001). There were so many questions. Why had Rose disappeared, and then returned to the area without making any contact with Didi? Why had Rose been living at a Zen Buddhist retreat under a false name? Had she set the fire that burned down the retreat house? Most important: who had killed her and why? Didi seemed out of control. Her behavior was so bizarre as to be inconsistent with her character. Charlie was bizarre, but that was a way of life for him.

The Nightingale narratives included unrelated veterinary cases, and numerous episodes involving Charlie and the other servants. They did not always advance the plots and occasionally interrupted them, but added humor and warmth.

Chicago Nordejoong

Author: Victoria McKernan

She might not rank with the top female investigators, but Chicago Norde-joong was no carbon copy. Her deceased mother was Trinidadian; her sea-going father, a Norwegian ship captain. Chicago, named after the city, was a tall, lithe, dark-haired woman, who shared her father's love of adventure. Her mother had died when Chicago was five, but she kept in touch with relatives in Trinidad. Years of travel with her father had provided her with little formal education, but a smattering of foreign languages and the ability to curse in all of them. Chicago made her home on her boat, which was harbored in U.S. and Caribbean ports as the whim and job opportunities took her. She taught scuba diving and captured rare fish for sea museums and aquariums. Her short but happy marriage to Stephen had ended when drug smugglers killed him. She had little interest in most domestic skills, but enjoyed weaving. Unconventional to the limit, her pet was an eight-foot boa constrictor named "Lassie."

As *Osprey Reef* (Carroll & Graf, 1990)) began, Alex Sinclair, a government investigator, rescued Chicago and Umbi, her Hawaiian assistant, from attacking sharks. Sinclair was researching the use of fish as receptacles for smuggled drugs. Chicago became a prickly and somewhat unreliable ally when Sinclair learned that local law enforcement officials were involved in the criminal activity. Before she was finished, Chicago suffered from the "bends" and a romantic attachment to Sinclair.

When Sinclair moved on to the Caribbean and a new career as a pilot for a small airline, Chicago felt rejected. However, in *Point Deception* (Carroll & Graf, 1992), he returned to find Chicago preparing for a two-year cruise. He had ferried a mutilated corpse identified by an U.S. Senator as that of his daughter. Chicago's trip was postponed while she and Sinclair tangled with munitions makers, industrial polluters, and crooked politicians. In the course of their struggle, Chicago learned more about the roots of Sinclair's inability to make a commitment.

Chicago and Sinclair were together as *Crooked Island* (Carroll & Graf, 1994) began, but she sensed his restlessness as they cruised the Caribbean. Conspiracies to locate and to conceal evidence that a living descendant of the Stuarts might threaten the legitimacy of the current British monarchy, came just in time. The discovery of a medallion in fish guts by a ten-year-old girl fed into the ambitions of a Scottish Jacobite group. Personal danger did not dissuade Chicago and Sinclair from playing a significant role in the outcome.

These were mystery adventures with a novel heroine and complex plotting.

Pat North

Author: Lynda La Plante

This was another of author Lynda La Plante's novelized television series. Although it covered territory similar to *Prime Suspect*, it neither attained the recognition, nor developed the female character of that series. It was perhaps more similar to the American television series, *Law and Order*, in that it followed a case through both the investigation and the prosecution.

Trial and Retribution (Pan, 1997) was an ensemble presentation that covered a case involving the family of five-year-old Julie Harris who was sexually abused and murdered near a low-income housing development. Attention was given to the police officers involved in that case including Detective Inspector Pat North and over-zealous Constable Colin Burridge and to the prosecutors and defense attorneys, particularly Belinda Sinclair, the novice defense counsel. At this point, Pat was thirty-five, lived with her boyfriend, Graham, and was stationed at the Southampton Street Station House in the Criminal Investigation Division.

In *Trial and Retribution II* (Pan 1998), the emphasis remained on the victims, suspects, and process. Inspector North and her supervisor, Detective Superintendent Michael Walker carried their roles as investigators with limited personal development. Walker was shown to have an unhappy marriage and some personal interest in Pat. Justice did not prevail in the courtroom, but the killer's wife rendered her own verdict.

Walker and Pat moved into an apartment in *Trial and Retribution III* (Pan, 1999). There seemed to be no potential conflict of interest because she had been transferred to the vice squad while Mike was stationed in the Metropolitan Area Major Investigating Pool. Then, fifteen-year-old Cassie Booth disappeared while delivering newspapers. Obsessive wine merchant Steve Warrington, who had demanded action from Pat on a possible brothel in his neighborhood, became a suspect. Walker and Pat dealt with different approaches to the case. Their relationship survived although Pat suffered considerable trauma.

Mike and Pat continued to live together although he had not divorced his wife by *Trial and Retribution IV* (Macmillan, 2000). The Home Office selected her for advanced placement. She was assigned to a team reassessing the conviction of James McCready. Mike, who had been the arresting officer, was accused on appeal of homophobia, suppressing evidence and having a personal grudge against McCready. There were consequences for both of them in the outcome.

As *Trial and Retribution V* (Macmillan, 2001) began, reclamation workers in a North London neighborhood uncovered the skeleton of a teenage woman in the backyard of 54 Hallerton Road. Mike Walker was assigned to the case at a time when Pat was relegated to administrative tasks. The initial investigation expanded, and received considerable publicity, as more skeletons were found. Enquiries and forensic results focused on the occupants of the house from 1981 to 1983. More difficulty arose in discovering the identity of the victims and their ties to the suspects. Pat showed an interest and made valuable suggestions. The personal relationship between Pat and Mike was in serious trouble: the divorce in abeyance, Pat's attraction to a more understanding man, and their inability to communicate with one another.

Tru North

Author: Janet McClellan

Tru North, a lesbian police detective in Kansas City, Missouri, had to work at it. She had taken a bachelor's degree at the University of Missouri-Kansas City before entering the police department. Unfortunately, she tested out in the bottom half of her police training class. Some real blunders on the job; e.g. shooting at her reflection in a department store mirror, didn't help. However, she was dedicated to her work and meticulous at a crime scene where she used a tape recorder to capture her impressions. Major O'Donoghue, a female professor of criminal justice at UM-KC, had encouraged her career. Fellow officers perceived Tru as obsessive-compulsive and overly assertive, but she worked companionably with partner Tom Garvan.

Possibly because she had attended a three-week FBI training course on serial killers, Tru was assigned to a case involving a series of bombings as *K.C. Bomber* (Naiad, 1997) began. Tru suspected that her supervisor wanted her to fail so she could be fired. Her personal life was in disarray. A three-year relationship had just ended, leaving her with a sense of rejection. Tru used her computer skills to identify a suspect, outlasted her supervisor, and found a new love.

A sense of unease kept Tru on the case, even after she had arrested a woman for the murder of her lesbian lover in *Penn Valley Phoenix* (Naiad, 1998). The lack of information about the victim puzzled Tru. Her computer and a set of fingerprints illuminated the victim's past and her probable killer.

As was shown in *River Quay* (Naiad, 1998), Tru had a problem with relationships. She had moved from a nine-month relationship with Eleanor to six-months with Marki, and then found herself involved with C. B. Belpre, an assertive arson investigator. They were initially hostile with one another while turf protecting on the death of a man in a burned-out building. Beyond their personal problems, they failed to properly identify the victim. The most stable element in her life was a cat, Poupon.

Fortunately, Tru's new supervisor ignored the negative personnel reports left by Captain Rhonn and gave her a fresh start in *Chimney Rock Blues* (Naiad, 1999). He offered her a choice assignment as the homicide representative on a Metro committee investigating serial murders. While checking out a scene of the crime, Tru saw a suspicious car, but was knocked unconscious and suffered amnesia, causing her to be restricted to desk duty for a while. Later, she was assigned to transport Valerie, a young alcoholic who had been housed in a rural jail because of crowding. The attacker who intercepted Tru and Valerie was probably the serial killer, but the conclusion left unanswered questions.

McClellan provided excellent background as to police procedures. There were detours into sexually explicit interludes.

Kali O'Brien

Author: Jonnie Jacobs

Kali O'Brien, a single attorney practicing in a large San Francisco law firm, had rarely returned to Silver Creek, California since her high school graduation. After her mother committed suicide, her father took the slower route, killing himself with alcohol. Nevertheless, when her brother John and sister Sabrina thought themselves too busy, it was left to Kali to clear up the estate and take on her Dad's springer spaniel, Loretta. Her relationship with her siblings was always tentative.

As *Shadow of Doubt* (Kensington, 1996) began, she took an evening off to attend a party held by old friends, Jannine and Eddie Marrero. When Eddie, a popular high school coach, was murdered, the local police focused on Jannine as the killer. At the request of Jannine's mother, and with the help of local publisher Tom Lawrence, Kali searched Eddie's life for other motives. Darryl Benson, the chief of police who had loved Kali's mother, was dubious, but the killer realized Kali was on his trail. Kali's big city job and her romance with a top litigator ended. She stayed on in Silver Creek, establishing a solo practice with the help of senior attorney, Sam Morrison.

When, in *Evidence of Guilt* (Kensington, 1997), Sam needed her help on a major murder case, Kali agreed. Defendant Wes Harding was the local "bad boy," the stepson of a prominent doctor. Kali remembered having a crush on him in high school. The crime, a vicious killing of a young mother and her daughter, was slowly tied to Wes by physical evidence. With little help from her client and Sam in the hospital, Kali persisted until again the murderer took action against her.

The trial attorney's worst nightmare is a client who lies to his lawyer. In *Motion To Dismiss* (Kensington, 1999), Kali had no choice but to take the case. Grady Bennett, the husband of Kali's best friend, was accused first of rape, then of murder. Based on diligent research, she managed a Perry Mason breakthrough in the courtroom to win the case. During the investigation, she lost a dear friend and reconnected with a former lover.

Kali had a history with psychologist Steven Cross. During *Witness for the Defense* (Kensington, 2001), she agreed to represent his sister Terri

Harper and her husband in an adoption proceeding. Right wing radio commentator Bram Weaver, who derailed the adoption by claiming to be young
Hannah's father, was murdered. When Terri was accused of the killing, Kali
took on her defense, even though that required her to work with Steven.
She had two strategies: (1) to weaken the prosecution case, and (2) to identify an alternative suspect in order to create reasonable doubt. In the end,
she was left with no doubt at all. Being around Hannah reawakened Kali's
desire to have a child.

A competent series set within a small town legal system.

Next books in this series: *Cold Justice* (2002); *Intent to Harm* (2002)

Rachel O'Connor
Author: Mary Freeman, pseudonym for Mary Rosenblum

Rachel O'Connor, the daughter of a Jewish mother, Deborah, and an Irish
father, Will, was raised in Oregon. The O'Connor family owned a prosperous orchard adjacent to the city of Blossom. After college and the death of
her father, Rachel's Uncle Jack had assumed she would return to work in the
orchard. Instead Rachel, aware that she would chafe under Jack's authority,
chose to set up a landscape business, Rain Country Landscaping, which
proved to be quite successful.

Within hours in *Devil's Trumpet* (Berkley, 1999), Rachel lost client
Henry Bassinger to violent death and signed a new client, Dr. Joshua Meier
who would profoundly affect her life. Jeff Price, Rachel's high school beau,
had returned to Blossom where he joined the local police force. Jeff, who
had moved to California after graduation, had been with the Los Angeles
Police Department. When Julio, Rachel's youthful assistant, became a suspect in Henry's death, she probed into the old man's past. A reclusive
dreamer at his death, Henry had spent a short interlude of his life away
from his domineering father. During that time he had enjoyed a career as a
musician, fathered a son, and laid the seeds for his own murder and the
death of a teenage boy. Jeff and Rachel found they still enjoyed one
another's company.

Plans to annex 200 acres of undeveloped land to the city of Blossom
in order to regulate its growth raised a storm in *Deadly Nightshade* (Berkley,
1999). Uncle Jack O'Connor who felt the prospects of the family orchard
would be damaged led opposition to the proposal. When Bob Dougan, the
swing vote on the city council was murdered, Jack was indignant because
Jeff, now chief of police, had questioned him. Jack laid it on the line with
Rachel; side with the family or with Jeff. A vicious attack on Jeff made it

clear to Rachel where her loyalties lay. A missing jacket, a Ponzi scam and a faked appointment led Rachel and Jeff to a crazed killer in time to prevent a second death. Rachel had introduced Dr. Meier to her mother early in the series but did not realize that their interest in one another would lead to an elopement.

Botanists Eloise and Carl Johnston had enjoyed a loving marriage, marred only by the death of their seventeen-year-old daughter, Linda. The widowed Eloise hired Rachel in *Bleeding Heart* (Berkley, 2000) to renovate the garden she and Carl had created. Her intention was to bequeath the property to a conservancy group. Eloise's sudden death by an overdose of digoxin focused suspicion on her caretaker, young April Gerard. Rachel was certain that the girl was innocent and that Eloise's biography in process had motivated the killer. She was half-right. Rachel was distracted by concerns that her mother might have tired of her marriage; the truth was equally disturbing but Deborah and Joshua faced it together. Rachel's own romance moved forward when she accepted an engagement ring from Jeff.

In all cases, suspicions cast on individuals about whom Rachel had come to care motivated her investigations.

Next book in this series: *Garden View* (2002)

Kendall O'Dell

Author: Sylvia Nobel

Kendall O' Dell was a tall redhead, living in Castle Valley, Arizona where she worked for the local newspaper, the *Castle Valley Sun*. She had originally come from the Philadelphia area, where her parents, and her brother Patrick and his wife still lived. Her father was a retired newspaper reporter, who had served as a foreign correspondent during the Vietnam War. She had inherited his love for the job. Her intense focus on her work doomed her early marriage to a pharmacist. Both the end of a subsequent romance and her asthma had been factors in the decision to move. Morton Tuggs, then editor of the *Castle Valley Sun*, owed Bill O'Dell a favor. He hired Kendall as a reporter for the paper, which was owned by his wife's family.

Kendall found relief from her asthma in Arizona, but in *Deadly Sanctuary* (Nite Owl Books, 1998), there were other hazards. Her predecessor at the *Sun* had disappeared in the midst of an investigation. Kendall walked a tight line. What had happened to unpopular reporter John Dexter? What might happen to Kendall if she continued to probe the deaths of two runaway girls? She was torn between the blandishments of attorney Eric Heisler and the challenges of reporter/rancher Brad Talverson.

On slight acquaintance, Kendall offered to drive young Angela Martin to an inherited mining claim in *The Devil's Cradle* (Nite Owl, 2000). They were not made welcome in nearby Morgan's Folly. Angela had presented herself as Audrey Martin, a child who had purportedly died along with her mother Rita fifteen years before. At stake was control of a decommissioned mine, that if reopened could provide jobs for the area. As Angela/Audrey struggled to make sense of who she was, Kendall investigated the death of the young woman's father.

Some of the romantic dialogue was fulsome, but the plotting was above average, clues well planted in the narratives. A good offering from a small press.

Next book in this series: *Dark Moon Crossing* (2002)

Maureen O'Donnell

Author: Denise Mina

A sexually abusive father made Maureen O'Donnell's childhood a living hell. Her alcoholic mother, Winnie, was into denial and was torn up with self-pity, leaving none for her daughter. As a child, Maureen had been discovered in a cupboard under the stairs with blood between her legs. Michael O'Donnell was never charged. She was not the only one of the children to suffer from his attentions, but it was never discussed among them. Maureen was labeled "crazy" when she had her breakdown, but received little professional treatment.

Given that background it was remarkable that she managed several years studying art history at Glasgow University before another breakdown caused her to drop out. She eventually finished her degree. She was the youngest of the O'Donnell children. Marie, the eldest had become a bank executive who married well and lived in London. Una, a civil engineer, dominated her kindly husband Alistair. Brother Liam, who was closest to Maureen, fared the worst. He dropped out of law school to become a drug dealer.

What treatment Maureen received after her college breakdown amounted to a four month period in Northern Hospital during 1996, followed by a referral to Rainbow Clinic where she was unsuccessfully treated as "Helen" by Angus Farrell. He referred her to Dr. Louise Wishart of Albert Hospital who provided help. At the time the series began, Maureen was working as a ticket seller at a movie theatre.

Maureen's liaison with therapist Douglas Brady in *Garnethill* (Bantam, 1998) ended when he was found dead in her apartment. Although his dalliance with Maureen was totally unprofessional, she was envisioned by the police, not as a victim, but as a suspect in his murder. Bolstered by her close friend Leslie Findlay and her brother Liam, Maureen chose not to be a victim, but to bring the culprit to justice on her own terms.

Maureen's helpful involvement in the Brady case did not win her any support from the Glasgow Police Department in *Exile* (Carroll & Graf, 2001). In a gesture of support to Leslie Findlay, Maureen looked for abused housewife Ann Harris, who disappeared from a Glasgow women's refuge, only to be found murdered in London. Maureen's reformed brother Liam warned her to stay out of it because "hard men" were involved, She traveled to London to learn more about Ann, her disappearance and her death. She was financially self-sufficient at this point, but deeply troubled. Her father Michael had returned to Glasgow and reconnected with her mother and her two sisters. Not everyone realized that Michael was still a dangerous man where children were concerned.

None of Maureen's problems had been resolved as *Resolution* (Bantam, 2001) began. Angus Farrell had been charged with two counts of murder, but there was a serious possibility that he would not be convicted. His release would put both Maureen and her vulnerable friend Siobhan McCloud, at great risk. The birth of her sister Una's daughter intensified Maureen's fears about her father. She had almost exhausted the windfall from Douglas Brady, only to learn that the Internal Revenue expected her to pay £6,000 in inheritance tax. Fighting her alcoholism, Maureen sought solutions that would not result in her arrest and imprisonment. The trilogy ended as she did so.

Jake O'Hara

Author: Noreen Wald

Jake O'Hara (baptized Jacqueline Grace after two of her mother's heroines of the times, Jackie Kennedy and Grace Kelly) preferred to be known as Jake. She had attended the finest schools her mother could afford: Convent of the Sacred Heart for high school and Manhattanville for college. She earned a bachelor's degree that she put to work as a ghostwriter, writing fiction and non-fiction to be published under the name of her client.

There was a support group in New York called Ghostwriters Anonymous where such writers gathered to share their contempt for their employers, bemoan the lack of credit they received for their work, and talk about plans to write their own books. Like AAA, the individuals referred to themselves at meetings only by first names and the initials of their last names. Over the series, the Ghostwriters who assisted Jake in her investigations narrowed down to morbid Modesty Meade, gay Too Tall Tom, and quiet but successful Jane Dowling.

Maura, Jake's mom was a constant presence in her life. Her marriage to Jack O'Hara, an ex-Marine who became a salesman, had not lasted. Jake loved her dad and mourned his eventual death. Maura and Jake managed quite well in an inherited co-op apartment in the exclusive Carnegie Hill area of New York City.

Jake's life was thrown into confusion in *Ghostwriter* (Berkley, 1999). She had become the center of attention for several handsome men, including a hypnotherapist, an attorney, and a NYPD detective. However, membership in Ghostwriters Anonymous was decimated by murder. The worst news was that the recent victims were all associated with Edgar-winning crime novelist Kate Lloyd Conners. Jake had just hired on to ghostwrite Kate's latest book. Although the modus operandi for the killings was quirky, the narrative read smoothly with witty dialogue.

The murder of caustic book critic Richard Peter in *Death Comes for the Critic* (Berkley, 2000) had enough suspects to fill a jury box. Jake benefited from Peter's death. Under the *qui bono* theory, she could have been included. The Ghostwriters pitched in, eliminating suspects. Unfortunately the killer eliminated several more. Jake juggled her feelings for high-powered attorney Dennis Kim and NYPD detective Ben Rubin. Her mother Maura would have settled for either one to get Jake married.

Two of the three celebrity panelists at a Greater New York Crime Writer's Conference died of poisoning in *Death Never Takes a Holiday* (Berkley, 2000). The holiday was St. Patrick's Day. The poison was administered in green beer served by a leprechaun. Motives abounded for the victims: a dying U.S. Senator and a former actress who promoted creative cruises. Jake went overboard in investigating the disparate motivations, which included theft of the Faith diamond, euthanasia services, and a thirty-four-year-old rape case. The Ghostwriters pitched in to help as always.

As *Remembrance of Murders Past* (Berkley, 2001) began, Maura O'Hara witnessed the murder of Father Billy Blake while waiting in the confessional. No way could Jake stay out of this case. Her mother, now engaged to former district attorney and prospective U.S. Senator Aaron Rubin, was in danger. The Ghostwriters had questions to ask. Jake's involvement was more personal. The murder of Karen Scanlon had coincided with Jake's birth thirty four years ago, and she felt her presence in her dreams and responses to people and settings. A spookier slant on murder.

There were flaws. Not everyone likes astral clues. The multiple suspects, helpers, and motivations cluttered the narratives. That should not keep a reader from having fun with Jake.

Next book in this series: *Enter Dying* (2002)

Freddie O'Neal

Author: Catherine Dain

Freddie O'Neal, who grew up in Reno, graduated from the University of Nevada-Reno. Fortunately, she did not gamble, except for an occasional Keno card, because she had no luck at all. After Danny, her unfaithful father, deserted his family, her mother married a man for whom Freddie had no affection. The man she loved, Rob McIntire, married someone else. A tall rawboned blonde, Freddie ran a small-time detective agency out of her home. Her support system consisted of political reporter Sandra Herrick, African-American veteran Deke Adams, now a guard at a local casino, and two cats, Butch and Sundance.

As a teenager, Freddie had a major crush on Mick Halliday, now a Los Vegas gambler. In *Lay It on the Line* (Jove, 1992), Joan, Mick's wife, hired Freddie to find the absconding caretaker for her ailing father. Freddie and Deke found the stolen car, but with a trunk full of cocaine. When Joan's prominent sister was murdered, Joan was the primary suspect.

Freddie's flying lessons came in handy in *Sing a Song of Death* (Jove, 1993). She flew the jet carrying singer Vince Marina when the pilot collapsed. Before she could determine the cause of the pilot's illness, Vince was murdered.

In *Walk a Crooked Mile* (Jove, 1994), it became vital for Freddie to locate her father. She began her search with Sam Courter, a Marine Corps buddy of Danny O'Neal. There were powerful forces who wanted Danny kept quiet, even if they had to kill him.

By *Lament for a Dead Cowboy* (Berkley, 1994), Sam had become the man in Freddie's life, but he had never forgotten the woman he married. On a shared trip to Elko, Nevada for a cowboy poet gathering, their relationship was tested. Sam was accused of murder, and he refused to discuss his case with Freddie.

In *Bet Against the House* (Berkley, 1995), Ted Scope's business flourished under his direction, but his death created consternation. His will left widow Gloria in control, and she reveled in it. Their three children disagreed on everything except to fight the will. Freddie was hired to get "dirt" on Gloria. By the time Gloria was murdered, Freddie had become her ally, and was determined to find the killer. Before her death, Gloria did Freddie a favor. She introduced her to an attractive university professor who made up for Sam's absence.

Professor Curtis Breckinridge helped Freddie face two crises during *The Luck of the Draw* (Berkley, 1996). When Al, her stepfather, had a heart attack, Ramona, Freddie's mom, moved in with her temporarily. Freddie's search for a student debtor involved her in university politics and murder.

Freddie felt contentment in her life with Breckinridge, but it all went up in gun smoke as *Dead Man's Hand* (Berkley, 1997) began. A Hispanic teenager held up Freddie and Curtis in a mall parking lot. Within minutes Curtis had been seriously wounded and Freddie had killed his attacker. Within days, Curtis was in the local hospital under the watchful eye of his aristocratic mother and Freddie was the darling of the right wing gun lobby. Her life was unalterably changed. She had to make major decisions, as did Curtis, but not today.

Above average for a paperback original. Author Catherine Dain has a new series featuring Faith Cassidy.

Allison O'Neil

Author: Lauren Wright Douglas

Blending in was not one of Allison O'Neil's goals. A redhead by nature, she dyed her hair assorted colors, had a pierced eyebrow and a black cat tattoo. Her clothes were shabby and funky. Her father, William Martin, had decamped when Allison was four. Mother Maureen returned to her maiden name. She died when Allison was a college senior. At that point Allison lost interest in graduation and dropped out. For a while she worked in a bookstore. As the series began, she was running a mail order mystery and science fiction book search business out of her home. The business was called Lorien, after the home of the elves in *Lord of the Rings*.

An unexpected bequest sent Allison to Lavner Bay, Oregon in *Death at Lavender Bay* (Naiad, 1996). The community was a gathering place for lesbians. Aunt Grace, with whom she had no contact since her mother's death, had left Allison $10,000 and an attractive bed and breakfast hostelry. Permanent residents who paid no rent inhabited the B&B. Allison's original intention was to sell the place and return to her California home. Her conviction that Aunt Grace had been murdered kept her there long enough to learn the truth and to delay plans to sell. Allison added a new boarder and a potential lover when she involved Kerry Owyhee, a Native American private investigator in her probe.

Aunt Grace was known for her generous hospitality to those in need. In *Swimming Cat Cove* (Naiad, 1997) Allison, plagued by empty rooms at the Bed and Breakfast, wondered if she could survive. Osie, the eleven-year-old daughter of the inn's caretaker, and private investigator Kerry persuaded a reluctant Alison to give sanctuary to a nine-year-old girl threatened by a neglectful father and his pornographic acquaintances.

Kathleen O'Shaughnessy

Author: Ruth Raby Moen

Kathleen O'Shaughnessy provided limited personal background. Her father, a Vietnam War veteran, had abandoned the family. She had been deflowered at her senior prom, had attended Kitsap Lutheran College where she took courses in journalism, and worked for a law office. She was described a having blonde curly hair and being very proud of her red 1973 Porsche.

Only One Way Out (Flying Swan, 1994) had the later copyright date but the events narrated preceded those in *Deadly Deceptions*. Kathleen accompanied her fiancé Casey on a Labor Day weekend trip into the Cascade Mountain range. By the end of the first day, they had become lost, found a corpse, and had their car disabled. Then it got worse. At the conclusion Kathleen changed boyfriends and careers, taking a job on the *Seattle Gazette*.

Kathleen was dissatisfied with her assignments at the *Seattle Gazette*. At thirty-one, she was ready for change. A phone call from Camille Cloud, a young mystic on the Suquamish Indian Reservation, during *Deadly Deceptions* (Flying Swan Publications, 1994) was a potential solution. Camille indicated that her father, a tribal leader who opposed leasing land to a gambling combine, had been abducted. En route via a car ferry, Kathleen noticed a family group in which two children were treated very badly. Kathleen's intervention brought her into contact with a handsome conniver who hoped to involve her in his schemes. She bumbled through kidnapping, child abuse, smuggling and twins split at birth, but she earned her scoop.

What had begun as routine coverage of the Skagit County Fair in *Return to the Kill* (Flying Swan, 1996) ballooned into sex scandals, murder, and the discovery of municipal corruption. Kathleen's sister Patti, whom she hoped to visit, had remarried. Her new husband was involved in a potentially violent militia movement. Kathleen's efforts to protect Patti's son Jeffrey and his young friend Bill put them all in danger. Billy's dad, Deputy Sheriff Benjamin Jack, was an attractive ally.

These were earnest narratives but the small print made them difficult to read.

Victory "Torie" O'Shea

Author: Rett MacPherson, pseudonym for Laurette Allen a.k.a.
Lauretta Dickhenber

Torie O'Shea's obsessive-compulsive strain, which can be a handicap, worked well for her as a genealogist, where attention to detail was important. It had helped in her prior job in a bank. If genealogy was her passion, her income came primarily from work at Gaheimer House, a historical society that also prized methodical precision. Torie was married to Rudy, had two daughters, and was pregnant with their third child as the series began. They lived on a two-acre piece of land near New Kassel, Missouri where they raised chickens. She sang privately with her Dad's band, although he has been divorced from her mother due to his chronic infidelity. In her early thirties, weight was another problem for Torie at 5' 2".

Torie's mother had contracted polio as a teenager, forcing her to spend her life in a wheelchair. She had been unable to finish high school as a result of the inadequate programs for the handicapped in West Virginia at that time, but was an accomplished artist. Torie's real name, Victory, was a celebration of her birth, because her mother thought she would never be able to bear a child. Torie had a tense relationship with her mother-in-law who blamed her because Rudy no longer practiced his Catholic religion. Torie did not have a close personal relationship with her boss, elderly Sylvia Pershing, president of the New Kassel Historical Society, but they had mutual respect. Enough so that Sylvia entrusted Torie with personal documentation of her youthful relationship with wealthy Hermann Gaheimer, which enabled Torie to release Sylvia from a sense of guilt.

Local businesswoman Norah Zumwalt made it clear in *Family Skeletons* (St. Martin's Paperbacks, 1997) that her purpose in seeking a five-generation genealogy was to find her father. Eugene Counts had served in World War II, leaving before he could marry her mother, and never returning. Before Torie could make Norah aware that Eugene was not only alive, but also lived nearby, she was murdered. Her current relationships, two estranged children and an unfaithful beau, provided as many suspects as did Torie's extended investigation of Eugene Counts. Torie was reminded that she had a husband and two vulnerable children to consider. The motivation of the killer seemed weaker than that attributed to other suspects.

Rudy was a very patient man in *A Veiled Antiquity* (St. Martin, 1998). He did not remonstrate with Torie when she searched a house in which a murder had been committed while their two children were present. Fortunately he was unaware that she had stolen (no other word for it) a packet hidden in victim Marie Dijon's home. Torie marshaled her genealogical materials, her history books, and her allies to trap a killer. Rudy did not know that Torie held back information as to where a treasure was hidden. They added a lost dachshund named Fritz to the household.

Torie was looking to her own family's past in *A Comedy of Heirs* (St. Martin, 1999). She had learned that her great grandfather, Nate Ulysses Keith, had been murdered fifty years before. His wife, Della Ruth had kept the family in the home at gunpoint as Nate died slowly outside. A clipping describing the murder sent Torie back into her family history. Her generation had no knowledge of the circumstances of the death. She wondered if it was too late to find Nate's killer. Torie's quest reunited her with her father and led her to accept the man who was to become her stepfather.

Torie had no idea why one-hundred-and-one-year-old Clarissa Holt had insisted that she be present at the reading of her will in *A Misty Mourning* (St. Martin, 2000). Clarissa was not even dead when the invitation was issued. She was murdered soon after Torie and Grandma Gert arrived. The will bequeathed a three-story boarding house plus ten acres of West Virginia land to Torie because of a kindness shown to Clarissa three generations earlier. Along with the bequest came the obligation to clear herself as a suspect in Clarissa's death. It did not help that Torie was seven months pregnant with her third child.

A good series.

Next books in this series: *Killing Cousins* (2002); *Blood Relations* (2003)

Laura Owen

Author: Louisa Dixon

At age thirty-eight, attorney Laura Owen had been appointed Commissioner of Public Safety in the state of Mississippi with the responsibility to enforce drug laws. She had attended "Ole Miss" for her undergraduate degree, earned a law degree at Virginia, and spent several years defending indigent clients in the criminal courts. Laura had married architect Semmes Owen and they had a young son, Willis.

Semmes died in a car accident during *Next to Last Chance* (Genesis Press, 1998). Laura's decision to leave a comfortable job as an attorney in the state auditor's office for a more politicized position in government brought chaos into her life. Her son's life was threatened and she was framed for the murder of a suspected drug smuggler. Fortunately during her brief tenure in office, she had gained the confidence of her appointee for head of the State Patrol. Her achievements made her a target of rivals within the Mississippi political community.

Time had passed by *Outside Chance* (Genesis Press, 1999). Laura had been appointed Commissioner of Public Safety and head of the State Highway Patrol. She still mourned Semmes death, but was showing an interest in Vic Regis, Chief of Staff to Governor Gibbs Carver. Although Laura was aware of political corruption in the state government, she did not play a central role in the purported death of Brent Wexler, Carver's chief fundraiser. Her primary contribution was in the investigation of financial irregularities. She had previously worked in the State Auditor's office and put that expertise to work.

Veronica Pace

Author: Philip Luber

The death of Veronica Pace's mother by a burglar had influenced her decision to become a prosecuting attorney after graduation from Harvard Law School. After serving as assistant district attorney for Bristol County, Rhode Island, she joined the FBI. Only a child when her mother died, she had been traumatized because she had seen the killer and felt guilty because she had survived. Her father had remarried a younger woman whom Veronica had difficulty accepting. She was a determined young woman, jogged regularly, set goals and attainted them ruthlessly. Not all of her desires could be met. She was unable to bear children.

Veronica was not the primary character in the series in which she appeared. He was Harry Kline, a widowed semi-retired psychiatrist, who had achieved notoriety for his book on Vietnam veterans and had independent means. When, during *Forgive Us Our Sins* (Fawcett, 1994), Harry researched family members of victims for a forthcoming book, he met Veronica. He contacted her on receiving pictures and notes sent by "Artie" who had killed a seemingly unrelated series of individuals. Together Veronica and Harry traced the deaths tied together by a penny left with the victims, but encountered the killer at personal risk. Kline decided not to write the book on victim's families, and began seeing patients again.

In *Deliver Us From Evil* (Fawcett, 1997), Veronica played an ancillary role, competing with a younger woman for Kline's attentions, but working out of the area on another case. Kline solved the mystery of a hit and run death, although concealing information from the police department, and forced a shoddy therapist to surrender his license. Veronica and her family had become very fond of Melissa, Harry's daughter. Melissa's initial resistance to Veronica as her father's romantic interest helped Veronica accept her own stepmother as a friend.

By *Pray For Us Sinners* (Fawcett, 1998) Veronica had moved into the housekeeper's vacant apartment on Kline's estate, although he was still mourning his deceased wife. The prologue returned to the night when Veronica entered her mother's room, and saw her killer who said, "Until we meet again" as he exited. She had never been able to erase this memory. Veronica took a leave of absence, reviewed the case file, revisited her family home now occupied by a Mafia don, and offered a substantial reward for information leading to the identification of the killer. It was Kline who made the decision as to the outcome of the case.

Exciting concepts and good characterizations.

Lorraine Page

Author: Lynda La Plante

Lorraine Page was a former police officer who subsequently ran her own investigation agency in Los Angeles. Upset by the death of her police partner, she had begun drinking. Under the influence of alcohol, Lorraine had caused the death of a young boy. Her guilt precipitated even heavier drinking which wrecked her marriage and ended her future in the police department. As the series began, Lorraine had been divorced from Mike Page for over five years, during which he had custody of their two daughters, Sally and Julie. She had no contact with the girls. Lorraine planned to deal with her scarred face by surgery sometime in the future. Her regular companion was a dog, "Tiger," part wolfhound and part Malamute.

As *Cold Shoulder* (Macmillan, 1994) began, Lorraine had been helped to recovery by Rosie, a fellow alcoholic. The need for money to buy liquor had led Lorraine into the clutches of a serial killer. After she escaped from him, she could not deny her responsibility to identify him. Her return to sobriety correlated with her role in his capture. The change in her life did not include a reunion with her children at this time.

In *Cold Blood* (Macmillan, 1996), Anne Louise Caley, indulged daughter of faded actress Elizabeth Seals and her husband, real estate developer Robert Caley, disappeared. The police and initial investigators had no luck in finding the girl. A chance encounter sent the case to newly founded Page Investigations, which consisted of Rosie and Lorraine. Their investigation was saturated with betrayal, voodoo, and death. They were the only happy survivors, emerging wealthy, but not necessarily healthier or wiser.

Cold Heart (Macmillan, 1998) was the final narrative in the trilogy. As it began, Lorraine seemed to have a new life. The one million-dollar bonus she had earned on the prior case subsidized a new office, a new truck and car, the down payment on a new home, and the financing for her plastic surgery. Her new client was Cindy Nathan, young wife of a major studio executive found dead in his swimming pool of gunshot wounds. When Cindy was found dead, the easy answer would have been suicide from guilt. Instead Lorraine uncovered art fraud and made plans for her own future. It would include a reunion with her daughters, and more time with a man who loved her as she was then, but she paid a price.

La Plante has had a stable of winners over the years, mostly BBC series that were novelized.

Charlotte "Charlie" Parker

Author: Connie Shelton

Charlie Parker and her brother, Ron, had been close since childhood, but the death of their parents in an air crash when she was sixteen deepened that relationship. Their father, a scientist, worked for Sandia Labs doing top-secret work during the Cold War. Their mother, a member of a wealthy and prominent family, spent her time in Junior League and country club activities. During the first years after the accident, Charlie lived with her grandmother. When old enough she moved next door into the home her parents had occupied before their death, sharing it with a mixed breed dog, named Rusty. She had become a tiny auburn-haired woman in her thirties without a husband or children. Another brother, Paul, occasionally visited with his wife and two rambunctious children. Charlie did not initially have a private investigators license. Her experience came when she uncovered theft in the trust fund left to her by her parents, and again when she assisted a neighbor who was being defrauded by an insurance agent. Bolstered by her accounting degree, CPA certification, and experience with a major corporation, Charlie opened an investigation agency with recently divorced brother Ron.

Loyalty was important to Charlie, so why in *Deadly Gamble* (Intrigue, 1995) did she agree to find a valuable watch for Stacy, the woman who "stole" her fiancé years before? When the man who had stolen the watch was murdered, Stacy needed help. Connie, realizing that Stacy was tied to a controlling husband, lent a hand.

That investigation left Charlie tired and depressed so she headed to Kauai, Hawaii in *Vacations Can Be Murder* (Intrigue. 1995). She spotted a corpse during a helicopter tour of the island. Charlie's personal interest in pilot Drake Langston drew her into the murder investigation. She must have failed to take the ethics course in business school. She entered private offices, read personal and business mail, and lied about her identity.

At the time of her parents' death, Charlie had asked few questions. Fifteen years later, in *Memories Can Be Murder* (Intrigue, 1995), she couldn't stop asking them. Why had reports of the Sandia plane crash been removed from the FAA office? Why had the fact that the crash had been caused by a bomb brought on board in the pilot's carry-on been concealed? Why were people even now willing to burn buildings and kill informants when the need for secrecy about the Sandia project was long past? People were getting hurt!

With heartache at her separation from Drake Langston and a headache from fourteen stitches in her head, Charlie returned to New Mexico in *Partnerships Can Kill* (Intrigue, 1997). High school friend, Sharon Ortega had financial and personal problems in her restaurant business—some of which stemmed from her partner, David Ruiz. Charlie's expertise was needed not only in auditing the books, but also in determining whether or not David committed suicide. The business insurance would be ineffective unless Charlie could find a killer, someone other than Sharon. In her spare time, Charlie protected Ron from a predatory female.

A casual visit to a small New Mexican town in *Small Towns Can Be Murder* (Intrigue, Press 1998) spurred Charlie's interest in the miscarriage and death of a young Hispanic woman whose husband might be an abuser. Combating the silence of the isolated community, Charlie uncovered a vicious conspiracy.

Drake had moved from Hawaii to New Mexico where he was building up a charter flight business. His plan to fly ski charters to Taos in the New Mexico mountains during *Honeymoons Can Be Murder* (Intrigue, 2001) had a dual purpose. Besides the income, it would provide him and Charlie a delightful place to spend the early days of their marriage. Included in the deal Drake had worked out was the rental of a secluded cabin in the woods. Because their own home was being remodeled, this fit into Charlie's plans too. Two new cases for RJP Investigations came with the site: the need (1) to prove their new friend Eloy Romero had not murdered his priest brother; and (2) to check a possible case of false identity. Charlie, as usual, had no compunction about stealing and reading privileged material; then concealing the information.

A light series from an enterprising publisher.

Next book in this series: *Reunions Can Be Murder* (2003)

Lily Pascale

Author: Scarlett Thomas

Lily Pascale, who made frequent references to the fact that she had one green eye and one blue eye, was, at age twenty-five, a lecturer in English Literature at a Devon University. Her area of specialty was mystery fiction. For a period of time due to a temporary vacancy she served as acting head of the department. While in London, Lily had hoped for a career as an actress. Her parents were divorced. "Mum," who coordinated the Women's Studies program at the University, was writing a novel. Henri, Lily's French-born father, practiced psychiatry in London where he entertained his many female friends. Her younger brother Nat, who had a different father, was attending the local university. For all of the cosmopolitan elements in her life, Lily remained rather innocent, and unaware of her impact on others. She disliked flying, but smoked. When younger she and her dearest friend Eugenie, now deceased, had learned magic and card tricks. She enjoyed puzzles and riddles. Lily shared her Devon home with a half-Siamese cat, Maude.

A sudden decision to flee London in *Dead Clever* (Hodder and Stoughton, 1998) sent Lily back to her maternal home and a part-time position at the University. She was to replace an instructor in Contemporary Literature who had quit suddenly. New to the faculty, she was appalled to learn that one member of her class had been savagely murdered and a second student had died of a drug overdose. The attractive man with whom she had a date might be connected to these tragedies. Something sinister was happening on the campus.

Lily's fifteen minutes of fame as a crime investigator caused former college friend Jess Mallone, now a freelance journalist, to ask for help during *In Your Face* (Hodder & Stoughton, 1999). Jess had written a magazine article about three women who had been stalked. The day it was published, all three were murdered. With time on her hands, Lily went to London to escape the end of a romance and meet with Jess. Not only had

Jess disappeared, but Lily also wondered if she had ever known her at all. The narrative was interspersed with the killer's responses to self-questioning.

Martha Patterson

Author: Gretchen Sprague

After a successful career in the Trusts and Estates Division of Reilly Whitman, a prestigious law firm, attorney Martha Patterson had too many skills to waste her time. The death of her husband Edwin, former owner of an airfreight business, had left her lonely but financially secure. Her son Robert was married and lived with his wife and two children in California. Martha had been born and raised in Nebraska, the daughter of a state Supreme Court Justice, but she intended to stay in New York City. A chance encounter with Howard Wallace, who had interned at Reilly Whitman but turned to public service work, led to her volunteer job at West Brooklyn Legal Services (WBLS). She had been warned to avoid the "Mother Teresa Syndrome." Still Martha took a personal interest in the people she served. She could not help contrasting their lives with those of her former wealthy clients. In her late sixties, she remained a physically active woman. Tennis was no longer an option but she chose to walk, rather than ride, whenever possible. She was interested in modern art and had a social life.

Meeting Wilma Oberfell at WBLS on her first day at the office in *Death in Good Company* (St. Martin, 1997) made an impact on Martha. Not only did Wilma seem distrustful of other staff members, but Martha was impressed by her excellent grammar. She was surprised that Wilma followed her home; then, left without speaking. When Martha went to Wilma's home to check on her, she was dead. Although she had other legal work to deal with, the murder of Howard Wallace, who had introduced her to the agency, convinced Martha that something was terribly wrong with WBLS.

Martha had moved on from WBLS by *Maquette for Murder* (St. Martin, 2000). She still volunteered for Sunny Searles' social services projects, but was also busy doing legal research for small firms. Because he had shown an interest in modern sculpture, she invited her accountant, Joe Gianni to accompany her to a showing by her friend, Hannah Gold. In the mid hours of the night, Martha was awakened by a frantic phone call from Hannah. She had been struck on the head, her maquette (a scale model of a larger piece) had been destroyed and her handsome young assistant, Kent Reed was dead. Fortunately, Phil Sharpman, who had worked with Hannah in the prior case, was involved. Unfortunately, Martha waited too long to share what she had learned with him.

A solid series.

Next book in this series: *Murder in a Heat Wave* (2003)

Dr. Andi Pauling

Author: Lillian M. Roberts

Andi Pauling, a tiny blonde, grew up in southern Illinois, near St. Louis. Her mother had a painful death from cancer while Andi was in college. She did not have a close relationship with her father, who had not been supportive of her career plans. Andi had never forgotten fellow veterinary student Ross McRoberts. He had been there to help her with her studies. The possibility of a romance between them ended when she rebuffed an overture, a decision she later regretted. Ross married Eastern socialite Kelsey Vallice shortly after graduation and moved to Kentucky. Andi joined Dr. Doolittle's Pet Care in Palm Springs California run by Dr. Philip Harris. Eventually she became a part owner of the business. Harris' death revealed serious financial problems. Andi ran the clinic alone for a while; then Dr. Trinka Romanescu, who had worked for the Animal Emergency Center, joined her. Trinka would be the managing partner in charge of finances. They occasionally disagreed as to the need for new equipment, hiring of additional staff, and Andi's overly generous nature. She had a problem saying "no," dressed very casually, and over the years had adopted numerous dogs and cats in need of homes. She did not, however, want children because they might bring heartbreak. Marriage was only a remote possibility in her plans.

Andi was still playing catch-up with her bills when Dr. Ross McRoberts reappeared in *Riding for a Fall* (Fawcett Gold Medal, 1996). His marriage had ended. He was planning to relocate, but was temporarily caught up in polo playing. He was also temporarily short of funds, so Andi offered him lodging. Andi's experience with animals had been directed towards small pets, rather than horses. Ross drew her into the wealthy world of competitive polo. She was unprepared for the vicious attacks on Ross' horses, a subsequent murder, and Ross' strange behavior.

When Andi saw the injured dog in *The Hand That Feeds You* (Fawcett, 1997), she realized that its condition was the result of a commercial dogfight. Within days the dog's owner had been viciously murdered and his mute eight-year-old daughter had disappeared. Andi, who had found the corpse, was unable to leave the matter to the authorities. Her instincts told her that dog fighting was minor compared to other aligned activities. Clay Tanner, the attractive owner of a neighboring horse farm, showed a personal interest. Until her health concerns were settled, Andi could not respond.

Andi had euthanized a seriously ill Sheltie belonging to philanthropist Gilda Hopkins several years before *Almost Human* (Fawcett, 1998) began. She was shocked to receive a videotaped plea from Gilda, asking for help in her own death. Andi had never forgotten her mother's painful cancer death. Her visits to Gilda made her vulnerable to charges that she had murdered the woman. The narrative gave close to equal attention to the treatment of Sally, a chimpanzee and her endangered infant. Too much monkey business.

Author Lillian M. Roberts did not hesitate to take on serious issues, i.e. animal and child abuse, drugs, and euthanasia.

Karen Pelletier

Author: Joanne Dobson

Karen Pelletier's parents were low-income emigrants from French Canada. She initially seemed destined to live a life much like her mother's. Married and pregnant by eighteen, she left her brutish husband when his anger spilled over on their daughter. Determined to make a life for herself and young Amanda, she went back to school part-time while working at a variety of menial jobs, eventually earning a Ph.D.

Her first professional work was at a New York City College where she began a significant affair with police captain Tony Gorman. Their relationship had real importance to Karen, but not enough to influence her decision to take a more prestigious offer from Enfield College in Massachusetts. Tony, who wanted a wife and children, accepted her decision and married someone else. As the series began, Amanda was a Georgetown University student; Karen, an untenured professor at the private school.

Karen's expertise in the works of Emily Dickinson was a significant factor in *Quieter Than Sleep* (Doubleday, 1997). It may have been the reason why Professor Randy Astin-Berger sought an opportunity to talk to her just before he was murdered. The exposé of a killer led also to new information about Dickinson's involvement with a libidinous historical figure. Karen's romantic interest in college president Avery Mitchell might have seemed mutual. However, Mitchell was careful to avoid a conflict of interest and hoped to reconcile with his wife. Karen's awe of the sophisticated Mitchell blinded her to the more humble talents of a local police lieutenant.

Karen was popular with most of her students, but she experienced considerable problems with the college administration in *The Northbury Papers* (Doubleday, 1998). The head of her department was disdainful of Karen's interest in the works of Serena Northbury, whose Nineteenth Century novels they considered unworthy of academic attention. Karen's discovery of members of the Northbury family in Enfield, coupled with the death of a wealthy descendant, made her a murder suspect. She was a collateral beneficiary of a trust that established a department at Enfield to explore the works of American women writers. While seeking an unpublished Northbury novel, Karen frightened a killer who thought she knew too much already.

The ultimate betrayal to academics, plagiarism, played a role in two separate mysteries in *The Raven and the Nightingale* (Doubleday, 1999). First, was the recent death of an arrogant and ambitious professor in Karen's department; second, the purported suicide of a young poetess involved with Edgar Allan Poe a century before. Karen's contacts with Lt. Charlie Piotrowski made a slight move towards friendship, but daughter Amanda strengthened her ties to her own past. The conclusion left untidy endings in the lives of supporting characters.

A flip remark, nominating *Oblivion Falls* as the outstanding book of the Twentieth Century during *Cold and Pure and Very Dead* (Doubleday, 2000) brought reclusive author Mildred Deakins to public attention after fifty years of anonymity. The attention was unwelcome and became worse when Martin Katz, the reporter who publicized Karen's recommendation, was murdered. *Oblivion Falls* had been a roman à clef. Karen believed that the motive for Katz's murder and a subsequent killing lay in events described in the book and reflected in Mildred's personal life. The killer was close enough to touch. The narrations were interspersed with excerpts from *Oblivion Falls*. Well done, but there were too many coincidences. The experience made Karen more understanding of her own mother.

These were literary mysteries, but Karen was free of the intellectual arrogance of some academic sleuths. She showed genuine interest in her students, particularly those who shared her background.

Next book in this series: *Maltese Manuscript* (2003)

Daisy Perika

Author: James Doss

Daisy Perika, an elderly Native American who had outlived two husbands, gradually tempered her Christian religion with a return to the shamanism of her Ute tribe. Her visions and signs alerted her when trouble was on the horizon.

The Shaman Sings (St. Martin, 1994) concerned the death of Priscilla Song, university researcher who had recently made a significant breakthrough. Scott Parris, the local police chief, and an attractive young reporter were unwilling to settle for the obvious suspect, Priscilla's lover, but it was Daisy who snared the killer.

Daisy had a larger role in *The Shaman Laughs* (St. Martin, 1995) when her friend and confidante, Nahum Yaciiti, disappeared. Her "favorite nephew," police officer Charlie Moon, searched for the old shepherd. Daisy, in peril of losing her homestead to a government proposal to store nuclear waste, also disappeared. Cattle mutilators and killers were no match for Daisy's dreams and her consultations with Pitukupf, a dwarf spirit who lived in the canyon.

Daisy was having visions as *The Shaman's Bones* (Avon, 1997) began, and she wanted Chief of Police Scott Parris to be aware of trouble to come. His decision to postpone his vacation based on her prophecy was fortunate. An ambitious Ute tribal member abandoned his wife Mary's corpse and fled with his daughter, Sarah, to the reservation and Daisy's protection. The bone of contention was a whistle, a sacred emblem of power. The manner of Mary's death and the prospective danger to Sarah caused Daisy to call upon her spiritual powers and Pitukupf.

The Sun Dancers of the Ute Mountain Tribe were tested for endurance. They fasted from food and liquids in a continuous dance, seeking a dream vision and the power it provided. During *The Shaman's Game* (Avon, 1998), two dancers died, seemingly of natural causes, but there were rumors of a witch. Charlie and his "Aunt" Daisy attended the summer dances on the mountain; he, in his professional capacity; she, because she was determined to deal with the witch. Another watcher sought revenge for the death of a young Shoshone dancer. At the end, Charlie did not know, or did not want to know, who had intervened to silence the witch, but he grieved.

Father-daughter relationships played important roles in *The Night Visitor* (Avon, 1999). Daisy provided foster care for an orphaned half-Ute child. The daughter of a greedy landowner had her eye on Charlie Moon. A father-daughter team sought accreditation to excavate a hairy mammoth. Last but not least, a young girl traveled the West with her father, whose devious kindness led to murder. Daisy played a diminished role, relinquishing her powers to a young successor. Buffoonery, archeology and Native American mysteries created an uneven mix and a tricky ending.

North American mysticism was diluted in *Grandmother Spider* (Morrow, 2001) by an infusion of Maggody-like humor. A series of unlikely events occurred in the territory next to the Southern Ute jurisdiction. Scott

Parris and Charlie Moon cooperated in the investigation of the murder of a patent attorney and the disappearances of two patients from the hospital. This tied in to sightings of a mysterious object that resembled a giant spider and to the Ute mythology of Grandmother Spider.

Author James Doss writes lovely mystic prose, enhanced by his descriptions of the Western landscape.

Next book in this series: *White Shell Woman* (2002)

Jane Perry
Author: Frances Ferguson, pseudonym for Barbara Perkins

Jane Perry had an eclectic background. Her father was a British Army general whose postings had taken them to Saudi Arabia, Sweden, Italy and Germany. She spoke several European languages, had a college degree and certification as an attorney. She had been deeply disappointed by her lack of opportunities to get into the Criminal Investigation Division in London.

Jane's move to a rural English police department seemed a good idea as *Missing Person* (Headline, 1993) began. Unfortunately, chauvinistic DCI Morland had just replaced the progressive female detective inspector. Nevertheless Jane with the help of a charming fellow sergeant solved serial murders, prevented an assassination, and identified an arrogant killer. She would bear scars from her efforts, but probably earned a promotion.

Jane's personal and personnel problems received considerable attention in *No Fixed Abode* (Headline, 1994). Her tempestuous relationship with veterinarian Adrian Reston was endangered when his partner was suspected in one of her cases. When her current superior officer, DI Dan Crowe resigned, Jane applied for the post, but did not receive serious consideration. Jane's persistence and independence worked against her. She investigated the death of Old Mary, a mentally ill vagrant after Crowe's replacement told her to drop the case.

In *Identity Unknown* (Headline, 1995), Jane's opportunity for promotion to detective inspector came...but at a cost. She had to leave the Criminal Investigation Division (CID) and move into Community Relations. In that role she attended the funeral of a local dignitary and witnessed the discovery of a headless corpse in the grave. Superintendent Annerley, who remembered her successes, insisted that she use her current post to gather information in the case. Jane found herself attracted to a mysterious cult leader at a time when she and Adrian were at odds.

The best part of Jane's new position was the opportunity to liase with European police forces and use her language skills in *With Intent to Kill*

(Headline, 1996). The abandonment of a truckload of immigrants on the highway took place as Jane drove by after such a meeting. The next morning while searching for the escaped immigrants, the police found the body of journalist Lionel Hughes. Hughes' current wife insisted that his prior spouse, now living in France, was the most likely suspect. Jane went beyond this supposition. She used a handsome Sûreté officer to develop another possibility. At least this time she arranged for backup when she ventured into danger. She would still prefer to work in CID, but not if it meant a transfer and leaving Adrian.

Karen Perry-Mondori

Author: Catherine Arnold

Karen Perry-Mondori's colleagues and adversaries perceived her as an adept criminal lawyer, who used trickery when necessary to give her clients the full benefit of the law. She did not do her own research nor factual investigations, but was skilled in courtroom tactics. A tiny brown-haired woman practicing in Clearwater Florida with an established firm (Hewitt, Sinclair, and Smith), she had earned her position. She had been estranged from her mother for years and never knew who had been her father. A good marriage to neurosurgeon Carl Mondori had made that less important in her life. They had a daughter, Andrea initially six-years-old who was cared for by au pairs while her parents worked.

Motivated by the courage of witnesses in a prior case who risked their jobs for the truth, Karen agreed to defend Jack Palmer in *Due Process* (Signet, 1996). There were many reasons not to do so. There seemed to be an open and shut case against Jack for killing the husband of a woman he had purportedly raped. The deceased and his wife were neighbors of Carl and Karen. Carl and the managing partner of her firm cautioned her to avoid the case. Jack Palmer probably could not pay her fees. The well-developed narrative provided credible courtroom scenes and an absorbing conclusion.

Karen could not explain, even to herself, why she agreed to defend aging Mafioso Angelo Uccello. He was admittedly a drug dealer, but in *Imperfect Justice* (Signet, 1997) she believed he had been framed on the current charges. State and federal investigators and judicial officials aligned themselves against her defense. Her mother Martha visited to insist that she withdraw. Karen and her family paid a price for her persistence. Even what seemed to be a final victory had a bittersweet twist.

There was no way for Karen to separate her personal and professional feelings in *Wrongful Death* (Signet, 1999). After receiving a videotape that portrayed him in pederast activity, her brother Robert was discovered shot in the head. Numbed with grief and trying to help Robert's widow and twin sons, Karen could not put aside her need for justice. She believed the tape had been faked, and intended to find out how and by whom.

The stakes for Karen escalated with each narrative. In the beginning she was protecting her client from being framed by an individual. By *Class Action* (Signet, 1999) she pitted herself against the federal government (CIA and FBI) in her defense of a vagrant accused of murder. At times, Karen's zeal for justice outweighed her responsibility to her husband and her daughter. In the conclusion she realized that she had been manipulated, but had enough faith in the American public to release frightening information.

Excellent at paperback prices.

Maddy Phillips

Author: R. D. Zimmerman

Blind and paraplegic, Maddy Phillips had isolated herself on a Lake Michigan island far from her former professional life in Chicago. Her vision problems arose from retinitis pigmentosa. Her physical injuries came as the result of a collision caused by a drunken bus driver. This ended her career as a forensic psychologist, but the insurance settlement made her financially independent. Maddy remained on the island year round with Alfred and Solange, husband and wife servants, and two mastiff dogs, Fran and Ollie. Maddy's father had been killed in a plane crash; her mother suffered from Alzheimer's. Maddy retained her interest in the world, her sense of humor, and her strong influence on her brother Alex. He allowed her to hypnotize him as to past activities and was guided by her questions. The relationship was close to unhealthy.

In *Death Trance* (Morrow, 1992), Alex's former lover Dr. "Toni" Domingo was killed, shortly after the death of her younger sister. Through hypnosis Maddy retrieved information that had defied Alex's conscious memory. When Maddy identified the killer, the knowledge was painful to her.

During *Blood Trance* (Morrow, 1993), former patient Loretta Long contacted Maddy in a panic. Alex, sent to bring Loretta to the island, found her standing over her stepmother's corpse with a knife. Attempts to injure Alex suggested that he had suppressed knowledge that would identify the killer. After the solution, Alex quit his job as a technical writer to work full time for Maddy.

The action moved from the Midwest to Russia in *Red Trance* (Morrow, 1994), and required an even greater suspension of belief. Maddy had corresponded for years with a wealthy Russian hypnotist from whom she concealed her accident and her confinement to a wheelchair. Alex returned to Russia where he had lived as a student, to find oppression replaced by commercialism at a level conducive to murder.

Quirky.

Joanna Piercy

Author: Priscilla Masters

Joanna Piercy's promotion from detective sergeant to detective inspector in a rural English police department was not universally popular with staff. On the positive side, she had the advantage of a college education with a degree in psychology and had recently scored a major success. Her ambition and coldness did not endear her to those whom she supervised. Nor did the fact that she was involved with married pathologist Matthew Levin. Joanna's parents had divorced. Her mother never recovered from her father's remarriage to a much young woman.

As *Winding Up the Serpent* (Macmillan, 1995) began, Joanna needed the respect and approval of her coworkers. Proving that the mysterious death of an unpopular nurse was murder could earn that respect. Joanna and Sgt. Mike Korpanski were under pressure to break through the silence of those who were glad the victim was dead. Over the series, Korpanski came to respect Joanna, which helped with other personnel. Unhappy with her private life, Joanna concentrated on her work, trying to end the affair with Matthew Levin.

Joanna and Mike's investigation into the death of a badly abused ten-year-old boy in *Catch the Fallen Sparrow* (Macmillan, 1996) produced many suspects, all guilty of something. Dogged persistence kept the police team working until significant clues appeared. It took a mother's devotion to get a confession. The intensity of the search kept Joanna's mind off the fact that Matthew was giving his marriage a second chance. At times, Joanna wondered if part of Matthew's allure was his limited availability. Did she really want him in her life full-time?

The rape and death by garroting of single mother Sharon Priest in *A Wreath for My Sister* (Macmillan, 1997) produced a quartet of possible suspects with whom she had been sexually involved. By the process of elimination, Joanna and Mike focused on a man who had killed before and might kill again. For a while it looked as though there might be a future with Matthew but she finally realized that it was not his wife Jane who was her rival for his affection. It was his daughter, Eloise. He was devoted to her and returned home when she went on a hunger strike.

Joanna, who resented Matthew's attachment to Eloise, learned more about parental love in *And None Shall Sleep* (Macmillan, 1997). After an accident while riding her bicycle, Joanna left her hospital bed to take over the investigation of the disappearance of solicitor Jonathan Selkirk, a patient on the floor below. The discovery of Selkirk's "executed" body necessitated the involvement of the Regional Crime Squad because his killer was presumed to be a paid assassin. The task of finding who had hired the killer remained the responsibility of Joanna and her staff. Two associated deaths emphasized for Joanna the devotion of parents to their children, particularly for an only child. The idea of a pregnancy distorting her body and limiting her activities was abhorrent to Joanna.

Even Joanna's cat ran away in *Scaring Crows* (Macmillan, 1999). An isolated rural family came to the attention of the police department. Elderly Aaron Summers, who was dying of cancer, and his mentally disabled son Jack had been shot to death. Aaron's daughter Rosie had disappeared, but Joanna was reluctant to treat her as a killer. Joanna was on the brink of purchasing a house with Matthew when she pulled back. His expectations that Eloise would spend considerable time with them and that they might have children of their own were unrealistic. She was honest about the fact that she did not like children and had no intention of getting pregnant.

Neither Joanna nor her assistant, Sgt. Mike Korpanski was in good humor as *Embroidering Shrouds* (Macmillan, 2001) began. At the office they were plagued by a series of burglaries that had escalated into vicious assaults. Mike had a visiting mother-in-law who upset his household. Joanna was dreading a visit from Eloise. She and Matthew had a shared residence and a loving relationship, but she knew he felt guilt at having divorced Eloise's mother. Eloise detested Joanna. When the most recent burglary included murder, it would have been easy to attribute it to the same source as prior incidents had it not been for the character of the victim. Nan Lawrence, a bitter woman, had tormented the lives of her siblings and a former lover and had twisted the character of her great nephew. Good police procedural although Joanna's treatment of Eloise seemed harsh.

Author Priscilla Masters has a new series featuring Dr. Megan Banesto. Next book in this series: *Endangering Innocents* (2003)

Anna Pigeon

Author: Nevada Barr

Widowed Anna Pigeon, mourning her handsome actor/husband, left their New York City apartment to rebuild her life. After training as a law enforcement officer in the National Park Service, she was assigned to the Guadaloupe Mountains Park in West Texas. The expansive park and the solo assignments provided solitude, perhaps more than was wise. The only link to her past was her sister Molly, a psychiatrist with whom she maintained regular telephone contact. Anna tried to fill the void in her life with alcohol and a lover, but was unsuccessful. At thirty-nine, she was a physically strong woman wearing her copper hair tinged with gray in a long braid, sharing her successive homes with her cat, Piedmont. Anna had attended a Catholic school system for academic reasons, but had no tie with organized religion.

In *Track of the Cat* (Putnam, 1993), Anna was jolted out of her isolation. While patrolling in search of wild lion spoor, she found the corpse of fellow ranger Sheila Drury. The official diagnosis was that the death resulted from an animal attack. Anna was convinced that a staff member had murdered the woman.

In *A Superior Death* (Putnam, 1994), Anna left her beloved desert behind for the rigors of Isle Royale in Upper Michigan. Now her mode of transportation was by boat, a new experience. The ranger post was rife with rumors about cannibalism by a husband whose wife was missing. Two Canadian divers found a sunken ship that had one more corpse than expected. It was at this point that Anna met FBI agent Frederick Stanton. He was the first man to whom she had been seriously attracted since her husband's death.

Anna returned to the Southwest in *Ill Wind* (Putnam, 1995), but the position at Mesa Verde, Colorado lacked the solitude she craved. She assisted in the rescue operations of injured or ill park visitors and policed domestic abuse and industrial theft by staff and contract workers. The local environmentalists and Native Americans resented park improvements that might damage Anasazi relics. When a series of tragedies occurred, some claimed that the ancient gods were angry. Anna saw human hands at work in the death of park employee Stacy Meters, and human greed in the illnesses that threatened the young and vulnerable. She faced her own vulnerability by finally admitting to herself and sister Molly, "My name is Anna, and I am an alcoholic."

Anna needed all of her wits during *Firestorm* (Putnam, 1996) when rangers from the Southwest responded to a major California fire. Not only did she and emergency medical workers have to abandon a seriously injured man as they fled from a firestorm, but a survivor from their group was murdered. The killer was someone whom Anna did not want to have punished for the crime.

Anna's next assignment was on the Cumberland Island Beaches off Georgia's coast in *Endangered Species* (Putnam, 1997). She and other National Park Services personnel helped volunteers who assisted rare turtles to spawn their eggs on the shore. When a drug interdiction plane carrying NPS personnel crashed, there was no doubt about sabotage, only about who had been the intended victim. While Anna investigated, the two most important persons in her life, her sister Molly and FBI agent Frederick Stanton faced a crisis of their own with implications for Anna.

Claustrophobia had always been a problem for Anna. It became unavoidable in *Blind Descent* (Putnam, 1998) when she entered a recently discovered extension of Carlsbad Caverns to rescue a survey team. One member of the team was Anna's dear friend Frieda who had been seriously injured in a suspicious fall. Curt Schatz, a member of the survey team, filled the void in her personal life since neither Molly nor Frederick had been close to her recently.

Molly's devastating illness brought Anna to her bedside in *Liberty Falling* (Putnam, 1999) where Frederick Stanton joined her. He had stayed away because Molly's love for Anna made her unwilling to return his love. Rather than spend her nights at Molly's apartment, Anna stayed with her friend Patsy Silva on Liberty Island in New York Harbor. Investigating the mysterious deaths of a teenage tourist and a friendly park policeman provided Anna with the diversion she needed as her sister lay deep in a coma. Anna's prodigious visual memory aided her as she roamed the island at night, uncovering a vicious plot but ending a valuable friendship.

In *Deep South* (Putnam, 2000), seeking career advancement, Anna moved up in the National Park system by accepting a district ranger position at the Natchez Trace Parkway. She anticipated hostility towards a Yankee female in a supervisory position. In investigating the murder of a teenage girl, Anna saw both the bigotry and tolerance of Mississippi, the cruelty and kindness, the weight of past history and glimmerings of hope for the future. Her awakening to potential love for Paul Davidson, the reverent sheriff, was accompanied by mistrust of his motives. The conclusion left her physically battered but at peace with herself.

What she had hoped would be an easy assignment to allow her to recuperate from her injuries turned out otherwise in *Blood Lure* (Putnam,

2001). She was detached to a DNA research project at Glacier National Park. Her experience and increased knowledge were to be useful on her return to Natchez Trace. Her superiors had a hidden agenda. Anna, who had always loved solitude and exposure to nature, was shaken by inexplicable behavior on the part of both humans and animals. The death of an abusive woman changed Anna's status from researcher to investigator. Solid police work tied together disparate clues: the value of "Boone & Crockett" trophies, the need for young boys to bond with pets and role models, and unusual bear activity. She returned to Mississippi and Paul, having done her best.

This has been a great series that has shown no signs of deterioration or repetitiveness.

Next books in this series: *Hunting Season* (2002); *Flashback* (2003)

Josie Pigeon

Author: Valerie Wolzien

Josie Pigeon had perceived herself as rejected by her parents and the father of her child when she became pregnant as a college freshman. She cut herself off from them completely. While employed as a waitress, she worked on a Habitat for Humanity house, where she met Noel Roberts. Noel changed her life. He rescued her at a time when she wondered how she would provide for Tyler Clay, her infant son. Noel offered Josie a job on his construction crew, Island Contracting, on one condition. She would commit herself to two years work. The work became a career. Tyler was thirteen when Noel died. He left the business to Josie and provided a trust fund for Tyler's education, which meant boarding at an off-island prep school. Josie had not been the only recipient of Noel's generosity. Each member of his all-female construction crew had been recruited at a time of crisis, offered a job, and a chance to change her life.

When Josie took over in Shore to Die (Fawcett Gold Medal, 1996), Island Contracting was remodeling a decrepit mansion that had recently been purchased by Mr. and Mrs. Cornell Firbank III. The Firbanks wanted cheap quality. Josie tried to meet their needs because, if this project were successful, it would bring in more business. She lost credibility for common sense when she hid a corpse found on her construction site. Sam Richardson, a former prosecuting attorney who recently purchased an island liquor store, collaborated with Josie. They decided the only way to avoid arrest by local police was to find the killer. It didn't help that someone removed the corpse. Interesting but there were loose ends never dealt with.

When finishing carpenter Amy Llewellyn, who worked for a competing construction firm, was murdered in *Permit for Murder* (Fawcett, 1997) the circle of suspects was small. It included members of Josie's work crew and her estranged lover Sam Richardson, because the corpse had been discovered on Josie's work site. Considering the resemblance to an earlier case, Chief of Police Michael Rodney focused his suspicions on the all-female crew.

Murder connected to Josie's crew occurred again in *Deck the Halls with Murder* (Fawcett, 1998). The victim was Caroline, a new employee. Even the incompetent local police knew where to look for the killer, i.e. among her coworkers. That didn't mean that they arrested the right one, of course. On a personal level, Josie was preoccupied with the coming holiday, her resumed romance with Sam, and Tyler's vacation. Her deadline for the remodeling of a home to suit a quadriplegic did not allow for workers to be murdered or arrested. Josie might know how Caroline died, but could she convince the authorities that her theory was sound.

Remodeling an A-frame house to suit an unknown client presented problems for Josie and her new crew in *This Old Murder* (Fawcett, 2000). She added to the complexities by agreeing to have their work taped for a Public Broadcasting series on home repair and renovation. Courtney Castle, the temperamental star of the show, had a history with Josie. This created problems when her corpse was located on site. Nothing new there. Along the way Josie reassessed her relationship with her parents. Chad Henshaw, son of Wolzien's other female sleuth, made a minor appearance.

Hurricane Agatha wiped out Point House, the site of Island Contracting's premiere project in *Murder in the Forecast* (Fawcett, 2001). Only Josie and one other person knew that the owner's corpse disappeared along with the building, the killer. As always a new member of her crew aroused suspicion. Something different occurred. Chief Rodney, now enamored of Sam's mother Carol, offered to help Josie find the killer.

There were admirable elements to the series; however, on occasion, Josie's identification of the killer was unsubstantiated by evidence that would sustain an arrest, trial, and/or conviction. Each narrative had a sub-plot concerning Tyler's teenage adjustments.

Next book in this series: *A Fashionable Murder* (2003)

Molly Piper

Author: Patricia Brooks

Molly Piper, a tiny woman at 4' 9" working as a Chicago police officer, was shot while acting inappropriately on duty; then allowed to resign. She went to the village of Grace on Prince Island, Washington where she became a private investigator. She had skills beyond her experience, was highly organized, and a former gymnast. She built up a coterie of friends, including Attorney Eugene Mulholland in Grace, and Simon Emmershaw, a semi-retired private investigator in Olympia. Timothy Gray, also a former Chicago police officer, had been there for Molly when she was raped at age twenty-one, and now lived nearby on the mainland. Molly's current home was an old camper, parked on land owned by Free, an African-American who owned a bookshop.

Mary Alice Abbott had only vague recollections of an older sister Alice, even when she received her letters in *Falling from Grace* (Dell, 1998). When Alice failed to appear for a planned meeting, Mary Alice hired Molly to find her. A serial killer known as the Crucifixer because of his methods resurfaced on Prince Island at this time. Mary Alice's dysfunctional family kept Molly preoccupied even as she almost became a victim herself.

In *But for the Grace* (Dell, 2000), unpopular businessman Edmond Anderson Bercain hired Molly to investigate the unknown members of the Liberation Brigade who had placed WANTED posters around town, alleging cruel and criminal behavior in his past. She began by contacting a group of squatters, many of whom had been evicted or felt cheated by Bercain. By the next morning, Bercain had been found dead after a citywide celebration of New Year's Eve. Her new client was Bercain's widow. Molly's personal life was in disarray because her current lover, Jake, had become disinterested. Feeling rejected, she concentrated on following up on anonymous letters slipped under her door relating to the murder, and on the problems of two suspects; a teenage squatter and a Native American youth both of whom had reasons to dislike Bercain.

How did she ever get into the Chicago Police Department at 4' 9"?

Jimi Plain

Author: Victoria Pade

Finances forced Jimi Plain into selling the home that she and her children had shared since the divorce eight years ago. Her former husband was referred to as "Uncle Dad' because, even though his biological connection to their two daughters was established, he withheld both emotional and financial support. By moving out of Colorado he managed to avoid paying the court-ordered child support. Whenever the law caught up with him, he moved again. The neglect affected each child differently: Chloe at nineteen eagerly sought contacts with her father; Shannon (seventeen) had written him off. The solution that presented itself was to move into the large family home owned by Jimi's grandmother (Gramma), a fierce Italian woman. She had already subdivided the place to provide a basement level apartment for Jimi's cousin, detective Danny Delvecchio. Jimi purchased the home from Gramma; then, shared the upper floors with her. The third floor provided Jimi with the office out of which she worked as a free-lance technical writer on catalogues, training material, etc. A miniature schnauzer, Lucy, completed the household. Jimi had been raised a Catholic but no longer practiced her religion to the dismay of both Danny and Gramma. She was approaching forty as the series began.

A divorce support group had provided Jimi with comfort. By *Divorce Can Be Murder* (Dell, 1999), she was beyond active participation, but assisted as a volunteer when called on by therapist Audrey Martin. The group involved in this narrative was disrupted by the interconnections among its members. After Bruce Mann was murdered, Jimi tried to balance her loyalty to the group (which included her best friend) and to the law (as represented by Danny). Subsequent deaths made the choice easier. The plot could be considered a wake-up call for wives to be knowledgeable about their husband's finances. However, Christians may be offended by the concept that while divorce is intolerable to some, murder may not be.

The membership in the New You Center for Dating in *Dating Can Be Deadly* (Signet, 1999) had been a gift to Jimi from Gramma, Chloe, and Shannon. She went reluctantly to avoid hurting their feelings. After Jimi's personal counselor Steffi Hargitay was murdered in her office, Jimi returned to check out the suspects for cousin Danny. She must have asked too many questions. The frequent reviewing of the potential suspects added length to the narrative.

Charlie Plato

Author: Margaret Chittenden

Charlie Plato had grown up in Sacramento. She was a tall redhead who had been on her own since her parents were killed flying their Cessna in a thunderstorm. She spent twelve years in Seattle where she married a young plastic surgeon, Rob Whittaker. She had met Rob when she applied to work in his office, but their lifestyles never meshed. At thirty, after they divorced, Charlie went in a totally different direction with her life. She invested her inheritance in a business. Along with TV western star Zack Hunter and two other friends, she purchased and managed a country and western tavern, "Chaps," located on the San Francisco peninsula. Zack was a silent partner with a half share. Charlie was an active manager helped by her best pal, Savanna Seabrook. Prudent for her age and state in life, Charlie did not engage in sex with Zack who was a womanizer. Allergic to cats and afraid of dogs, she shared the loft over the tavern with "Benny" her Netherland dwarf rabbit.

With time on his hands, Zack ran for the local city council in *Dead Men Don't Dance* (Kensington, 1997) and convinced Charlie to be his campaign manager. The discovery of deceased Gerald Senerac, Zack's opponent in the race, in Zack's car trunk created political and legal problems. His alibi was Senerac's wife!

While attending her self-defense class in *Dead Beat and Deadly* (Kensington, 1998), Charlie noticed bruises on Estrella Stockton, a mail order Philippino bride. Suspecting an abusive husband, Charlie offered her help. Estrella's murder prompted her husband Thane to enlist Zack and Charlie in proving that his innocence; that in fact, he had been physically abused and threatened with murder by Estrella. Research into Estrella's checkered past revealed that she was capable of murder, but who killed her?

The aftershock from an earthquake in *Dying to Sing* (Kensington, 1996) uncovered the skeleton of an older man in the Chaps flower garden. He had been dead for several months, just about the time that Zack purchased the property. Damages to police department computers made it difficult to identify the victim, but someone knew. A mysterious phone caller demanded $5,000 owed him by Mr. X. (later identified as Walt Cochran, once a popular singer, more recently a vagrant who read the Wall Street Journal at the public library). Zack and Charlie sought nformation. Someone else destroyed it, killing an elderly librarian. Along the way, Savannah got a new beau. Zack got a new series. Nothing for Charlie except satisfaction. Zack made moves on her but was too unreliable to consider after marriage to an unfaithful husband.

Charlie had been aware that bartender and partner Angel Cervantes had a deep secret in his past. In *Don't Forget To Die* (Kensington, 1999), she learned that his mother had been murdered. His father, Vincenzo the primary suspect, had fled with a younger woman. When Vincenzo's corpse of was discovered in the area, the police questioned Angel and his brother Miguel. All mysteries were solved except whether or not Charlie finally succumbed to Zack's seductive powers.

Savanna Seabrook graduated from an alternative high school where teacher Reina Diaz had motivated many of the students. Reina's murder in *Dying To See You* (Kensington, 2000) took place at Chaps during a twenty-year class reunion. Which of her devoted students had killed this highly regarded woman? Charlie and Zack found the answer deep in the past but not before serious damage to their business.

A light, bouncy series. Don't expect significant character studies or intricate plotting.

Stephanie Plum

Author: Janet Evanovich

Being unconventional had become a way of life for Stephanie Plum. To her mother's dismay, she had shown no interest in marriage since her divorce from Dickie Orr. Her Italian-Hungarian heritage was not responsible for her quirks: beer for breakfast, disinterest in physical possessions, and devotion to a pet hamster. She was tall, brown-haired and currently out of work. Behind on car payments, Stephanie blackmailed her cousin Vinnie into a job as a skip tracer for his New Jersey bail bond business.

As *One for the Money* (Scribners, 1994) opened, Vinnie set her on the trail of police detective Joe Morelli, accused of murdering an unarmed suspect. Stephanie preferred to believe that Joe was merely seeking a witness to prove his innocence. She had always let Joe sweet-talk her, even when they were high hormonal teenagers. Armed with pepper spray, handcuffs, and a gun, Stephanie set out in the car she stole from Morelli.

Morelli continued to play a major role in Stephanie's investigations. In *Two for the Dough* (Scribners, 1996), her search for an absconding defendant turned into a murder probe. Grandma Mazur's absorption in local wakes provided Stephanie with an opportunity to observe the suspects; Gran's 1953 Buick became transportation when Stephanie's Jeep was stolen. Morelli's special assignment to trace stolen army equipment dovetailed with Stephanie's search for the missing defendant.

Cousin Vinnie was not interested in the fact that candystore owner "Uncle Mo" was popular with all the neighbors in *Three to Get Deadly* (Scribners, 1997). All that concerned him was that Mo had disappeared, failing to appear in court in a case in which Vinnie had posted his bail bond. With the help of "Ranger" her coinvestigator, Stephanie reluctantly sought Mo, earning the disapproval of her extended family, until she found a corpse on the store premises. While evading the police, including Morelli, Stephanie had a hair-raising experience, had to deal with her ex-husband, and fought off attackers while defending her hamster, Rex.

The first three books were combined in *Three Plums in One* (Scribners, 2001)

Stephanie was led on a merry chase in *Four to Score* (St. Martin, 1998) by a bail jumper who had vicious killers on her trail. Stephanie acquired a new assistant and a new enemy (who torched her car and apartment) driving her into the willing arms of Joe Morelli. Business as a bail enforcer was depressed and so was Stephanie.

Stephanie and Morelli ended their affair because of divergent plans for their future. He had no intentions of marrying. In *High Five* (St. Martin, 1999), she took on odd jobs: (1) at her family's request to look for missing Uncle Fred who may have blackmailed a killer and (2) to assist Ranger in a series of funny escapades which may be illegal, but to Ranger were "morally right." Author Evanovich teased her readers with "the tiger or the lady" ending. Whom did Stephanie invite to share the evening? Morelli or Ranger?

Ranger had been a friend and mentor to Stephanie. In *Hot Six* (St. Martin, 2000), she refused to execute Vinnie's order to find him. Ranger had jumped bail when questioned about the death of a gangster in a burned building. The action was non-stop from that point on. The narrative mixed a voracious Golden Retriever, a semi-suicidal friend, and at least two sets of rival gangsters. Cars blew up. Joe and Stephanie suffered from repeated coitus interruptus. Lula, the ex-hooker, and Grandma Mazur added to the distractions.

Eddie DeChooch was an old man with limited hearing and vision. He should have been an easy pick-up for bounty hunter Stephanie in *Seven Up* (St. Martin, 2001). However, Eddie was a retired gangster used to solving problems with a handgun, and well able to elude both Stephanie and Ranger throughout the narrative. Stephanie freed three hostages, replaced a human heart and overpowered a deranged widow, but she couldn't bring Eddie in without making a deal with Ranger.

Murder is not funny but Evanovich has added a lot of quaint touches to the series. She sets her scenes well, combining realistic ethnic dialogue with action and humor.

Next books in this series: *Hard Eight* (2002); *Visions of Sugarplums* (2002); *To The Nines* (2003)

Rachel Porter

Author: Jessica Speart

The educational background for her entry into a career in the U.S. Fish and Wildlife Service seemed skimpy, but Rachel Porter received basic training at the Academy in Glynco, Georgia before her assignment to the New Orleans area. She had sought a placement in the Slidell office where Charlie Hickok was in charge after being inspired by a television program on his achievements. Not only was Charlie a misogynistic curmudgeon, but Rachel underestimated the cultural differences between New York City and Louisiana. Her prior experience had been as an actress, struggling for small roles on Broadway, television and in commercials. Now, Rachel, already in her thirties, raised by a Jewish mother and stepfather, had to learn a new way of life. Her stepfather, Dr. Sandy Berman, had adopted Rachel, but graciously insisted that she retain her birth father's last name. Rachel actually got along better with Sandy than with her formidable mother.

Charlie Hickok routinely sent Rachel out on cold and unsuccessful attempts to catch poachers. Even when caught, the local authorities rarely prosecuted small time offenders. Nepotism, graft, and political manipulation were taken for granted. Although the official Fish and Wildlife station was in Slidell, Rachel lived in the French Quarter of New Orleans. She and Terri, her gay landlord who was a professional female impersonator, became close friends. The area had experienced an increase in right wing politics. Neo-Nazi groups demonstrated against gays and minority groups who received little protection from the police department. Over the series, her supervisors perceived Rachel as a wild cannon. They were right.

Once the reader accepts the improbabilities inherent in Rachel's career change, *Gator Aide* (Avon, 1997) moved swiftly. The presence of a dead alligator at a murder site necessitated the attention of an agent from the Fish and Wildlife Service. Charlie Hickok must not have realized that once Rachel got on an exciting case, it would be impossible to get her off...particularly when she was working with attractive homicide detective Jake Santou. The victim of the murder was Valerie Vaughn, a topless dancer who had suspicious connections to local politicians and businessmen.

Anyone who thought all they could lose in Las Vegas was their money, had better read *Tortoise Soup* (Avon, 1998). Rachel wanted to leave the bayous, but was lonely for Jake Santou. Federal agents were unwelcome in the Nevada deserts, hated by ranchers because of the emphasis on endangered species, by mine owners for regulations, and by real estate developers because the government owned most of the land. When an elderly recluse was murdered, Rachel challenged the local, state, and federal governments to find the killer.

Rachel picked up new allies wherever she relocated; next, the Miami area in *Bird Brained* (Avon, 1999). They were rarely coworkers or police. Her crusades led her far beyond the bounds of her job description, when she investigated the murder of smuggler Alberto Dominguez. Dominguez had been involved in the exotic bird trade, but Rachel smoked out additional culprits. Terri Tune, her former landlord in New Orleans, joined her, and partied with her current lesbian landladies, Sophie and Lucinda. Add in a retired military man and a smart mouthed cockatoo for help in solving the murder. Colorful characters, yes. Careful plotting, not necessarily.

Rachel's next transfer was to the El Paso, Texas area in *Border Prey* (Avon, 2000). Her immediate concern was the death of her only snitch, Timmy Tom Tyler, an entrepreneur who smuggled animals across the Mexican border. Timmy Tom was small-time, but Rachel moved on to bigger game, i.e. erratic scientist Dr. Martin Pierpont and powerful rancher Frederick Ulysses Krabb (better known by his initials). Unfortunately, Krabb was currently married to Rachel's long time friend, Lizzie Burke.

During *Black Delta Night* (Avon, 2001), Rachel was reunited with her former supervisor Charlie Hickok and Jake Santou, the man she couldn't forget. Having Charlie available made it easier to get unofficial permission for a dangerous undercover mission. Fishermen on the Mississippi River were hired to catch the endangered paddlefish, whose roe was similar to caviar. Santou made an undercover appearance as a shady character. Pooling their resources they ended up without egg on their faces.

Author Jessica Speart took on worthwhile causes in her narratives; i.e. the protection of endangered species including female émigrés. She implicated the business and government interests, which not only tolerated abuses, but also benefited from them. The historical backgrounds and physical descriptions were credible.

Next books in this series: *A Killing Season* (2002); *Coastal Disturbance* (2003)

Kathleen "Kit" Powell

Author: Julie Robitaille

Kit Powell had eclectic tastes: boxing and Jane Austen. A redhead whose father ran a sports bar, and whose ex-husband had been a jock, she reported sports for a San Diego television station. She had previously worked as a television writer, but moved on screen when the regular sportscaster was too drunk to appear.

Kit's assignment put her on scene in *Jinx* (Council Oak Books, 1991) when the general manager of the Sharks football team was killed in a fall out of a skybox. The victim's mother Daphne Collier had inherited the team when her third husband was killed in an accident. She moved the team from Galveston to San Diego. The victim's widow owned stock in the team, but did not live to dispose of it. Someone was taking sports too seriously.

Iced (St. Martin, 1994) involved Kit in the serial murders of homeless persons in San Diego. It was in her role as sportscaster covering the skating championships that Kit met Therese Steiner. Her death was somehow tied to the killings of the homeless and the bigotry of the "White Nation." Kit's underground work put her in danger, but not out of action.

Kate Power

Author: Judith Cutler

The British police system allowed accelerated advancement for recruits with college degrees. In her late twenties, Kate Power, who had a master's degree from Manchester University, was a sergeant in the Birmingham CID (Criminal Investigation Division). She attended the local Baptist church at the urging of her Aunt Cassie, but had been involved with a married man, now deceased. When Aunt Cassie entered the nursing home, Kate had the use of her house and was busy fixing it up. In her spare time, she coached a youth football team. There was some evidence that Kate had a drinking problem but was working on it. As the series developed, there was even more evidence that she fell too easily into romantic and/or sexual affairs with coworkers and superior officers, not recommended in any line of work.

The move to Birmingham was a flight from Kate's memories of Robin, her lover who had been killed. She could not mourn him properly, that was for his wife and children. In *Power On Her Own* (Hodder & Stoughton, 1998), Kate encountered a new set of problems: the hostility of fellow workers at the West Midlands CID, the adjustment of Great Aunt Cassie to the nursing home; and the renovation of the old woman's house for her use. Most chilling was the probability that among her new friends at work and in the community were members of a pederast ring and a killer.

By *Staying Power* (Hodder & Stoughton, 1999), Kate had moved from London and made friends on the Birmingham force. She contended with Detective Constable Selby's insubordination and misogyny. She was not his only victim. DC Colin Roper, who kept his homosexuality in the closet, was Kate's partner. They tied together several major cases involving pharmacy thefts, drug dealing, family violence and fraud. Selby's behavior eventually accelerated to the point where charges could be brought.

Kate's transfer to the specialized Major Incident Team during *Power Games* (Hodder and Stoughton, 2000) might have offered professional opportunities. Instead it placed Kate under hostile supervision from Inspector Nigel Crowther whose spectacular advancement on the force had been fostered by his politically prominent mother. Kate had her own admirers in Inspector Graham Harvey and Superintendent Rod Neville to protect her reputation. When she discovered an unidentified body at her tennis club, she sought the woman's identity and her killer with a persistence that created problems for Crowther.

Another transfer, this time to the Birmingham Fraud Squad, brought more misery to Kate in *Will Power* (Hodder & Stoughton, 2001). Her immediate supervisor, Inspector Lizzie King was volatile to the point of hostility, a problem recognized but not understood by others in the squad. Kate's assignment to a forgery case expanded to a murder investigation, allowing her to liaise with the CID unit to which she had previously been attached. Again working with her secretive and guilt-ridden lover Graham Harvey and under the direction of Rod Neville, who had no qualms about office romances, she needed to get her personal priorities in order.

Next book in this series: *Hidden Power* (2002). An American publisher has recently issued the series.

Narcissa Powers

Author: Ann McMillan

Narcissa Powers' mother died when she was fifteen and her father died when she was nineteen. Her husband, Rives Powers had tutored her brother Charley. Rives died of tuberculosis, leaving her a widow at age twenty-one. Their baby died shortly after birth. At twenty-three, Narcissa became one of an ensemble which included Judah Daniel, a former slave who had expertise as an herbalist; Dr. Cameron Archer, the supervisor of the Medical College of Virginia Hospital; and Brit Wallace, an English reporter.

The terminal illness of her beloved brother Charley, a medical student, had sent Narcissa to Richmond in *Dead March* (Viking, 1998) in time to realize that he might have been murdered. After a brief visit in the home of Dr. Edgar Hughes, Charley's professor, Narcissa moved in with her sister-in-law Mirrie, an outspoken opponent of secession. The State of Virginia made its choice and prepared for war while Narcissa focused on activities of the "resurrection men" who stole corpses from their graves for medical research. Her sensitivity to the plight of African-Americans was heightened by attendance at a slave auction and her alliance with free African-American Judah Daniel. Narcissa and Judah worked together as practical nurses at the overflowing army hospital, while investigating Charley's death.

In *Angel Trumpet* (Viking, 1999), Narcissa and Judah worked in the Medical College of Virginia Hospital under Dr. Archer. They were expected to watch over Archer's headstrong young female cousin, Jordan who had returned from a Maryland boarding school for young ladies. They also had the task of interrogating slave servants who were suspected of killing members of their plantation families. Although Judah's herbal skills and Narcissa's probing affected the plot, Cameron and Brit identified the killer.

Civil Blood (Viking, 2001) was an ambitious narrative, fueled by the fear, greed and passion of a dozen characters. Narcissa and Judah, with a common goal—preventing the spread of smallpox in Richmond—set out to locate a jacket and a considerable amount of money that carried the smallpox virus. Rival youth gangs, a philandering entrepreneur, and the women he betrayed complicated their search.

Next book in this series: *Chickahominy Fever* (2003)

Patricia "Pat" Pratt

Author: Bernie Lee

Ignoring the unfortunate choice of surname, this was another "couples" series. Patricia Pratt, the mother of two college age children, was a successful financial consultant, who lived in Oregon with husband, Tony, a freelance mystery writer. In *Murder at Musket Beach* (Fine, 1990), the couple rented a cottage in a small Pacific coast town. Although Tony wanted a vacation from mysteries, they tripped over a corpse shortly after they arrived.

A Japanese film company hired Tony to make location arrangements near an Indian reservation as *Murder Without Reservation* (Fine, 1991) began. When Pat joined him, her role was more that of victim than investigator. Even with such action standbys as stampedes, kidnapping, robberies, and the murder of a handsome Japanese actor, the narrative failed to hold together.

Murder Takes Two (Fine, 1993) took the Pratts to London where an advertising executive was murdered during the filming of commercials. Only on their return to Oregon did they identify the killer. Pat took an active role in protecting Tony when he confronted a suspect, but the killer was obvious, and the motive was weak.

Dr. Amy Prescott

Author: Louise Hendricksen

Dr. Amy Prescott was a slim divorcee who had been raised by her father and followed in his footsteps as a forensic pathologist. She initially worked in the Western Washington State Crime Lab; later, she formed a consulting firm with her father. Amy maintained an apartment in Seattle, but spent much of her time on an offshore island where the family owned property. Her mother had left the family when she was eleven. Amy was fiercely independent of all men, even her father, which may have contributed to her failed marriage. She shared her island cottage with Cleo, a black Cocker Spaniel, and Marcus, a Manx cat. Amy was described as tall and brown-haired. One of her closest relationships was with her Aunt Helen, who had become a substitute mother.

Cousin Oren, Helen's son, was a murder suspect in *With Deadly Intent* (Zebra, 1993) when his provocative fiancée Elise disappeared. The sheriff of Lomitas Island resented the Prescott family, and was uninterested in any other explanation for the missing woman. Amy teamed with Simon Kittredge, formerly Elise's lover, to disclose the truth about the disappearance.

Simon remained important to Amy in *Grave Secrets* (Zebra, 1994). He was kidnapped in Idaho after he investigated unfortunate investments made by his father. He had left a message on Amy's answering machine. She went to look for him, even though he was interested in another woman. Rock Springs, Idaho was controlled by elements who did not intend to share their secrets with Amy.

Amy was four-months pregnant by her Native American lover, Nathan Blackthorn, as *Lethal Legacy* (Zebra, 1995) began but had no intentions of telling him he was the father. Nathan had returned to the reservation and married within the tribe. Yet she needed his help when her friend and fellow doctor, Cam Nguyen, was accused of murdering his wife. The police solution was too simplistic for Amy; so she followed a trail of Asiatic intrigue through back alleys and topiary gardens.

These were paperback originals, which were worth the price.

Gin Prettifield

Author: Cecil Dawkins

Although Gin (Ginevra) was part-Sioux Indian, she rarely mentioned the fact because it had become so politically correct to be Native American. That was not her style, although she frequently wore an expensive silver conch belt. She was a tall, dark woman who had been raised in the Mora Valley of New Mexico, and now worked as assistant director of the Waldheimer Museum in Santa Fe, which had an unusual collection of Old Masters. Gin rented a small unit in a compound where the inhabitants shared a semi-communal existence and an interest in the arts. Before settling down, she had attended Barnard College, earning a degree in art history, and traveled extensively through the British Isles.

In *The Santa Fe Rembrandt* (Ivy, 1993), even though she was competent, Gin wondered why she had been hired by the Museum for such a responsible position. Her confidence was shaken when she discovered that forgeries had been substituted for priceless artwork. When a visitor was murdered, Gin was not sure whether or not the crimes were connected.

In *Rare Earth* (Ivy, 1995), Gin vacationed at her family home in the Sangre de Cristo Mountains where she discovered a mutilated body over which a bear hovered. The ranger to whom she reported the incident returned with her, but the body had disappeared. The victim was probably a member of a well-known rock band expected to perform at an area festival, but which one? Complex motives and unexplained relationships early in the narrative diminished the impact of the action.

Tina Martinez and Reuben Rubens, members of the communal group to which Gin belonged, were featured in author Cecil Dawkin's *Clay Dancers* (Ivy, 1994). She did not appear.

Laura Principal
Author: Michelle Spring a.k.a. Michelle Stanworth

The daughter of a truck driver dad and hairdresser mom, Laura Principal managed an advanced degree from Cambridge, which qualified her as an academic historian and teacher. Her father Paul died after a long illness. She ended her marriage when it no longer met her needs. Then, she became a private investigator working for her divorced lover, Sonny Mendlowitz. Laura owned a Cambridge home, and a shared-interest in a renovated Norfolk barn cottage (Wildfell) with university librarian Helen Cochrane. While in London, she lived in Sonny's apartment. Although she loved Sonny, she had a need for Wildfell and friendships with other women. During her investigations, Laura frequently compared herself to fictional detectives.

As *Every Breath You Take* (Orion, London, 1994) opened, Laura and Helen lowered the Wildfell expenses by taking in a third party, Monica Harcourt. However the threesome was tense, and Monica's murder was no solution. Because Laura had involved herself in the affairs of several other friends, when she was attacked at her office, it was unclear whether or not the attack was connected to Monica's death. Laura and Helen risked further danger before the culprit was found. Too many ambitious plots tripped over one another.

A similar problem existed in *Running for Shelter* (Orion, 1995). Laura was managing the office and caring for Sonny's sons while he was in

Europe. She accepted an assignment to find the thief plaguing the theatre where producer Thomas Butler was preparing a new play. She agreed to trace the missing paintings from Marcia Shields' home without involving the police. She involved herself in the plight of immigrants whose services were abused by their employers. Laura risked personal injury and police charges to rescue a victim when the police were reluctant to act on her information. She resolved the conflict between her relationship with Sonny and her need for privacy.

During *Standing in the Shadows* (Ballantine, 1998), Laura was hired not to prove the innocence of foster child Daryll Flatt who had allegedly murdered his widowed caretaker, but to learn his motive. Detective Inspector Nicole Pelletier, a former student of Laura's, who had worked the case, had no sympathy for the boy even though he came from a deeply disturbed background. Laura probed the social services management of Daryll's case and those of other lonely women, which placed the "facts" in a different light.

With Sonny obsessed with expanding the agency to Europe, Laura immersed herself in the disappearance of a young college student in *Nights in White Satin* (Ballantine, 1999). The cruel treatment experienced by Katie Arkwright at the hands of sadistic Cambridge men was enough to drive her away, but had she committed murder before she left?

Laura had given little thought to having a child until *In the Midnight Hour* (Orion, 2001). Olivia Cable had seen a teenage boy who resembled the young man her missing son might have become. She and her husband Jack had spent twelve years searching for their child. Jack did not want Olivia crushed by another disappointment so he hired Laura to check the young man's background. Laura's awareness of Olivia's deep sense of loss caused her to confront her own feelings about having Sonny's child.

E. J. (Eloise Janine) Pugh

Author: Susan Rogers Cooper

E.J. Pugh, a tall redhead, had no taste for violence. She was a happily married young woman in her thirties with children living in small town Texas. Her parents, an over-involved mother and a passive father, lived in Houston. She had three sisters. The older two, Liz who managed a small theatre, and Nadine, a nurse, had never been close to E.J. Cheryl, a few years older, had been too close for comfort. Over the years, E.J. had contributed to the family income by writing two dozen romance novels. Her husband, Willis, an engineer, was a stabilizing influence in her life.

But in *One, Two, What Did Daddy Do?* (St. Martin, 1992), E. J. had no choice. Drawn to the neighboring house, she found a family slaughtered with only Bessie, a four-year-old girl, as a survivor. The local police were content to file the case as murder-suicide but E.J. knew the family well. She would not take the chance that Bessie was in danger, and eventually persuaded a female police officer to help trace the clues found in a teenager's journal.

In *Hickory, Dickory, Stalk* (Avon, 1996), E.J. returned by which time Bessie had become a part of the Pugh family in the process of adoption. The house formerly occupied by Bessie's parents had been purchased by a strange family, whose elder son, Brad, was found stark naked and definitely dead in E.J.'s car. He was no favorite of E.J.'s who suspected him of vicious pranks. Whoever had been harassing E.J. set about framing her for Brad's death.

Home Again, Home Again (Avon, 1997) was Willis' book, not E.J.'s. At a time when he was dealing with his fortieth birthday, he had developed a compulsion to climb Enchanted Rock. His disappearance after he and a friend set out to make the climb set E.J. on his trail with the help of their friends. She had to do some soul searching about her role in the deterioration of their relationship. Equally interesting was Willis' adventure among rural Texans who could not afford to let him go, but were reluctant to kill him. He weighed the quality of his marriage and his need for some validation for his forty years of life.

E.J. had stopped Brenna McGraw from killing herself. Now she had to bring security into the teenager's life. But, in *There Was a Little Girl* (Avon, 1998), that became more difficult when Brenna was accused of killing her mother, recently released from prison. E.J.'s mother-in-law Vera, formerly hostile, became an ally. Police officer Elena Luna, E.J.'s friend and neighbor, had no sympathy for E.J.'s amateur antics and neither did Willis.

During *A Crooked Little House* (Avon, 1999), figures from the past threw Willis and E.J.'s lives into turmoil. Willis and Vera had always blamed the death of her younger son, Dusty, on his immature wife, Juney. Vera had cared for Juney during her pregnancy, then took sole care of baby Garth when Juney left. Vera had been devastated when Juney reappeared and took little Garth away after a year. When Juney dropped Garth off a second time, Vera was determined to seek custody of the boy. After Juney was accused of murder, Vera put aside her feelings and helped E.J. prove her innocence.

E.J.'s involvement in murder investigations was very hard on Willis. Aware of this, she discussed with her therapist, Anne Comstock, why she allowed herself to be drawn into these matters when it so obviously created a problem for her husband. *Not In My Back Yard* (Avon, 1999) confronted two of the most terrifying fears of a mother: (1) the possibility of terminal illness and (2) proximity to a child molester. E.J. was torn between her repugnance for a convicted pederast and compassion for his wife and nine-year-old son. Her tactics when the man was murdered went over the line. She lied, made unfounded accusations, and bullied suspects.

Only E.J.'s mother, Louise, thought a vacation shared by her daughters would lead to bonding in *Don't Drink the Water* (Avon, 2000). The enmities among the siblings had begun in their childhood and were too serious to be erased in a week, even in the lovely Virgin Islands. The discovery of a woman's corpse in a cistern exacerbated the problem. E.J.'s history of involvement in crime put her on the suspect list of the local police. While investigating the victim's background, E.J. reviewed her childhood, seeking clues to the rivalry between her and her sister, Cheryl.

A good series and a bargain at paperback prices. Author Susan Rogers Cooper has another major series featuring Deputy Sheriff Milton Kovak.

Sarah "Quill" Quilliam
Author: Claudia Bishop, pseudonym for Mary Stanton

Sarah "Quill" Quilliam had established herself as an artist in New York City, but her personal life was in disorder. She turned her back on urban life, and joined her recently widowed sister, Meg, in operating the Hemlock Falls Inn. Quill served as the business manager for the Inn located in rural New York State, while Meg, a petite trained chef, ran the kitchen. They relied on a dedicated staff including the part-Native American manager John Raintree and the "born again" head housekeeper, Doreen Muxworthy.

When, during *A Taste for Murder* (Berkley, 1994), a guest was injured after a fall from a balcony, and car dealer Gil Gilmeister was killed in an accident, there seemed to be no connection between the incidents. A third death was obviously murder. John Raintree may have been one of the targets of a dead blackmailer. Quill found a killer who tried to put her out of business.

The inn needed a public relations coup, so when television hostess Helena Houndswood came to stay in *A Dash of Death* (Berkley, 1995), the staff catered to her every mood. She came to the Inn, because she was considering the purchase of land in the area and was to interview the winner of a design contest sponsored by her program. Unfortunately the winner was a group (employees of a local paint manufacturer), which gradually decreased in size as members were murdered. Quill solved the mystery before her beau Sheriff Myles McHale could. He was surprisingly constant, given that she frequently withheld information needed to solve the murders.

Their relationship was threatened in *A Pinch of Poison* (Berkley, 1995) when Myles sought marriage and a family. Marriage was acceptable to Quill, but she did not believe she could continue her career if she became a mother. The continued existence of the Inn was threatened when the members of the Rudyard Kipling Condensation Society revived a long buried hatred. Myles and Quill worked together well enough to declare a truce.

The varied plot lines of *Murder Well-Done* (Berkley, 1996) were hard to swallow. A gender issue had divided the local Chamber of Commerce into feuding sections. The Inn was to host the wedding dinner of deposed Senator Alphonse Santini to the heiress of a Scottish-Italian Mafia clan. Myles had been defeated for reelection and his successor was less tolerant of Quill. The new town justice sentenced her to jail. Too many ingredients of dubious quality to go down easy. Not up to the standard of prior books.

During *Death Dines Out* (Berkley, 1997), a pseudo-vacation in West Palm Beach turned into a disaster for Quill and Meg when they were caught between a vengeful socialite and her powerful ex-husband. What was anticipated to be Meg's chance to earn back her third star as a chef ended up in a murder/kidnapping. On their return home, good times were back in upstate New York and particularly for tourism.

Among the few guests at the Inn during *A Touch of the Grape* (Berkley, 1998) were a quintet of elderly ladies who merchandized craft kits. A series of arson/murders thrust suspicion on Quill and Meg as owners of heavily mortgaged property, but money was not the motive for the crimes. Revenge was.

Quill was betwixt and between during *A Steak in Murder* (Berkley, 1999). Her lover, Sheriff Myles McHale was doing industrial espionage for General Electric. Her suitor, John Raintree, was available to help with business decisions and crime solving. The restaurant (the Palate Gourmet) that she had received in trade from Marge Schmidt was operating at a profit. In turn, Marge was doing well with the Inn at Hemlock Falls, which she had purchased, mortgage and all. So why was Quill miserable? The consensus from sister Meg and friends was that Quill used these distractions and the murder investigations to avoid the real problems in her life. An acknowledged artist, she no longer painted. Unimpressed by these insights, Quill involved herself in a triple murder that featured Texas cattlemen and Russian venture capitalists. Then she turned back the clock.

Quill was not at her best during *Marinade for Murder* (Berkley, 2000). It was understandable. The negotiations for the Finnish acquisition of a minority interest in the Inn, enabling the sisters to repurchase, were not going well. Meg, whose participation in the Inn's future was essential, had been offered a lucrative position at a New York City restaurant. Horvath

Kierkegaard, the Finnish representative who loved American fast food, was insisting upon changes in the Inn's menus. Quill's relationship with Myles had ended with John Raintree as a probable successor. She had too much on her plate. To make it worse, her dog was accused of murder!

Next book in this series: *Fried by Jury* (2003)

Garner Quinn

Author: Jane Waterhouse

Garner Quinn's preoccupation with true crime may have resulted from watching her father, a criminal defense attorney. Dudley Quinn had rejected Garner's alcoholic mother He had provided for his child's financial needs, but showed little personal interest in the girl. He was a hedonistic egotist who filled his home and his life with beautiful people. Garner's upbringing was watched over by Cilda Fields, the African-American housekeeper. As a child Garner had fantasized that attractive sculptor Dane Blackmoor, who frequented the Quinn home, might be her real father, and that she might be the product of her mother Gabrielle's affair. Blackmoor's interest was far from paternal, even with Garner in her preteen years. None of this prepared her for marriage. Her short-term union with attorney Andrew Matera produced little happiness, except for her daughter Temple who shared her New Jersey home. Her focus was on her career. As one project ended, she became desperate to begin another book. When she covered a trial, she became a part of the defense, even contributing to their plans.

As Garner left behind the legal team that had won the acquittal of Jefferson Turner, putative serial killer, in *Graven Images* (Putnam, 1995), she was contacted by Dane Blackmoor, who offered himself as the subject of her next case. He was suspected of killing a young woman whom he had used as a model for his work. The narrative explored Garner's need to know more of her mother, now deceased, to connect with her dying father, and to cope with her continued fascination with Blackmoor.

Garner was thirty-seven as *Shadow Walk* (Putnam, 1997) began, burned out by her short but highly successful career and determined to move her life in another direction. She could not, however, turn her back on what had been one of the most intensive relationships in her life, a high school friendship with Lara Spangler. Lara, her mother, grandmother, and two brothers were killed by her father, who then disappeared. Shortly before his "suicide," T.J. Sterling, a rival author, had hinted that he had located Gordon Spangler. Convinced that Spangler had killed Sterling, Garner set out to hunt him down.

The letter from Dane, eagerly awaited by Garner, never arrived in *Dead Letter* (Putnam, 1998). Instead there were threatening, erotic messages from CHAZ. Garner was referred to the Corbin Security Agency for protection from the unknown stalker and found a loving friend in its owner, Reed Corbin. When the agency was unable to provide the safety it had promised, Garner made her own plans.

Garner was a flawed but fascinating character.

Imogen Quy

Author: Jill Paton Walsh

In her thirties, Imogen Quy settled contentedly into her deceased parent's home in Cambridge, England. She had abandoned her plans to become a doctor; and entered nursing school instead. After graduation she secured a position with the University. She dated, but remained single. Her first love, a fellow medical student, had rejected her, and the right person had never come along. Boarders, primarily students and staff at Cambridge, supplemented her income.

As *The Wyndham Case* (St. Martin, 1993) opened, Imogen was called to the library in her capacity as university nurse. The librarian in charge of the exclusive Wyndham collection had discovered the body of a first-year student. Imogen's continued involvement came at the request of Sgt. Mike Parsons. She discovered how a practical joke and an unfortunate scuffle ended in death; then found the plunderers of the Wyndham case.

In *A Piece of Justice* (St. Martin, 1995), Fran, one of Imogen's roomers, was hired to ghost the biography of Gideon Summerfield, an otherwise undistinguished mathematician whose single great discovery made him a candidate for the Waymark Prize. Imogen learned that the three prior ghostwriters had either disappeared or died mysteriously. The origins of Summerfield's discovery became apparent to Imogen, as did the reasons why murder was necessary to hide the truth.

These were intricate narratives. The characterization of Imogen was not broadly developed, but the plotting was excellent.

In another series, author Jill Paton Walsh took on a formidable task, continuing the Lord Peter Wimsey/Harriet Vane series.

Caro Radcliffe

Author: Carole Hayman

Caro (Caroline) Radcliffe experienced more than a physical change in life during her forties. She had been a researcher for a television production company when she married Sebastian. Twenty years of his infidelity had produced one daughter, Jade, now off to Oxford, and considerable dissatisfaction. Sebastian was a prominent television producer, who had returned from one liaison during the Christmas holidays, only to disappear. Caro resided in the coastal town of Warfleet.

　　Missing (HarperCollins, 1996) concentrated on Caro's evolution into a novelist and a lesbian. The only corpse was an individual not closely connected to the primary characters. Sebastian, who had left Caro, found happiness with Delia Henderson. Delia was the guardian of Sebastian's son by a deceased lover. A sub-plot involving young Warren Peabody, son of the Radcliffe housekeeper, was convoluted.

　　By *Greed, Crime, Sudden Death* (Vista, 1998), Warfleet and Caro had their hidden depths revealed. She had used the events of her recent past as the background for her first successful novel. Jade was now working for the television production company where Sebastian had held a prominent position. She had discarded Warren who married very well, but was shocked to learn that he was having an affair with her mother, Caro. Warfleet reeled under the news that the estate of the Marquis of Tolleymarch might be turned into a theme park. This time there clearly was a murder. The victim, Charlie Fong, had made a dramatic entry into the media business and was behind the plans for the theme park. There were also rumors of drug and gun smuggling in the taverns and hotels, now filled with reporters, police and FBI agents. Cluttered.

Agatha Raisin

Author: M. C. Beaton, pseudonym for Marion Chesney

Agatha Raisin had always pushed herself, leaving school at fifteen to work in a local biscuit factory; then, attending business college. Beginning as a secretary, she achieved management status in a public relations agency. The child of alcoholic parents, she married Jimmy Raisin, who had a drinking problem. They had separated, but neither had taken the ultimate step of divorce. Agatha was in her early fifties when she sold her lucrative public relations business.

The self-centered, competitive Agatha Raisin responded to life in the Cotswold village of Carsely with a series of learning experiences and disasters. She learned that the qualities that made for success in the business world were not held in high esteem among the locals. She disliked housework, was totally inept in a kitchen, and knew little or nothing about gardens. Yet she wanted to be included in the life of the village. She possessed none of the small talk or courtesies that might have attracted acquaintances, but in the way of small towns, she gathered a circle of friends. She added cats to her household, and enjoyed swimming. A stocky woman with brown hair and eyes, Agatha was no beauty, but was definitely interested in men, and particularly in neighbor James Lacey.

When, in *Agatha Raisin and the Quiche of Death* (St. Martin, 1992), she learned of the quiche competition, it seemed an opportunity to make her presence felt. And so it did. The purchased spinach quiche, which she entered as her own, poisoned the contest judge later in the day.

In *Agatha Raisin and the Vicious Vet* (St. Martin, 1993), her overtures to Lacey were counterproductive. Veterinarian Paul Bloden took her to dinner, but made an appeal for his new animal hospital. However, when Bloden was killed by equine medication, Agatha found an interest she could share with Lacey—murder.

The two early themes, Agatha's competitiveness in local contests and her interest in Lacey, combined in *Agatha Raisin and the Potted Gardener* (St. Martin, 1994). She had returned from a European vacation to find Lacey had diverted himself with Mary Fortune, a newcomer who excelled in cooking and gardening. Agatha sold herself into six months servitude with a London public relations firm in an effort to win prowess as a gardener and regain her rapport with Lacey. After her rival was brutally murdered, Agatha and Lacey teamed to find the killer.

Six months in London was about all Agatha could handle. During *Agatha Raisin and the Walkers of Dembley* (St. Martin, 1994), she was relieved to return to the countryside. Her tour de force with Lacey, finding the killer of an aggressive leader of a local hiking group, brought him to a proposal.

It would be too much to expect a wedding to go smoothly for Agatha. In *Agatha Raisin and the Murderous Marriage* (St. Martin, 1996), Jimmy, her first and current husband, was the uninvited guest. When he was murdered near Agatha's home, she and the now-estranged James combined to learn who else had a motive to kill him.

James left Carsely, taking the planned Greek honeymoon alone. In *Agatha Raisin and the Terrible Tourist* (St. Martin, 1997), she set out in pursuit. Her companions in the Turkish sector of Cyprus included two couples and two singles attached to the couples. They formed an ill-sorted group, but within it were a victim and a killer. Agatha encountered James during the murder investigation; however, it was tightfisted but attentive Sir Charles Fraith who offered his support.

A commercial plan to purchase a share of the water from a century-old spring that flowed onto public property aroused considerable controversy in the community during *Agatha Raisin and the Wellspring of Death* (St. Martin, 1998). Agatha's discovery of the body of a member of the Anscombe Parish Council just before a deciding vote brought her into the fray. She accepted a position as public relations manager of Anscombe Water, the group seeking a franchise, and a personal relationship with a co-owner of the company. James and Agatha conducted individual probes but coordinated their efforts in the end. This cooperation did not extend to a romantic future. Maybe it was time for Agatha to move on.

Agatha had a hair-raising experience in *Agatha Raisin and the Wizard of Evesham* (St. Martin, 1999) when she and Charles interfered in a police investigation. They believed that hairdresser Mr. John was seducing and blackmailing female clients. His murder whetted their appetites for detecting until they discovered the naked truth.

Depilated to her roots, Agatha headed for a seaside resort in *Agatha Raisin and the Witch of Wyckhadden* (St. Martin, 1999). It was a dismal place during off-season. Elderly singles who spent the evenings playing Scrabble populated the Grand Hotel. Agatha's presence and her visit to a local psychic provoked excitement, followed by two murders. She regained her looks but not her spirits. Romance with a kind local inspector did not survive. Her only acquisition was another cat, named Scrabble.

Agatha never did discover the source of the strange lights at the end of her garden during *Agatha Raisin and the Fairies of Fryfam* (St. Martin, 2000). She did stumble upon the killer of an upstart businessman. She had rented a cottage in the small village in Norfolk in the hope that her absence would kindle James Lacey's interest. Although she succeeded in that respect, her friends predicted a marriage would not last.

Regular readers aware of Agatha's strong personality and the entrenched habits of James Lacey would not be surprised at the travails of their marriage in *Agatha Raisin and the Love from Hell* (St. Martin, 2001). Less predictable would be the shared suspicions of infidelity, the public quarrels, and James' departure leaving behind evidence of a bloody struggle. James, at first thought of as a victim, became a suspect when Melissa, with whom he had an affair, was found dead. Agatha was aroused from her depression by Sir Charles and dear Mrs. Bloxby, the vicar's wife, who assisted in locating James and flushing out the killer.

Agatha was pugnacious, unrepentant, and crude; and those were her positive characteristics.

Next books in this series: *Agatha Raisin and the Day the Floods Came* (2002); *Agatha Raisin and the Case of the Curious Curate* (2003); *Agatha Raisin and the Haunted House* (2003)

Gwen Ramadge

Author: Lillian O'Donnell

Gwen Ramadge, a tiny blonde who had been a model, became a private detective. The only child of a wealthy New York family, she had graduated from Barnard College. During an unfortunate love affair, she became pregnant, ending her work as a model and initiating her career with Hart Security and Investigations. When her lover showed no interest in marriage and her child miscarried, Gwen stayed on at the agency, eventually becoming the owner.

She preferred corporate work, but Gwen could not turn down an important client. In *A Wreath for the Bride* (Putnam, 1990), Anne Soffey asked her to investigate a murder that had occurred at the wedding of her daughter Mary. When the wedding car blew up, a bridesmaid then checking the luggage, was killed. Mary disappeared at sea on the honeymoon. A second new bride was found dead while her drunken husband slept. Gwen was piqued by the similarities among the cases.

This experience convinced Gwen that she wanted no more to do with murder. In *Used to Kill* (Putnam, 1993), she had no choice. Businessman client Douglas Trent had informed his office that he would be returning early from a business trip. No one had told his wife, Emma, a dance teacher. When she returned from her studio and found him dead and the safe robbed, she was stunned. She was also suspected because of a report by Hart Security. Later Gwen needed a vacation and a chance to assess her relationship with Sgt. Ray Dixon, so she spent time in Cuernavaca at her parent's home.

By *The Raggedy Man* (Putnam, 1995), Gwen was bored and ready to take on new challenges. Her first case, suggested by Dixon, was to prove the innocence of a young policewoman who had been suspended for drug possession. Jayne Harrow had broken the code, turning in fellow police officers for dealing drugs obtained in raids. Gwen hired her. On her first assignment, Jayne was found dead. The police preferred to label her death a suicide. Gwen and Ray proved that Jayne died because she knew too much. Disturbed by the police corruption, Sgt. Ray Dixon retired and was considering a career as a private investigator.

Gwen was hired to probe thefts on board the cruise ship *Dante Alighieri*, in *The Goddess Affair* (Putnam, 1997), but was diverted into the investigation of the drowning in the ship's pool of Minerva Aldrich. Minerva, whose cancer was in remission, was in the center of a family squabble over control of Goddess Designs, the firm founded by her deceased mother. Theft, smuggling, drugs, and financial mismanagement were entangled in a murky plot.

Readers may remember that Lillian O'Donnell was also the author of the Norah Mulcahaney and Mici Anhalt series covered in Volume 1.

Carmen Ramirez

Author: Lisa Haddock

Carmen Ramirez, the daughter of an Irish-American mother and a Puerto Rican father, had been raised by a loving but strait-laced Baptist grandmother in Frontier City, Oklahoma. Her father was still alive, but her mother had died when Carmen was young. After graduation from journalism school, she remained in her hometown, working at the local newspaper, sharing her apartment with two cats. Carmen had accepted her lesbian orientation, but had no expectation that her grandmother or the community would do so.

During *Edited Out* (Naiad, 1994, but set in 1985), Carmen and her lover, Julia Nichols, investigated the death of a lesbian teacher who had died when suspected of killing a twelve-year-old girl. They questioned whether the teacher's death was correctly labeled suicide, or if there had been a cover-up. It was too serious a matter to cover up, if the murderer of the child were still at large.

During *Final Cut* (Naiad, 1995, but set in 1987) Julia, a student at Frontier City University, was one of a group starting a lesbian/gay organization. A visit from Toni Stewart, a bisexual friend from Carmen's college days, ended in her death. Toni's family wanted the matter settled quietly. Carmen uncovered an anti-homosexual group that enforced their views with murder.

The narratives had excellent plotting, but evidenced a strong and offensive anti-male bias.

Lucia Ramos

Author: Mary Morell

Lucia Ramos, one of the early Chicana series sleuths was a lesbian police officer working in San Antonio, Texas. After a stint in juvenile, she had been assigned as a rookie detective in homicide.

In *Final Session* (Spinsters, 1990), her investigation of the death of psychotherapist Elizabeth Freeman showed that Freeman was a destructive personality who had seriously damaged patients by sexual abuse. Lucia looked for the killer among current and former patients and members of their families until she discovered a tie-in to Freeman's personal and professional life. Lucia became sexually involved with an older woman psychologist who worked with her on the case.

In *Final Rest* (Spinsters, 1993), Lucia went to Alabama to assist her lover's Aunt Meg who had been arrested for murder. Amy, Lucia's lover, and her aunt were both lesbians and victims of incest. Lucia's credentials as a police officer gained cooperation from local officials while Amy rallied the gay community for further support. The plot had merit, but the explicit sex will deter some readers.

Precious Ramotswe

Author: Alexander McCall Smith

Precious Ramotswe had been the only child of her prosperous father, a man who had worked the mines and suffered lung damage as a result. He had built up a substantial cattle ranch over the years. Her mother died when she was only four. Precious had an excellent education for a female in Gaborone, Botswana (formerly Bechuanaland Protectorate). A cousin had taught her preschool. She continued through regular classes and Sunday school until age sixteen. By then she excelled in art and mathematics, assisted by a remarkable memory. Her interest in detection asserted itself in her first full time job. While doing office work for a bus company owned by a family member, she caught an employee stealing.

Precious had no intention of continuing her father's cattle business. She sold the extensive herd, which included white Brahmin bulls. With the proceeds she purchased a small building at the outskirts of Gaborone and established the No. 1 Ladies' Detective Agency, the first of its kind in Botswana. Adding to her fame was the fact that she did not charge clients for whom she failed to get satisfactory results. Her methods of detection were based on a book by Clovis Anderson: observation, deduction, and then analysis. Her personal beliefs centered on the god Modimo who rewarded and punished appropriately in the hereafter.

Precious was a dark, heavyset woman in her thirties when the series began. She loved her country, loved Africa, and wanted to be nowhere else. Precious had not been fortunate in her marriage to musician Note Mokoti. They had been immediately attracted to one another, but she could not abide his life style. After the loss of a premature infant, she made a life on her own. She had no problem finding suitors. A wealthy factory owner proposed but was rejected. Mr. J.L.B. Matekoni, mechanic at the Tiokweng Road Speedy Motors, was successful on his second offer of marriage. All of this information was gradually introduced in *The No. 1 Ladies' Detective Agency* (Polygon, 1998), which included a series of cases, both humorous and serious.

The path of true love did not always run smoothly in *The Tears of the Giraffe* (Polygon, 2000). J.L.B. and Precious had to choose a house in which to live. Hers was in better condition. Florence, J.L.B.'s lazy maid was unacceptable to Precious so became a formidable enemy. As a gift to his bride, J.L.B. surprised her with two children in need of a home: Motholali, an eleven-year-old handicapped girl and her brother, Puso, age five. He was a very kind man and she appreciated that quality in him. At work, Precious had added an assistant Mma Makutsi. There were moral questions in the cases she handled: how much to tell of what she learned in an investigation and the appropriateness of blackmail to learn the truth.

The couple's happiness was shattered in *Morality for Beautiful Girls* (Polygon, 2001) when J.L.B succumbed to depression. His business was going well and could be turned over to an assistant. Precious cut her caseload, adjusted her expenses by moving into a smaller office in J.L.B.'s garage and renting out her building. She continued to take a few cases, (possible domestic poisoning, investigating potential candidates in a local beauty contest) but her real concern was her husband's recovery.

These were charming stories in a new setting.

Next books in this series: *The Kalahari Typing School for Men* (2002); *The Full Cupboard of Life* (2003)

Sonja Joan "Sunny" Randall

Author: Robert B. Parker

As a feminist Sunny Randall's mother had talked the talk, but never walked the walk. She was horrified by her daughter's decisions. She had not approved of Sunny's marriage to Richie Burke, whom she had known and loved since grade school. The Burke family was notorious then, and still held sway over criminal operations in part of the Boston area. Nor had she approved of their divorce or understood their continued close relationship.

Sunny earned a degree in social work, but never used it. She had joined the police force following in her father's footsteps, but that did not last either. Becoming a private investigator allowed her more independence. That seemed to be the byword for Sunny. She could not handle being controlled. Richie had come to realize this, although not necessarily understand it. He could be forgiven his confusion, because when push came to shove, Sunny often turned to him for help in her investigations. Their divorce had been unusually congenial. She refused alimony. He insisted that she have full ownership of their home, although she could not afford the upkeep. The only possible controversy was placement of their bull terrier, Rosie. Sunny was granted custody with visitation rights for Richie. As the series began she was working on a master's degree in fine arts and selling some of her paintings.

Sunny had close friends, although her perfectionist sister Elizabeth was not among them. Julie, a psychiatric social worker, and Spike, the gay part owner of Beans & Rice, a bar-restaurant, were always there when she needed them.

As *Family Honor* (Putnam, 1999) began, Sunny still needed to be with Richie. They met for dinner once a week (which eventually included more intimate weekends). Her assignment to locate Millie, a runaway fifteen-year-old girl, pitted Sunny against professional criminals. To save Millie, vulnerable because she had overheard a conversation that led to murder, Sunny not only took personal risks but she invoked the power of the Burke family. Her role as mentor to Millie paralleled a similar relationship that Spenser had with Paul Giacomin in Parker's other series.

Millie had disappeared from the scene by *Perish Twice* (Putnam, 2000). Most of Sunny's time was occupied by pro bono work. It was unclear how she survived without alimony, personal wealth, or paid employment. She proved to no one's satisfaction that her sister Elizabeth's husband was unfaithful. She comforted her dear friend Julie whose therapeutic skills were ineffective to deal with her own drinking and infidelity. Finally, although she was initially paid for this one, she located the man who was stalking feminist Mary Lou Goddard. Sunny continued on the case after Mary Lou fired her. A woman resembling Mary Lou had been found dead in her office. The stalker was shot subsequently, leaving a confession indicating he had killed himself. The presence of pimps and hookers in the case brought Sunny into conflict with African-American criminal elements. Again Richie (who was not personally involved in crime), and his father and uncle (who were) came to her rescue. Independence went just so far for Sunny.

Author Robert B. Parker's dialogue and warm relationships enriched the series.

Next book in this series: *Shrink Rap* (2002)

Tammi Randall

Author: E. L. Wyrick

Tammi Randall was not born in Patsboro, where she practiced law. However, she had been raised in a Southern Georgia town about the same size. Her rigidly religious mother and alcoholic father had left her with a spiritual belief that was unconnected to church membership. Her undergraduate degree had been in psychology and her law degree was from local Catledge University.

Her strong feeling for the underdog led Tammi to the practice of public law in the Teal County Legal Aid Society. Frequently this meant the dirty and scurrilous, the poor and undereducated, the petty crimes and repeated complaints. Occasionally, she and her friends Mitch Griffith, an African-American businessman, Dan Bushnell, a school administrator, and Dan's wife, Meg, became involved in criminal investigations. Tammi was mentored and supported by Bernard Fuchs, a seasoned attorney who worked part-time for Legal Aid. Her salary was average to low. She drove a Yugo which barely made it through the Georgia hills, and lived rent-free in an older home, acting as house sitter. At twenty-seven, she remained single, cautious about her relationships with men after a badly handled sexual interaction in the back seat of a car at age seventeen.

During *A Strange and Bitter Crop* (St. Martin, 1994), Tammi represented a young African-American man against charges of double murder. When one of his accomplices tried to end Tammi's investigation by vehicular assault and rape, she defended herself. Her distrust of men was exacerbated by the betrayal of a man she had come to love.

By *Power in the Blood* (St. Martin, 1996), Tammi was working out at a self-defense class, swimming several days a week, and practicing with a pistol, determined never again to be defenseless. Her therapist, Dr. Josie Beam was concerned that Tammi might overreact to a threat. A request to handle a lucrative real estate matter was tempting; however, her client was dead on arrival. Tammi had to understand actor Lawton Fletcher and why he wanted to buy the nearby town of Warrendale, Georgia before she could identify his killer. She did meet an attractive man along the way, and found friends to share her home.

Claire Rawlings

Author: Carole Bugge

Claire Rawlings was well established in New York City as editor for mystery books at Ardor House. She had a comfortable life: drove an old brown Mercedes, exercised with hand weights, and enjoyed classical music and national public radio. Initially she shared her apartment with Ralph, an all white cat. That changed when she teamed up with a fellow redhead, a thirteen-year-old girl who, like herself, had never come to terms with her mother's death. Meredith Lawrence more or less adopted Claire who had known her mother in college. Detective Wally Jackson eventually became part of their "family," adding a much needed balance.

Claire's social circle in New York City during *Who Killed Blanche DuBois?* (Berkley, 1999) included old friends from her college days in North Carolina. Blanche DuBois was more than a friend; she was a best selling author on Claire's list. When first Blanche, then another member of the group, were murdered, Claire felt vulnerable. Meredith and Detective Wallace Jackson were there when Claire realized that not every friend could be trusted.

Rejected by her stepmother and ignored by her passive father, Meredith became Claire's ward as *Who Killed Dorian Gray?* (Berkley, 2000) began. Claire was still suffering nightmares from her near escape from death. An invitation to spend a pleasant week at Ravenscroft art colony near Woodstock seemed likely to provide the relaxation she needed. Her only task would be to lecture to the artists and writers attending the camp. The campers included some who had previous ties. During a late night ramble to the bathhouse, Claire found the body of Maya Sorenson a.k.a. Dorian Gray. She had help in solving this and a subsequent murder from Meredith, who ran away from summer camp to join Claire.

Claire and Wally Jackon might have benefited from a travel guide in *Who Killed Mona Lisa?* (Berkley, 2001). Instead they relied upon a recommendation from Claire's boss, Peter Schwartz, in selecting a vacation hideaway. Hide away from whom? Not only did Meredith join them, but they were also stuck with a sorry group of staff and residents at the Wayside Inn in South Sudbury, Massachusetts. As in a Golden Age mystery, when beautiful young waitress, Mona Lisa Callahan was murdered, the group was isolated by a snowstorm. Claire and Meredith found clues through an historic Secret Drawer Society.

These were well written books. Claire was portrayed as an intelligent, well-educated woman who had a strong sense of history and literature. Meredith, who was looking for a mother substitute, grew throughout the series. Author Carole Bugge has a second series based on Sherlock Holmes.

Savannah Reid

Author: G.A. McKevett, pseudonym for Sonja Massie

Food was a major focus of Savannah Reid's life. About thirty pounds overweight at age forty, she compensated by scrupulous attention to her appearance. While a police officer, she had earned a black belt in karate. The oldest of nine children of an irresponsible mother and assorted fathers, Savannah remained single, sharing her San Carmelita, California apartment with two black cats (Cleopatra and Diamante). Her mother remained back in Georgia, but the travails of her siblings were frequently brought to Savannah's attention.

In *Just Desserts* (Kensington, 1995), Savannah, then a police officer, felt sandbagged in her efforts to find the killer of Jonathan Winston, husband of an activist city council member. When her investigation threatened local public figures, Savannah was fired on the excuse that she had failed physical standards by not losing weight. Beverly Winston, Jonathan's wife and chief suspect, hired Savannah to continue. Her efforts were hampered by the arrival of Atlanta, her youngest sister who had become uncontrollable in her mother's home. In her new roles as substitute mother and private investigator, Savannah showed promise, founding her own Moonlight Magnolia Agency.

During *Bitter Sweets* (Kensington, 1996), Savannah's morale was severely tested when her search for Lisa Mallock, the "sister" of a client, ended in the woman's murder. Not only had she been duped by the man who pretended to be a brother, but Lisa's daughter Christy was missing. With the help of her two gay assistants and police detective Dirk Coulter, who had been her partner, Savannah made the best of a bad case.

In *Killer Calories* (Kensington, 1997), Dirk was in charge of the investigation wherein a middle-aged actress, Kat Valentina, died in a sleazy health spa. The victim, who was a part-owner of the facility, had a high alcohol content, so an accidental death was assumed, but an anonymous client hired Savannah to review the case. Savannah went undercover at the Royal Palms Spa where the staff included several with serious motives for wanting Kat dead. The least likely outcome was a letdown.

A series of vicious rapes escalated into the murders, not of the victims, but of police officers who worked the cases. During *Cooked Goose* (Kensington, 1998), Captain Harvey Bloss of the San Carmelita police did not want Savannah participating in his department's investigation of the local rapist. He could not maintain his opposition when his estranged daughter Margie turned to Savannah for help after escaping the rapist. The deaths and disappearances of several police officers and the rapes were tied together by the presence of ornamental rings on victims. Savannah and officer Dirk Coulter exposed Bloss' reason for opposing their investigation. On a personal level, she delivered her sister Vidalia's second set of twins. The exposure of the rapist was unusual because the man had none of the obvious characteristics of a serial rapist.

Regular business had to be put aside in *Sugar and Spite* (Kensington, 2000) when Dirk Coulter, Savannah's best friend and former partner, was arrested for the murder of his ex-wife, Polly. Dirk might be foul mouthed, sloppy, and inconsiderate, but he did not kill Polly. Savannah's loyal band (John Gibson, Ryan Stone, and Tammy Hart), rallied around when the top brass at the police department showed little interest in other suspects.

Savannah, noted for her healthy appetite and generous girth did not usually spend time at Beauty pageants. In *Sour Grapes* (Kensington, 2001), she had two good reasons for attending the Miss Gold Coast Beauty Queen Contests. She was working security there with her friend Ryan Stone. Her sister, Atlanta Reid, thinner than ever, was a contestant. Savannah might be faulted for focusing on the wrong suspect, but Atlanta came through with a bang.

Next books in this series: *Peaches and Screams* (2002); *Death by Chocolate* (2003)

Cassandra Reilly

Author: Barbara Wilson

Cassandra Reilly was a free spirited translator of Romance languages. She was described as a tall, middle-aged woman, with hazel-green eyes. She received most of her education through her travels, having left her

Michigan home at sixteen. Her widowed mother had seven children, but Cassandra never liked her siblings, and had few contacts with them. Essentially rootless, she maintained a rented room in Hampstead, England, another in Oakland, California, but roamed Europe on an Irish passport.

During *Gaudi Afternoon* (Seal, 1990), Cassandra found work translating a book, but was diverted into the search for Frankie Steven's husband. Somewhat later Cassandra realized that her client was a transsexual, fighting his/her former spouse for custody of their child. Neither one came across as a responsible parent, although they finally reached an accommodation.

Cassandra returned in *Trouble in Transylvania* (Seal, 1993) en route to China via Vienna. She encountered a strange group of acquaintances traveling to a Romanian health spa, and decided to join them. The inventor of a youth serum was electrocuted while demonstrating a treatment.

The Death of a Much-Travelled Woman (Third Side Press, 1998) was a set of short stories during which Cassandra unmasked killers, but could not always bring them to justice. She wrote her own book but lost the credit as she traveled in Hawaii, rural England, Central Europe, Scandinavia, and Russia. She stayed with friends, lived on a shoestring, and found lovers and former lovers along the way.

As *The Case of the Orphaned Bassoonist* (Seal, 2000) began, Cassandra had just returned from an unrewarding journey to a tropical island, only to be urged to come at once to Venice. Her friend and landlady Nicola Gibbons, currently attending a symposium on Vivaldi, was in danger of arrest. Someone had stolen a valuable bassoon left in Nicola's care. Cassandra had no contact with the local police; nevertheless, she investigated the personal, sexual, and professional lives of the musician-suspects. Background included art history insights into the Pieta, the female orphans trained by choirmaster Antonio Vivaldi and the possibility that among them had been unrecognized composers of musical scores for bassoonists. The best of the series.

Nina Reilly

Author: Perri O'Shaughnessy, pseudonym
for Pamela and Mary O'Shaughnessy

When she lost her job as an appellate attorney and her marriage became unbearable, Nina Reilly moved to Lake Tahoe, temporarily living with her younger brother Matt and his family. She brought along her eleven-year-old son Bobby, who knew that Nina's husband was not his father. At that point Nina had withheld information about the man who was. She realized a day would come when Bobby would demand the information.

During *Motion to Suppress* (Delacorte, 1995), Nina reassessed her original intention of practicing only civil law when her secretary, Sandy Whitefeather, brought in Misty Patterson as a client. Misty knew she had struck her husband; believed he had left the house on his own; but denied that she had killed him and deposited his body in Lake Tahoe. Misty's pregnancy reminded Nina of her own vulnerability before Bobby was born, so she took the case. With the help of Paul van Wagoner, a San Francisco investigator, she not only handled the courtroom battles, but also probed Misty's past to relieve her of guilt. Although van Wagoner had no affinity for either marriage or fatherhood, he fell in love with Nina and wanted more than a casual affair.

In *Invasion of Privacy* (Delacorte, 1996), Bobby's need to know became unbearable when Terry London, a treacherous client forced the issue. Terry's murder brought back into Nina's life the man who had left her pregnant and alone a decade earlier. When he was arrested for Terry's murder, Nina fought a rival attorney for the right to prove him innocent.

Having discouraged Paul van Wagoner's romantic interest, Nina reached out to Collier Hallowell, a widowed prosecuting attorney in *Obstruction of Justice* (Delacorte, 1997). Hallowell had never recovered from the hit and run death of his probation officer wife Anna, three years before. When he and Nina climbed Mount Tallac, they encountered the contentious de Beers family whose expedition ended in the death of the father, Ray. Paul's investigation of Anna's death intersected with the possibility that Ray's death had not been an accident. Hollowell and Nina faced one another in the courtroom and at the edge of death. Paul, who responded to Nina's rejection by an obsession with a seductive artist, was there when Nina needed him.

The potential of a multi-million dollar contingency fee was not Nina's only motive for taking a complex palimony case in *Breach of Promise* (Delacorte, 1998). She felt compassion for Lindy Markov whose business and personal relationship with her partner/lover had never been legalized. Lindy's stake in their successful business disappeared when Mike left her for a younger woman. The palimony trial was disrupted when a juror died of an allergic reaction to delivered food.

Nina's chance at happiness in *Acts of Malice* (Delacorte, 1999) was endangered by her representation of James Strong, a man accused of killing his brother. Collier Hallowell, who had returned from a period of mourning for his deceased wife, ready to renew his relationship with Nina, had warned her off the case. She waited too long to scrutinize her obligations to a client when they conflicted with her sense of justice. Paul who had left the area to work in Washington, D.C. remained in waiting for Nina, protective of her interests even from a distance.

Nina's son Bob was probably the only friend that sixteen-year-old Nikki Zach had. In *Move to Strike* (Delacorte, 2000), Bob talked Nina into representing the girl when she was accused of murdering her uncle, Dr. William Sykes. Nina needed something to jolt her out of her mourning, but she needed help. Paul van Wagoner, when contacted, was reluctant to be with Nina again, a mixture of pain and guilt. Paul's investigation into a plane crash and mining claim combined with Nina's courtroom skills to unearth a triple killer.

On reflection, Nina should have realized in *Writ of Execution* (Delacorte, 2001) that Jessie Potter was not the ideal client. Only reluctantly did she even reveal her identity. As the recent winner of a seven million-dollar jackpot at Prize's casino, she had obligations to the Internal Revenue Service, which could not be ignored. Her solution, marriage to a mere acquaintance, Kenny Leung, would provide her with another name. However, this brought a new set of problems. Jessie feared vengeance from the father of her deceased husband. She had another equally insidious enemy, the men who had arranged to win the jackpot themselves. Paul van Wagoner was on scene to help, but the on-again, off-again connection was becoming tedious.

These were excellent narratives, combining competent legal background with romance and mystery.

Next books in this series: *Unfit to Practice* (2002); *Presumption of Death* (2003)

Regan Reilly

Author: Carol Higgins Clark

Regan Reilly was the daughter of a funeral director and a suspense novelist whose maiden name had been Regan. A trim brunette, she had spent her junior year abroad at Oxford. She became a private investigator located on the West Coast.

As *Decked* (Warner, 1992) opened, Regan was attending the tenth reunion of her classmates in St. Polycarp's hallowed halls, remembering the disappearance of her roommate, Greek heiress Athena Popolous. After Athena's skeleton was discovered, Regan's disclosure that she had a journal and pictures of that period brought the entire Reilly family into the case.

During *Snagged* (Warner, 1993), Regan attended a Florida wedding, only to become enmeshed in the problems of another guest, the bride's uncle. Richie Blossom, a long time inventor, should have known that the hosiery industry would not welcome runless pantyhose. Luke and Nora, Regan's parents, were along to justify the "mortuary jokes," but could not resuscitate the weak plot.

Iced (Warner, 1995) found Regan and her parents in Colorado where rival art thieves plundered the rich, including their host and hostess. Eben Bean, a missing ex-convict, was assumed to have committed the crime, but Regan believed him innocent. She did not throw in the towel but used them to rescue Eben and restore him to his family.

Twanged (Warner, 1998) was as overcrowded as a New York City cocktail party. The reader barely had a chance to know any of the wacky characters. Regan had been hired to bodyguard Brigid O'Neill, Her story and that of the historic fiddle that was bringing her fame underpinned a charming plot that survived the confusion of murder, accident, and theft.

Regan had a dozen interesting suspects to consider in *Fleeced* (Scribners, 2001). Her friend, Thomas Pilsner, manager of the formerly prestigious Settler's Club, needed help to locate missing diamonds that were to have been donated to the Club. The donors, two retired jewelers who were club members, both died the night the jewels disappeared. Jack Reilly (no relative), the New York police detective with whom Regan had planned to spend time, had been sent to London. She had other resources in sorting out what began as theft but included arson and murder.

Author Carol Higgins Clark combined her talents with those of her mother, Mary Higgins Clark in *Deck the Halls* (Scribners, 2000) during which Alvirah Meehan and Regan Reilly shared a Christmas story. A pair of disgruntled bumblers kidnapped Luke Reilly and Rosita, his driver from the funeral home. Hints dropped by Luke in a phone message and clues from friends brought about a rescue in time to save Luke and Rosita from a frigid death.

Next books in this series: *Jinxed* (2002); *Popped* (2002)

Maggy Renard

Author: Barbara Sohmers

Maggy Renard's career as an actress had languished after her marriage to Fred Renard. He continued to be successful as a television and stage actor, a playwright, and author of thrillers. They preferred spending time together to working separately but at times it could not be avoided. Maggy was deeply in love with her husband who was twenty years older than she. Yet, at times she regretted the missed opportunities to advance her own career. They had met when Fred, then divorced, directed Maggy in her first appearance on stage. References to "The Fox" in the titles were to Renard, the French word for "fox."

Ile de Marees (Island of Tides) off the French coast had always been a special place for Fred. He and Maggy had vacationed there in their own cottage, but in *The Fox and the Puma* (Sodef Press, 1997), Fred purchased a bar-restaurant. His residuals were such that he could afford to take time off. The planned "vacation" deteriorated into a lot of work, complicated by (1) the murder of a promiscuous summer visitor; (2) the disappearance of the victim's daughter; (3) the escape of a convicted rapist from the local prison; and (4) a second escape, a puma from a visiting circus. Fred and Maggy found real life drama to be more nerve wracking than writing fiction.

While Fred was shooting a film in Provence during *The Fox and the Pussycat* (Sodef, 1998), Maggy made an unusual career decision. Disappointed at her lack of opportunity for dramatic roles, she signed on as singer and mistress of ceremonies at The Pussycat, a strip tease joint in Paris. It was a learning experience, not the least of which was increased awareness of ritual female mutilation in some African countries. Maggy wanted to be the heroine, not the victim, but when performers at the Pussycat were murdered, Fred stepped in to save the day.

Although the narratives and dialogue were witty, both dwelt upon serious sub-themes: anti-Semitism and female circumcision.

Worthy efforts.

Susan "Sukey" Reynolds

Author: Betty Rowlands

Sukey Reynolds had been an English police department photographer working at crime scenes until her divorce from Paul. She found it impossible to care properly for their son Fergus while on the force. Instead she became a civilian employee of the local police department. Paul, who had remarried, was no longer part of her life. During the series, she dated divorced Inspector Jim Castle.

As *An Inconsiderate Death* (Severn House, 1997) began, the prologue revealed that of three men who had robbed a bank, two had been arrested and convicted. Neither the identity of the third man nor the location of the stolen money had ever been discovered. Sukey's position as civilian photographer for the scene of the crime unit did not have official status.

Nevertheless, she played a prominent role in sorting out two murders, aided by pictures she had taken. Inspector Jim Castle, who had known Sukey when she was on the force, did much of the investigating and volunteered to fill the vacant space in her life.

It was unfortunate that Sukey discovered the corpse of her former husband's current wife in *Death at Dearley Manor* (Severn House, 1998). Naturally, she had to be removed from the case asserted her lover, Inspector Jim Castle. Naturally, according to Castle's supervisor, he too had to be removed. That created problems because Paul Reynolds was the primary suspect and their son, Fergus, insisted that Sukey prove his innocence.

By *Copycat* (Severn, 1999), Detective Inspector Jim Castle was accepted as Sukey's lover although they maintained some discretion in the presence of her fifteen-year-old son. Her role as a civilian scene of the crime officer differed from Castle's but they frequently worked the same cases. Castle was certain that Manuel Rodriguez masterminded a series of art thefts, a theory confirmed by Pepita, an undercover female agent. Sukey's close resemblance to "Pepita" made her a target of a vicious international gangster. She rebelled against Jim Castle's personal authority.

The deaths of two participants in the RYCE (Restore Your Cosmic Energy) program seemed more than a coincidence to Sukey in *Touch Me Not* (Severn, 2001). Using her own time, encouraged by son Fergus and family members of the deceased, she signed up for the therapeutic sessions. Sukey was experiencing real benefits until day four when "Xavier," the cult leader was murdered. Whatever positive influence the program may have had until then, it did not deter Sukey from taking independent action without a backup. She had a tight line to walk on a personal level. She remained bitter against her former husband Paul, who had abandoned her and Fergus years before, but recognized that Fergus loved his father.

Readers may also be interested in the Melissa Craig series by author Betty Rowlands.

Emma Rhodes

Author: Cynthia Smith

Emmy Lou Rhodes dropped her birth name early on, choosing Emma in honor of Emma Peel, a character in *The Avengers* television series. Her early life had been exemplary—wonderful parents, educational achievements, the potential of her 165 IQ, an almost photographic memory, and a law degree that led to a coveted position in a Wall Street law firm. Yet Emma wanted something different. A life of excitement, freedom from financial concerns, the ability to pick and choose her assignments, and work that could be accomplished within two-week spans because she was easily bored. Emma's impatience showed in her serial monogamous relationships with men, but she retained many of her former lovers as friends. She parlayed a degree in art history from Sarah Lawrence, her law degree, ease with languages, musical skills, and a sympathetic persona, into a unique vocation, private resolver. Her standard plan included no retainer but a $20,000 fee payable only on success within two weeks. She always succeeded. Among her possessions were apartments in New York City and London, plus a villa in Portugal. The homes were embellished by valuable art works and furniture given her by grateful clients. Her own tastes were expensive. She purchased Porthault bedsheets at $1,000 apiece, bought designer clothes and indulged her taste for jewelry. She attended the theatre, but preferred ballet and opera.

Emma developed a network of powerful friends who assisted in her investigations. Abba Levitar, a Mossad official was a resource but never a lover. Black Scotland Yard Inspector Caleb Franklin was both. Interestingly, she maintained an excellent relationship with her parents who lived in Rye, New York. They had always encouraged her, supported her decisions, and relished hearing of her important clients and friends.

As *Noblesse Oblige* (Berkley, 1996) began, Emma earned the gratitude of the Belgian royal family by rescuing a small boy from an attempted kidnapping. The introduction led to a two-pronged case: to end attempts to kill a Spanish diplomat and to discover where he had fled. Moving seamlessly throughout Europe and England, Emma solved two murders and a series of abductions.

She sought relaxation in her Portuguese casita where she mingled with an assortment of expatriates in *Impolite Society* (Berkley, 1997); then, acquired a new case almost immediately. An American couple refused to believe their son had committed suicide. The young man, a minister, had become involved with a maladjusted single mother. Emma's probe expanded to drug traffic in the area. With Abba and Caleb's help, she solved multiple problems. They could not help the fact that she had fallen deeply in love with a man whom she could not bear to marry.

An encounter on an English train started Emma's next case in *Misleading Ladies* (Berkley, 1997). She earned a double fee by saving a marriage, identifying a misguided killer, and securing an inheritance for a young woman. Although Emma varied from her serial monogamy in this episode, her heart still belonged to Lord Mark Croft, heir to a dukedom. She postponed decisions as to marriage because she had little respect for titles or the lifestyle of the nobility. She retained family values, e.g. believed that parents, not servants, should raise children.

A casual visit to Sotheby's auction house in *Silver and Guilt* (Berkley, 1998) set Emma on an extended adventure. First, to reclaim an heirloom candelabra for a member of the English nobility; second, to solve the murder of its most recent owner Bootsie Corrigan, a personal friend. Bootsie had been poor, became rich, and still drove a hard bargain, perhaps too hard. Along the way, Emma stabilized a marriage, arranged a political career, and restored dignity to an impoverished family. Not bad for a two week job.

Emma's assignment in *Royals and Rogues* (Berkley, 1998) took her to Russia to evaluate conditions in a factory subsidized by an American foundation. She was startled by the pervasiveness of the Russian mafias, the corruption of the criminal justice system, and the tolerance of these conditions by the community. When her young friends were murdered, Emma was advised to return home. This was a crucial decision for her. Was she a dilettante to abandon a case when it became hazardous? No, she was a professional, and remained.

As awed as the reader may be with Emma's skills, equal credit should be given to the broad knowledge of the author in art, music, European history, architecture, and literature. An interesting series and wonderful buy at paperback prices. Author Cynthia Smith's plotting was above average. Her clues tracked and were valid for the arrest, trial and conviction of criminals unlike many other light mysteries.

Schuyler Ridgway
Author: Tierney McClellan, pseudonym for Barbara Taylor McCafferty

Schuyler Ridgway had survived her divorce and the need to support a family with limited work experience and two years of college. She found work as a real estate agent. Her two adult children were college dropouts without any real purpose in life. Schuyler's life in Louisville, Kentucky was dull, but at least she no longer had to put up with her ex-husband's upper class pretensions.

Schuyler's life took an unexpected turn in *Heir Condition* (Signet, 1995). She was notified of a bequest from wealthy developer Ephriam Cross. The members of the Cross family were equally surprised and assumed that Schuyler had an affair with the deceased. No one believed she had never met the man, particularly since she had no alibi for his murder. In fact someone tried to frame her for the crime. Matthias Cross, son of the victim, was determined to learn the truth about his father and Schuyler.

Matthias, a college professor, remained an important part of Schuyler's life in *Closing Statement* (Signet, 1995). So did detectives Reed and Costello who once again were called upon to investigate a crime in which Schuyler was involved. She had discovered the corpse of a former client who was suing her. The victim's last words should have identified the killer, but a misunderstanding and the passage of time delayed the solution.

Schuyler's difficulty in expressing her feelings for Matthias finally resolved itself in *A Killing in Real Estate* (Signet, 1996) during which she discovered another corpse when taking clients to view a house for sale. The victim was a rival real estate agent who had been "stealing clients" from Schuyler. That left her as either a suspect or the next target.

By the time Schuyler met murder again in *Two-Story Frame* (Signet, 1997), the gimmick of having the same police detectives handle the case and consider her a suspect had worn thin. The more interesting angle was that the victim was Kim, the fiancée of Schuyler's former husband Ed, to whom Schuyler was showing a house for sale. Schuyler spent a considerable portion of the narrative complaining about Ed and their children, before she came up with a conclusion that competent detectives could have reached earlier.

Lil Ritchie

Author: Phyllis Knight

Lil Ritchie, a Virginian by birth, had worked for years in Texas; then, settled in Maine. A tall rawboned lesbian with graying dark hair, she had been a country musician before she became a private investigator. Her musical career was ruined by a false accusation that she had murdered a friend and member of her band. She still enjoyed music (especially early jazz, blues, and rock), cooked Southern style, and swam for recreation.

In *Switching the Odds* (St. Martin, 1992), Lil was hired to find young Jesse Cooper who ran away from prep school to find his alcoholic birth father. Jesse could run, but he could not hide, because he and his friend, Greg, had witnessed a murder.

During *Shattered Rhythms* (St. Martin, 1994), Lil helped Andre Ledoux, a guitarist whose work she had always admired. Ledoux's erratic behavior and eventual disappearance worried the other members of his combo, who thought he might have relapsed into drug addiction. Lil followed his trail to Northern Maine, and into Canada. She was unable to prevent his death, but she resolved to turn his killers over to the police.

Sophie Rivers

Author: Judith Cutler

By her thirties, Sophie Rivers had become a lecturer at Murdoch College in Birmingham, England. She led a simple life: enjoyed cooking (excellent curries); did the Canadian Air Force Exercises, sang with the Midlands Choral Society, was an excellent pianist, as well as a cricket fan (her father had played professionally). Scared off by the thefts of automobiles in Birmingham, she had no car. She used public transportation, walked, or rode her bicycle to the college campus. There were a few problems. Sophie liked her gin a little too much and her taste in men had been unwise. William Murdoch bore no resemblance to the famed British universities. The students were primarily from immigrant homes, eager to rise above their parent's status. A kind woman, Sophie was frequently drawn into their personal problems.

When, during *Dying Fall* (Piatkus, 1995), an ambitious student was murdered on campus, Sophie discovered the corpse. A short time later, she was devastated by the death of her close personal friend, George Carpenter, the bassoonist in the local symphony orchestra. With help from a college porter, Sophie avoided becoming another victim. Sophie had enjoyed the company of DCI Chris Groom, but he was too bland for her taste.

By *Dying To Write* (Piatkus, 1996), Sophie was focused on a writer's workshop where unfortunately the male attendees offered little interest. Moreover the week at the isolated institute was very hard on the females involved. One woman had died, one disappeared, and there had been several attacks on females. Chris Groom was called in, but was unable to save Sophie from a dreadful incarceration and the knowledge that her latest beau had a wife and two children. She might be scholarly, but she learned slowly out of the classroom.

In *Dying On Principle* (Piatkus, 1996), a temporary assignment to George Muntz College for a computer project provided Sophie with a more convenient commute, but put her on someone's hit list. The College's top management staff was anti-union, rarely available, and on the take. Sophie removed Simon, a musician, from her list of admirers, but added a randy fraud squad inspector and a ruthless entrepreneur. Inspector Chris Groom remained at the top of the list but Sophie was not ready to make any commitments.

Sophie's attachment to her slightly younger cousin, rock star Andy Rivers, was a pivotal factor in *Dying For Millions* (Piatkus, 1997). Chris Groom was away for training when, after a series of malicious acts, a worker on Andy's final performance was murdered. A parallel assignment, finding technical internships for students, placed Sophie in a dangerous conflict of interest. This forced her to balance her feelings for Andy against her loyalty to Chris.

As *Dying For Power* (Piatkus, 1998) began, Sophie had returned to William Murdock College tanned and refreshed from a vacation. What she found there was chaos. Ethnic groups clashed as to proper attire and the appropriate behavior of female students and staff. Some minority groups were harassed by others. This was no minor problem for Sophie whose own attire was criticized. There were fires, attacks on staff, and murder. The new administration could not or would not take proper action; in fact, it supported charges against Sophie.

Chris had been promoted to Chief Superintendent in a nearby jurisdiction as *Dying To Score* (Headline, 1999) began. His relationship with Sophie had diminished to friendship. Good thing because at this point Sophie met the man she had been waiting for, cricket player Mike Lowden. Not even the accusation that Mike had killed a fellow player could change Sophie's feelings. At the conclusion, she was a happy woman, facing the future, secure with the two most important men in her life, one a minor surprise.

It had seemed like a well-coordinated decision in *Dying By Degrees* (Headline, 2000). Mike would be in Australia for cricket matches; Sophie would take a sabbatical from William Murdock College to earn a masters degree at the University of West Midlands. She would join Mike for the Christmas holidays. They would have a small wedding on his return to England. Sophie had always enjoyed her teaching, and felt confident that she had done a good job. She was assigned to part-time work, teaching English to Asian women, and failed miserably. Could it be because the membership in the group changed regularly? Were her students qualified for the course? She had to rely on Chris Groom when her problems connected with murder.

Sophie's participation in the Big Brum Bookfest was intended to be casual volunteer activity during *Dying By The Book* (Piatkus, 2001). Her commitment quickly expanded when the project director became seriously ill at a time of crisis. Authors who were to headline the event had been threatened. One was murdered. Someone was stalking attractive blondes and Sophie fit the description. Her personal problems were resolved along the way.

Next books in this series: *Dying in Discord* (2002); *Dying to Deceive* (2003)

Nan Robinson

Author: Taffy Cannon

Nan Robinson, who had been divorced for three years, lived in a condo in Playa del Ray near Los Angeles. A graduate of the UCLA Law School, she worked as an attorney/investigator for the California State Bar. Leon, her former husband, had remarried and there was no contact. Her father, who died in a car wreck, had been an alcoholic. She still attended meetings of the Adult Children of Alcoholics. In her mid-thirties, Nan remained unsure of what she wanted to do with the rest of her life.

Before *A Pocketful of Karma* (Carroll & Graf, 1993) began, Nan had befriended computer expert Debbie Fontaine, a young woman from her hometown. When Debbie's mother contacted the Bar office in search of her daughter, Nan was surprised. Debbie no longer worked there. For old time's sake, Nan tried to find Debbie, who had become involved with an obscure cult, "Karma, The Past Lives Institute." First Debbie's corpse, then that of her abusive former husband were found. The police would settle for murder/suicide, but Nan believed that Debbie had been a danger to someone at PLI. She hoped it was not the man with whom she had fallen in love.

In *Tangled Roots* (Carroll & Graf, 1995), Nan left her work behind to visit her sister Julie, who ran a small flower and orchard business with her husband, Adam. When Shane Pettigrew, the heir to his primary competitor, was murdered, Adam was charged even though he and Shane had been friends since childhood. There were other suspects, but no one seemed interested in pursuing the investigation, even when Shane's domineering father died mysteriously. Nan took on the challenge, prodding defense attorney Ramon Garza until she discovered the killer.

When Nan's high school class in Spring Hill, Illinois announced their twentieth reunion, she attended during *Class Reunions Are Murder* (Fawcett Crest, 1996). She was not the biggest surprise at the gathering. That was Brenda, the "class tramp," who had left town pregnant. The father of her child was the obvious suspect when she was murdered, but Brenda had more than one secret that gave her power over fellow classmates.

Author Taffy Cannon created memorable characterizations and interesting plots. She completed Rebecca Rothenberg's manuscript for *The Tumbleweed Murders* and, writing as Emily Toll, has a new series featuring travel director Lynne Montgomery.

Benedetta "Bennie" Rosato

Author: Lisa Scottoline

Bennie Rosato made her living as a defense attorney in criminal actions or as a plaintiff attorney in civil cases, specializing in matters which involved civil rights and police brutality. She had an adversarial relationship with the Philadelphia police. Benny had never had it easy. She was the child of Carmella Rosato, a single mother who had never identified her daughter's father. Although Benny had a good income, her mother was chronically mentally ill and required twenty four-hour care. Carmella lived in Benny's home, where a nurse cared her for during the daytime. This did not leave much time for a personal life.

For a time after Bennie and her law partner, Mark Biscardi, ended their affair, they continued to practice together. But, as *Legal Tender* (HarperCollins, 1996) opened, Benny learned that Mark, now seriously involved with Eve Eberlein, an associate in their firm, was preparing to leave. Angered by the secrecy of his betrayal, Bennie blew her top. When Mark was murdered during a period of time when Bennie had no alibi, she found herself dealing with the Philadelphia police department.

By *Rough Justice* (HarperCollins, 1997), Bennie headed a small all-female law firm. Rosato and Associates. The firm served as local counsel for hotshot attorney Marta Richter in her defense of slumlord Elliot Steere when he was accused of murder. The case had already gone to the jury and Marta was confident of an acquittal, when Steere bragged of his guilt. Marta returned to the Rosato firm, determined to undermine her own case with the assistance of two young attorneys. They were unaware of why she wanted further investigations, but risked their reputations and safety. Bennie, who kept in touch with the case at crucial moments, did not play a major role in the narrative. She saved Marta from making a serious mistake.

Bennie could not separate her private life from her profession during *Mistaken Identity* (HarperCollins, 1999). She defended a woman who was probably her twin sister on a murder charge. Bennie had been raised by her chronically ill mother in the belief that she was an only child abandoned by her father. Neither was the truth. That still left the question: did sister Alice kill police officer Anthony Della Porta? If not, who did?

The Vendetta Defense (HarperCollins, 2001) was only a peripheral part of the Rosato series. Attorney Judy Carrier was a member of the firm headed by Bennie. Judy took on the defense of an Italian septuagenarian who considered murder to be a necessity given the wrong that had been done to his family. Judy carried the narrative, but it was Bennie who showed her how to win.

Attorney readers may swallow hard at the histrionics and questionable legal practices. (See also Mary DiNunzio, another member of Benny's staff). Benny also appeared in a supporting role in a stand-alone book—*Courting Trouble* (2003). She will return in a book of her own, *Dead Ringer* (2003).

Danielle "Dani" Ross

Author: Gilbert Morris

Dani Ross' life had taken several different directions. She had studied to be an accountant at Tulane University and worked for the Attorney General's Office in Massachusetts. She fell in love with Jerry, a divinity student. When he died in a tragic accident shortly after they had quarreled, her guilt led her to believe that she should take his place in the missionary field. Her graduate work at Hayworth Divinity School was interrupted by news that her father was ill. Dan Ross ran a detective agency in New Orleans, but could not continue after a serious heart attack. His wife, Ellen, and two younger children, Rob and Allison, were incapable of keeping the business afloat. Dani saw a different responsibility, one that she could not ignore. She was a devout Christian who did not take these matters lightly. Dani was tremendously proud of her great-great-grandfather, a colonel in the Confederate Army, and drew inspiration from his courage at Pickett's unsuccessful charge at Gettysburg.

In *Guilt by Association* (Revell, 1991), she knew that she would have to hire additional staff at the agency but Dani was hesitant about hiring rebellious Ben Savage. He had been recommended by a police chief but with the comment that he had lost his job as a Denver detective for insubordination. It turned out to be a wise choice. Within a month Dani had been abducted and imprisoned in a silo along with ten others. They were to be punished for an unknown transgression. Ben, who followed up on her disappearance, was added to the group. She imparted her religious beliefs to members of the group suffering from their captivity and danger. Ben's physical skills, gained when he worked as an aerialist in a circus, led to their escape. Together they figured out which of their fellow prisoners was the killer.

Well-known actor and playwright Jonathan Ainsley convinced Dani to come to New York City in *The Final Curtain* (Revell, 1991). There had been threats, followed by attempts on his life as he began production of his comeback play. Dani was to go undercover as a wardrobe mistress, prompter and understudy. When the leading lady was murdered, Dani assumed her role. Ben joined the crew in time to save more than one life. Dani's religious beliefs transformed several characters. Her deductive skills uncovered five members of the group who had committed crimes.

During *Deadly Deception* (Revell, 1992), Dani took her Christian beliefs (and her .38 revolver) into the home of a crime syndicate boss. Dominic Lanza. He hired Dani and Ben to guard his four grandchildren against attacks by a rival gang. The closeness between Dani and Ben made it possible for them to communicate when she and a four-year-old boy were kidnapped.

Someone was extorting money from men and women on the rodeo circuit. Ben's sister came to him for help just as he and Dani had another of their quarrels in *Revenge at the Rodeo* (Revell, 1993). She heard next of Ben when he turned up in a Dallas hospital. Luke Sixkiller, currently on suspension for alleged abuse of a prisoner, accompanied her. Both took undercover jobs on the rodeo circuit until they identified the "creeps" who had gone beyond threats to mayhem and murder. Luke had a conversion experience which brought him closer to Dani in Ben's absence.

Dani faced her biggest challenge in *The Quality of Mercy* (Revell, 1993). Tommy Cain was out of prison, determined to kill those who had caught and convicted him, including Dani's father. When he succeeded, Dani's pain was so great that she lost touch with her faith. She wanted revenge, not consolation, ignoring the advice of those who loved her: Ben, Dominic Lanza, and Lt. Luke Sixkiller.

An innocent man facing execution in a Mississippi prison reached out to Dani in *Race with Death* (Revell, 1994), the conclusion of the six book series. Only a gubernatorial pardon could save Eddie Prejean and Governor Layne Russell wanted Eddie dead. Ben and Dani found the trail that led to Russell's personal connection to the victim. Dani, helpless in a swamp, had found her way to safety. Ben, desperate with fear that she might be dead, found his way to faith in God.

The narrative placed considerable emphasis on religious values. They were well plotted with interesting characterizations. Continuing characters were used to illustrate the power of Dani's intercession even if not immediately effective; e.g. two criminals who did not seek repentance in their first appearance, died after a change of heart in subsequent books.

Ruby Rothman

Author: Sharon Kahn

Although she could never escape her role as the widow of a rabbi, Ruby Rothman was a skilled computer consultant and became part-owner of The Hot Bagel in Eternal, Texas. Her only child, Joshua was a college student. The Rothman household had shrunk to Ruby and a three-legged golden retriever named Oy Vey. Members of her former husband Stuart's congregation, particularly Essie Sue Margolis, kept their eyes open for an acceptable beau for Ruby. She was a warm and witty woman, who was less comfortable in larger groups. The Rothmans had lived in Eternal for twenty-one years, but Ruby loved New York City and enjoyed her visits there. She had a support system: members of the Temple; her Lebanese partner in the bagel shop, Milt Aboud; and Nan, a legal secretary and law student with whom she corresponded on the Internet. Ruby's e-mail letters were utilized as part of the narrative.

Ruby had almost accepted her widowhood when, in *Fax Me a Bagel* (Scribners, 1998), a tragic event made her aware that Stu Rothman might have been murdered. A prominent temple member (Essie Sue's sister) died of cyanide poisoning after eating a bagel at Milt's shop. The possibility that the bagel might have been intended for Ruby and subsequent "accidents" confirmed her suspicions. Two trips to New York City, during which she learned the traditions of the bagel business and probed the relationships among members of a prominent bagel-making family, enlightened her as to possible motives. When the killer threatened her, a book saved Ruby's life.

Essie Sue's relentless campaign to sell matzo balls to raise money for a statue to honor her sister provided an opening for more unscrupulous dealings in *Never Nosh a Matzo Ball* (Scribners, 2000). While Essie Sue spent her time sponsoring a marriage for Rabbi Kevin Kapstein, Ruby sought the connection between a recent murder and the residents of the Fit and Rural Ranch. Ruby, peddling her computer skills, infiltrated the Ranch, which provided a weight reduction plan, but received a cool reception.

The hot pastrami in *Don't Cry for Me, Hot Pastrami* (Scribners, 2001) was only the second prize. The first prize in Essie Sue's moneymaking lottery, a cruise in the Caribbean, was won by Ruby. She would go as part of a tour group from her Temple headed by Rabbi Kevin Kapstein. The professor who was to deliver the lecture series on "Jews of the Inquisition" died while boarding. Rabbi Kapstein retained possession of his materials and, thanks to Essie Sue, was named as his replacement. Kapstein, a less than fluent speaker, needed help so Essie Sue volunteered Ruby. This gave her an opportunity to learn more about the Diaspora of the Spanish Jews, but again made her a target for a killer. Ruby proved to be a survivor. She also met an attractive Jewish travel writer who promised to keep in touch.

Next book in this series: *Hold the Cream Cheese, Kill the Lox* (2002)

Mary Russell

Author: Laurie R. King

The Beekeeper's Apprentice (St. Martin, 1994) was a compilation of notes left behind by an elderly woman, relating to incidents in her youth. Mary Russell had been a fifteen-year-old orphan, living near the Suffolk Downs with a disgruntled aunt, when she met Sherlock Holmes. She was tall, blond, athletic, and lonely, tortured by guilt because her ill humor might have contributed to the death of her parents and brother. During a stroll on the Downs, she met Holmes, now retired and began a relationship that shaped her life. Mrs. Watson became a second mother; Sherlock a mentor and friend. Gradually she joined in his investigations, traveling disguised as a gypsy to rescue a missing American child.

Once freed from her aunt, she moved from being Holmes' pupil to acting as his associate. They incurred the wrath of a criminal who targeted Watson, Holmes and Mary for death. With Holmes' powers fading, Mary, by then an Oxford student, persisted until they faced their adversary. By her twenty-first birthday, Mary was almost six feet tall, a student of the martial arts, and increasingly devoted to Holmes.

In *A Monstrous Regiment of Women* (St. Martin, 1995), their personal relationship changed, frightening both with its sexual implications. Mary involved herself in the charismatic religious movement of Margery Childe, which explored the female component of God. The deaths of devotees to the New Temple of God provided funds for Margery's movement, causing Mary to wonder whether she was victim or killer? A vicious and greedy murderer dragged Mary to the depths of drug addiction before Holmes rescued her. The ending may shock Holmes' fans.

Mary did not consider herself a Christian. Her mother had been Jewish. Still, she shared Holmes interest in *A Letter of Mary* (St. Martin, 1997). An amateur archeologist, Dorothy Ruskin, contacted them regarding a papyrus message from Miriam (Mary) from the town of Magdala re Joshua (Jesus). Dorothy, because her sight was failing, turned custody of the letter and the carved wooden box in which it had been contained over to Holmes. The provenance of the letter seemed authentic. Its impact on the Christian world would be to indicate that women played a strong role in the early life of the Church. A short time later, Mary and Sherlock learned that

Dorothy had been killed in a traffic accident. Convinced that she had been murdered, each went undercover to investigate major suspects. There was an interesting appearance by "Peter" (Wimsey?) who recognized Mary, but did not betray her.

Although Sherlock and Mary had been married for over two years in *The Moor* (St. Martin, 1998), she was still learning about him. His peremptory telegram summoning her to the home of aging scholar Rev. Sabine Baring-Gould distracted Mary from her work, but she acquiesced. The moor (Dartmoor) had no attraction for her at first. As she and Sherlock investigated first rumors, then murder, reminiscent of his prior case, *The Hound of the Baskervilles*, its bleakness and the people who inhabited the moor enthralled her. The narrative moved slowly. Perhaps like the moor, it required time and attention to develop a real interest.

Nursing their physical and emotional wounds, Mary and Sherlock left England as *O Jerusalem* (Bantam, 1999) began. The narrative was out of sequence, covering a period before Mary and Sherlock had married. Mycroft, Sherlock's brother, had offered several alternative locations in which they could serve England. Mary chose Jerusalem, the homeland of her people, then occupied by British troops. She and Sherlock traveled together with Mary dressed as a young man under the auspices of suspicious British allies. They noted the contemptuous treatment English soldiers gave to occupants of Jerusalem. Their relationship moved to a different level during their travails.

Next book in this series: *Justice Hall* (2002)

Amelia Sachs

Author: Jeffrey Wilds Deaver

Lincoln Rhyme, former head of the forensics unit at the New York Police Department, was a quadriplegic confined to a wheelchair. He wanted to die and his doctor had agreed to help. Three factors intervened: (1) a difficult case which he may be the only person able to solve; (2) a fearsome enemy, "The Bone Collector," who dangled clues to taunt Rhyme, his ultimate target; and (3) Amelia Sachs, who made his life worth living.

A tall attractive redhead, she had been an advertising model; then, became a patrol officer like her father. The onset of arthritis limited her choices to retirement or transfer to the information unit. Her personal life had been on hold since her lover Nick, a bent detective, ended their relationship. When his criminal affiliations were discovered, Nick cared enough about her to put distance between them. Her father had been dead for three years. Mother Rose lived near Amelia's apartment in Brooklyn. Amelia was an excellent pistol shot, cast her own bullets and reloaded her own ammunition. She also carried a switchblade that she learned to use as a kid in Brooklyn.

It had been Amelia who discovered the first victim as *The Bone Collector* (Viking, 1997) began. By the time Rhyme's former comrades on the police force went to him for help, Amelia had been accepted as a member of the scene of crime team. Rhyme was impressed enough to insist that she become his contact with the police. She would be his eyes at the scene of the crime, wearing an earphone connection to keep in touch. Their relationship grew, a fact noted by the Bone Collector, whose modus operandi was based on that of a killer described in a book *Crime in Old New York*.

The federal government's efforts to prosecute arms dealer Phillip Hansen were hampered when he dropped evidence into the ocean from a plane. Of the three witnesses against Hansen, a contract killer known as the Coffin Dancer had eliminated one, Edward Carney of Hudson Air Charters. Rhyme's cooperation was assured in *The Coffin Dancer* (Simon & Schuster, 1998) because the Coffin Dancer had killed his laboratory assistant Claire Trilling, the woman he loved. The first responsibility for Rhyme's special squad was to protect the remaining witnesses: Carney's widow, Percey and top Hudson pilot, Brit Hale. The second was to capture and convict Coffin Dancer. Rhyme wanted more than justice. He wanted vengeance. Amelia was very much a part of the action, angry with herself because during one contact she had an opportunity to kill Dancer and failed to do so, angry at Rhyme because he resisted her sexual overtures.

When Rhyme went to the University of North Carolina's Medical Center in *The Empty Chair* (Simon & Schuster, 2000), he was aware of the risks involved in the experimental treatment he would receive. It was worth it if the end result would be increased mobility. He did not expect to be drawn into the hunt for a teenage boy accused of murder and kidnapping. Nor did he anticipate that Amelia would dispute his findings and those of the local authorities. Her independent actions caused her to be indicted for murder. She was saved before sentencing when Rhyme uncovered a sinister plot. She repaid his efforts, by saving his life.

These were spellbinding narratives; different in tone from Deaver's other series featuring Rune.

Next books in this series: *The Stone Monkey* (2002); *The Vanished Man* (2003)

Dr. Maxene St. Clair

Author: Janet McGiffin

Maxene St. Clair was a M.D./Ph.D., meaning that she had earned both a medical degree and a doctorate in science. Her marriage to another doctor failed. After six years of teaching and research, she left the academic setting, taking an equally high-pressure job as an emergency room doctor at St. Agnes' Hospital in Milwaukee, Wisconsin. A redhead in her late thirties, Maxene used photography as a relaxation, and her cat, "Ruby" for company.

During *Emergency Murder* (Fawcett, 1992), Maxene worked the late shift when the wife of a prominent surgeon arrived close to death dressed as a hooker. The immediate diagnosis was heart failure. An autopsy indicated that she been poisoned by an obscure substance, last known to have been used in Maxene's college lab. Investigator Joe Grabowski, who had dated Maxene before her marriage, was inclined to give her the benefit of the doubt.

In *Prescription for Death* (Fawcett, 1993), Joe played a larger role. Among the regular admissions to the emergency room were prostitutes brought in by their pimps after hard sex and abuse. Maxene made a personal visit to the rooming house where Latoya was close to death. Before the ambulance could arrive, a drive-by killer had wounded another hooker and artist Wyoming Syzinski, Joe's boyhood chum. Joe and Maxene were present later when a heavy wooden sculpture fell and injured artist Soren Berendorf who subsequently died. They connected the incidents.

Maxene joined the ranks of politicians in *Elective Murder* (Fawcett, 1995) when there seemed to be a bounty on female legislators in Wisconsin. Her primary goal was to protect state funding for emergency room treatment, but she had to solve a murder to do so.

Laney Samms

Author: Carol Schmidt

Laney Samms co-owned a bar in California that attracted a lesbian clientele. Her constant companion was a German Shepherd called "Radar." Her business partner was a female veterinarian with whom she had lived for twenty years. She was described as a woman in her forties whose hair had turned from dark to silver.

In *Silverlake Heat* (Naiad, 1993), Laney found her long time affair stultifying and ended it. She became involved in a destructive relationship and a murder investigation in which the killer manipulated her.

Laney bought full control of the bar, but left it to be managed by a friend in *Sweet Cherry Wine* (Naiad, 1994). She moved to a guesthouse on the Los Angeles estate of Kitt Meyers, a music entrepreneur. Kitt provided Laney with free rent and a small salary for housesitting and minor clerical work. Laney and Kitt intervened in an attack on a young woman whom they recognized as a former rock star. The recovery of Hayley Malone needed more than financial and medical assistance. A malevolent ghost had pursued her from childhood.

By *Cabin Fever* (Naiad, 1995), Laney's relationship with Hayley was floundering. Her stay at Kitt's estate ended when she was almost killed by a bomb placed in Kitt's car. Laney moved again, this time to Upper Michigan where she worked to establish a lesbian summer camp, threatened by the hostility of the local residents.

Charlotte Sams

Author: Alison Glen, pseudonym for Cheryl Meredith Lowry and Louise Vetter

Although she had a financially successful husband, Walt, Charlotte Sams wanted more. Their son, Tyler, was twelve, and she had time on her hands. Her best pal, Lou Toreson, had retired from her position at Ohio State University to carry on a private psychology practice. Charlotte, who lived in Clintonville, a suburb of Columbus, Ohio, decided on her own career as a freelance journalist concentrating on feature stories about the area. Once on the scene, murders occurred, and Charlotte and Lou solved them.

In *Showcase* (Simon & Schuster, 1992), the setting was a local art show, which might be displaying copies, not original art-works. The guest who raised the question died the next day. His death was accepted as a heart attack by the authorities, but Charlotte and Lou knew better.

Columbus' zoo was highlighted in *Trunk Show* (Simon & Schuster, 1995) when an animal handler whom Charlotte was to interview was found dead in the elephant yard. Neither vandalism to her car, nor the efforts of African-American homicide detective Jefferson Barnes, kept Charlotte and Lou from interviewing suspects, rifling files, and interfering in the investigation. There were some interesting suspects. The narratives were run-of-the-mill.

Dr. Meredyth "Mere" Sanger

Author: Robert W. Walker

Meredyth Sanger a.k.a. Mere was a silver-blonde psychiatrist, born and raised in Seattle, Washington, but practicing in Houston, Texas. Her parents had been educators. Mere had attended Duke University. The primary protagonist in the series was Lucas Stonecoat, a Native American who had been relegated to the "Cold Room" of the Houston Police Department. His job was to check unsolved murders to see if they had been mishandled or if new information made it wise to reopen the case.

Lucas had been disabled since a drunken driving accident while working for the Dallas Police Department. After that, there was no future for him in Dallas. He moved to Houston where he started as a rookie, but had not conquered his drinking problem. He had contempt for laws and regulations that enhanced the rights of the accused. On occasion Mere, in her job as psychiatrist for the 31st Precinct, pushed to have Lucas involved in her cases. They became his cases, not hers. His viewpoint, personal life, and actions dominated the series.

Lucas hoped that Mere would be part of his future. Her assistant was Randy Oglesby, a computer nerd who helped Lucas on the sly. Although she had an interest in Lucas, Mere had other lovers, but no marriages. She carried a weapon and was proficient with it, unusual for a police psychiatrist. Mere's police salary was only a portion of her income as she also had a lucrative private practice.

Randy, Lucas and Mere became interested in a series of mutilations and deaths by crossbows during *Cutting Edge* (Jove, 1997). Randy knew something about bows because he had constructed a computer game based on crossbows. Mere met Lucas in the records unit when she went there to research murders stretching back ten years and taking place in a variety of locations. A recent victim had been local judge Charles Mootry. Not only were their efforts unappreciated by Lucas' superior officers, but they were decoyed first out of the area, then, into danger. The narrative was extremely violent with villains and protagonists both quick to kill.

FBI agent Dr. Kim Desinor (who also appeared in author Robert W. Walker's Jessica Coran series) added her visions to Mere's psychological insights and Lucas' Native American mysticism in *Double Edge* (Jove, 1998). Another serial killer terrified a segment of Houston's community, the families of young African-American males. Lucas could not resist keeping tabs on the latest victim, Lamar Coleson who had disappeared but might still be alive. Guided by Kim's dreams and visions, Lucas and Mere raced against the clock. Lucas made time to reinvestigate the death of a young Native American woman, whose son could not rest until her killer was identified.

Cold Edge (Jove, 2001) was not for the faint of heart, or for those who believe that police officers should abide by the civil rights of those who have been suspected of or arrested for crimes. Lucas and Mere joined in the hunt for a depraved serial killer, or perhaps two separate killers, the Scalper and the Beheader. Lucas, under heavy pressure at work, juggled his romantic and family connections. He was angry that the authorities assumed the Scalper was a Native American, but he behaved like a savage to get information from a suspect.

A reader who enjoyed Mere should try Walker's other series featuring Jessica Coran.

Hillary Scarborough

Author: Paula Carter (A possible pseudonym)

See: Jane Ferguson, page 207.

Dr. Kay Scarpetta

Author: Patricia Daniels Cornwell

Kay Scarpetta had been raised in a poor Italian-Catholic home, marred by her father's illness, then death, from leukemia. She grew to be a petite blonde, extremely bright, and having almost total recall of written material.

She had an impressive resume: an undergraduate degree at Cornell, a medical degree from Johns Hopkins, plus a law degree. As the series began she was employed as the chief medical examiner in Richmond, Virginia, which was stated to have the second highest per capita rate of homicide in the United States.

Her childless marriage to Tony Benedetto ended in divorce, but Kay had an endearing relationship with her niece Lucy who became an integral part of the series. Lucy, from the time she was ten years old, was tied more closely to Kay than to her own feckless mother. Kay added other supports to her life as the series progressed, the most important of which was her affair with Benton Wesley, an FBI profiler. The job consumed Kay's life despite her efforts to keep an emotional distance from the murder victims, yet retain compassion for their survivors. Her idea of a good time was a small dinner, usually Italian-American food, which she cooked for friends.

Privacy, a sense of separation, was important to Kay so she lived on a one-acre suburban lot.

In *Postmortem* (Scribners, 1990), Kay searched for a pattern in the serial murders of women. The investigation after the fourth death focused on the victim's husband as the logical suspect but Kay was unconvinced. At risk from office politics, she received help from Lucy, who was already precocious at the computer, Benton Wesley, and an ambitious reporter.

Body of Evidence (Scribners, 1991) introduced Kay's former lover, attorney Mark James who represented deceased author Beryl Madison and Beryl's mentor Cary Harper. Madison's work in progress mirrored her relationship with Harper, leading Kay to puzzle over the human aspects of Beryl's life and death.

By *All That Remains* (Scribners, 1992, Kay had developed additional allies: reporter Abby Turnbull and police officer Pete Marino whose initial resentment of Kay became wholehearted acceptance. All worked with Kay while investigating a series of "couple" killings. The most recent disappearance of the daughter of a high-ranking federal government spokeswoman put heavy pressure on agencies for quick results. Scarpetta's persistence and knowledge of blood types pinpointed the killer.

During *Cruel and Unusual* (Scribners, 1993), bureaucrats tried to stifle Kay's investigation of the death of a savagely mutilated child. The incident was similar to a crime for which a man had been sentenced and executed. Fingerprints could not lie, or could they? Lucy visited in time to help Kay pursue an enemy through agency computers that had been manipulated to conceal data.

Lucy was a college student by *The Body Farm* (Scribners, 1994) working as an intern in a highly secret FBI unit at Quantico. Kay, Benton Wesley, and Pete Marino were simultaneously assigned to a child murder that resembled earlier atrocities by the elusive Temple Gault. Kay fought Marino to find the real killer, and the FBI to prove that Lucy was not a security risk because of her sexual orientation.

In *From Potter's Field* (Scribners, 1995), Gault returned with a personal vendetta using for his own purposes a computer system designed by Lucy, which connected the FBI to municipal police departments. He was suspected of killing an unidentified young woman in Central Park. Benton (by now Kay's lover), Marino and Kay were consultants. Kay discovered the motive behind "Jane's" death, delving into the Gault family history to trap the man who taunted her with his killings.

Serial killers were not a primary concern in *Cause of Death* (Putnam, 1996), during which Kay investigated the murder of a reporter poisoned while diving in a restricted area. She battled local authorities to tie the death to the activities of a religious cult, only to learn that her probe was second-ary to a federal effort to thwart illegal munition sales. Kay's relationship with Benton was on hold as his marriage ended. Her ties to Lucy weakened as the younger woman developed her own personal and professional lives.

Another serial killer occupied Kay's attention during *Unnatural Exposure* (Putnam, 1997). An ambitious FBI agent was eager to connect a recent corpse to prior cases, but Kay found significant differences in the modus operandi. Her probe was complicated because Deadoc, the series killer, had singled Kay out. He familiarized himself with her life and tanta-lized her with picture clues on his murders. Kay found Deadoc, who did not fit the usual profile of a series killer. She also freed herself from the memory of her deceased lover Mark James, making room for Benton in her life.

Scarpetta's Winter Table (Wyrick, 1998) was a diversion, appealing primarily to Cornwell devotees or cooks. A modest holiday tale served as the vehicle for recipes purportedly used by Kay, Lucy, and Pete Marino.

It was back to the hard stuff in *Point of Origin* (Putnam, 1998). Carrie Grethen had spent almost five years in a psychiatric hospital, plan-ning revenge on Kay, Benton, and her former lover, Lucy. Carrie's escape coincided with a difficult arson case, which bore the marks of a serial killer, and enticed Kay, Benton, and Lucy. They followed a trail with Carrie always a step ahead of them, reaching a shocking end, which changed Kay's life forever.

As *Black Notice* (Putnam, 1999) began, Kay was given a letter that Benton had written before his death, forcing her to evaluate where grief had taken her. Protected by her friends, she became the target of an ambitious rival, deputy police chief Diane Bray. Kay and Marino focused on a murder, which pitted them against an international smuggling ring run by the pow-erful Chandonne family. The struggle awakened Kay's professional interest, but her personal life did not benefit from a short-term love affair. Lucy had also suffered from Benton's death, but her problems were magnified as she struggled to balance her duties with the Alcohol, Tobacco and Firearms Bureau and her responsibility to her current lover.

The Last Precinct (Putnam, 2000) could be compared to an old-fash-ioned icebox soup in which the cook utilized a meat bone, and then added all the leftover vegetables in the refrigerator. Kay's relationship with her dying father, with her husband Tony Benedetto, lovers Mark James, and Benton Wesley were all explored. Her conflicts with the criminal Chan-donne family, with Carrie Grethen and Newton Joyce were woven into the plot. She faced new antagonists within the criminal justice system, notably Jaime Berger, a New York City prosecutor. There were connections to Kay's feud with Diane Bray. The accumulation of stresses had left Kay vulnerable when she was accused of killing Bray. Lucy, Marino, and Dr. Anna Zenner remained staunch allies but their ill-timed interventions were not always beneficial.

A second Scarpetta cookbook *Food to Die For* (Putnam, 2001), coauthored with Marlene Brown, tied individual recipes to dishes that appeared in particular narratives, and recipes from favorite restaurants. The pictures were terrific.

Personal happiness eluded Kay throughout the series. She had frequent struggles within the criminal justice system. Although Cornwell became an international favorite, her narratives grew longer and longer, each more dependent on prior books for understanding.

Next book in this series: *Blow Fly* (2003)

Goldy Bear Schulz

Author: Diane Mott Davidson

See: Goldy Bear, page 50.

Cynthia Chenery "C.C." Scott

Author: Pele Plante, pseudonym for Patricia Planette

C.C. Scott, in her fifties, had a stable lesbian relationship with teacher Barbara Bettencourt. Her family life had been unremarkable, although her father suffered from depression. As an adult C.C. had wrestled with her own alcoholism, but had been dry for seventeen years thanks to her involvement with Alcoholics Anonymous. She worked as a therapist in California on a part-time basis. Barbara had some difficulty in the work place due to parental concerns about her sexual orientation.

C.C.'s interest in the elderly motivated her in *Getting Away with Murder* (Clothespin, 1991). She suspected that a pseudo-supportive agency was duping older people through "living trusts."

While on vacation, C.C. was wary of local reactions to her lesbianism. In *Dirty Money* (Clothespin, 1993), she met other lesbians and male homosexuals at Abalone Beach. Unfortunately she also encountered her share of drug dealers, and a blackmailing killer from whom she had to be rescued. When she came too close to the killer, intervention by her friends made a difference.

Nicolette "Nick" Scott

Author: Val Davis, pseudonym for Robert and Angela Irvine

Scientific achievement was taken for granted in Nicolette "Nick" Scott's family. Her father was a distinguished professor of anthropology at the University of New Mexico, focusing on the Anasazi Indians. She had a Ph.D. in archeology, had earned kudos for her discovery of World War II airplanes in the Pacific, and was seeking tenure as a professor at the University of California-Berkeley. This concentration of energy on the past had its destructive aspect. Nick's mother Elaine suffered from chronic mental illness, a fact ignored by her father. Nick's childhood had been devoted to managing the household and concealing her mother's aberrations so as to avoid angering her father. Despite lingering resentment of her father's cavalier attitude, Nick spent her summers working with him in the New Mexico desert or on Pacific islands.

During *Track of the Scorpion* (St. Martin, 1996), Nick was skeptical of elderly prospector Gus Beckstead's claim that he had located a World War II plane in the desert. Her expertise told her that such an event was unlikely. Nevertheless, she accompanied him to the site where the B-17 and its occupants were buried. The mission of the plane had been a secret one. Its exposure even now would be threatening to military and government officials. Nick needed her father and the survival skills he had taught her to combat the pressures placed on her investigation.

For all her complaints about her father's obsessions, Nick exhibited her own in *Flight of the Serpent* (Bantam, 1998). The narrative was about "Annie," a World War II B-24 bomber and the men who had flown in her. The plane had brought her crew back from 25 missions over Germany and the Ploesti oil fields of Rumania. When she was decommissioned, former pilot John Gault purchased the plane. Before Gault's grandson Matt was blown to bits in his Cessna, Nick had heard a helicopter, seen its shadow, and noted Matt's physical appearance. She became a part of Gault's reconstructed crew bent upon learning why Matt died and taking revenge.

Nick's suspension by the her hostile department head, Ben Gilbert, made her available to accompany her father and his college classmate Prof. Curt Buettner on an expedition in *Wake of the Hornet* (Bantam, 2000). The lure included a search for World War II airplanes located on Balesin, a neglected Pacific island. Villagers on the island adhered to the "cargo cult," a belief that if they built runways and decoy airplanes, others would come bringing valuable goods. The jungles on Balesin had secrets that Buettner intended to uncover, but that others would kill to conceal. Ingenious plotting.

Nick's father had always warned that airplanes would be the death of her. In *The Return of the Spanish Lady* (St. Martin, 2001), they nearly were. Her first assignment at the Smithsonian Institute was an expedition to northern Alaska to reclaim a World War II Japanese Aichi bomber. She and the Institute's administration were unaware that the sponsors of this quest, a pharmaceutical group, had a hidden agenda, one that put not only members of the expedition but society at risk. Fortunately in her misspent youth, Nick had learned some very handy lessons, including how to hotwire a vehicle.

Next book in this series: *Thread of the Spider* (2002)

Claudia Seferius

Author: Marilyn Todd

Claudia Seferius had considerable business ability, but in 13 B.C., she had limited opportunities to use it. A lesser woman would have devoted herself to the management of the house servants. Claudia was ambitious. She was an outrageous heroine; a former harlot/dancer who assumed the identity of a widow, Claudia Posedonius whose family had died of the plague. Actually her father had been an army orderly and her mother had committed suicide. Under this cover, she married Gaius Seferius, a wealthy wine merchant who had secrets of his own. When she met Security Agent Marcus Cornelius Orbilio she had neither the life experience nor the temperament to recognize a good man when she saw one. She didn't want Orbilio, but she discouraged any woman who did. The only true affection she seemed able to give was to an Egyptian cat, Drusilla, which she took everywhere.

In *I, Claudia* (Macmillan, 1995), she pitted her wits against Orbilio. He was a member of a noble Roman family who intended to pursue a political career when he had established his reputation. He had access to powerful members of the Augustinian government. Both Orbilio and Claudia sought the serial killer of six prominent Roman citizens. For him, it was part of his job. For Claudia, it was an effort to conceal the fact that the victims had purchased her services. She was addicted to gambling, and this time she won.

The death of her elderly husband Gaius provided Claudia with what should have been a comfortable inheritance in *Virgin Territory* (Macmillan, 1996), but she was unable to leave well enough alone. Within a short time she had gone into debt with her gambling and her right to Gaius' real estate was contested. In search of a solution she visited Sicily, escorting a former vestal virgin to her family home. The Collatinus estate was unsafe for virgins; not that Claudia had any such pretensions. Nevertheless, she benefited from having Orbilio on her trail.

Claudia should have learned that she was safer in Rome, but, in *Man Eater* (Macmillan, 1997), her bailiff Rollo summoned her to her vineyards. Set upon by hoodlums, she sought refuge at the nearby home of Surges Pictor. What a zoo that place was! Not just the animals either. Orbilio came to the rescue but had a difficult time convincing Claudia that the murders on the premises were designed to destroy her. In the larger world, the death of Agrippa, the premier general of the army and close friend to Augustus, created uncertainty.

A serial killer terrorized the Roman streets during *Wolf Whistle* (Macmillan, 1998). Rich merchants sought to take advantage of the civil unrest following the death of Agrippa to undermine Augustus. Orbilio was needed everywhere. He concentrated on saving two women whom he treasured: his youthful cousin Annia who was a potential victim of the serial killer and Claudia, who had acquired an obsessive admirer. She had little appreciation for Orbilio's efforts, but Claudia showed a warmer side to her personality in her treatment of an abandoned child.

Plague created panic in Rome during *Jail Bait* (Macmillan, 1999), but Claudia had more to fear. She had been stealing money from the repository of Sabbio Tullus. Orbilio, always mindful of her activities, secretly arranged a vacation for Claudia at Atlantis, an opulent resort. Once there, Claudia was enmeshed in murder investigations and the attentions of an attractive Spaniard. With Orbilio's help, she survived both.

To keep her wine business afloat in *Black Salamander* (Macmillan, 2000), Claudia joined a caravan of artisans and merchants visiting Gaul. She couriered a segment of a treasure map to rebellious tribal leaders as part of a deal to enhance wine sales. The expedition was a disaster. Orbilio, who joined the group belatedly, warned Claudia that her behavior could be considered traitorous. She was going to lose her head if she wasn't careful. Gaul was divided into more than three parts in this one.

Whatever credibility the background material on early Rome might establish was dissipated by Claudia's vocabulary. In the First Century, Women were unlikely to ask, "What part of the word 'no' don't you understand?"

Next books in this series: *Dream Boat* (2002); *Dark Horse* (2002)

Beth Seibelli (Cole)

Author: Ed Stewart

Beth Seibelli was an investigative reporter who eventually married Reagan Cole, a San Francisco police sergeant. Beth's parents had always been seriously religious, but only experience led her to that state in her life. Activity had been more important than reflection for Beth. She played college level basketball and rode a motorcycle. Beth and Reagan each made serious religious commitments, but could not always mesh their professional assignments.

At times overwhelmed by its sheer length, *Millenium's Eve* (Victor, 1993) contained an interesting character study of television evangelists who, with some reservations, agreed to meet on Millennium Eve, December 31, 2000 in a show of Christian unity. Their exposure to a rescue mission, which practiced what they preached, and to bomb threats by a religious fanatic were powerful influences on the evangelists. Changes also occurred in the lives of Beth, a doubter, and Reagan Cole who learned to pray when there was no other alternative.

Shelby Hornecker Rider, one of the evangelists whose lives had been changed by their millennium experiences, gave up her television work to serve at Dr. No's King's House Rescue Mission during *Millennium's Dawn* (Victor, 1994). She and her new husband, Dr. Evan Rider, faced unexpected problems from a secret in Rider's past. Beth had drifted away from Reagan, partly due to his spiritual transformation. Tracking down a professional killer with Reagan provided her with a conversion experience that brought them together in spirit. The lives intersected in a dramatic conclusion. Some pruning could have made the book more interesting.

A near death experience gave pilot Cooper Sams a sense of destiny in *Doomsday Flight* (Victor, 1995). Under the influence of religious guru Lila Ruth Atkinson, he came to believe that the Second Coming of Jesus would occur on February 20, 2002 and that an airplane populated by believers could be spared the destruction of the earth. Beth was given an opportunity to interview the prospective passengers, even to accompany them on their journey. Her decision took into consideration Reagan's feelings and her pregnancy. The extended narrative covered the motivations of the passengers on the Doomsday Flight.

Desiree "Dez" Shapiro

Author: Selma Eichler

Desiree Shapiro continued as a New York City private investigator even after the death of Ed, her husband-partner, but she limited her practice to routine cases. She was a short plump woman who had accepted her weight and dealt with it by carefully choosing her clothes and accessories, but touched up her auburn hair. Ed and Desiree had no children, but she was close to his niece, Ellen Kravitz. Stuart Mason, a divorced friend, had become a regular date and casual lover, but with no plans for a more structured relationship.

Desiree was unsure that she was capable of working a murder case until *Murder Can Kill Your Social Life* (Signet, 1994), when two deaths occurred in Ellen's apartment house. Neither Ellen nor Desiree knew the victims; but Desiree was concerned about Ellen's safety. Early on Desiree selected the brutish building custodian as her candidate for killer, but the final solutions were more complex and more painful for her.

She could not resist a handsome young man, particularly the younger brother of a childhood friend, so in *Murder Can Ruin Your Looks* (Signet, 1995), Desiree promised Peter Winters that she would discover which of twins had survived a vicious attack. Peter was engaged to Mary Ann Foster, but no one knew whether she was the patient in the hospital, or the corpse in the morgue. Desiree learned the motive for the murder before she could understand why the bodies had to be defaced.

Doomed by her inability to say "no" even after she had been seriously endangered in earlier murder investigations, Desiree assumed risks again in *Murder Can Stunt Your Growth* (Signet, 1996). Elderly Evelyn Corwin insisted that her granddaughter did not die a natural death. The Corwin family was so dysfunctional that there was no dearth of suspects.

Ellen, Desiree's niece, was one of a group invited to the gracious home of newly divorced Sybil Miller in *Murder Can Wreck Your Reunion* (Signet, 1998). An unexpected guest was Raven Eber who not only had not been sent an invitation, but was heartily disliked by other members of the group. Her death by a plunge into the pool from an upstairs window could have been an accident, but the police were not taking it for granted. When the detectives questioned Ellen, Desiree took a hand.

Murder Can Spook Your Cat (Signet, 1998) focused on the death of a popular author of children's books, formerly married to Desiree's friend, Kevin Garvey. Kevin suspected his ex-wife had been killed by one of her three stepdaughters, but, prompted by a cat's water dish, Desiree took another look around.

Bruce Simon had been nothing but trouble for Desiree when they shared an affair. In *Murder Can Singe Your Old Flame* (Signet, 1999), suspected of murdering his wife, he was even worse as a client. Desiree made the same mistake the victim had, trying to have her cake and eat it too.

Desiree's comfortable relationship with dentist Al Bonaventure took a blow in *Murder Can Spoil Your Appetite* (Signet, 2000). She investigated the murder of Frankie Vincent, a politically inclined chiropractor. Her client, mobster Vito da Silva had mentored Frankie's career and would not take "no" for an answer. He arranged the full cooperation of the Riverton, New Jersey police department, including a working relationship with attractive Lt. Lou Hoffman. Desiree was out of her territory and blindsided by the killer.

Desiree's brief encounter with philanthropist Miriam Weiden had left her with admiration. The news of her death in *Murder Can Upset Your Mother* (Signet, 2001) caused guilt. Miriam had sought Desiree's help when she felt threatened, but too late. Too soon, she learned that Miriam's charity was a façade; her friendships, in tatters; her lover, disenchanted. She was a woman whom only a mother could love. Personal plotting included Ellen's wedding plans.

A frequently used pattern in the series was a set number of suspects provided by the client and an ending when an attempt on Desiree's life revealed the killer. Yet in others, she developed her material and let the police take over.

Next books in this series: *Murder Can Cool Off Your Affair* (2002); *Murder Can Rain on Your Shower* (2003)

Claire Sharples

Author: Rebecca Rothenberg

Claire Sharples, one of the new breed of highly educated sleuths, had a Ph.D. in microbiology but had burned out during her postdoctoral experience at MIT. On a more personal level, the end to an affair had left her depressed. An opening at the University of California Citrus Experimentation Field Station in Central California came at the right time.

During *The Bulrush Murders* (Carroll & Graf, 1992), arson and murder marred Claire's arrival at the Station. The valley was torn between the major landowners and the small orchards. The California fieldwork was a totally different experience than Claire's laboratory experiments. Sam

Cooper, the abrupt extension agent, helped Claire acclimate and solve a murder.

The relationship with Sam was stressed by his strong commitment to the sons of his first marriage during *The Dandelion Murders* (Mysterious Press, 1994). Claire had befriended lonely Emil Yankovich, an organic farmer, but found his ambitious brother Bert's heavy use of pesticides unacceptable. The Yankovich brothers became suspects during a half-hearted investigation of the deaths of two immigrant farm workers and a Los Angeles reporter. Dissatisfied with the police department's commitment, Claire moved into the reporter's apartment in a marginal neighborhood and allied herself with the field workers who were exposed to potent pesticides and sexual harassment.

Sam and Claire were estranged in *The Shy Tulip Murders* (Mysterious, 1996). He had someone else in his life, a woman who wanted to share his two children. Claire had made it clear from the start that mothering was not part of her life. She opened new directions for herself: fixing up an isolated cabin, taking on extension duties in the California Central Valley, and an attraction to a young activist. She could not isolate herself from the ill feeling between the environmentalists and loggers, or from the violence that erupted. Sam, visiting the Valley as an expert during the murder investigation, convinced Claire to buy a weapon, but did not invite her back into his life.

Taffy Cannon's *The Tumbleweed Murders* (Perseverance Press, 2001) was a seamless rendition of the book begun by Rebecca Rothenberg. The descriptive material was as lovely as before. The pain and growth of Claire as she moved towards a new relationship was handled with delicacy. The discovery of a long buried skeleton that might be the lost love of aging country music singer Jewell Scoggins captured Claire's sympathy and curiosity. Jewell's subsequent death only amplified Claire's need to know. She found a new ally, Ramon Corarrubas' cousin, Yolie who had been harassed for years for her attempt to focus public attention on an unscrupulous businessman. Claire never really got over Sam Cooper, but she and Ramon were headed for a commitment.

Lori Shepherd

Author: Nancy Atherton

See: Dimity Westwood, page 693.

Rei Shimura

Author: Sujata Massey

Rei Shimura's parents (her Japanese father, a psychiatry professor and American mother, an interior decorator) were permanently located in California. They might not understand Rei's need to move to Japan indefinitely, but they respected it. Their offer of a one-way airline ticket "home" was ongoing. Rei's father had a sister living in Japan who, along with her son Dr. Tom, was a resource at times of trouble. As the series began, Rei was twenty-seven, a small dark-haired woman who subsisted on a vegetarian diet and shared her apartment with a fellow employee. Her Phi Beta Kappa key and master's degree in Asian art history had been of no immediate value. She supported herself by teaching English at Nichiyu (a kitchenware corporation that wanted bilingual employees). Eventually, Rei developed her own business as an "antique shopper" for wealthy Japanese collectors and foreign tourists.

Her insistence on making her own way in Japan still allowed Rei to splurge on a vacation trip to Shiroyama in *The Salaryman's Wife* (Harper-Collins Paperbacks, 1997). The discovery of the nude body of Setsuko, wife of a middle management businessman, in the snow outside the local inn thrust Rei into controversy. She did not believe Setsuko's death to be accidental or suicide. Whom could she trust among her fellow vacationers: the elusive Scottish solicitor Hugh Glendinning; the effusive American widow, Marcele Chapman; certainly not Setsuko's offensive husband? She found answers in Setsuko's personal heritage and a career in an antique wooden box.

Rei's new profession as an antique shopper was at risk in *Zen Attitude* (HarperCollins, 1998). Her expertise fell short when she purchased an expensive *tansu* (dresser) for a client only to learn that she had seriously overestimated its value. She returned to the seller, only to find he had vacated the premises. When he was discovered dead, Rei followed up on the consignee of the *tansu,* who died shortly after her visit. Hugh Glendinning, by now Rei's lover, was preoccupied with the escapades of his younger brother, Angus. Her investigation of the two deaths led to an even more valuable discovery.

Since Rei's affair with Hugh Glendinning had ended, Aunt Norie felt it was time for her to seek an appropriate Japanese husband in *The Flower Master* (HarperCollins, 1999). To that end, she enrolled Rei and herself in the flower arranging class at the Kayama School. Norie was well acquainted with the art of Ikebana and the staff. Too well, perhaps, because teacher

Sakura Sato was found dead with a pair of Norie's pruning shears in her body.

The Floating Girl (HarperCollins, 2000) was a more complex narrative. To earn extra income, Rei took a part-time job as a columnist for the *Gaijin Times*, a publication directed to foreign readers. The owner intended a switch in focus transforming the paper into manga (comic strips). Rei's assignment, a history of manga, led her into doujinski Showa, parodies of the commercial Mars Girl comic. Three former college students produced the Showa. One was murdered after talking to Rei. The case eventually involved the Yakuza (Japanese crime syndicate).

Rei displayed courage but a lack of wisdom in *The Bride's Kimono* (HarperCollins, 2001). A unique kimono, one of those she couriered from a Tokyo museum to the Museum of Asian Art in Washington, D.C., was stolen from her hotel room. A young Japanese woman who may have been connected with the theft was subsequently murdered. The D.C. police department and the Japanese Embassy were suspicious of Rei who had delayed notifying either the authorities or the museum. She measured a new romance against her feelings for Glendinning.

The narratives provided excellent background and a sense of the perplexities faced by someone trying to be loyal to two cultures.

Next book in this series: *The Samurai's Daughter* (2003)

Marla Shore

Author: Nancy J. Cohen

Marla Shore had been haunted by an incident that occurred in her late teens. While babysitting a small child, she had answered an important telephone call, unaware that Tammy had left the house and fallen into the pool. The parents never forgave Marla for their child's death and she never forgave herself. They sued, but the price she paid went higher than that. She spent years educating people about the dangers of unenclosed pools, sought legislation to force owners to fence in pools, and encouraged swimming lessons. It had been very important to Marla's family that she marry well and that she marry a Jewish man. Attorney Stan Kaufman of the firm hired to defend Marla had seemed a perfect choice. Too late, Marla realized that her attraction for Stan was her docility and youth.

After her divorce, she used the settlement money to finance her education and the establishment of a beauty salon in Palm Haven, Florida. By this time, Marla's father had died, but her mother Anita lived nearby. Her only brother was married with children.

Marla's best friend was Tally Riggs, owner of a dress shop. She needed friends, particularly one who owned a dress shop because she was extremely conservative in her attire. The divorce had left her leery of entanglements. She spent considerable time working on environmental causes. Her former interest in gourmet cooking had to be abandoned when she became over-involved in causes. Stan who had remarried pressured Marla to sell jointly owned rental property. She wanted the continued income. His new wife wanted a more expensive home so he wanted the cash.

The events surrounding Tammy's death continued to shadow Marla's life in *Permed to Death* (Kensington, 1999). She and Bertha Kravitz, owner of Sunshine Publications, had been alone in the beauty parlor when Bertha ingested poison. Detective Dalton Vail said only lack of motive kept him from charging Marla with placing the poison in the powdered coffee creamer that was kept at the shop for Bertha's personal use. The motive existed and Marla needed to find the killer before Vail discovered an envelope that disclosed why Marla might want Bertha dead. The killer was aware that Marla who lived with only a small dog (Spooks) for company was vulnerable.

Marla learned very little from her prior experience with murder. In *Hair Raiser* (Kensington, 2000), she used her recovery time from an injury to help her cousin Cynthia in recruiting chefs for a benefit. Someone was determined to sabotage the project—possibly someone on the board of directors of the environmental group holding the benefit. Heedless of Dalton Vail's warnings (they were dating) and undaunted by two murders, she made herself an easy target for very determined criminals.

Marla's connection to murder victim Jolene Myers was merely that of beautician to client, but, as she admitted to her mother, in *Murder by Manicure* (Kensington, 2001), she was bored. Moreover she had been at the Perfect Fit Sports Club when Jolene drowned in the whirlpool. So had a half dozen others who had reason to want Jolene dead. Some good came of her involvement. She bonded with Brianna, Dalton Vail's twelve-year-old daughter.

Next book in this series: *Body Wave* (2002)

Kate Shugak

Author: Dana Stabenow

Kate Shugak was an Aleut Indian in her late twenties when the series began, only five feet tall, 110 pounds, but well able to take care of herself on land and at sea. Her skin was bronze, her hair black, and her eyes light brown. Her father Stephan, who had died when she was a child, had raised Kate to be independent and courageous. Her grandmother, Ekaterina Shugak, who raised Kate, no longer had an official position, but remained the most significant person in the community. Ekaterina, now eighty, and family friend Abel Int-Hout had shared her guardianship after her parents died. Kate left the tundra behind long enough to graduate from the University of Alaska in Fairbanks, but was drawn back to her people and the land they occupied. When arresting a child molester, whom she was forced to kill, Kate's throat had been slashed not only leaving her with an ugly scar, but also impairing her vocal chords. She resigned from the Anchorage District Attorney's office, ended an affair with fellow investigator Jack Morgan and returned to her family village. Kate could handle isolation. She enjoyed chocolate, read extensively, liked The Nashville Network, and had "Mutt," her Malamute for company. After the injury, Kate retreated to land homesteaded by her father.

As *A Cold Day for Murder* (Berkley, 1992) began, Ken Dahl, who had been assigned to find the environmentalist son of a prominent Congressman, had been missing for two weeks. Morgan convinced Kate to search for him because of her superior knowledge of the area. Her special assignment again cost her dearly.

An unidentified killer appeared early in *A Fatal Thaw* (Berkley, 1993) leaving a trail of seemingly unrelated murders, which almost included Kate. Ballistics indicated that the death of a seductive young woman did not fit into the pattern. The intimacy of the community meant her quarry was someone whom Kate knew.

Kate took a different tack in *Dead in the Water* (Berkley, 1993). Tempted by the chance to earn money on a crab fishing boat, she boarded the *Avilda* as a deck hand. Two men had disappeared on the last voyage and the District Attorney's office had to know why.

John King, the CEO of a major oil company in Alaska, was disturbed by evidence that his employees had easy access to drugs during *A Cold-Blooded Business* (Berkley, 1994). Once she was hired as a roustabout, Kate quickly became well enough acquainted with coworkers and staff, to learn that there could be no friendships with drug dealers.

Play with Fire (Berkley, 1995) sent Kate, paraplegic Bobby Clark, and photojournalist Dinah Cookman into the regrowth of a great forest after a fire. While hunting for morels, she found murder and religious mania, but could not bring herself to identify the killer. Like many of those who cherish their isolation, Shugak was critical of vacationers who wanted to share the wilderness for a short time but left it damaged.

Kate's sense of responsibility emerged in *Blood Will Tell* (Putnam, 1996). Her grandmother, a major figure in tribal politics, had been the dominant person in Kate's life. Nevertheless Kate had rejected any suggestion that she might take an active role in the affairs of the native people of Alaska. Ekaterina's age, the efforts to bribe her fellow council members, and the suspicious deaths of two supporters of native rights forced Kate to investigate forces that would open the wilderness to uncontrolled development.

Breakup (Putnam, 1997) described the coming of spring to Alaska; the emergence of the bears from hibernation, often with cubs; the relief of the residents from days of limited sunshine; and the resumption of outdoor life for Kate. Her sense of optimism was dampened when parts of an airplane dropped causing serious damage to her home, garage, snowmobile, and truck. Even more frightening was the discovery of a corpse by representatives of the National Transportation Safety Board while searching the forest near Kate's home. The apprehensive parents of Kate's friend Mandy could not understand why their daughter had abandoned her social position and wealthy lifestyle for Alaska. While giving the visitors a tour, Kate came upon Richard Stewart fleeing from a bear that had attacked and killed his wife, Carol. Kate had the intuitive, deductive skills and the persistence to tie these incidents together while doing some domestic counseling on the side.

A greedy brutal man was murdered in *Killing Grounds* (Putnam, 1998). Still what readers may remember best after reading the narrative is the rush of excitement when the salmon returned, the stubborness of commercial fishermen who plied their trade although hampered by government regulations, and the plight of the elderly natives who needed the fish to survive. Kate wrestled with her distrust of clergymen after her experience with a fanatic pastor. State trooper Jim Chopin came to realize that even though Kate had no official status many tribal members perceived her as the successor to her grandmother's authority.

Nine men and a woman, top executives of a German software corporation, comprised the hunting group that Kate and Jack Morgan guided into the wilderness in *Hunter's Moon* (Putnam, 1999). While Jack and Kate resolved their differences to plan a life together, the hunters exploded into violence, motivated by ambition and greed. Jack's violent death led Kate to the brink of suicide, thwarted only by Mutt's intervention.

As *Midnight Come Again* (St. Martin, 2000) began, Sgt. Jim Chopin of the Alaska State Troopers had failed to locate Kate who had left her homestead, providing no information as to her destination. An undercover assignment with the FBI sent Jim north to Bering. Kate was working there under an assumed name. It took them both to outwit an alliance between Russian terrorists and greedy Americans. It took a near death experience to teach Kate that she wanted to live and to make Chopin aware that he wanted to share her life.

Gradually Kate reembraced life remembering Jack's plea that she care for his son, Johnny. As *The Singing of the Dead* (St. Martin, 2001) began, the boy had hitchhiked from Arizona to Alaska, determined to remain. Kate provided a haven. The next step would be to fight for his custody, as his mother had relinquished his care to an unsympathetic grandmother. For that she would need money. Anne Gondaeff, a candidate for the Alaska State Senate, needed a bodyguard. As murder followed murder within the campaign entourage, author Dana Stabenow skillfully wove in the story of a hardworking hooker during the Gold Rush days. Ethan Int-Houk, a figure from Kate's own past, became a part of her future. A terrific read.

The material about Alaska and its native inhabitants provided an interesting background to well plotted stories. Kate was a credible tough investigator.

Next book in this series: *A Fine and Bitter Snow* (2002)

Jo Beth Sidden

Author: Virginia Lanier

Jo Beth Sidden was a wild, wild woman. Her childhood had been impoverished and her parentage uncertain. Her early marriage to Bubba, a battering psychotic, ended in divorce and his imprisonment. At age twenty-nine she was described as a tall, well-muscled woman. Jo Beth had built a life for herself as the breeder and trainer of bloodhounds in the southern Georgia area where she was raised. She not only bred the dogs, but also schooled police officers to use them. She assisted law enforcement officers in finding victims, killers, and persons lost in the nearby Okefenokee Swamp.

She would not take police referrals to locate bootlegger's stills or marijuana grower's fields. On occasion, she protected friends by destroying such evidence before the federal agents could gather it. Jo Beth did not have an alcohol problem, but she lit one cigarette after another, subsisted on a high caffeine intake when working, and, when under pressure, used "speed" tablets. She never cooked, survived on fast food, and paid a price with indigestion.

With self-assurance and insensitivity, Jo Beth interfered with the marriages and relationships of friends and guests, possibly in one instance, causing a suicide. Her reluctance to share information with the police may have led to a triple murder. She did not hesitate to involve others in her deceptions, including police chiefs and sheriffs with whom she had personal relationships, and a computer hacker "Little Bemis" who provided illegal access to information. Jo Beth had earned many of her enemies, but was innocent of the hatred from Bubba's father, a prominent local citizen. She made efforts to trace her own parentage.

Death in Bloodhound Red (Pineapple Press, 1995) was episodic, detailing Jo Beth's experiences with a boy who died while lost in the swamp, the abuse of an elderly couple, and a returned Southerner whom she helped reclaim his inheritance. The profits enabled Jo Beth to add to her staff at the kennel. She disproved charges that she had attacked Bubba and forced a corrupt sheriff out of office.

The House on Bloodhound Lane (HarperCollins, 1996) had a half-dozen subplots, but focused on the search for a wealthy man whose disaffected sons plotted his kidnapping and potential death.

Jo Beth's disdain for the law extended to Judge Sanford Albee in *A Brace of Bloodhounds* (HarperCollins, 1997). The judge had taken advantage of his housekeeper, Clara Ainsley for years. Her daughter, Gilly, suspected he had also caused Clara's death. Jo Beth was sympathetic to Gilly and provided her with needed refuge. Her more immediate concern was finding the kidnapper of a small boy who had been camping with his family. Locating the child was only the first step; the "good old boys" were reluctant to believe that one of their own could be the culprit.

During *Blind Bloodhound Justice* (HarperCollins, 1998), Jo Beth kept a lot of secrets. Sheriff Hank Cribbs did not believe in coincidences, but he did not want to stir up a controversy. The medical parole of Samuel Debbs, convicted thirty years before of a double murder, was followed by the return of a now adult victim of kidnapping connected to the murders. Debbs sought Jo Beth's help. It seemed unlikely that a bloodhound could bear witness to a crime committed three decades before. Once convinced of Debb's innocence, Jo Beth found a way to pinpoint a killer, yet spare an innocent victim from disclosure. Bubba returned with his leaded baseball bat, but Jo Beth kneed him effectively.

Perhaps Jo Beth's need to be alpha dog in the kennel and on the trail had affected her to the point where she had to dominate in her personal relationships. In *Ten Little Bloodhounds* (HarperCollins, 1999), she paid a price for her disregard for the feelings of those who loved her. Hired first to find a cat, then to identify the killer of the cat's owner, Jo Beth solved her personal problems in a manner that may leave some readers uncomfortable.

Lanier has great imaginative and descriptive powers.

Phoebe Siegel

Author: Sandra West Prowell

Billings, Montana may seem a strange location for an Irish/Jewish private investigator, but Phoebe was no stereotype. She was a member of a large family which included a dead Vietnam veteran, a Catholic priest, a police officer whose death had been ruled a suicide, and a former drug addict. March was always a difficult time for Phoebe because her brother Ben's "suicide" had been attributed to an accusation that he took advantage of a juvenile. Her siblings with whom she maintained a prickly relationship called her "Fee." She had loved her father, a deceased police officer, deeply and still drove his 1949 Chevy truck. Phoebe was in regular contact with her mother, but shared her home only with a truculent cat, "Stud."

During *By Evil Means* (Walker, 1993), Mary Kuntz, mother of Jennifer who had made the accusation against Phoebe's brother, Ben, sought help. Jennifer, then receiving treatment at a nearby sanitarium, had undergone a personality change. Phoebe's investigation gave her a chance to clear Ben's reputation.

The conflicts within the Native American community in Montana surfaced in *The Killing of Monday Brown* (Walker, 1994). Matthew Wolf, leader of a traditional faction, was accused when suspected grave robber Monday Brown was murdered. The Wolf family hired Phoebe to prove Matthew's innocence, giving her custody of artifacts discovered in Matthew's truck. Relying on her dreams and information from hookers, Phoebe believed that a German collector was the killer, but learned otherwise. The killer, when cornered, took her own life.

When Wallflowers Die (Walker, 1996) was exceptional. Phoebe investigated the decades old death of a vulnerable young woman She connected it to the death of an ex-convict whose sister had been killed that same day. Sustained by her family, then in the throes of a religious crisis, and by Deputy Kyle Old Wolf she found an unrepentant killer and exposed a conspiracy to delay justice. Kyle's platonic friendship had become very important to Phoebe.

Phoebe was competitive with most current private investigators.

Emily Silver

Author: Carol Brennan

Emily Silver had never adjusted to the structured life forced upon her at age nine by a rigid grandmother. Until then she had shared her parents' erratic lifestyle. Tuck, the father whom she adored had been an unsuccessful playwright subsidized by his wealthy mother. Celia, her mother, an actress, kept the family afloat by working as a waitress. Their deaths had been officially designated as murder/suicide. As soon as she could, Emily ran off to seek a career as an actress. After limited success in Hollywood, she moved in with trucker Mike Florio, who provided safety within freedom, something she needed. He was seventeen years older and divorced, tolerant and patient, warm and accepting.

During *In the Dark* (Putnam, 1994), Emily's vague recollection that a third person with an unusual raspy voice had been in the apartment the night her parents were killed was reawakened. She heard that same voice in a darkened movie theatre. Mike calmed her hysteria by promising to investigate, but his visit to New York ended in his death. With only the name of "Dev," Mike's best friend as a lead, Emily went to New York City to solve Mike's murder and the deaths of her parents. She reconnected with her dying grandmother, and located Dev, a.k.a. Paul Hannagan, now an investigator for a legal firm. After interviewing friends of Tuck and Celia, Emily came to know her parents as individuals, flawed in ways she had not expected. Emily and Dev's investigation and their sexual relationship forced her to rethink who she was.

In *Chill of Summer* (Putnam, 1995), murder again struck close to home. Emily and Dev lived in the house her grandmother had bequeathed her. Zach Terman, a womanizing author married to Emily's high school roommate, was left dead in the basement food locker. Emily investigated the tangled relationships of her friends until she found the guilty parties. On a personal level she coped with the presence of Liam, Dev's abusive father who now reeked of repentance and alcohol; and Dev's writer's block, which had plagued him since his first successful book.

Margo Simon

Author: Janice Steinberg

Margo Simon had stress at home and at work. As the series began, she was a part-time reporter for San Diego's public radio station, KSDR, hoping for full time work. Her husband Barry Dawes, a professor at the Torrey Institute of Oceanography, expected their life to include regular visitation by the children of his first marriage: Jenny, a volatile teenager, and David, more amenable at age eleven. The household also included a golden retriever (Frodo) and a cat (Grimalkin).

She had been a rebellious student at the University of Wisconsin in Madison, where protests were commonplace; then, dropped out of college to follow her lover Rick to New Mexico where they subsisted on her pottery and his painting. When that relationship ended, Margo moved to San Diego. Work in a bookstore led to appearances on public radio. Enthusiastic about radio journalism, Margo returned to college and graduated from San Diego State. Her great personal enjoyments were dance and pottery, both of which relaxed her high-strung personality.

Margo covered a major art exhibition at the Capelli Foundation in *Death of a Postmodernist* (Berkley, 1995). Her prior research on the displaying artists provided insights into their personal lives. When installation artist Susana Contreras was killed on site, KSDR kept Margo on the story. The suspects were an eclectic group of artists, promoters, administrators, and critics. The most crucial observer might be a homeless woman whom Susana had befriended. Margo's success in the Capelli murder led to a full-time position on the staff, extended to include general news.

Her assignment in *Death Crosses the Border* (Berkley, 1995) was to evaluate the impact of maquiladoras, American-owned factories located across the Mexican border. The death of a clergyman, who had disclosed the miserable living conditions of the workers, was the beginning of Margo's journey into corporate deceit, religious duplicity, and political guile.

Margo's friend Paula Chopin glimpsed, but did not recognize, a killer/arsonist as *Death-Fires Dance* (Berkley, 1996) opened. Margo was drawn into the deaths of several "healers," not only through her reporting, but also as stepmother to Jenny, whose troubled boyfriend was a suspect. She almost lost her life to a forest fire while trailing the serial murderer.

Margo's interactions with Barry and the safety of her stepson David were at risk in *The Dead Man and the Sea* (Berkley, 1997). A cruel and seductive faculty member at Torrey Institution of Oceanography had been murdered. The problem was the large number of persons who had feared and hated the victim. Margo had finally realized that her nightmares and flashbacks were symptoms of Post-Traumatic Stress Syndrome.

Leaving her marital problems unsolved at home, Margo journeyed to Israel in *Death in a City of Mystics* (Berkley, 1998). She and her sister Audrey were concerned because their mother Alice had been poisoned. The sisters were aware that Alice had partial amnesia when she became conscious. They were not totally satisfied with the explanations of Batsheva Halevi, Alice's mentor in Israel. When he was murdered, Audrey was suspected until a letter sent by Alice before her illness was discovered. Margo's newfound connection with her religion released her from feelings of panic, fear and resentment. She left determined to make her marriage work. There was interesting background material as to the conflicts within the Israeli community.

Margo was an interesting, if not always endearing, sleuth who accepted challenges and persisted in her investigations, wondering at times if she had become too preoccupied with professional success. Author Janice Steinberg is an excellent writer.

Barbara Simons

Author: Carole Epstein

Barbara Simons had been terminated as vice president in charge of public relations at Pan Canadian Air when it was absorbed by an American corporation. She was looking for something to do. Her parents had reached a happy level in their marriage. Her father was a retired women's sportswear designer, and her mother waited on him hand and foot. Her mother was a terrible cook, but her dad never seemed to notice. Barbara was addicted to Coca-Cola and cigarettes, but did not drink alcohol. She was a tall auburn haired English-Canadian, as distinguished from the French Canadians among whom she lived and had worked in Montreal, Quebec. She was fluent in both English and French. Barbara had no tolerance for provincial nationalism, but had to be careful whom she offended.

In her forties, Barbara was unmarried, but had maintained a long-term peripatetic relationship with Sam Levine, who lived with his significant other in Connecticut. That part of her life was also close to crisis. Sam wanted to meet with her in Chicago to discuss their future…marriage…the end of the relationship…or something in between with more structure than they currently shared. Barbara was used to living well after many years of profitable employment. Her severance package allowed her to continue the good life for two years, and she had no incentive to make decisions as to her career future. She was sensitive to speech patterns as indicating the social class and educational background of others, and had disdain for those who did not meet her standards. She had one weakness, her great affection for her godchild, eight-year-old Robert, the son of a friend.

In *Perilous Friends* (Walker, 1996), Barbara showed herself capable of loyalty to her friends. Susan Porter's estranged husband Frank shared an apartment with a "Blonde Bimbo." Joanne Cowan, an investigative television reporter, was probing rumors of a gay tobacco smuggling ring. Her assistance was not without risk. After she and Susan searched Frank's apartment, someone murdered him. Barbara's undercover role as a lesbian gangster infiltrating the cigarette smuggling put her at odds with major

Mafia figures. She surmounted considerable odds to survive this turmoil; then awaited Sam's visit with a Scarlet O'Hara like attitude of "I'll deal with that tomorrow."

Sam's visit never came off as *Perilous Relations* (Walker, 1997) began. Instead, she renewed her acquaintance with handsome Sgt. Greg Allard. While "riding along" in a police car, she became embroiled in the death of Walter Whitestone, who had been her boss at Pan Canada Airlines. His wife, sister, past and current mistresses, all of whom were suspects, sought Barbara's help in proving someone else guilty. The police considered Barbara as just another suspect so she had personal motivation for finding the killer. She managed to subdue him without police assistance.

Cecily Sinclair
Author: Kate Kingsbury, pseudonym for Doreen Roberts

Cecily Sinclair was the primary protagonist of the Pennyfoot Hotel series. She and her husband had transformed a deteriorating country estate house into a charming hotel frequented by the rich and idle of the English Nineteenth Century. Unfortunately, her husband, Major James Sinclair, died of malaria soon after the project was completed. He left his friend and manager Baxter to assist Cecily. Baxter came to care for Cecily, but he was almost as frigid as the coastal weather, and could not think of her in such personal terms. Cecily, a tall warm-blooded woman in her early forties whose light brown hair was beginning to gray, was lonely. She was unsuccessful in her efforts to induce Baxter to be more informal in their contacts. She did pressure him into sharing his light cigars with her, although he thoroughly disapproved.

Cecily, who had five brothers, was an active daring woman with little formal education but extensive experience traveling with her husband during his military service. She and James had two sons, both of whom were serving overseas as the series began. The series regulars from the village included Phoebe Carter-Holmes, mother of the vicar who assisted in social events at the hotel; Madeline Pengrath, whose special powers aroused fear in the villagers; and several regular guests. Each narrative had at least one semi-humorous subplot connected with guests and one involving relationships among the servants. The hotel, which catered to those seeking discretion, offered gambling and secluded accommodations for men who were accompanied by women to whom they were not married.

In *Room with a Clue* (Jove, 1993), loose bricks from a hotel parapet were believed to have caused the death of a member of the nobility recently married to a younger, poorer man. The bereaved husband was arrested for the murder, but Cecily and Baxter proved his innocence.

In *Do Not Disturb* (Jove, 1994), Madeline was suspected when two men died amidst quarrels relating to a new lighthouse intended to inhibit smuggling. A loyal friend, Cecily burglarized a corpse to get a list of victims, and picked up enough medical knowledge to explain the mysterious deaths.

Service for Two (Berkley, 1994) had an aura of evil, beginning with the substitution of a corpse in Dr. McDuff's casket. The body was that of a London criminal. Using Baxter to gather information from the villagers, Cecily noted that a series of robberies had taken place at the homes of hotel guests.

The Radley family had gathered at Pennyfoot during the off-season in *Eat, Drink, and Be Buried* (Berkley, 1994). The corpse of Lady Sherborne was found tied to a maypole on the Grange. The Maypole Dance was a vital spring festival in the area. Cecily questioned other family members even though they resented her interference.

During *Check-out Time* (Berkley, 1995), Michael, Cecily's son, returned to the village with an African bride who became a suspect in the murder of an obnoxious hotel guest.

In *Grounds for Murder* (Berkley, 1995), housemaid Gertie awaited the delivery of her child (turned out to be twins); Baxter inched closer to a personal relationship with Cecily; and a multi-personality maid created confusion among the staff. Nevertheless, Cecily involved herself and Baxter in the murders of gypsy women in the area, using her friend Madeline Pengrath as bait.

Kilted Scotsmen invaded the community during *Pay the Piper* (Berkley, 1996). They stayed at the Pennyfoot en route to a London competition. After a hotel footman found a corpse in the butcher shop cellar, the proprietor was charged with murder. His wife begged Cecily to prove otherwise, and she did. She was less successful in working out her relationship with Michael and his pregnant wife. They returned to Africa.

An even greater blow to her pride awaited Cecily in *Chivalry Is Dead* (Berkley, 1996). She discovered the unwitting killer of a staff member and solved a kidnapping, but her hopes for the future were dashed by Baxter's announcement that he was seeking employment elsewhere.

Baxter returned in *Ring for Tomb Service* (Berkley, 1997). He had changed. He was self sufficient and ready to approach Cecily as an equal. She had come to realize how important he was in her life, but was far too busy hosting a bicycle club, securing the return of a sacred vessel, and finding a killer, to listen to his plans.

Cecily introduced Baxter to staff as her business partner in *Death with Reservations* (Berkley, 1998). She had a more serious problem to consider. Among her guests were a pregnant music hall singer, her titled lover, and his wife. Murder must be avoided, if possible.

Turnover at the Pennyfoot accelerated as illness and ambition struck. In *Dying Room Only* (Berkley, 1998), when a magician's assistant disappeared and was discovered dead, Cecily could not leave the solution of the case to the incompetent police. Times had changed in England and the clientele at the Pennyfoot had deteriorated in numbers and in quality.

In *Maid to Murder* (Berkley, 1999), the servants looked elsewhere for their futures as one final killer wreaked havoc with the downstairs staff. The series ended with grace. Multiple murders were not good publicity for an establishment.

These were light and entertaining, worth the paperback price, but the romance wore thin as the slow dance between Cecily and Baxter dragged on. Diversions like maid Doris' hopes for a musical career helped. Cecily and Baxter, now married, returned in *No Clue at the Inn* (Berkeley, 2003). Kingsbury, a.k.a. Roberts, has a new series featuring Elizabeth Hartley Compton.

Sydney Sloane

Author: Randye Lordon

Sydney Sloane was a tall strawberry-blonde private investigator in her late thirties, who lived in New York City. She had been a police officer before opening an agency with partner, Max Cabe. Max, a chronic philanderer, deluded himself that he could woo Sydney from her lesbian orientation. Sydney's lover, a sculptor, had left her to study in Europe. Her mother had died of cancer. Her father, an attorney, was murdered in a courtroom by a pedophile. Sydney had never believed that her older brother David, who had a criminal record, had been killed in Israel.

In *Brotherly Love* (St. Martin, 1993), Sydney recognized David as an escaped murder suspect pictured in the newspapers. He had been cruel and sadistic, but she did not believe he was a killer. She set out to prove his innocence with the help of Gilbert Jackson, a family friend in the Police Department and her Aunt Minnie, an unconventional senior citizen. In the course of her investigation, Sydney became involved with the victim's daughter, and discovered that she had a nephew.

Sister's Keeper (St. Martin, 1994) continued the focus on personal relationships. Caterer Zoe Freeman had grown up within the Sloane family, so her death in a traffic accident captured Sydney's attention. Even more so, because Zoe had built up a second identity, which indicated that she might be planning to disappear. The extended narrative also involved Sydney's sister Nora, who formed an attachment to a possible killer.

Father Forgive Me (Avon, 1997) found Sydney depressed. Debi, the fifteen-year-old girl whom she had traced for her family, jumped off a rooftop to her death. This might not have been the right time for Sydney to take on an investigation of the death of young Peter Long, found with drug paraphernalia on the scene. The police were willing to accept a suicide determination. Peter's sister Vanessa said he had been murdered. Either way, his death was an inconvenience to Wallace, his wealthy father, preparing to run for governor of his state, and about to introduce an improved computer chip that would enhance his business. Sydney took considerable personal risks to explore the relationships within the Long family and Wallace's business associates.

During *Mother May I* (Avon, 1998), Sydney reached out to a friend of her beloved Aunt Minnie. She proved that young Dr. Michael Callahan was innocent of the death of his wife. If so, of what was Callahan guilty? He had preferred prison to disclosing where he had been (and with whom) at the time his wife died. Sydney's affection for a ninety-two-year-old client was tinged with an awareness of her own vulnerability to the aging process. On a happier note, she and her current lover Leslie added a stray mixed breed pup, Auggie to their household.

Uncle Mitch had been dear to Sydney in her childhood, but totally rejected her when she revealed her homosexuality. Nevertheless, when Mitch was charged with arson and homicide in *Say Uncle* (Avon, 1999), his children came to Sydney for help. The family tie prevailed but led her into mayhem, more murder and an escape from a harrowing new career. Uncle Mitch had secrets of his own.

Sydney had to be coerced by Leslie to travel abroad in *East of Niece* (St. Martin, 2001). She took consolation in the fact that she could visit her niece Vickie and Vickie's fiancé, Gavin Mason. As she and Leslie traveled the treacherous roads along the Mediterranean, they passed an accident. Even before Sydney learned that the victims were Gavin's parents, she suspected foul play. Gavin's disappearance after a secret marriage brought him to the attention of the police. They had discovered that the brakes on his parents' car had been damaged. Sydney received attention herself when her companion at a bistro died after eating a poisoned croissant. The investigation answered two questions for Sydney. "Yes," she wanted to continue as a private investigator, but "no," never again outside the United States.

These were above average narratives.

Next book in this series: *Son of a Gun* (2003)

Grace Smith

Author: Liz Evans

By age twenty-eight, Grace Smith had undergone a considerable amount of rejection. Raised by a dedicated police officer father, she had joined the force. When she was set up in order to free a guilty defendant, her father and the police department both believed her guilty of accepting a bribe. She became a private investigator but the police officers she encountered in her cases remembered why she had been forced out. Her father, now confined to a wheelchair by an injury incurred in the line of duty, was even less forgiving. He has not spoken to her since her dismissal. Grace had one sister, married with children, and one brother.

The life she had put together since then was haphazard. Her professional status was as part of Vetch International Associates, a commune of six self-employed detectives all paying Mr. Vetch for the space and services provided. Vetch tossed his least rewarding cases to Grace. Her home in Seatown on the English coast was equally unstable, a basement apartment in a four story Edwardian house. Rent free, but hardly secure. Over a period of time she developed friendships, but it wasn't easy. She was well known for scrounging the use of phones, food, and equipment from other members of the commune.

Without money to pay her share of the office expenses as *Who Killed Marilyn Monroe?* (Oriel, 1997) began, Grace had no choice but to take on the investigation of Marilyn Monroe's death, even after she learned that Marilyn was a donkey. December Drysdale ran the family business—donkey rides for children on the beachfront. He was devoted to his beasts, naming them after his favorite American film actresses and actors. The fact that Marilyn had her throat slashed on the same night as a young prostitute convinced Grace to concentrate on the human murder. No one was paying her for this line of investigation. She managed to irritate both December and the police department. She remained one step ahead of everyone but the unsuspected killer. She did meet December's son Kevin who ran the Electric Daffodil, a popular pub, and found him very stimulating.

Even though she ended up with some doubts about her abilities as a private investigator in *JFK is Missing!* (Orion, 1998), Grace had every reason to be proud of herself. She had tied together two complex cases: Henry Summerstone's search for a woman he hardly knew (or so he said) and a spoiled teenager's search for a married workman for whom she had a fancy. Even when her mistakes in deduction made her vulnerable, Grace persisted. Finally, she had her personal life in sufficient order that she could reject a role as "the other woman."

Barbra Delaney, Grace's new client in *Don't Mess with Mrs. In-Between* (Orion, 2000) could be charitably referred to as eccentric. Married first to a philanderer who left her with two children, one of whom died of leukemia, Barbra struck it rich with her second husband from whom she inherited a fortune. An accident caused her to consider a will. She intended to disinherit her only living child and divide her fortune among three strangers, identified only by pictures she had taken of them. Grace's assignment was to identify the prospects and evaluate their worthiness for the bequests. There were subjective decisions to make since cross-dressing, Native American enthusiasts, and murder were included in the mix.

Plotting was as devious as ever in *Barking* (Orion, 2001) when Grace agreed to help accountant Stuart Roberts investigate the connection between a decades old murder and his own repressed memories as taped by his therapist. Aided by a flatulent part-bulldog, Grace worked her way through four separate murders, stretching back into the past. Amazing Grace.

Jane Smith

Author: Christine T. Jorgensen

See: Stella the Stargazer, page 616.

Marguerite Smith

Author: Marie Lee

Marguerite Smith began life as a Southie, the daughter of an Irish-American father and a French-Canadian mother. She moved out of South Boston when she was granted a scholarship to Radcliffe College. During college she met Joseph Smith, scion of a wealthy and prominent New England family, and with misgivings from both sets of parents, they married. After a seemingly happy marriage, which produced son Cornelius (Neil) and Alexandra (Alex), Joe sued for divorce to marry a younger woman. Marguerite could earn her own living as a teacher and was granted the house in the divorce proceedings, but her way of life was irreparably altered. Joe provided for the children, even subsidizing college, but Marguerite was deeply hurt by his rejection.

Marguerite had taken early retirement in her fifties as *The Curious Cape Cod Skull* (Avalon, 1995) began. She had been preparing for a visit from her niece Portia's husband, Jeb, and their children, when she discovered a corpse in her shed. Jeb's insistence that he had not been on the premises put him high on the list of suspects when his alibi was broken. With an assist from her dog Rusty, Marguerite also found an ancient skull that tied into a list of library books found on the victim, archeologist Dr. Peter Dafoe. For Portia's sake, Marguerite delved into the books re Viking travels in America, until she discovered a motive that matched the crime.

Although she no longer taught, Marguerite kept an interest in her former students. She and her family were present at the internment of an elderly Native-American when a fresh corpse was discovered in the gravesite as *The Fatal Cape Cod Funeral* (Avalon, 1996) began. The victim, Ethan Quade, was the father of Rose, whom Marguerite had taught years before. Rose became a bone of contention as her maternal grandfather sought custody, as did Ethan's sister. Was Ethan guilty of embezzling funds from his employer? Red herrings abounded as Marguerite set herself to help Rose and clear Ethan's name.

Longing for the past and the temptation for a new romance brought Marguerite trouble in *The Mysterious Cape Cod Manuscript* (Avalon, 1997). Joe, her former husband, sought her help in finding an obscure book that would restore him to wealth. A handsome stranger made Marguerite look ridiculous in the eyes of the police when Joe was murdered. It took their daughter Alexandra, her husband Preston, and niece Portia to defend Marguerite from charges of double murder. Even the unpleasant police sergeant who suspected her was more effective than Marguerite in this case. She never suspected the killer even though she was on the trail of the mysterious journal.

A pleasant series with plotting difficulties that can be overlooked.

Guadalupe "Lupe" Solano

Author: Carolina Garcia-Aguilera

Lupe Solano was a tiny dark-haired Cuban-American, the U.S.-born daughter of refugees from Castro. Although her mother died of cancer, Lupe's father became a prosperous contractor, eager to gather his family together on his lavish Florida estate. Lupe had two sisters: Fatima, who moved back into the family home with her two children after a divorce, and Lourdes who became a nun. After two years in college and a six-year apprenticeship, Lupe opened her own investigative agency. Ostensibly a Catholic, she shared her sexual favors with a select and seemingly non-competitive group of lovers.

In *Bloody Waters* (Putnam, 1996), Jose Moreno, an adoptive father, came to Lupe for help. His cancer-stricken daughter Michelle needed a bone marrow transplant. Lupe had met a child suffering from a similar illness while at her dying mother's bedside, and could not refuse. However, she had no idea then what a task she had undertaken: sleazy adoption attorneys, corrupt doctors, but happily, a mother superior who would deal with them.

When Lupe met with her best friend, Margarita, as *Bloody Shame* (Putnam, 1997) began, she seemed distraught but would not share her concerns. Preoccupied with assisting her sometime lover/attorney Tommy McDonald on a murder case, Lupe did not insist. When the pregnant Margarita died in a car accident, Lupe concentrated on charges against Tommy's client, a jeweler who claimed self-defense in the death of a purported burglar.

Luis Delgado, the Cuban refugee who repaired Lupe's Mercedes in *Bloody Secrets* (Putnam, 1998), did not share all of his past with her. His father had been defrauded of his share of diamonds smuggled into the United States by Miguel de la Torre, now a wealthy and prominent Cuba-American. Someone hired a professional killer to assassinate Luis after he came to the United States. Luis persuaded the man to take a diamond instead. The de la Torre's were friends of Lupe's family, sharing her father's obsession of returning to a capitalist Cuba. Lupe became so enamored of Luis that she was willing to embezzle funds for him. Good friends, including a call girl who would like to become a private investigator, helped Lupe, in spite of herself.

Two major conflicts in Lupe's life surfaced in *A Miracle in Paradise* (Avon, 1999). Although she did not practice her faith, she remained emotionally attached to the Catholic Church. Her Cuban heritage was extremely important to her, but, as with others of her generation, she realized that the past could not be regained. News that a miracle would occur at the Shrine of the Cuban Virgin on October 10th, a significant date in Cuban history, put these loyalties to the test. The rationale for the murders that followed the announcement tested credulity.

Lupe had never been to Havana. In *Havana Heat* (Morrow, 2000), it took two murders and the chance to recover a priceless tapestry to motivate her to make the trip. She risked her life and her current relationship with left-wing Cuban attorney Alvaro Mendoza to get there. Then she had to fight her way out.

The loyalty of many Cuban exiles to their homeland and to one another was very powerful. In *Bitter Sugar* (Morrow, 2001), Lupe agreed to help her father's childhood friend Tio Roman Suarez. Suarez had been contacted by a nephew with regard to an offer to purchase family interests in

Cuban sugar mills appropriated by the Castro government. When the nephew was murdered after a quarrel, Tio Roman was charged with murder. As Lupe learned, loyalty could go only so far. There were problems in the Suarez family that had nothing to do with land or money.

Lots of local color; good but not great.

Bretta Solomon

Author: Janis Harrison

Her mother, Lillie, now deceased, had raised Bretta Solomon. Her father, who had tired of farming, deserted his family when she was eight. He did not totally forget them when his invention of a branding "gizmo" made him rich. Until Lillie died he sent an annual check. After that, Bretta merely received a birthday card and grapefruit for Christmas. She was unaware of whether he had remarried and/or had other children. Her husband, Carl, a deputy sheriff, had shared his cases with Bretta, valuing her insights. He gave her credit when she assisted in an investigation, which did not sit well with his boss, Sheriff Sid Hancock. Carl died of a heart attack, leaving Bretta a childless widow in River City, Missouri.

Bretta opened a flower shop and made other changes in her lifestyle. By nature she was a highly organized person, self-described as a "planner." Formerly addicted to sweets, she cut back and lost weight. In an effort to keep her slimmer figure, she became an innovative cook.

In *Roots of Murder* (St. Martin, 1999), the death of an Amish farmer who had grown many of Bretta's flowers reawakened her interest in criminal investigations. Neither the ire of the Amish bishop nor a python in her car could stop Bretta once she made up her mind. Two little girls, one whose life she altered and one whose life she saved, had reasons to be grateful.

Using Carl's insurance money, Bretta purchased the Beauchamp mansion in *Murder Sets Seed* (St. Martin, 2000). Her plan was to turn it into a boarding house. The seller, Cameo Beauchamp-Sinclair, had an agenda of her own—bypassing her daughter Topaz, and adding Bretta to the sinister line of Beauchamp women. At a holiday dinner, Cameo announced that she was being blackmailed. Within hours, she had been strangled with Christmas lights. Cameo cancelled Bretta's house debt, but the murders had not ended. Bretta had ignored an invitation to visit her father in his Texas home. He came to hers.

During *Lilies That Fester* (St. Martin, 2001), Bretta expected hard work and challenges to her authority as head of the design contest at the Southern Missouri Flower Arrangers convention in Branson. She did not anticipate becoming involved in the desperate pleas of an elderly couple who wanted justice for the death of their daughter, nor more pleasantly meeting a man who turned her thoughts to a romantic future. She realized that Carl would want her to go on living. The plight of overweight women was handled with insight and compassion.

Next book in this series: *A Deadly Bouquet* (2002)

Helen Sorby

Author: Karen Rose Cercone

Helen Sorby went beyond unconventional for Pittsburgh in 1905. She was a feminist, pro-temperance, pro-union, and a socialist in a city controlled by industrialists. Since the death of their parents, she and her twin brother Tom, mapmaker for a fire insurance company, shared a residence, but not political views. Tom, deeply devoted to his sister, was far more accepting of the conditions. Both siblings were closely connected to their aunt, Patricia McGregor a.k.a. Aunt Pat, a comfortably situated widow. She was a strong supporter of the South Side Temperance League and had enlisted Helen to serve as her secretary.

Although she had only perfunctory allegiance to her Catholic upbringing, Helen had an elderly cousin, Father Regis Gillan, who counseled her at times. Helen's socialist views did not keep her from accepting help from Aunt Pat who had many valuable ties in the financial and industrial community, or from recruiting Tom to help her in her independent investigations. She showed great disdain for Milo Kachigan as an employee of a corrupt county detective service, but worked with him regularly. Her personal feelings were divided. She harangued him; then, was irritated when he did not come back for more.

Helen had a "marriage" that she initially sought to have annulled. The annulment became unnecessary when she learned that James Foster Barton was a bigamist. He had, in fact, made a habit of marrying well-to-do young women. Helen was not wealthy; however, she and Tom had expectations from Aunt Pat. They managed on Thomas' salary and the income Helen received from her freelance writing for New York City magazines. This connection provided her with access when she investigated. The local media were controlled by the oligarchy. She was writing *The Benefits of Socialized Pension Systems for Laboring Men*, a topic not likely to be a best seller. Helen lacked Thomas' training, but she was an excellent artist and draftsman. Her sketches were valuable to the police department in several cases. In her spare time she volunteered at Carey Settlement House.

Over the narratives, Helen developed a personal and professional alliance with Milo Kachigan, a detective with the Pittsburgh police department and later with the Allegheny County detective bureau. Milo had his own secret, his Armenian background. To be hired and promoted in his profession, it was obligatory to be Irish. The name Kachigan, Americanized at immigration, sounded Irish enough to get him hired. His presence at the Ancient Order of Hibernian hangouts didn't hurt. By the time he was "outed," he and Helen had been successful in their joint cases.

In *Steel Ashes* (Berkley, 1997), Milo and Helen met at the site of an arson/double murder. Based on his position and Irish sounding name, Helen expected him to be a mendacious bigot, oppressing more recent immigrants. Still they made a truce to learn who killed steelworker Josef Janczek and his socialist wife Lide. Bernard K. Flinn, slum landlord and head of the industrial police, was an obvious threat to learning the truth. Attempts to kill or injure Milo and Helen failed but not for want of trying. They were less surprised to find betrayal from coworkers than they were by support from unlikely allies.

Helen's disdain for authority, including Milo, made it difficult for her to cooperative with him in *Blood Tracks* (Berkley, 1998). Milo contended with police corruption in a more personal way. He was framed on charges of bribery, but was never prosecuted so that his boss, Big Roge McGara could hold that possibility over his head. Both Helen and Milo were determined to find the killer of a brilliant inventor on the payroll of Westinghouse Electric. The clashes between Westinghouse and the Penn railroad, a primary consumer of Westinghouse products, formed the background for the case. In this troubled atmosphere, Helen and Milo worked together. They got close enough to count.

Coal Bones (Berkley, 1999) had as many twists and turns as the coal mines. Milo investigated the murder of a coal company employee, initially without knowing the identity of the victim or of the young Italian man apprehended near the body. It was a revelation to him that Helen's Italian relatives had a hand in much of the local villainy. She was balancing two projects: locating the missing daughter of a coal baron and coverage of a coal strike by desperate miners. One impediment to a marriage between Milo and Helen was removed, but she clung to her belief in free love.

An excellent series.

Anna Southwood

Author: Jean Bedford

Anna Southwood, the daughter of an Australian solicitor and his wife, had graduated from a Sydney University without any strong career goals. She married Clyde, a businessman whom she had met while in college, without much scrutiny as to what business he was in. Their life together floundered and they were separated when he died. The death left Anna a wealthy widow with an expensive home in Balmain. A tiny redhead who had been a "tomboy" as a child, Anna decided to spend Clyde's ill-gotten money to help others. She underwrote a monthly investigative newspaper for her friend, Lorna Temples, dabbled in Cordon Bleu cooking, radical politics, and detecting. The latter she accomplished by subdividing her home into residence and office, and employing an out-of-work actor to front as the primary detective.

When, in *Worse Than Death* (HarperCollins, 1991, cowritten with Tom Kelly), Anna investigated the disappearance of a fourteen-year-old girl, it was to defend the child's mother from a charge of murder. Her efforts to connect the missing child with a similar incident in the past brought her into danger, but uncovered a nasty scandal. Undeterred by the risks, Anna continued both her altruism and her struggling agency.

A police officer sent Hilda Trelawney to Anna in *To Make a Killing* (HarperCollins, 1994). Hilda had never accepted the police decision that the death of her environmentalist husband was an accident. Among the potential suspects were right-wing fanatics, real estate developers and tame politicians. They fought environmental legislation and the location of group homes for the developmentally disabled. Anna traced the family relationships that were the real cause of the murder, and met attractive police sergeant Ian McNeath, who became her lover.

By *Signs of Murder* (Angus & Robertson, Australia 1994), Anna realized that she needed her own qualification as a private investigator. Hearing-impaired social worker Fiona Galloway hired Anna because she had been receiving threatening letters. Fiona connected the threats to Jackie Sims, a developmentally disabled adult who had been convicted of rape and murder. When Fiona was badly beaten, Anna coopened the Sims case to find the real killer.

Anna matured into a hard-edged investigator. The Australian series showed promise.

Diana Speed

Author: Tony Gibbs, pseudonym for Wolcott Gibbs, Jr.

Diana Speed, who had investigative experience from ten years in U. S. State Department Intelligence, was currently occupied as a troubleshooter for reclusive billionaire Roger "Rajah" Channing. She was a tall ash-blonde, educated at Wellesley and a member of a socially prominent family. Her mother was a French Vicomtesse. Diana's former husband had been a Congressman. Disliking the artificiality of the Washington scene, she relocated in New York City as an executive in Channing's publishing company, Wild-Freeman.

Patrick Sarsfield, writer of historical romances, came to Wild-Freeman with an unusual offer as *Shadow Queen* (Mysterious Press, 1992) opened. An elderly woman and her daughter, Marie, who were purported to be direct descendants of Mary, Queen of Scots, had possession of documents in which startling revelations were made. Sarsfield was murdered before he could deliver. The documents attracted both those who wished to save the British monarchy from embarrassment, and those who realized their commercial value. Diana sacrificed her relationship with Englishman Alan Trowbridge to uncover a plot to steal the material and dispose of Marie, the young "pretender."

During *Capitol Offense* (Mysterious Press, 1995), Diana developed a special rapport with recovering alcoholic Eric Szabo, another of Channing's investigators. They had not been expected to cooperate. Szabo was placed in Wild-Freeman as an editor, from which position he and Diana probed the death of a power-hungry U.S. Senator. The killer of the politician could be a young woman with whom Rajah Channing had close ties.

Author Tony Gibbs was also the author of series featuring Lt. Tory Lennox in this volume and Gillian Verdean in Volume 2.

Lee Squires

Author: Christine Andreae

A mid-life crisis posed by the death of her four-year-old daughter, Rachel, from leukemia and the dissolution of her marriage, caused Lee Squires to abandon her career as an English professor and poetess and her opulent lifestyle in Washington D.C. She managed without a permanent residence, housesat on a short-term basis, and took jobs whether they were academic or culinary as they came along. When under pressure, Lee contacted her mother, a practicing psychotherapist who lived in a communal setting back East.

In *Trail of Murder* (St. Martin, 1992), Lee signed on as cook for a Montana wilderness expedition. She knew little about the tour operator, an Native American entrepreneur, or the wealthy participants. A series of accidents occurred, one fatal, within the close-knit group, exposing their fears and disloyalties. The adventure produced a romance with police officer Luke Donner, who was separated from his wife.

In *Grizzly* (St. Martin, 1994), tired of reading student papers, Lee took a break to serve as the cook at the J-E cattle ranch, where she and her family had often spent vacations. Lee had never forgotten the Fife brothers, whose parents had owned the J-E. Dave and his wife were now running the dude and cattle ranch, while "Mac," who had inherited the land, was obsessed by his study of grizzly bears. Lee entertained Japanese guests who were interested in purchasing the property. She located a grizzly killer, who had murdered a persistent reporter. Lee's affair with Donner ended when he returned to his wife and family. She resumed teaching on a part-time basis and returned to her poetry, but the lure of the wilderness was still a potent influence in her life.

As *A Small Target* (St. Martin, 1996) began, old friend Pete Bonsecours convinced Lee to cook for a small group journeying up to Lost Pipe Lake near the Flathead Indian lands. The party included a Los Angeles developer who wanted to locate a ski resort in the area and an environmental activist. Both were murdered at the site. Luke Donner reappeared to conduct the investigation with the help of Lee's insights and negotiating skills. She had misgivings about her role in capturing a wounded suspect.

Lee was not a happy heroine, but was a memorable character.

Stella the Stargazer a.k.a Jane Smith

Author: Christine T. Jorgensen

Jane Smith, bored and burned out by her work as an accountant, made a radical change in her appearance, outlook, and employment. She became Stella the Stargazer, an astrologer and advice columnist for a second-rate weekly Denver newspaper. The pinstripe suits were exchanged for wildly colored voluminous outfits; the regular salary, for an irregular income with no benefits. Jane provided little information about her past: parents still alive, one brother and one sister; the education needed to be an accountant. Attention was given to her idiosyncrasies: an extra sense which affected her not only when she met people, but even in touching their correspondence, a fascination with lingerie, and a pet chameleon to whom she confided her problems. She had done volunteer work with a literacy program. The atmospheric conditions of mile high Denver cannot explain all this, but a reader who can accommodate the eccentricities will enjoy the Stargazer series.

In the opening narrative, *A Love to Die For* (Walker, 1994), Jane made the move to the *Daily Orion*. She fabricated some of the early letters. Others came from people she already knew. When Jane "saw" the corpse of the woman who produced her lovely lingerie, she was unsure whether she saw a real body or only an aura. Either way, the police saw her as their number one suspect.

Two disturbing letters began the mystery in *You Bet Your Life* (Walker, 1995). The first was a letter from a woman seeking to avenge the death of her mother. The second was from a husband whose wife left him on Stella's advice. Then, a rush to marriage by an old friend sent Stella off to visit an old West gambling hall in Silverado.

Jane felt threatened in *Curl Up and Die* (Walker, 1997), but not enough to stay out of the love affair between her best friend, Meredith Spencer and a creative hair stylist at an exclusive salon. She had every right to be afraid: more threatening letters, "spells," and an astrological prediction in which she sensed doom for Meredith. When the stylist was murdered while both Meredith and Jane were on the premises, their problems had just begun.

Jane did not discount the story of abduction of his nanny, Elena, told by young Steven Holman in *Death of a Dustbunny* (Walker, 1998). Unlike the police and Dustbunnies (the agency which had placed Elena in the household), she knew that the farewell note left by Elena was a fake. Based on her volunteer work, she was aware that Elena was illiterate. Steven's father was a reclusive man, isolating his motherless son. Jane took a special interest in the child, working as Elena's replacement until she figured out what was happening.

Even though she had an initial warning of tragedy, it was not Stella's extra-sensory power that led her to uncover a murderer in *Dead on Her Feet* (Walker, 1999). Instead she was motivated by her sympathy for a lonely teenager. She invaded the privacy of suspects while working as an assistant director at the Magic Circle Theater where the victim, a hot-tempered stage mother, had been killed. A second job was necessary because her publisher would not raise her salary. Stella had other concerns, Lips, the chameleon, had laid an egg.

These were simplistic narratives conducive to light reading.

Delta Stevens

Author: Linda Kay Silva

Delta Stevens was a lesbian police officer in California. After taking a bachelor's degree in social science, she initially planned to go to law school. She entered the police force with the plan that she would earn the money for tuition and then resign. However, she found police work so interesting that she stayed on. She loved to dance, collected baseball cards, but her job was her primary focus. Delta was not a team player. She risked dismissal from the force on more than one occasion for her failure to share information with detectives on the case.

During *Taken by Storm* (Paradigm, 1991), when Delta's patrol partner and close friend Miles Brookman was shot in the line of duty, Delta did not accept the official line of "cop-killer" as an explanation. Miles had been checking drug thefts from the police department's evidence room. During his investigation, he had worked with Megan Osbourne, a childhood friend who had become a prostitute. Police computer expert Connie Rivera joined Delta in ferreting out which of their fellow cops were involved in drug dealing. They were aware that their investigation could lead to ostracism and retribution. In the course of the narrative, Delta began an affair with Megan.

Connie Rivera had graduated first in her class at Massachusetts Institute of Technology. Her involvement in humiliating practical jokes against a rival brought tragic results in *Storm Shelter* (Paradigm, 1993). Delta sensed a pattern in the escalating crimes in her patrol area. Only after several incidents did Connie tie the bizarre events to a video game left for her at the station. The obstacles that had to be overcome to win the game at each level were mirrored in the savage murders taking place. Knowing the identity of the perpetrator was not enough. They had to convince the homicide investigators of their theory. Meanwhile the crimes escalated to endanger those whom Delta and Connie loved.

Weathering the Storm (Paradigm, 1994) explored Delta's promise to Miles Brookman that she would protect children during the course of her work. Rogue behavior by Delta led her new captain to assign her as a patrol-training officer to Tony Carducci, a rookie with a directional handicap. Remembering how Miles had borne her early inadequacies, Delta tolerated a lot as they investigated a child pornography ring. Delta's personal heroism in the face of danger was weighed against her disregard for official orders. She won the approval of her new supervisor. Megan, needing space from their relationship, left for a time-out in Costa Rica. Delta had urged her to take part in a "marriage" ceremony.

In *Storm Front* (Paradigm, 1995), Delta had two concerns: an assassin determined to kill the female district attorney who wanted to be more than a friend to Delta, and a female jewel thief who left a trail of clues for Delta to follow.

Delta had not approved of Megan's decision to accept an internship in the Costa Rican forests. In *Tropical Storm* (Rising Tide, 1997), her fears were realized when Megan became a prisoner of Colombian smugglers. The gangs kidnapped women to work in gold mines. Delta recruited Connie Rivera, Sal (an electronics expert) and Josh (a former Vietnam veteran) to enter the tropical forest. All were aware that besides the smugglers, the forest held poachers and remnants of the Bribri, an indigenous tribe.

There were episodes of explicit lesbian sex during the narratives. Baseball fans will be annoyed to note that Mickey Mantle's name was misspelled and old time radio listeners will be irked to read that *Fibber McGee and Molly* was a children's program. A little research would eliminate such generational errors.

Blaine Stewart

Author: Sharon Zukowksi

Recovering alcoholic Blaine Stewart chose a difficult profession for a woman who needed to limit the stress in her life. She was a tall, redheaded private investigator, working in New York with her attorney/sister, Eileen. Drug dealers had killed Blaine's husband Jeff, a government agent. Her subsequent miscarriage triggered her descent into alcoholism. Work, hard work, had been a blessing and made both sisters financially secure. The agency had an elite clientele; banks, insurance companies, and large corporations.

But, in *The Hour of the Knife* (St. Martin, 1991), Blaine was close to the edge. Eileen insisted that she take a vacation. Instead Blaine investigated the disappearance of a college friend, who enjoyed hacking into computer networks. Blaine held nothing back. She challenged the local authorities and broke into an office, while fighting off her recurrent nightmares with cigarette, coffee, and a compassionate doctor.

In *Dancing in the Dark* (St. Martin, 1992), Blaine divided her attention between a pro bono investigation into police harassment of African-American bodega owner Hurley Blake, and a far more lucrative case for Faradeux Industries. Faradeux sought a listing on the New York Stock Exchange, but W.A.R.M. (Worldwide Animal Rights Movement) was prepared to picket the announcement celebration. Blaine went undercover as a convert to the animal rights movement, where respect for life did not always extend to humans. Violence erupted in both cases. Eileen was seriously disabled when the agency office was bombed. Blaine did not seek relief in a bottle, although she cruised the toughest bars in the area for information.

Leap of Faith (Dutton, 1994) was a letdown from the earlier crisp narratives in its reliance on coincidences. Casual acquaintance Judith Marsden hired Blaine and Eileen to trace the surrogate mother who was bearing her child. Their investigation explored the potential abuses in the surrogate system as it developed into a business operation.

Blaine's marriage to FBI agent Dennis Halstead was in its fourth month when she received a call from her brother Dick in *Prelude to Death* (Dutton, 1996). Dick, who had been out of touch for two years, was charged with raping and killing the poetess with whom he lived in Key West, Florida. Blaine rallied to Dick's defense instinctively, but risked Dennis' career and her own life when she challenged Cuban expatriates and powerful conservative forces within her own government.

The presence of a corpse on Blaine's doorstep drew her into the cutthroat world of international finance in *Jungleland* (Signet, 1997). The victim, George Walden, had managed funds at investment bank Kemble Reid. Blaine set out to learn what kind of man George had been. Was he involved in the theft of $500,000,000 in government securities or had he been about to expose the perpetrators? These questions consumed Blaine's work time until a more personal crisis occurred, the kidnapping of her niece Sandy. Now the question was: had Eileen's estranged husband taken his daughter, or was Blaine too close to finding George's killer.

A dauntless woman, fighting her alcoholism in situations often beyond her control.

Dr. Kellen Stewart

Author: Manda Scott

Dr. Kellen Stewart had begun her professional career as a medical student. By the time she had completed the requirements to practice, she discovered that she did not want to do so. Diverted for a short time into medical research, she left it all behind to become a psychiatrist. Her private life was nearly as chaotic. After the death of her widowed mother, Kellen inherited a three-story building in Helensburgh. She sold the building and used the proceeds to purchase a country place where she and her then lover, Bridget Donnelly could raise ponies and keep a stable. Somewhere along the way,

Bridget and Kellen's relationship got off track. Kellen walked out, promising to come back.

As *Hen's Teeth* (The Women's Press, 1996) began, Kellen shared a Glasgow apartment with Canadian computer journalist Janine Caradice. Caroline Leader, a childhood friend and Bridget Donnelly's current lover, called Kellen to tell her that Bridget was dead. She believed that Bridget's death and the recent death of Bridget's brother Malcolm were connected. Kellen could not walk away this time.

The ties between Kellen and veterinary surgeon Nina Crawford had been two-way. After a suicide attempt, Nina had been referred to Kellen for therapy. Kellen, who now ran the stables with the help of elderly Sandy Logan, went to Nina when her livestock needed attention. In *Night Mares* (Headline, 1998), problems multiplied on both sides of the equation. Nina was coping with a series of unexplained equine deaths at her surgery. While Kellen monitored Nina's mental health, her mare that had just given birth to a prize foal was struck with the same symptoms as the dead horses. Someone wanted Nina either terrified or dead. Kellen, who had come to care for her more than she should for a patient, could not allow this to happen.

The discovery of friend Dr. Eric Dalziel's body while rock climbing was only the beginning in *Stronger Than Death* (Headline, 1999). Over short intervals, other medical associates of Kellen Stewart died under strange circumstances. Det. Stewart MacDonald focused on Eric's housemate, Dr. Lee Adams. Lee and Kellen were long time friends, but Kellen could not prove Lee's innocence unless she would cooperate. The lesbian aspects of the relationships were not sexually explicit. Controversy might arise as to the appropriateness of assisted suicide.

Scott is an excellent writer. Her sense of place, and descriptive powers were exceptional.

Teal Stewart

Author: J. Dayne Lamb

Teal Stewart, whose birth family had been poor and disorganized, was upwardly mobile at all costs. Her mother had trained as a concert pianist, but little was said about her father. By her thirties, Teal had parlayed her MBA from Stanford into work as a certified Public Accountant at Clyborne Whittier. A tall, chestnut haired woman, she owned a three-unit town house on posh Beacon Hill in Boston. She had shared one unit with unconventional architect Huntington Huston a.k.a. "Hunt" for several years. Their affair cooled down to friendship with occasional bursts of loneliness, which brought them back together. They could not live with one another, regardless of their need. Argyle, the Scottish deerhound, who remained in Hunt's custody, suffered from the separation.

As *Questionable Behavior* (Zebra, 1993) opened, a dying man collapsed in Teal's arms as she waited for the elevator in her office building. Her connection with the murder investigation hinged upon her developing relationship with the victim's best friend, her status as a witness, and her professional services in auditing the financial accounts of suspects. Her casual contact with a literate hit man and some assistance from a savvy secretary and a fledgling police detective enabled Teal to identify the killer and save herself.

In *A Question of Preference* (Kensington, 1994), Teal was preoccupied with her need to testify in an embezzlement case. Her dearest friend artist, Nancy Vandenburg, asked her help with threatening letters. Nancy's death left Teal feeling guilty, even when she learned that Nancy had a life she had never shared. Lt. Dan Malley, now engaged to Teal's secretary, saved the day in an action filled ending. There were strong female characters explored during the narrative. Partnership at Clyborne Whittier had been Teal's goal, but, once achieved, it presented a new set of problems.

During *Unquestioned Loyalty* (Kensington, 1995), office politics formed the background for a series of tragic deaths. Hunt disapproved of changes he saw in Teal as she accommodated herself to the system. Teal was torn between personal loyalties to coworkers and the firm's welfare. Working with Dan Malley, now married to her secretary, Teal went far afield to discover an unsuspected motive and killer.

These were not easy books to read because of the technical jargon and multiple suspects.

Emily Stone

Author: Kathryn Buckstaff

Emily Stone wanted to forget Blue Eye, Missouri, where she lived until she was six. Her dad, a quiet man who enjoyed his fishing and his booze, had left his failing hardware store behind, and moved his family to a Jacksonville, Florida trailer court. Her mother, an uneducated woman, became an embarrassment because of her limited interests and country philosophy. Emily was lonely in Florida, rejected because of her accent and appearance, but she persisted until she received a college education and a job as travel writer for the *Tampa Tribune*. She maintained a long-term relationship with an architect, but at thirty-eight felt unprepared for marriage and a family.

No One Dies in Branson (St. Martin, 1994) presented Emily with an unwelcome assignment covering the "Hot Country Awards" show in the tourist inflated town of Branson, Missouri, a short distance from Blue Eye. While investigating the death of Stella Love, a budding country singer, Emily uncovered hidden relationships among the suspects, but also came to appreciate the positive aspects of country and country music. The narrative was flawed by gushing comments about the "stars" that Emily met while in Branson (Johnny Cash, Louise Mandrell, and Glen Campbell).

By *Evil Harmony* (St. Martin, 1996), Emily had not only moved to Branson, but had also become the acknowledged sweetheart (but not lover) of country star Marty Rose. Awed by the glitter of his life and his personal charisma, Emily was slow to realize that Marty was haunted by events in his past. The murders of two friends caused Marty to hire security guards, but his solution to the problem was unacceptable to Emily.

Lucy Stone

Author: Leslie Meier

Lucy Stone, a native New Yorker, moved to Tinker's Cove, Maine because of her interest in the environment and her marriage to carpenter Bill Stone. Although busy with three pre-teenaged children, she worked at Country Cousins, a Land's End clone, processing mail orders.

While on a break in *Mail-Order Murder* (Viking, 1991, also published as *Mistletoe Murder*), Lucy noticed an occupied car in the parking lot with the motor running and an exhaust pipe in the window. The managing director of the company had been knocked unconscious, and subsequently died. Lucy was a potential witness who might be in danger.

Another pregnancy ended Lucy's employment, but left the family in financial straits, as *Tippy-Toe Murder* (Viking, 1994) began. This did not keep Lucy from investigating when "Caro" Hutton, a retired ballet teacher disappeared. Lucy juggled her concerns about Caro with the murder of a hardware storeowner who had suffered from theft, and the problems of a battered wife. No wonder she had limited time for preparing meals, attending Little League games, and sewing ballet costumes.

Lucy was still nursing her new daughter when she embarked on a third murder investigation in *Trick or Treat Murder* (Kensington, 1996). A series of fires, the last of which had caused the death of a summer visitor, seemed targeted at historic properties. Buildings within the historical zone of the community could not be renovated without approval by a local commission. Lucy focused on the marital difficulties of the dead woman until forced to deal with a killer who had money, not romance, on his mind.

With three of the children back in school and handy daycare available for the baby, Lucy was restless as *Back to School Murder* (Kensington, 1997) began. A temporary job at the local newspaper and a night course in Victorian literature offered her chances for self-development. Instead she focused on a mysterious bombing at the elementary school, which fit a pattern of past crises. Local police arrested Josh Cunningham, a popular teacher who had roused the ire of right wing parents, for the death of Carol Crane, the heroine of the bombing. A handsome college professor was a distraction to Lucy, but she returned to home and hearth without compromising herself.

Libraries ought to be safe places and library board members ought to be pillars of the community, but in *Valentine Murder* (Kensington, 1999) neither was true. At her first meeting as a board member, Lucy discovered the corpse of Bitsy, the librarian. Since access to the building was limited, board members, including Lucy, were suspects. Her investigation placed the Stone children in danger amidst the snowstorm of the century.

The annual cookie exchange had been a tradition for Lucy and her friends. In *Christmas Cookie Murder* (Kensington, 1999), the event was a washout. Personal jealousies, rivalries and insecurities among the participants destroyed the holiday spirit. The murder of a young childcare worker was attributed to her affair with an unfaithful husband. Lucy's personal knowledge of the suspect caused her to look further, perhaps too far for her own safety. More than the usual amount of action with smugglers, SWAT teams and corrupt officials.

When Native American activist Curt Nolan was killed after protesting against a gambling casino in *Turkey Day Murder* (Kensington, 2000), Bill, Lucy's husband took a firm stance. She was not to investigate. On the other hand, Miss Julia Talley, long time friend of the family, urged Lucy to get involved. That, and her own curiosity tipped the balance. Curt had made so many enemies. Lucy looked in all the wrong places. When she identified the killer, it was a turkey that saved her neck. Toby was off to college; but Lucy added Nolan's Carolina dog to her household.

As *Wedding Day Murder* (Kensington, 2001) began, Sidra Finch, daughter of Lucy's best friend Sue, was engaged to marry Ron Davitz, an Internet entrepreneur whom she had met in New York City. Ron's overbearing mother substituted elaborate and expensive touches to the simple wedding that Sidra's family had envisioned. When Ron was found dead in the water before the ceremony, there were startling revelations about his financial empire. The ending was contrived.

The narratives were expanded with domestic details, and will be enjoyed best by those who like their mysteries seasoned with warmth and humor.

Next books in this series: *Birthday Party Murder* (2002); *Father's Day Murder* (2003)

Dr. Michael Stone

Author: Anna Salter

Despite the name, Michael Stone was a female, named by her father while he was too drunk to realize his error. She became a forensic psychologist who specialized in child abuse, battered spouses, and custody cases. She devoted 80 percent of her time to a staff position at the Jefferson University Mental Health Clinic, and the rest to private practice in Vermont. Michael was the daughter of a gentle alcoholic father who practiced law in Wilson's Pond, North Carolina and his strong-minded wife. Michael's marriage to Doug ended after their daughter, Jordan, died of SIDS (Sudden Infant Death Syndrome).

Michael's life changed with Jordan's death. She maintained an interest in professional football, played in pickup coed basketball games, and rode on horseback, but she separated herself from ownership. She occupied an isolated home that she stocked with 250 items, no more. Michael had serial relationships with married men after her divorce, but avoided any commitments. Under considerable pressure in her work, she returned on vacations to the inner coastal waters of North Carolina to refresh her spirit.

Shiny Water (Pocket Books, 1997) was an absorbing narrative, describing Michael's involvement in a child custody case in which allegations of child abuse had been made against the father. After he was awarded primary physical placement, the children were murdered, and the mother charged with their deaths. To protect her professional reputation and personal stability, Michael intervened in the investigation. She willingly accepted help from a convicted child molester, but feared dependence upon Adam Bowman, an attractive chief of police who shared her conviction that the mother was innocent.

In *Fault Lines* (Pocket, 1998), Attorney Carlotta Young, Michael's best friend, warned her that the release from prison of Alex B. Willy, a former minister convicted of abusing children, could place her in danger. Michael had testified against Willy in court. Willy had won the right to a new trial on technical grounds, but the state would probably not retry the case. Willy's vendetta endangered not only Michael, but also the confidentiality and stability of her patients. A trained Rottweiler saved her life. A confused patient might put Willy back behind bars.

Personal relationships played a large role in the dilemma that faced Michael in *White Lies* (Pocket, 2000). Her respect for a former mentor influenced her to evaluate the competence of his son, an anaesthetist who was accused of sexual improprieties with his patients. Then a long-term friendship with psychiatrist Marv Gliesen drew her into a case involving recovered memories of incest. Her never forgotten loss of a daughter to SIDS made it impossible for Michael to ignore the vulnerability of another woman's child. Finally her near death opened her up to a closer relationship with Adam Bowman, the Jefferson police chief.

Salter, a forensic psychologist, created an intriguing heroine and credible plots. Not for the squeamish.

Next book in this series: *Prison Blues* (2002)

Sergeant Stone

Author: Sarah J. Mason

Ponderous rural police Superintendent Trewley, and his brighter, younger, and better educated assistant Sergeant Stone were the protagonists in this series. Stone received chances to display her skills—a black belt in judo and medical training. She shared her private life with a traffic cop referred to as "What's his name" by Trewley. The couple were close enough to share a mortgage. "What's his name" had a degree in civil engineering. Stone was described as dark-haired with hazel eyes, capable of eating endless snacks without gaining weight to the dismay of her corpulent, always hungry superior officer.

Murder in the Maze (Berkley, 1993) offered rural English stereotypes and little action. The locals were gathered on the estate of newcomer Montague Rowles to celebrate their annual church bazaar when Isabel, the domineering wife of the local doctor, was murdered in the maze. After extensive questioning by Trewley, Stone's awareness of an obscure medical syndrome assisted in the solution.

In *Frozen Stiff* (Berkley, 1993), the incompetence, union stonewalling, and resistance to change in Tesbury's grocery chain headquarters hampered the efforts of management consultant Ken Oldham. When someone dispensed with him entirely, Trewley and Stone followed regular procedures.

Friday always seemed to bring weird cases, as in *Corpse in the Kitchen* (Berkley, 1993). A local aristocrat demanded police support in her efforts to evict a communal cult occupying adjacent land. A feud erupted between a bootier and a major manufacturer. These stresses might or might not account for the discovery of a corpse in the kitchen of a nearby lodge. The methods of murder were ingenious, but the motive was weak.

During *Dying Breath* (Berkley, 1994), Stone's understanding of mercury poisoning helped Trewley in the determination of death of a prominent scientist. Neither officer used much common sense in handling suspects.

Two murders in quick succession at a prominent girls' school confounded Stone and Trewley in *Sew Easy to Kill* (Berkley, 1996). A third occurred before they sewed the case up.

As *Seeing Is Deceiving* (Berkley, 1997) began, young "What's his Name" was busy directing traffic when three bank robbers drove past him. The cruel, well-organized thieves avoided detection for a considerable period of time even though a documentary film producer had videotaped their escapade. Their emphasis on crimes against oculists eventually solved the cases.

Stone (last name only provided) was an underdeveloped character with glib dialogue in a series in which other characters were better developed. The series had excellent plots.

Writing as Hamilton Crane, author Sarah J. Mason was also the final author in the Miss Emily Seeton series.

Dr. Sylvia Strange

Author: Sarah Lovett

Sylvia Strange, a divorced woman, was described as a tall attractive brunette in her thirties who had earned a Ph.D. in psychology. Relationships had been difficult for Sylvia. Her father, besieged by alcoholism and depression, left when she was thirteen. Her next few years were notable for problems with drugs and the legal system. As an adult, she had infrequent contacts with her mother. An early marriage had ended in divorce, and an affair with an older man ended with his death. She was more successful professionally. Her practice, which included the evaluation of convicts under consideration for parole, led to a book on pathologies in prison inmates.

In *Dangerous Attachments* (Villard, 1995), Sylvia worked closely with her married friend Rosie Sanchez, an investigator at a New Mexico penitentiary. Sylvia had been hired by Attorney Herb Burnett to examine Lucas Watson, a seriously disturbed convict. Rather than parole, Sylvia recommended transfer to a psychiatric unit, earning not only his enmity but also that of his equally unstable brother and his father, a state senator. A parallel plot revolved around Rosie's search for the demented collector of body parts from prison inmates.

As *Acquired Motives* (Villard, 1996) began, Sylvia had ended her affiliation with the state prison, entering practice with Forensics Evaluation Unit, a private enterprise. Her employment as a defense witness in the trial of confessed rapist, Anthony Randall was distasteful. Randall's release on a legal technicality fueled vengeance by a serial killer, whose identity was uncovered only after Sylvia delved into the childhood abuse of two lonely children. Her current affair with Police Officer Matt England was endangered by his desire for a long-term commitment, including a child.

It was a fluke that Sylvia was called to the hospital to work with Serena, a mute child, in *A Desperate Silence* (Villard, 1998). Serena was bright, but terrified. She had eluded a killer, driven her protector's car into a train, and survived. Sylvia and Serena developed a bond, which made Sylvia's involvement necessary to Serena's recovery. Sylvia fought off the authorities, possible relatives of Serena and the killer until she was sure that the child was safe. Matt surprised Sylvia with an engagement ring; she surprised him by accepting it.

Perhaps Sylvia should have refused to take part in John Dantes' psychological evaluation during *Dantes' Inferno* (Simon & Schuster, 2001). She had not come to grips with a personal crisis, the suicide of a patient whose release from the hospital, she had authorized. John Dantes had been convicted as a bomber, but authorities suspected he had valuable information about other possible terrorist activities. Sylvia served with a group of experts (FBI, Los Angeles Police Department, and independent forensic guru Edmond Sweetheart) who suspected that Dantes had engineered the bombing of the Getty Museum and planned further depredations. How was he contacting his accomplices on the outside? Sylvia found Dantes attractive, worth saving, and her feelings were returned. Very complex characterizations and a narrative requiring close attention.

Next book in this series: *Dark Alchemy* (2003)

Jane Stuart

Author: Evan Marshall

Jane Stuart came from the Midwest and attended the University of Detroit, but had few ties there. Both of her parents were dead. She was an only child. She met her husband Kenneth at her first job after college. He was her supervisor at

Silver & Payne, a major literary agency in New York City. Because of stresses at Silver & Payne, partly due to the predatory nature of major executive Beryl Patrice, Kenneth quit his job and formed his own agency. He and Jane, by now his wife, moved their offices and home to a small New Jersey town, Shady Hills, about 25 miles west of New York City. Kenneth was able to take most of his writers along with him. His death in a traffic accident not only left Jane personally bereaved, but also decreased their client base. By this time she was in her late thirties and their son, Nicky, was nine. His favorite companion was Winky, a tortoiseshell cat who figured in several of the mysteries. Jane was comfortable in Shady Hills. She belonged to a knitting group, which provided her with emotional support and the best gossip in town.

Things had not been working out for Jane as *Missing Marlene* (Kensington, 1999) began. Her top author, and romantic interest, Roger Haines was experiencing burnout. His latest book sold badly. His publisher dropped his option. Jane felt that his current manuscript needed a major overhaul, causing him not only to fire her, but also to undermine her reputation. Marlene, the nanny whom Jane hired out of affection for the young woman's mother, disappeared. Jane realized that Marlene had engaged in reckless behavior since joining her household in Shady Hills. She felt guilty that she had made so little effort to help Marlene get acquainted. The guilt and calls from Marlene's mother prompted Jane to delve into what might have happened to Maarlene.

Jane could not deny the loneliness in her life since Kenneth's death, but she became too involved to be obsessed by it during *Hanging Hannah* (Kensington, 2000). A *People* magazine profile of Jane as "Agent of Justice" tied her and other Shady Hills residents to the death of Hannah, a young developmentally disabled woman. Hannah's killing was followed by the murder of editor Holly Griffin who had arranged for Jane to represent superstar Goddess. Jane allowed attentive detective Stan Greenberg to chauffeur her as she questioned and researched but she did not share her findings with him. Winky earned her keep in this one. The premise that an indigent woman would have been allowed to stay on at a private facility without payment was incredible. Reality check, please.

The memory of Kenneth, whom she had loved dearly, motivated Jane to accept his cousin, Stephanie Townsend into her home in *Stabbing Stephanie* (Kensington, 2001). According to Stephanie she needed a place to stay until she could find an apartment. Carson & Hart, a publisher newly relocated in Shady Hills, would employ her. Stephanie convinced Jane to go undercover at the publishers. She was sure that something was wrong there. Stephanie was a big part of what was wrong, but it took Jane a while to figure that out. Winky, who visited the publisher to pose for a picture, opened the door to the solution. Light humor came from Jane's efforts to stay on the difficult Dr. Stillkin Diet. She was dating Detective Stan Greenberg regularly, and had improved her business status.

The behaviors that provided motivation in the narratives were not closely linked to the way characters were presented.

Next books in this series: *Icing Ivy* (2002); *Toasting Tina* (2003)

Liz Sullivan

Author: Lora Roberts

As the series opened, Liz Sullivan's decision to live out of her 1969 Volkswagen van, avoiding relationships and subsisting well below the poverty level, seemed quixotic, even paranoid. She was hiding from Tony, her brutal former husband. She had divorced him while she was in prison for shooting him in self-defense. Hiding was not paranoid. It was prudent, because he continued to stalk her. A regular job or a permanent address would have limited her ability to move regularly, so she subsisted in the van, writing freelance articles using the public library as a resource, She managed on thrift shop clothes and cheap food, supplemented by her section of a Palo Alto community garden plot.

Liz was a short, stubby woman with nondescript hair who found it easy to lose herself in the crowd. Her ties with her extended Irish family in the Denver area had been damaged when she dropped out of college to marry Tony. They had offered no support during the difficult period of her trial and imprisonment. Her husband's brutality had left her cautious in her relationships with men, but she taught writing at a senior center, enjoyed the companionship of other writers, and swam daily at a community pool.

The discovery of the corpse of a local street person under her vehicle during *Murder in a Nice Neighborhood* (Fawcett Gold Medal, 1994) brought Liz to the attention of the police, and eventually led Tony to her van, but she survived.

However tenuous Liz's ties were with her family, she could not ignore the news that her mother was ill. In *Murder Mile High* (Fawcett, 1996), she returned to Denver. When someone deposited Tony's corpse on her parents' front porch, Liz protected herself and her family from hasty conclusions by the police department and the machinations of the killer.

An unexpected visit by a runaway teenage niece in *Murder in the Marketplace* (Fawcett, 1995) continued her prickly family relationships. Young Amy Sullivan's visit was tolerable because Liz had inherited a small home and income from the sale of adjacent property. Liz's entry into temp work as a clerical exposed her to murder and caused her to be suspected by her coworkers. Not so with Police Officer Paul Drake, who became a friend and neighbor. Eventually Liz relaxed enough to have a nondescript black and white dog named Barker, probably for good reasons.

In a moment of weakness during *Murder Bone by Bone* (Fawcett, 1997), Liz agreed to care for a friend's four children. Her strained domesticity was fragmented by the discovery of old bones and a new corpse. The continued intimacy with Drake who provided overnight, but chaste, protection for Liz and the children aroused both positive and negative feelings in Liz.

She enjoyed growing, and sometimes selling, the vegetables she grew in a community garden. For Liz, gardens were a serene place, but when shared, they could become a source of wrangling and territorial disputes, as in *Murder Crops Up* (Fawcett, 1998). When murder did occur in the communal garden, an old enemy suspected that Liz was the killer. Her close observation provided Liz with an alibi when a second death occurred. Niece Amy survived a personal crisis, but her life was changed. Paul's absence because his father was ill made Liz realize how important he had become in her life.

In *Murder Follows Money* (Fawcett, 2000), Liz's temporary employer warned her that her new assignment would be difficult. Escorting culinary expert Hannah Couch on her San Francisco tour went beyond difficult. Hannah's entourage included a killer, a kidnapper, and a potential suicide. Paul Drake was there for Liz and they moved closer to a commitment.

Considering the price, these books were a real bargain.

Dr. Evelyn Sutcliffe

Author: Leah Ruth Robinson

Dr. Evelyn Sutcliffe was a third-year resident working the emergency room at Manhattan's University Hospital on the upper west side of New York City. Prior to taking up medicine, Evelyn had been ABD (all but dissertation) towards a Ph.D. in English. As part of her studies, she had spent a semester at Oxford University. Her father, Evan Sutcliffe, had died in a car accident. Her mother Joan, a formidable personality who had served as a MASH nurse in Korea, had remarried. Joan's second husband, Dr. Sandy Berman, a pediatric neurologist had adopted Evelyn although he insisted that she keep her birth father's last name in his memory. He was the man whom Evelyn thought of and referred to as "Dad." Sandy Berman had suffered a severe heart attack recently. Joan, who had been serially unfaithful, pulled herself together and paid more attention to him. Evelyn had two half-brothers: Alan, who was gay, studied at the Culinary Institute, and Craig, an assistant district attorney, had marital problems.

The man in Evelyn's life was Dr. Phil Carchiollo, a staff psychiatrist. Initially they both had apartments at the Doctor's Residence, a building that housed staff and provided office space for attending physicians' private practice. Phil moved out, wanting a more permanent home, and a more committed relationship. Evelyn felt pressured, unsure of her willingness to either move in with Phil or marry him. He had not always been that eager for commitment. He had dual relationships with Evelyn and another woman for some time. Beth resided in London but returned to New York City on a regular basis. When she did, Phil was there for her. Beth's marriage changed the arrangements.

Evelyn was attracted to risk-taking charismatic men. She described herself as tall—six feet in shoes, with light brown hair. She was only minimally observant but shared the Jewish rituals of her mother and stepfather. Evelyn prided herself on her ability to focus on her work tasks, clearing herself of any emotional involvement in the patient. She described herself and other emergency room staff as "adrenaline junkies."

First Cut (Avon, 1997) could be compared to a six-hour miniseries with an ensemble cast, members of which were described in detail. Evelyn had management responsibilities over other staff members, several of whom had professional or personal problems. Treatment of the third victim of a serial killer brought Evelyn and her staff into a murder investigation. The death of a medical student, whom Evelyn had mentored, could be attributed to the "Babydoll Killer" or might be a copycat. Evelyn was unsure of whom she could trust among her associates. The clues to the identity of the killers were artfully inserted in extensive details.

As *Unnatural Causes* (Avon, 1999) began, the relationship between Evelyn and Dr. Phil Carchiollo was disrupted by Elise, a neurotic young woman who had inflated a minor contact into a belief that she and Phil were lovers. Not surprisingly Evelyn cast Elise as the prime suspect when poisoned mushrooms were delivered to her apartment, causing the death of a dear friend. The final outcome took place in the emergency room. Maybe a trifle too many trauma notes.

Doctors are not supposed to provide services to family members or close friends, but in *Blood Run* (Avon, 1999, but previously published in a different form in 1988), Evelyn had no choice. She was on duty in the emergency room when her friend, Dr. Shelley Reinish, arrived as a patient and left as a corpse. Evelyn, with her background in writing, was polishing up Shelley's book on emergency room physicians. Overcome by grief that she might have failed to note serious changes in Shelley's behavior, Evelyn probed until the connections came together.

The narrative over-focused on Evelyn's perceptions and feelings, and Phil's professional analysis of her feelings.

Cassandra "Cassie" Swann

Author: Susan Moody

Author Susan Moody who had a long running series about globe-trotting, English-African photographer, Penny Wanawake, switched to Cassandra Swann, a former biology teacher who taught bridge. Cassandra had been raised first by her pub-keeper father and grandmother, and then by an uncle in a rural vicarage. She had family: cousins Hyacinth and Primula, twins who were unbearably thin. Cassandra, who finished university in three years, had a strong visual memory that helped in playing bridge but also assisted her in solving mysteries. She was described as a divorcee in her thirties, who accepted her "womanly figure."

When, during *Death Takes a Hand* a.k.a. *Take-out Double* (Penzler, 1994), Cassandra arrived late for a bridge session, she found her fellow players dead at the table. They were members of a larger group, vacationing in a country mansion as part of a bridge tournament. Others in the group had connections based on their personal or professional lives, but it was the placement of the cards that directed Cassandra to the killer.

Grand Slam (Penzler, 1995) connected Cassandra's volunteer work teaching bridge to inmates at the local prison with her job as a paid partner for a professional bridge player. When discharged by her partner, she tripped over a corpse. Someone wanted her dead and she had to know why.

The death of Cassie's father haunted her throughout *King of Hearts* (Scribners, 1995), which had little or nothing to do with bridge. The mention of a horse named "Handsome Harry" set her to work questioning witnesses of Harry Swann's demise. Cassie became convinced that a quarrel outside his bar had been staged; the motive, murder. Her parallel investigation of the death of an immigrant doctor was transparent to a careful reader.

By *Doubled in Spades* (Scribners, 1997), Cassie and her friend Natasha had started a bridge sundries business. She met amateur bridge player Naomi Harris who believed her husband wanted to kill her; and Lucy Benson, the child Naomi had given up for adoption. Male family members had preyed upon both women. Cassie involved faithful friend, Charlie Quartermain, in her investigation of Naomi's death, but she and Lucy subdued the killer at the conclusion. Charlie got no respect or affection from Cassie so it was not surprising that someone else recognized his worth.

In *Sacrifice Bid* (Headline, 1997), Cassie noted that a bridge acquaintance was more than willing to assist Charlie in his fund raising for the local nursing home. She was too busy worrying about Lolly Haden-White to care. Lolly, who also played bridge with Cassie, seemed distracted, making errors inconsistent with her skill level. When Lolly died mysteriously, Cassie believed her death was motivated by an incident decades before in Africa. She focused on the wrong suspect, but was rescued by an old age pensioner whom she had befriended.

As *Dummy Hand* (Headline, 1998) began, a passerby had found Cassie badly injured by a hit and run driver. Charlie Quartermain, determined to find the offender, did not accept a voluntary confession by Bernard Price, a local schoolteacher. His investigation continued as Cassie slowly recovered her health and her memory. Then, the man who had blackmailed him into confessing one offense rather than face exposure for another murdered Price.

Bridge had become peripheral in the later Swann books, but the cool mind and intense focus that made Cassie an exceptional player worked to her advantage in solving mysteries.

Kathryn Swinbrooke
Author: C. L. Grace, pseudonym for Paul Harding a.k.a. P. C. Doherty

This historical series centered on the relationship between a young female physician and a rough Irish mercenary during the Fifteenth Century. Kathryn Swinbrooke, who had been trained to follow in her widowed father's footsteps, had married Alexander Wyville, an attractive but faithless man, who was missing in the War of the Roses. In her late twenties, she was dark-haired with blue gray eyes and lived in Canterbury.

Kathryn met Colum Murtagh during *A Shrine of Murders* (St. Martin, 1993) when current pilgrims to Canterbury were poisoned in methods reminiscent of Chaucer's work. Kathryn, whose husband had allied himself with the losers in the War, became interested in Colum, aware that her husband might still be alive.

Colum worried about his countrymen in *The Eye of God* (St. Martin, 1994) because, as an Irishman allied with an English King, he was perceived as a traitor. The Eye of God, a valuable sapphire stolen by Richard of York from Ireland contained a secret that men would kill to protect or to learn. True to her own integrity and the spirit of the times, Kathryn remained chaste as she sought an annulment from her marriage. The War of Roses had ended by 1471.

In *The Merchant of Death* (St. Martin, 1995), Kathryn and Colum deduced that the suspects in a murder at the local inn were not brought there by chance but under pressure from a blackmailer. Kathryn took the lead in solving this murder, absolving Colum from blame in a purported death, and concealing the truth in another family tragedy.

Colum lived in Kathryn's home as a lodger, as *The Book of Shadows* (St. Martin, 1996) began. Two years and a day would have to elapse from Alexander's disappearance before she could seek permission to remarry within the church. Shortly after Kathryn attended a dying former sorcerer and learned of the *Book of Shadows*, Tenebrae, its current possessor, was murdered. He was an admitted necromancer who used the book not only for its spells, but also to blackmail. In addition to his death, the disappearance of the book was of concern to local officials, including Colum.

Although the War of the Roses had ended by 1472, with Edward IV on the throne, the potential for disruption still existed within the York faction as *Saintly Murders* (St. Martin, 2001) began. Neither of Edward's surviving brothers could be trusted, a source of great concern to their mother, Duchess Cecily. When Roger Atworth, a former soldier who had entered a monastery to repent for his sins, died, Cecily had two worries: had Roger destroyed the letters she had sent him, and had he died a natural death. Kathryn was selected by the archbishop of Canterbury to serve as Devil's Advocate in the process of proposing Atworth for sainthood. Implicit in that assignment was a close look at the circumstances of his death. The reward dangled before Kathryn was a search for Alexander Wyville, dead or alive.

This continued to be an interesting series, with documentary material to illuminate the period.

Next book in this series: *A Maze of Murders* (2003)

Dodee Swisher

Author: Peter Abresch

Attendance at Elderhostels, short-term educational programs for persons age fifty-five or older, constitute one of the enjoyable perquisites of growing old. Individuals or couples share college dormitory or hotel accommodations, attend classes without the pressure to achieve, and make new friends. Jim Dandy, a recent widower, had only promised to attend the Elderhostel in Bolder Harbor, New Jersey, to accompany an uncle. When the uncle died, his children convinced him to go anyway, although he had limited interest in bonsai. There he met Dodee Swisher, a tiny gallery owner and artist. After their first unplanned contact, they arranged to attend the same programs. Their intimacy grew accordingly. Her habit of sketching during classes provided them with clues when they encountered a mystery. He was the viewpoint character, but Dodee was the aggressor both in their physical relationship and their investigations.

Among the skills that Jim learned in *Bloody Bonsai* (Worldwide/ Writeway, 1998) were how to steal trees, burgle hotel rooms, and rescue damsels in distress. The damsel was Dodee who taught Jim that he had not lost his interest in, and aptitude for, lovemaking.

Dodee and Jim were reunited in Baltimore when they attended a culinary Elderhostel during *Killing Thyme* (Write Way, 1999). They were on the same wavelength as to resuming their physical relationship, but only Dodee's pressure kept Jim on the trail of a chef-killer. A senior citizen version of Ivan and Nan Lyons' *Someone Is Killing the Great Chefs of Europe*, but with a flavor of its own.

By the time Dodee and Jim met in *Tip a Canoe* (Write Way, 2001), he was evaluating their relationship. This was a very active Elderhostel in South Carolina's Santee Lakes Region. They added canoeing to their usual tasks of discovering corpses and identifying killers. By the conclusion, Jim was ready to make a declaration of love, to which Dodee responded wholeheartedly. A foul-mouthed attendee whose off-color sexual comments were inappropriate marred the cast of characters.

Next book in this series: *Painted Lady* (2003)

Alex Tanner

Author: Anabel Donald

Alex Tanner's work as a freelance researcher for television programs provided her with investigative experience. Her family background, an unknown father and an institutionalized mother, gave her empathy, but not pity, for the disadvantaged. She had spent her childhood in foster homes, buoyed up by her plan to become a private investigator like those she knew from reading mysteries. Her education, both college and secretarial training, prepared her for a career. By age twenty-eight, she owned a co-op apartment in London and had an independent pension plan. Unfortunately she had acquired no social graces and limited ability to bond with others. Alex was not over-scrupulous. On occasion, she stole books from libraries and read the papers on desks when she was left in an office. She was a shrewd judge of people, and capable of changing her mind.

In *An Uncommon Murder* (St. Martin, 1993), Sarah Potter's plight aroused Alex's sympathy. Sarah, after a lifetime of service as a governess to the Sherwin family, had been dismissed. Alex researched the death of Lord Rollo Sherwin in Africa during the Fifties and the disappearance of Lord Rollo's granddaughter, whom Sarah had taught.

During *In at the Deep End* (St. Martin, 1994), Alex was hired by a posh London firm of solicitors to investigate the "state of mind" of seventeen-year-old Olivier de Savigny Desmoulins before he drowned in the pool at his boarding school. Using her television research connections as a cover, Alex became embroiled in the "evil" that pervaded Rissington Abbey, where a paramilitary curriculum was used to control unruly students. She and her assistant uncovered deceptions at several levels, and risked Alex's life in the endeavor. Television producer Barty O'Neill was the man in Alex's life, but without commitment.

In *The Glass Ceiling* (Macmillan, 1994), Barty and Alex hit some rough spots when he misunderstood her relationship with old friend Peter Barstow. A social worker friend convinced Alex to house and mentor Nick, a withdrawn teenage girl who would rather be homeless than fostered. These diversions did not deter Alex from following up on letters from a killer who wanted to be stopped. Alex explored the current lives of four young women who had been "pranksters" during their university days, and who were still playing games.

Alex planned to use her time in the United States during *The Loop* (Macmillan, 1996) visiting the sites where her favorite fictional sleuths had lived. Instead she fended off Barty's proposal of marriage and involved herself in model Jams Treliving's search for the love of her life...and the father of her unborn child. Both pursuits followed Alex back to England where she added a third concern. She needed to identify her biological father. That done, maybe she could move on in her life.

In *Destroy Unopened* (Pan, 1999), just when Alex most needed her under-aged assistant Nick, she (Nick) disappeared. That left Alex with the intriguing case of the unsigned love letters found by a recent widow. The love letters made reference to a serial killer. Nick had left behind an unfinished case, the disappearance of a young developmentally disabled woman. Barty was off in Africa, possibly in danger. She needed him to help her make an important decision about her future. The result was an intriguing narrative that left a reader with an appetite for more.

Alex was a no-nonsense investigator, who could go far. There were excellent reviews in England, but the series was not well known in the United States.

Mary Alice Tate (Sullivan, Nachman, Crane)
Author: Anne George

See: The Tate Sisters, page 638.

Patricia Anne Tate (Hollowell)
Author: Anne George

See: The Tate Sisters, page 638.

The Tate Sisters
Author: Anne George

The Tate sisters were a study in contrast. Narrator Patricia Anne Tate Hollowell (nicknamed Mouse) was a petite, reflective, and well-organized mother of three, happily married to Fred Hollowell for forty years. She had taught high school English until she was sixty in a suburb of Birmingham, Alabama. After retirement she tutored children. Patricia Anne was careful about what she ate, promoted a vegetarian life style, and was allergic to alcohol. She continued to vote the Democratic ticket even after the Republican resurgence in the South, and had a soft spot for the hippies of the Sixties. Her dog, a mongrel named "Woofer," completed the household.

Mary Alice Tate Sullivan Nachman Crane, five years older, enjoyed life to the fullest with little concern for the future. Her lifestyle was subsidized by the considerable wealth she had inherited from her three deceased husbands, each of whom had been considerably older and to each of whom she had provided great joy and a child. She voted the straight Republican ticket, ate whenever and whatever she pleased, enjoyed a cocktail, and entertained lavishly. She shared her luxurious home with an overweight cat, "Bubba," and—for a time at least—with a "boyfriend." Physically, Mary Alice (called "Sister" by Patricia Anne) was a tall woman weighing at least 250 pounds. Her originally brunette hair had undergone subsequent variations. Mary Alice had two daughters and a son from her marriages. Son Ray had left the United States after being caught raising marijuana in a national forest. He ran a dive boat in Bora Bora. The sisters were one another's best friends, and their dialogue will resonate with anyone who has a loved sister.

Author Anne George has subtitled each book in the series "A Southern Sisters Mystery."

As *Murder on a Girls' Night Out* (Avon, 1996) began, Mary Alice had purchased a country western bar. Shortly after she showed her new venture off to Patricia Anne, the seller was murdered. Combining their skills and resources under protest from Fred, the sisters proved the innocence of a young man whom Patricia had taught in high school. On the side, they scouted for prospective husbands for their daughters among the suspects and investigators.

Although less hilarious, *Murder on a Bad Hair Day* (Avon, 1996) was enjoyable. The sisters' interest in primitive art involved them in the murder of a gallery owner and an art critic. Again Patricia Anne's sense of loyalty to a former student motivated her to take considerable personal risks to identify the tormented killer.

Mary Alice's daughter Debbie married Chef Henry Lamont as *Murder Runs in the Family* (Avon, 1997) began. The guests included Dr. Philip Nachman who matched up with Haley, Patricia Anne's widowed daughter. Another guest was Meg Bryan, the groom's cousin and a professional genealogist. Meg died precipitously after Patricia Anne requested information about Henry's family. The negative side of genealogy emerged as the sisters investigated judicial high jinks and family skeletons.

As *Murder Makes Waves* (Avon, 1997) began, Patricia Ann was bored by the routine of her life. She, her daughter Haley, and family friend Frances Zata accepted Mary Alice's invitation to visit her Florida condo. Mary Alice, who would be attending a Writer's Conference, had many friends in the area; more than one of whom were killers. Fred prepared to merge his business with a major corporation, providing a future life of leisure and comfort for Patricia Ann. However, given the past, she might get bored again.

Weddings took the spotlight in *Murder Gets a Life* (Avon, 1998). Haley, Patricia Anne's daughter, announced her plans to marry Dr. Philip Nachman (his father had been one of Mary Alice's husbands). Ray, Mary Alice's son in Bora Bora, had married Sunshine Dabbs, who had won a trip to the island on *Wheel of Fortune*. Sunshine, a member of an extended family housed in a five-trailer compound back home, disappeared. A corpse was found, but it was not Sunshine's. Her family matched the sisters' in its complexity so keeping them all straight may be a problem for the reader.

Murder Shoots the Bull (Avon, 1999) when judged on its interesting characters and dialogue came off a winner. The narrative focused on the woes of Patricia Ann's happily married neighbor, Arthur Phizer. He was accused of murdering Sophie, the woman he had briefly married as a teenager. The couple had remained friends even after the annulment. Dying, Sophie Sawyer had appointed Arthur to serve as executor and trustee of her extensive estate. There were too many coincidences for credibility, but then that's not what the series is all about.

A power struggle within a church and unrequited love were the motivations for murder in *Murder Carries a Torch* (Morrow, 2000). The narration was enlivened by contrivances such as artificial testicles as aids to childbirth, snake handling preachers, and Cousin Luke's wife, Virginia who danced her way out of his life. On a more serious level, the sisters tripped over a corpse in their efforts to help their unlovable cousin Luke.

Mary Alice had opted for a fourth marriage to Sheriff Virgil Stuckey as *Murder Boogies with Elvis* (Morrow, 2001) began. The planning drew her and Patricia Ann into the problems of the groom's family. Stuckey's son and son-in-law were members of the Elvis kick line at a benefit performance when a fellow dancer was murdered. Not only had Patricia Ann been watching from a front seat, but someone put the murder weapon in her purse. Had it not been for Mary Alice's trained karate kick, things could have been worse. The narrative glowed with the affection between the sisters and the love between Patricia Ann and Fred.

Bert and Nan Tatum

Author: Barbara Taylor McCafferty and Beverly Taylor Herald,
themselves twins

As twins, Bert (Bertrice) and Nan Tatum may have been physically identical, but their attitudes were different. Nan, still single, worked as a disk jockey on a country music station in Louisville, Kentucky and enjoyed a casual lifestyle. Bert's husband had left her after twenty years of marriage. She had been highly domesticated, but was now alone. Her son Brian and daughter Emily were in college. She found employment through a temp office service, and lived in the other half of a duplex occupied by Nan. This provided her with an oversight into Nan's personal life, of which she did not approve.

Nan hated to shop; Bert loved it. Nan remembered the unhappy parts of childhood. Bert saw it all positively. Nan went to work dressed in ragged jeans and a T-Shirt and had a foul mouth. Bert wore professional clothing and had a professional attitude.

When *Double Murder* (Kensington, 1996) began, the existence of the Sandersen family, killed twenty years before, had faded in the twins' minds. They vaguely remembered that the couple for whom they had baby-sat had been murdered while on vacation. So why were Bert and Nan being threatened, followed, and their homes ransacked by a person connected to that past incident? The alternating narrations distracted from the flow in an otherwise interesting plot.

As *Double Exposure* (Kensington, 1997) began, Nan had a problem with a persistent caller to her program, whom she had come to call "Looney Tunes." The woman, having heard of her prior success as an investigator, wanted Nan to solve a mystery. Nan was preoccupied with a new man in her life, also a twin. He aroused her sympathy describing his grief at the suicide of his brother. The sadly mourned brother may have committed the murder that Looney Tunes wanted solved. Bert came to rely on Hank Goetzmann, the stolid police officer who had dated Nan for a while.

The twins had promised never again to switch places because it got them in trouble. In *Double Cross* (Kensington, 1998), they did it again. They switched places and they got in trouble. Their shenanigans made it more difficult for the police to solve the murder of beautiful, but aggressive divorce attorney Stephanie Whitman. The only solution was to find the killer themselves. Bert's romance floundered over whether or not she was willing to "do it."

Although the explanation as to how Emily, Bert's daughter, confessed to murder was contrived, the dialogue or double monologue, in *Double Dealer* (Kensington, 2000) was witty. The twins harassed enough people while trying to learn who killed a dishonest antique dealer to force the murderer to attack them.

Nan pushed the envelope in *Double Date* (Kensington, 2001). She used Bert's name to enter an Internet dating service. Then she approached Derek Stanhope, whom she believed to be a respondent, as Bert. His wedding ring and obvious lack of recognition should have clued Nan into the fact that someone else might also have appropriated his name. When Stanhope was murdered, detective Hank Goetzman with whom Bert was considering marriage, suspected Bert of betraying their relationship and of murder. E-mail caused the problem but it also drew out the killer.

Light reading. Barbara McCafferty also wrote the Schuyler Ridgeway series as Tierney McClellan.

Aurora "Roe" Teagarden

Author: Charlaine Harris

Unlike many other librarian/sleuths, Aurora "Roe" Teagarden did not fade into the background as the series progressed. She became financially independent, had several meaningful relationships that went nowhere, and played a major role in each book. She was described as a tiny woman (4' 11") with brown hair and eyes. As the series began, Roe lived in, and managed, a Lawrencetown, Georgia town-house complex owned by her mother, Aida. Her father, a newspaperman, had moved after her parent's divorce and remarried. Like many librarians, Roe was addicted to books, most particularly to those based on actual crimes.

In *Real Murders* (Walker, 1990), Roe joined a club that met monthly to discuss true crime. Each member was responsible for preparing one program per year, researching a specific crime. Roe's assignment was the Wallace case, the factors of which were replicated when Roe found a club-member's corpse in the VFW kitchen. It seemed logical that a member of the Real Murder Club was involved. Roe, police officer Arthur Smith, and crime writer Robin Crusoe focused on them. When Roe's six-year-old half brother visited, she feared a repeat of a child-killing case, and followed through until the boy was safe.

In *A Bone to Pick* (Walker, 1992), retired school librarian Jane Engle bequeathed Roe a home plus over one half million dollars. Convinced that Jane had some special reason for her bequest, Roe searched the house, finding a human skull. With the help of police officer Arthur Smith's pregnant wife, Roe drew out a killer who was ready to strike again. Roe had met an attractive man with only one perceived flaw: he was a clergyman.

Encouraged by her successful mother, Roe was working on a real estate broker's license as *Three Bedrooms, One Corpse* (Scribners, 1994) began. When showing an expensive home to new plant manager Martin Bartell, Roe discovered the corpse of a rival realtor. Bantam sized Roe used her eye for detail and a rock to clear Martin from suspicion. She had developed a passion for him.

Roe's marriage to Martin, a man of mystery, in *The Julius House* (Scribners, 1995) included a surprise gift from her new husband. Martin purchased "The Julius House," from which a family had disappeared six years before. He was a sophisticated man, who was determined to protect Roe from the potential violence of his own business, the details of which he did not always share with her. Martin should have realized that Roe could not resist pursuing the mystery of the Julius family. Martin, aware of potential danger, arranged to have special security for his home, a married couple who lived on the premises.

Angel Youngblood was almost a bodyguard for Roe, but in *Dead Over Heels* (Scribners, 1996) she could not protect her from a corpse dropped from a low flying plane. The victim was a police officer who had been hostile to Roe. Subsequent incidents made it likely that the killer was someone who had an obsessive love for Roe.

In *A Fool and His Honey* (St. Martin, 1999), Martin was having health problems. Someone was slipping drugs into medication bottles. Martin's niece Regina descended upon the Bartell household without her husband but with a six-week-old baby. That should have been enough but at that point things went seriously wrong in Aurora's life. When Regina's husband showed up he was dead on arrival. Not much room for humor in this narrative.

Author Charlaine Harris made Roe an engaging heroine, furnishing her with clever plots, but too often solutions depended upon mentally unstable killers.

Next books in this series: *Last Scene Alive* (2002); *Poppy Done to Death* (2003)

Sydney Teague

Author: Anne Underwood Grant

After her divorce, Sydney Teague made a life for herself and two children, Joan and George, Jr., as owner of a small advertising agency "Allen Teague" in Charlotte, North Carolina. She denied herself alcohol, which had been a problem, but relieved tension with an occasional cigarette. Her former husband George paid little attention to the children, so Sydney made every effort to attend Joan's volleyball games and George, Jr.'s soccer matches.

Sydney's father had been a defense attorney. His moral courage in representing a young man accused of the rape and murder of a high school student was resented by Sydney. Her understanding came too late. They had been very close, but he died without resolution of the estrangement. Her widowed mother had moved to Asheville. Her family support came from her brother, Bill, a corporate attorney who had failed at three marriages himself. She had good friends: her secretary Sally Ball, agency art director Hart Johnson, and real estate dealer Barbara Cates. Detective Tom Thurgood, who had been a lover, became a friend, and a frequent tennis partner. She pushed her body's tolerance for stress. Frequent abdominal pains hinted at an ulcer.

The death of her good friend Crystal Ball and the arrest of Crystal's husband Fred were a shock to Sydney as *Multiple Listing* (Dell, 1998) began. Crystal was in the process of divorcing Fred, whose sister, Sally Ball, was Sydney's secretary. Sydney did not believe that Fred had raped and killed his wife. With some professional and more personal help from widowed detective Tom Thurgood, Sydney connected the fact that Crystal's house had been on a multiple listing with local real estate dealers, and that several other women whose homes were also on the list had been attacked and raped. This discovery did not end Sydney's conflict of interest as she had friends in the business.

Seth Bolick's obsession with the SNAKE project, developing a non-carcinogenic cigarette, touched Sydney in *Smoke Screen* (Dell, 1998). Seth's desire to continue his father's crusade appealed to Roe's need to absolve herself from guilt as to her own father. Seth's death by nicotine poisoning, so closely patterned on his father's suicide, did not end the professional relationship. The Allen Teague Agency was still responsible for promoting the project. The local sheriff's decision to treat Seth's death as another suicide was well accepted by his family. Sydney believed he had been murdered. The narrative explored the plight of rural communities heavily dependent on tobacco as a cash crop, reminiscent of the Southern dependence on slavery in another century. A lost cause with dedicated adherents.

Cuttings (Dell, 1999) presented an interesting background, a gathering of floral designers in the Charlotte Convention Center, but the ending came across as contrived. Sydney had an interest in having FloraGlobal go well. Allen Teague had made the preliminary arrangements for the events and had ongoing clients who took part. One, two, and finally three significant participants were murdered. She and Tom Thurgood had different reactions to the possibility that Sydney might be next.

Grant's final book in the series, *Voices in the Sand* (2000), may have been self-published. It was remarkably different in its narrative style, more introspective and more descriptive of the setting. Sydney had no idea what she was getting herself into when she agreed to represent her Aunt Nan at the annual meeting of Dune's End Condominium Homeowners. The seaside and water had always been special to Sydney and her Uncle John but he was dead. With few allies on whom she could rely, she thwarted the plans of a powerful corporation.

Jane Tennison

Author: Lynda LaPlante

Little physical description was provided as to Jane Tennison in the novelizations of the popular *Prime Suspect* series. She could be nothing but what actress Helen Mirren portrayed her to be: a slim woman of medium height who wore her sandy colored hair in a short casual style.

Jane, initially assigned to white-collar crime, demanded the chance to head a major investigation. In *Prime Suspect* (Dell, 1993), she had her opportunity only because popular DCI Sheffield died of a heart attack while a case was in progress. The unit, which had strong loyalties to Sheffield, resented Jane from the start. She fought their passive/aggressive behavior, heightened when she ordered the release of their suspect. Only after she directed the team to credible evidence, did she win acceptance.

In *Prime Suspect 2* (Dell, 1993), Jane had just ended an affair when she met black detective sergeant Robert Oswalde at a training session and shared a one-night stand. Her ambitious supervisor, Mike Kernan used the incident by assigning Oswalde to Jane's team currently investigating a murder with racial overtones. She and Oswalde managed the case successfully, but credit went elsewhere and Jane was passed over for promotion.

In *Prime Suspect 3* (Dell, 1994), the men in her new supervisory assignment resented Jane. She terminated a pregnancy, which at times she had seemed to welcome. Her professional skills were tested by official interference in an investigation of child pornography and prostitution. Jane used inside information to wrangle a favorable new assignment. She might not be one of the boys, but she had learned to play hardball.

It was not unusual for popular series to be novelized, but less frequently has the author of the television script done it. Actress Helen Mirren won an Emmy in 1993 for her role as Tennison, while the production won the award for best dramatic miniseries or special production in 1994. A possible additional season in the television series was announced early in 2003.

Iris Thorne

Author: Dianne G. Pugh

Iris Thorne was an overachiever, who arrived at work by 6 a.m. to get an early start at her West Coast stock brokerage. After a dirt-poor childhood and her father's abandonment when she was fourteen, Iris earned an MBA from the University of California at Los Angeles. She took a vacation in

Paris before starting a job. There she met and fell in love with charming American photographer, Todd Fillinger. On her return to the United States, she poured herself into her career. Iris drove a Triumph sports car, and was referred to as the "ice princess" by her fellow workers. She drank too much. There was a lighter, softer side to Iris, who had been a special education teacher working with deaf children. She wondered about having a child of her own.

In *Cold Call* (Pocket, 1993), she was devastated when a street gang stabbed Alley, a handicapped "gofer" at the office, to death. Iris had been unaware of ties between her agency and a major Mafia family. When she learned of financial misbehavior, she concealed money and information from the police. Iris was not overburdened with scruples even after her best friend was killed in her stead.

Slow Squeeze (Pocket, 1994) failed to show Iris in a more favorable light. She was angry and vindictive when her lover's wife and child sought a reconciliation. At work, she competed with a young Mexican broker for the business of Barbie Stringfellow, a widow with money to invest. When Barbie was murdered, Iris solved the case to protect herself.

In *Fast Friends* (Pocket, 1997), Iris renewed acquaintances with Dolores Gaytan De Lacey ("Dolly"), the mother of a childhood friend, Paula. Dolly was having memory problems, not the least of which was that she couldn't remember executing a will in which she left valuable family land to her husband, Bill. Dolly was sure she would never have bequeathed the property to Bill against her deceased father's wishes. When Dolly died, presumably a suicide, Iris had mixed loyalties. Bill, who had employed Iris' father, had helped to underwrite her college expenses. Bill wanted Iris to locate Paula, ostensibly so she could attend her mother's funeral, but did he have a more sinister motive? Complex, but interesting if read carefully.

Bridget Cross, the practical partner in the marital and professional relationship with her husband Kip, a computer genius, had serious problems in *Foolproof* (Pocket, 1998). Bridget, having caught Kip being intimate with their daughter's nanny, intended to divorce him. Their financial ties were not so easy to end. Bridget owned the majority stock share of Pandora, the software corporation built on Kip's creativity. Bridget came to Iris to launch an IPO (switch from private ownership to a public stock corporation) with T. Duke Sawyer, a major dealmaker having a substantial interest. Kip opposed both the IPO and the involvement of Sawyer. When Bridget's murder was discovered, Kip was the obvious suspect. Iris had been named administrator of the Pandora stock fund; making her a target for a fantasy killer.

When Iris and Todd Fillinger met again as *Pushover* (Headline, 1999) began, it was at his invitation. He was now an entrepreneur in Moscow, seeking investors. She made the trip not only to check out the financial opportunity, but also because she still had a sense of guilt as to how their affair ended. She had a rewarding career and a solid relationship with her former boss Garland Hughes, but Iris still needed closure. Within hours after he met her at the Moscow airport, Todd had been murdered. When Iris returned to Los Angeles, she could not let go. She learned more than she wanted to about Todd and about herself.

Judith Thornton

Author: Patricia D. Benke

After graduation from Stanford Law School in the Seventies, Judith Thornton worked her way up to Assistant (eventually Chief Assistant) in the San Diego District Attorney's Office. Her personal life did not fare as well. Marriage to a fellow attorney did not survive her workaholic behaviors. She and Steven developed a mildly congenial relationship for the sake of their daughter, Elizabeth, but Judith never reconciled to his second marriage. Whatever marital problems she may have had, Judith was a fond mother and a devoted daughter. When her widowed mother declined into dementia, Judith designed an apartment for her in the home she and Steven had shared. She used her money to pay for nursing care, and spent leisure time at her mother's bedside. At times, Judith felt exhausted by her professional and personal responsibilities. She had her mind set on becoming a judge, using that goal to justify her concentration on work. There was no room for a relationship with a man after Steven left.

Judith's highly political supervisors in the District Attorney's office handed her a sensitive case in *Guilty By Choice* (Avon, 1995). Robert Dean Engle was clearly the brutal killer of a young girl, but inexperienced police officers had gathered vital evidence without a warrant. The community would have had little tolerance for a failed prosecution, so it fell to Judith to develop admissible evidence.

In *False Witness* (Avon, 1996), Judith's ambitions for a vacancy on the California appellate court system were stymied by her devotion to duty. An elderly "tagger" who would identify the killer only if allowed to complete a mural on the hillside retaining wall had witnessed the death of a prosperous resident of Silverado Estates. The face of the killer was recognizable to Judith and to other Silverado residents, but could she prove her case?

In *Above the Law* (Avon, 1997), Judith's role was subordinate to that of two male Hispanics. Serafino Morales, a migratory worker, crossed the border each year to work the fields in order to provide for his family. When a brutal coworker was murdered, the authorities were unsure whether Serafino was the killer or a witness. Perhaps both. Young attorney Peter Delgado had been assigned to Judith's major crimes unit as a trainee. Peter had avoided dealing with the problems of migratory workers. He no longer had that option. It changed him.

The death of her mother caused Judith to be out of town in *Cruel Justice* (Avon, 1999) when the decision was made to prosecute Tom Russell for the sexual assault on his daughter. Judith did not consider it a viable case, but rather a political decision because the district attorney was up for election. Another factor was the animosity between Judith and prosecutor Aaron Mercer. She balanced her sense of personal ethics against loyalty to the district attorney's office.

Alix Thorssen

Author: Lise McClendon

Alix Thorssen, although American, made frequent references to her Norwegian background to which she attributed her stoicism. She had grown up and gone to high school in Montana, but attended St. Olaf's College in Minnesota. That was a fine place to steep herself in her Norwegian heritage. She collected the comic book adventures of "Mighty Thor," a Nordic hero. Although Alix's original goal had been to support herself by painting, she accepted her limitations and opened an art gallery in Jackson Hole, Wyoming together with handsome Paolo Segundo. There she could continue her affiliation with art, but enjoy riding her horse, Valkyrie, and kayaking the white waters of the Snake River. Alix's income was supplemented by her work as an art fraud investigator.

In *The Bluejay Shaman* (Walker, 1994), an art fraud investigation made Alix available to her sister, Melanie, when her husband, Wade, was arrested for murder. Wade, a college professor with a special interest in Native American traditions, had quarreled with Shiloh, a former graduate student. She was deeply involved in Manitou Matrix, which combined feminism with Native American mythology. Whoever set Wade up for murder, also framed Alix for charges of vandalism. Fortunately, Alix found detective Carl Mendez who believed in her, and rescued her when she spied upon the Manitou ceremonies. Alix set a trap for the person she suspected as a killer, but was surprised at her catch.

In *Painted Truth* (Walker, 1995), Alix, her friend and kayak instructor Pete Rotondi, and art gallery owner Eden Chaffee were returning from the river when they realized that the Chaffee gallery was on fire. Only later did they learn that the corpse found inside might have been that of artist Ray Tantro, whose work was being displayed. He had hoped for a comeback with his showing sponsored by Eden. Alix overcame her panic when Paolo announced that he wanted to sell his share of the gallery. McClendon's conclusion was downbeat and unconvincing.

The Scandinavians have claimed with great pride that Vikings, not Christopher Columbus, first reached and traveled in North America. In *Nordic Nights* (Walker, 1999), the possible discovery of an historic runestone put Alix's stepfather in jail for murder, her mother in the hospital, and Alix under ice. With Carl Mendez away for training, she was tempted by an attractive Nordic skier, but resisted.

The image of a wolf seen after her father's death had haunted Alix's memories. In *Blue Wolf* (Walker, 2001), the death of a wolf occurred about the same time as a request from painter Queen Johns. Queen Johns' son Derek had been killed in what had hastily been declared an accident. Years later, still distrustful of the police department and perceived by the locals as an eccentric, Queen John asked Alix to reopen the case. The pressures created by her probe brought unexpected results, one of which Alix deeply regretted.

Abigail "Abby" Timberlake

Author: Tamar Myers

Fifty years before, a divorced woman in her forties might have been considered too old for a new life, but Abby Timberlake lived in the 1990s. She had always been a rebel; e.g. an anti-war protestor in the Sixties. Disaster seemed to dog her family. Her father, a traveling salesman for a clothing mill, had been killed when a seagull struck him while he was skiing.

Her husband Buford had exchanged her for a "blond bimbo" named Tweetie. Abby, a tiny woman who had the gray streaks in her brown hair tinted, lived in a rent-free home near Charlotte, North Carolina. She had turned her knowledge of antiques into a business enterprise, the Den of Antiquity. Buford, an attorney, had gained primary physical placement of their two children: Susan, now nineteen and at college, and Charlie, a seventeen-year-old high school student. Abby had close relationships with both children. She also spent time with her widowed mother who lived in nearby Rock Hill, South Carolina. Mama could be a comfort but she was excessively rude, made inappropriate choices in her male friends, and demanded a lot of attention from Abby. Buford also retained custody of the family dog, Snuffle. Abby had the cat, Dmitri. Her dear friend, C.J. (Jane) Cox figured in many of the narratives. C.J.'s whimsical (and probably incorrect) stories about her family became tiresome. They were a mistake to omit however because occasionally one contained a significant clue.

Abby's Aunt Eulonia had organized the Selwyn Avenue antique dealers, but they no longer considered her an asset in *Larceny and Old Lace* (Avon, 1996). She had let her store, Feathers 'N Treasures, deteriorate, but why would anyone strangle the old woman? Circumstantial evidence pointed to Rob, a gay member of the Association, but Abby did not believe him capable of murder. Six-foot-tall detective Greg Washburn came to agree with Abby and to value her personally. Their joint solution left Abby richer, although she lost the rent-free house.

Prompted by his diversion with a big-busted blonde, the romance with Greg had cooled by *Gilt By Association* (Avon, 1996). When Abby found a corpse in an armoire she had purchased from a dealer, she renewed her contacts with Greg in his official capacity. She was convinced that the murder related to a secret contained within the four-piece-set of which the armoire was a part. Abby interviewed the members of the Barnes family. A second murder and burglaries at the "Den" confirmed her suspicions but did not limit her investigation. Rob and his lover shared their expertise and were lifesavers when needed. When Greg proposed, Abby was skeptical of his fidelity.

Abby had been too busy to talk to June Troyan when she stopped into the shop carrying a gray vase in *The Ming and I* (Avon, 1997). Only after the exiting June had been struck and killed by a car, did Abby find the vase had been left behind. It was a Ming, valued at well over $10,000. She was eager to keep the vase. There were others who were interested enough to vandalize her store, steal the vase, threaten her on the phone, and commit murder.

Greg took off on a vacation, to "clear his head" as *So Faux, So Good* (Avon, 1998) began. Abby was too busy to mind. First, their wedding announcement was found in the wallet of a dead man. Then her vaunted purchase of an antique tea service, turned out to be questionable, sending her and three of her fellow antique hunters up North. There she became acquainted with Magdalena Yoder (a sleuth in author Tamar Myers other series). Abby needed all the help she could get, because the killer was at hand.

Suspension of belief was required in *Baroque and Desperate* (Avon, 1999). Was it likely that a casual contact on an airplane would lead to an invitation to take part in a treasure hunt? Or that the maid at the wealthy

Latham estate had been murdered at least once, and that C.J., Abby's dear friend, confessed to the killing? Someone stole everything in the Den of Antiquity in Abby's absence, and her insurance had lapsed. The credibility was missing too. Something good had occurred, her restless brother, Toy, was now top of his class at the Episcopalian seminary.

In *Estate of Mind* (Avon, 1999), an impetuous bid at the white elephant sale at the local Episcopalian church left Abby as the proud possessor of a missing Van Gogh. While she focused on how much the painting could sell for, others concentrated on taking it away from her.

In *A Penny Urned* (Avon, 2000), a surprise inheritance sent Abby, Mama, C.J., and her older friend, Wynell, to historic Savannah, Georgia. There were more surprises: a cousin who became an aunt; hidden family secrets, and coin tricks. Greg's offer of an engagement ring forced Abby to make a decision.

Abby must have forgotten to take her estrogen when she held her Halloween party during *Nightmare in Armor* (Avon, 2001). She invited guests whom she did not like or whom she hardly knew. Eccentric costumes and overindulgence in alcohol proved hazardous to the guests and setting alike. Finally in a huff, Abby sent them all home. Among the items left behind was an antique set of armor enclosing the corpse of Tweetie Timberlake, Buford's second wife. The new police detective, an attractive blonde, was not as impressed by Abby's explanations as her fiancé, detective Greg Washburn might have been.

Zany characters.

Next books in this series: *Splendor in the Glass* (2002); *Tiles and Tribulations* (2003)

Elena Timofeyeva

Author: Stuart Kaminsky

Undoubtedly Inspector Porfiry Rostnikov was the dominating figure in the police procedural series in which Elena Timofeyeva appeared. He was a principled police official who had been shunted aside by political influence, but whose skills and intelligence made him valuable when difficult cases arose. Rostnikov built an ensemble within his unit (much like the Ed McBain stories he so admired). Like McBain, the group created by author Stuart Kaminsky was exclusively male, primarily featuring the dour Emil Karpo and the libidinous Sasha Tkach, until a single woman broke the barrier. For McBain, it had been Eileen Burke; for Kaminsky, it was Elena.

Elena had ties with the police bureaucracy. Her father had worked in military intelligence. Her Aunt Anna, a staunch Communist, had served as procurator, a post that made her Rostnikov's supervisor. When Elena moved to Moscow, Anna, though retired because of ill health, had sufficient influence to find her a position in the Special Investigations Office under Rostnikov. This was during the transitional period in Russia from the U.S.S.R. to Russia, a nation in which powerful commercial and criminal forces challenged the power of the government. Elena was described as a brown-haired, rather plump woman, very intent upon her career. At one time she had attended college in Boston. She and Aunt Anna shared a tiny apartment.

In *Death of a Russian Priest* (Ballantine, 1992), Elena was assigned to work with Tkach whose former partner had been injured. Rostnikov and Karpo were assigned to the murder of a rural priest who challenged the government, leaving Tkach and Elena to deal with the disappearance of a young woman, the daughter of a Syrian diplomat. The pattern of two or more plots, in one of which Elena played a role, continued.

During *Hard Currency* (Ballantine, 1995), Elena's skill in Spanish made her the logical choice to accompany Rostnikov to Cuba where they assessed the guilt of a Russian engineer in a murder case. Elena fended off an ardent Cuban police official while Rostnikov dealt with the political implications of the investigation. She questioned witnesses, visited a model Cuban prison, surveyed the scene of the crime, and shared with Rostnikov a private interview with Castro.

During *Blood and Rubles* (Fawcett Columbine, 1996), the unit was busy. Three cases were asssigned to the officers. Elena and Karpo had been present when a tax squad invaded the home of an elderly woman whose brother had collected Czarist treasures. When Karpo was reassigned, Elena remained on the case because the treasures disappeared overnight. The other two subplots were more dramatic.

In *Tarnished Icon* (Ballantine, 1997), the murder of Russian Jews preoccupied Rostnikov. Emil and Iosef (Rostnikov's son) sought a letter bomber. Elena worked with Sasha to find a serial rapist whose violence was escalating. Their success came when the attacker was determined to be a policeman. Elena and Iosef became lovers.

The Dog Who Bit a Policeman (Mysterious Press, 1998) sent Elena and Sasha undercover to investigate dogfights and other criminal activities carried out by the Russian Mafia. Elena was considered dangerous and had to be rescued by Rostnikov. Iosef wanted to marry Elena. She cared for him, and felt no prejudice against his Jewish mother, a factor that had hampered Rostnikov's career.

The most significant strand of *Fall of a Cosmonaut* (Mysterious, 2000) was Rostnikov's assignment to find a missing cosmonaut who had served on Mir, the Russian space station. Rostnikov soon learned that his quarry would be killed to protect a state secret. Elena, still engaged to Iosef, worked with Sasha Tkach on a theft meant to disguise a murder.

The dominating story line in *Murder on the Trans-Siberian Express* (Mysterious, 2001) was the recovery of valuable information from a courier by Rostnikov and Sasha Tkach while traveling across the nation. Each member of the Office of Special Investigation squad had a role in the narrative. Iosef set himself up to entice a serial subway killer, but it was Elena who was attacked and injured, leading to plans for an immediate wedding.

Jacobia Tiptree

Author: Sarah Graves

Jacobia Tiptree's parents disappeared from her life when she was three. Her father, an anarchist, mishandled the bomb with which he planned to blow up a Brink's truck. The blast killed his wife. Jacobia returned to her mother's family in Tennessee hill country until she was grown. When she was sixteen, she took off for New York City where she fended for herself for several years. Not a great deal was revealed as to how she managed or where she obtained the funds and grants that enabled her to go to CCNY. However, she always had sympathy for young girls and women unhappy in their setting.

It was impossible for Jacobia to change her activity level completely, but she made a mid-life correction in her setting. She quit her job as a well-paid money manager to move to tiny Eastport, Maine where she purchased a large, rundown mansion to serve as a bed and breakfast inn. Her move preceded the drop in the money market. Whenever possible she managed her own repairs and renovations, providing much of the humor in the series. Her husband Victor, a brain surgeon who had made a habit of infidelity, chose to follow her to Eastport. Both were deeply involved in the life of their son, Sam whose dyslexia had led him into drug abuse. Sam's needs had been a primary reason why Jacobia had moved. Jacobia entered into a domestic partnership and eventually marriage with harbor pilot Wade Sorenson. The household also included Monday, a black Labrador.

Ellie White had become more than household help by *The Dead Cat Bounce* (Bantam, 1998). She was a friend, too good a friend to allow her to confess to a murder that Jacobia was certain Ellie had not committed. The victim had been Threnody McIlwaine, a former resident of Eastport, who had ruined Ellie's father financially. Knowing Ellie's dedication to her dad, who cared faithfully for Hedda, his irascible invalid wife, Jacobia wondered whom Ellie was protecting. She challenged an ambitious investigator for the state district attorney's office and prodded local police chief Bob Arnold, but could not get Ellie to cooperate.

Jacobia, determined to renovate the sagging wreck of her home into a livable house, was changing herself by *Triple Witch* (Bantam, 1999). Part of the change came from her satisfying relationship with Wade Sorenson. She also had accepted that Victor had the right to be involved in Sam's life. She had adapted to Eastport where guns served a real purpose, friends could be counted on, and everyone knew more than they should about everyone else. This became important when Ellie and Jacobia found the body of Kenny Mumford, local ne'er-do-well, but a friend of Ellie's. Within a short time, Kenny's father and his girlfriend had been murdered. Jacobia learned that, even in Eastport, greed and infidelity existed and could lead to murder. She took a great risk to save Sam's life with an unexpected result.

Victor's reasons for moving to Eastport were unclear to Jacobia as *Wicked Fix* (Bantam, 2000) began. She accepted his concern for Sam, but there was more to it. Putting aside their unhappy marriage, she helped to finance Victor's plan for a trauma clinic. Eastport needed the clinic. Jacobia needed Victor busy and out of her life. What she had not anticipated was the return of local bully Reuben Tate, who even as a boy had terrified his schoolmates. Tate's death did not end the problem. Instead it spawned a series of murders with Victor as the primary suspect in at least two.

Jacobia had been suspicious of Jonathan Raines from the moment they met in *Repair to Her Grave* (Bantam, 2001). He presented himself as a penurious graduate student seeking information on Jared Hayes, the Nineteenth Century musician, who had owned Jacobia's house. When Jonathan disappeared, his girlfriend Charmian Cartwright turned up. She claimed that he had been murdered while seeking a Stradivarius purportedly owned by Hayes. Jacobia was not sure she believed Charmian either. Amidst confusing clues, Jacobia coped with Sam's infatuation with a seductive teenager.

Faye Anne Carmody's abuse at the hands of her husband was well known in Eastport. In *Wreck the Halls* (Bantam, 2001), he was murdered and she was discovered in a bloody and confused state. Faye Anne received considerable public sympathy when she was arrested. Jacobia and her friend, Ellie Valentine, had a problem. Faye Anne did not claim self-defense. She insisted that she had not killed Merle. There were layers of intrigue among newcomers to the community, false names and appearances, stalking and blackmail. Other attacks took place before the killer went too far and had to be stopped. A side effect of the investigation was a restored memory of a fleeing car. Jacobia had a recollection of a car leaving her parents' home after the explosion. Could her father have survived? If so, was he still alive?

Several of the book titles were Wall Street slang phrases, but explained in the text. Graves imbued her series with a great love of place similar to that of Margaret Maron and Sharyn McCrumb in southern locales.

Next book in this series: *Unhinged* (2003)

Nicky Titus

Author: Eve K. Sandstrom

Nicky Titus depicted the Oklahoma landscape and its sparse beauty, as seen through the eyes of a stranger in the land. She was a small woman with curly dark hair and brown eyes. The daughter of a widowed Army general, she had spent most of her adult life in urban areas, often in foreign countries. Nicky suffered agoraphobia when confronted with the flat, sparsely populated plains of the Southwest, and felt threatened by the closeness of the rural community. Her husband, Sam, an intelligence officer stationed in Germany, had taken inactive status when needed on the family ranch. Nicky, an artistic photographer, accompanied him, expecting their sojourn to be a short one.

In *Death Down Home* (Scribners, 1990), Sam bypassed the local sheriff to discover why his father had been attacked and his brother killed. Sam's preoccupation with the investigation left Nicky feeling abandoned, but her pictures of the accident scene provided a significant clue. By the time Sam decided to remain in Oklahoma, Nicky felt accepted.

Sam became county sheriff in *The Devil Down Home* (Scribners, 1991). Nicky, irritated by Sam's taciturnity, made herself useful by taking photographs for his department, recording interviews, even studying law enforcement at a nearby college. A corpse in a benefit "Haunted House" unearthed local scandals ranging from closet Gothic authors to satanic pranks.

Meanwhile, back at the ranch....In *The Down Home Heifer Heist* (Scribners, 1993), ranch hand Johnny Garcia became the number one suspect in cattle theft and murder. Even without a black hat, the villain was evident to readers, but the narrative was warm and enjoyable. Note: author Eve K. Sandstrom's other series featuring Nell Matthews.

Rev. Ziza Todd

Author: David McCullough

Redheaded Ziza Todd, initially a student pastor wore the clerical collar but no specific denomination was mentioned. Ziza (long "i") had attended Oberlin College, then a Rochester, New York seminary.

In *Think on Death* (Viking, 1991), the Olde Smyrna utopian community held its annual meeting just as ninety-three-year-old Nan Quick, last of the founding family, died. Aunt Nan could not have been a killer, but there were bones and a corpse in her home. Ziza came to officiate at the funeral but remained to solve the mystery.

Ziza relocated in Quarryville-on-the-Hudson during *Point No-Point* (Viking, 1992). Single at twenty-nine, she was assigned to provide youth services for a consortium of Protestant churches. She found herself caught between redevelopers and proponents of a deceased sculptor as to the use of property. The local pastors approved Ziza's plan to take her youth group to New York to assist vagrants, but drew the line when the street people returned the visit.

Nikki Trakos

Author: Ruby Horansky

Nikki Trakos was the darling of a large Greek family. Her father had retired to Florida but there were dozens of aunts, uncles and cousins in New York. Six-foot tall with big bones, long brown hair and blue eyes, Nikki could take care of herself. Bored by business school, she entered the Police Academy, where she distinguished herself by her intelligence and her interviewing skills. After working as a street cop, she became a detective investigator in Brooklyn. Still unmarried, she had adopted her nine-year-old niece Lara.

In *Dead Ahead* (Scribners, 1990), Nikki and middle-aged widower Dave Lawton were expected to solve the murder of gambler Frank Sunmann in three days or "turn it over," so they cooperated. Nikki worked out the solution, but had to be rescued by her new partner.

In *Dead Center* (Scribners, 1994), startled by Dave's proposal, Nikki insisted that they work separately to give her time and space. She needed his professional skills when the death of a local politician revealed an identity he had hidden from the voters and his family.

Ginny Trask

Author: Lee Wallingford

Recently widowed Ginny Trask coped with grief and loneliness and the need to support her nine-year-old daughter, Rebecca. Finding it impractical to continue her art studies, she became a fire dispatcher for the Forest Service, while training for investigatory work. She met and became involved with fellow employee, Frank Carver, a divorced former police detective, who served as a law enforcement officer for the Forest Service in Oregon.

In *Cold Tracks* (Walker, 1991), Ginny called on Frank officially when coworker Nino Alvarez failed to appear. Ginny found Alvarez's body, but the murder investigation moved slowly. They discovered that Alvarez's death had important ties to an influential family and to the Forest Service. Ginny's participation as Frank's assistant brought her daughter, Rebecca into danger.

By *Clear Cut Murder* (Walker, 1993), Ginny had applied for transfer into the law enforcement division. Carver assigned her to the Coffee Creek district. A logging company was preparing to cut a prime section of old timber, the sale of which had been vigorously opposed by environmental groups. When the mediator was killed, Frank and Ginny coped with bumbling local officials and a killer's long repressed need for vengeance. In contrast to many couples in mysteries, Ginny and Frank were cautious about their personal relationship. Perhaps because he was older and her supervisor, but also because his marriage had ended in divorce, Frank postponed intimacy.

Tory Travers

Author: Aileen Schumacher

After the death of her husband, Tory Travers was fortunate to have her training as a structural engineer to provide for her and her teenage son, Cody. She had been raised in a wealthy family in central Florida, but became estranged from them. At nineteen, she had married one of her college professors, a man twice her age. During the series, her father, State Senator Tom Wheatley, contacted her. He arranged to have Cody spend a summer with him in Florida.

Nine years of marriage to Carl and several years of widowhood had transformed Tory into a competent businesswoman. In *Engineered for Murder* (Write Way, 1997), aware of the potential consequences to her company, she reported flaws in the construction of the new University football field. What she had not anticipated was that a technician would be murdered on the site. El Paso detective David Alvarez was assigned to the case. In working out her problems, Tory revealed the background of her estrangement from her father.

As *Framework for Death* (Write Way, 1998) began, Tory hadn't heard from David in months. When he needed a structural engineer, she responded immediately. A wealthy but domineering woman and her unidentified companion were found dead in a secret basement room. The floor above them had collapsed by accident or design. When an explosion seriously injured David, Tory took him home to nurse him. Good characterizations and plot.

In *Affirmative Reaction* (Write Way, 1999), the quality of Tory's engineering skills was called into question when her report on an abandoned development sharply disagreed with earlier tests. While inspecting storm sewers, she came upon a corpse. Det. David Alvarez, currently on disability leave, was more than willing to share Tory's investigation. He was responsible for most of the evidence uncovered. The narrative took on the controversial issues of affirmative action to remedy past injustices to minorities, and reverse discrimination.

In *Rosewood's Ashes* (Intrigue, 2001), when a heart attack struck Tom Wheatley, a retired Florida state senator and Tory's father, she and David Alvarez flew to his bedside, unsure of their welcome. There were complications beyond Tom's health. Amy Cooper, a historian whom they had met on the plane, was struck down by a hit and run vehicle as she exited the airport. Cooper was connected to historical research and the legislative efforts to redress the harm done to the African-American residents of Rosewood by a vigilante attack twenty-three years before. Tory needed to know why her father, well known for his right wing viewpoint, supported the review of Rosewood's destruction. This was a mature, well-written book, the best of the series.

Melanie Travis

Author: Laurien Berenson

Melanie Travis was divorced from Bob, the father of her four-year-old son, Davey. Both of her parents had been killed in a car accident. She had supported herself and Davey as a teacher and camp counselor in Connecticut.

In *A Pedigree to Die For* (Kensington, 1995), Melanie responded when she was contacted by her Uncle Max's widow. Max had helped her father repeatedly over the years. Aunt Peg had two problems: Max's death of a heart attack which she believed had been provoked; and the disappearance of their kennel's top dog, Beau. Melanie posed as a potential purchaser of a stud poodle, bringing her into contact with those most likely to steal Beau or to antagonize Max. There were surprises ahead for Melanie (fewer for the reader) in disturbing news about Beau and Max, but a "beau" of her own in suspect Sam Driver.

The show class puppy given Davey by Aunt Peg interested Melanie in purebred poodles during *Underdog* (Kensington, 1996). The death of professional dog handler Jenny Maguire shortly after her best dog Ziggy had been killed aroused Melanie's suspicions. They were intensified when she realized that Ziggy was still alive. She concealed this information from Jenny's family. They were her primary suspects.

As *Dog Eat Dog* (Kensington, 1996) began Sam and Melanie were compatible. Then, a telephone call from her ex-husband created problems. Bob's oil well had come in. He was ready to play a major role in son Davey's life. Aunt Peg wanted Melanie to solve a murder and theft among the elite members of the Belle Haven Kennel Club. Barry Turk, a disreputable dog handler, had earned no kudos for his treatment of dogs or women. Melanie's sympathy for his pregnant lover caused her to investigate his death. There were lots of motives, but it is fair to say the killer, was not only least likely, but improbable.

Melanie's limited knowledge of dog breeding was sufficient to trap a killer in *Watchdog* (Kensington, 1998). She had promised Sam Driver that she would stay out of dangerous situations, but could not reject her brother Frank's plea for help. Frank had blithely gone into business with a notorious land developer. When the developer was murdered on the premises of Frank's new coffee house, he had no alibi and lied to the police.

Melanie's new position as a special tutor at exclusive Howard Academy did not seem likely to lead to murder and arson. However, in *Hush Puppy* (Kensington, 1999), that was what followed her research into the history of Josuah Howard, founder of the school. Melanie was devastated to learn that Sam Driver's former wife was in town, seeking a reconciliation. She busied herself rescuing a neglected young girl and finding hidden treasure.

Melanie, Sam, Sam's former wife Sheila, and her current partner Brian made for tense dinner companions in *Unleashed* (Kensington, 2000). Within weeks Sheila and Brian, who were developing a dog show magazine, were dead. Sam and Melanie's plans to marry were jeopardized. Melanie looked for Sheila's killer at Sam's request, but with concern that the solution to their personal problems would be more difficult.

Melanie had good reason to feel sorry for herself during *Once Bitten* (Kensington, 2001). Sam had taken time off to come to grips with Sheila's death. Not only was Melanie's brother Frank about to marry dog groomer Bertie Kennedy, but Melanie was expected to play an active role in the planning. Initially her assignment was to keep Aunt Peg from meddling. It expanded when the wedding planner disappeared. Melanie had to find her, or do the planning herself. Bob, her former husband, returned for the wedding with an agenda of his own.

Technically well versed as to the competition among dog owners, trainers, and handlers, but no blue ribbons. Too often the bits of interesting dog information sit like undissolved lumps in the narrative.

Next books in this series: *Hot Dog* (2002); *Best in Show* (2003)

Elizabeth Anne "Betty" Trenka

Author: Joyce Christmas

A tall, graying unmarried woman in her early sixties, Betty Trenka had been dismissed as out of date when her lifetime employer retired. He had been more than an employer to her. With an adequate pension and savings, she moved from Hartford, Connecticut to a rural setting in East Moulton. Needing to fill her time and reassert her usefulness, she sought employment. As much as she wanted to be known as Elizabeth, she always became "Betty" to new employers. Betty was feeling the aches and pains of growing old, but stayed active doing volunteer work at the library and taking part-time jobs.

In *This Business Is Murder* (Fawcett Gold Medal, 1993), Betty posted a notice card in the local grocery store, indicating her availability for clerical work. Jerry Preston, president of a local computer software firm, hired Betty to fill in for a few days during Denise LeGrand's vacation. When Denise was killed by a hit and run driver, Betty accepted a longer assignment, but not the official version that Denise's death was an accident.

As *Death at Face Value* (Fawcett, 1995) began, Betty was tutoring a young grocery store checker in how to improve her employment opportunities. This activity connected with Betty's job—typing the autobiography of eccentric literary critic Crispin Abbott—and the unexpected visit of a hometown friend who was fleeing from suspicion of murder. Lots of threads, but very tangled.

Sid Edwards was the only man Betty had ever loved. She wondered when she didn't hear from him after his retirement to Arizona. She learned in *Downsized to Death* (Fawcett, 1997) that he had been rendered helpless by a stroke. Eager to have access to Sid, Betty agreed to help his son, Sid Jr. check his father's files. While Betty was in Hartford, Sid's wife, Mary was murdered. Betty possessed special knowledge that enabled her to tie motive to opportunity. Reminiscent of a great Patricia Highsmith thriller.

Back in East Moulton, Betty was restless. As *Mood for Murder* (Fawcett, 1999) began, she hired young Tommy Rockwell to work on her yard while she took a short-term position at the local schools. Robbery and assaults in the community aroused suspicion against Brad Melville who had been treated badly by East Mouton residents. He and his black clad consort, Raven, were believed to have a Fagin-like control over disaffected teenagers, including Tommy Rockwell. Betty found herself in an insular village, cruel to strangers and outcasts.

Joyce Christmas is also the author of the Lady Margaret Priam mysteries. In *A Better Class of Sleuth* (Fawcett/Ballantine, 2000), the two women met. Betty was asked by neighbor Ted Kelso to size up software billionaire Gerald Toth. Toth wanted Ted, an accomplished computer programmer, to test a valuable new software system, ERP. While in New York City, Betty met Margaret who escorted her to glittering social events. The two became friends while solving a mystery that began with the death of a beautiful woman caught in a power struggle between software companies.

Next book in this series: Priam and Trenka work together again in *Forged in Blood* (2002)

Rose Trevelyan

Author: Janie Bolitho

Rose Trevelyan had been widowed after twenty years of marriage to David, a mining engineer. Her marriage had been a happy one. Left alone in her fifties, Rose took comfort, even joy, in her work as a painter and photographer. She had attended Art College as a young woman, but started again slowly with photography and watercolors; then, progressed to oil painting. The photography was her living; the painting, her passion. She lived by the sea in Newlyn, Cornwall, a wonderful place for an artist and a cook. Her parents were still alive. There had been no brothers or sisters. She and David had no children.

As *Snapped in Cornwall* (Constable, 1997) began, Rose's new friend, Gabrielle Minton, invited her to a dinner party. They never reached the main course. Rose found Gabrielle dead in her garden, seemingly the victim of a fall from her balcony. Barry Rowe, who used Rose's photographs on cards he sold in his shop, wanted to be a more important person in her life, but her feelings for him had not risen above affection. She received the attentions of Gabrielle's widower and the investigating officer, Detective Inspector Jack Pearce.

Her husband David's death had narrowed Rose's vision of her future. Ironically it was the death of dear friend Dorothy Pengelly in *Framed in Cornwall* (Constable, 1998) that awakened Rose to the need to reset her priorities. Dorothy, a reclusive woman who died suddenly, had two sons: Peter, dominated by an avaricious wife, and Martin, a developmentally disabled adult. The narrative explored how Dorothy's death changed her sons' lives. Rose, determined to prove that Dorothy had not taken her own life, persisted against the admonitions of Barry Rowe and Jack Pearce and the threats of the killer. She returned to painting with oils, opening a new chapter to her life.

In *Buried in Cornwall* (Constable, 1999), Jenny Manders, an artist's model that Rose had met at a private showing was murdered. Initially Rose did not connect her death to a prior psychic experience when she heard screaming from a mineshaft that contained an old skeleton. Rose added Nick Pascoe, formerly Jenny's lover, to her list of admirers. She continued to meet with Inspector Jack Pearce in the investigation of Jenny's murder.

Regardless of her beaus—faithful Barry Rowe, exciting Jack Pearce, and flirtatious art dealer, Geoff Carter—Rose placed a high value on her independence in *Betrayed in Cornwall* (Constable, 2000). She was enjoying the first showing of her oil paintings but found time to help her friend, Etta Chynoweth. Etta coped with a rebellious daughter, a married lover, and the death of a beloved son. Rose was determined to locate Etta's daughter, Sarah, but it was Jack Pearce who paid the price for her efforts.

Next books in this series: *Killed in Cornwall* (2002); *Caught Out in Cornwall* (2003)

Hannah Trevor

Author: Margaret Lawrence, pseudonym for M.K Lorens

Hannah Trevor would never have survived physically or emotionally without her Aunt Julia and Uncle Henry. Three children had been born to the marriage of Hannah and her husband James Trevor, a loyalist during the American Revolution. He was a domineering man, who thwarted her efforts to remove the children from a disease-ridden area. All three children died. James was willing to move to Maine when the Revolutionary War ended in defeat for his cause, but only as a stop on his way to Canada. Determined to have another child, Hannah seduced a married man. Their child, Jennet, was afflicted with deafness. Aunt Julia and Uncle Henry provided a home for Hannah and her child, but they were growing old. Johnnie Markham, their son and heir, might not be so generous. Hannah, who learned midwifery from Julia so she could support herself in the future, despised the inept Dr. Clinch who also served as coroner.

As *Heart and Bones* (Avon, 1996) began, Hannah and the local constable and blacksmith Will Quaid discovered the raped and murdered Anthea Emory. She was a reclusive young woman whose husband was on an extended surveying trip. A note describing three nights of abuse by local men (including Daniel Josselyn, father of Hannah's child) focused local attention on Josselyn as the probable killer. He was of distinguished English descent, but had given his loyalty to the revolutionary forces, serving with many of the local men under his command. Their war experiences had left him, and others, deeply disturbed. Hannah did not believe him capable of rape and murder; nor did his invalid wife, Charlotte. Hannah had survived loving Daniel by staying away from him, although allowing him access to Jennet.

In *Blood Red Roses* (Avon, 1997), the body of her husband, who had been living in the area under an assumed name, was discovered. A killer had slaughtered James Trevor's bigamous second wife and their three children. The authorities, already intent upon placing Jennet in indenture, focused on Hannah as the probable killer, forcing her and Daniel together to save themselves and their child.

The prelude to *The Burning Bride* (Avon, 1998) explored the tensions in the community that eventually led to rebellion by local farmers. They were forced to pay their taxes in non-existent silver, rather than the scrip with which they had been paid for their war services. Hannah was pregnant and preparing to marry Daniel, when the community exploded into violence. Daniel's recollections of the war and Hannah's bargain to save his life made it necessary for them to leave their homes behind and strike out for Canada. This was intended to be a trilogy, ending with this narrative.

Very well written, with absorbing historical details and characters. A subsequent book, *The Iceweaver* (Morrow, 2000) followed Jennet into adulthood. During that narrative Hannah, by then a widow, died.

Lucy Trimble (Brenner)

Author: Eric Wright

Lucy Trimble disposed of Geoffrey Brenner, her controlling husband of twenty-three years, the conventional way. She divorced him and left Kingston. She had prepared for the separation by carefully concealing an inheritance from her mother, buying a house in Longborough, Ontario, and finding working as a part-time library assistant. The house was ample for a Bed and Breakfast business. Her adult daughter Jill, who lived in British Columbia, was a dental hygienist. Lucy enjoyed a mutually satisfying relationship with the "Trog," Ben Nolan, an occasional guest at her Bed and Breakfast. Lucy was proud of her long-time Canadian heritage. Her father's family had been Loyalists during the American Revolution who then moved to Canada. Her mother's Welsh family moved from the British Isles before Confederation.

After a therapist encouraged her to get a life, she did just that. A bequest from David Trimble, her gambling addicted cousin, gave Lucy a second opportunity. At age forty-seven, she inherited his detective agency after years of reading mystery stories. Her first major case in *Death of a Sunday Writer* (Foul Play Press, 1996) was the exploration of David's death. He had been writing a mystery novel centered on horse racing. How much of it was fact? How much was fiction? Her other cases involved an agoraphobic wife, and a legacy left to a young boy who was transported to Canada in 1940, one of many who were removed from England during the bombings. Leaving the prosaic affair with the Trog behind, Lucy moved on to the more exciting and dangerous Johnny Comstock, a horse trainer of dubious morals.

In *Death on the Rocks* (St. Martin, 1999), Lucy's client, Greta Golden, learned that the man she had considered a stalker was Michael Curnow, a British private investigator. He had been checking her for a possible inheritance. Financially independent, Greta was less concerned about a legacy than in the question of her parentage. To her knowledge her father had died as a result of a fall on a cliff in Cornwall at a time when her mother was in a nearby maternity hospital. Rival legatees questioned whether Aubrey Golden had been her father. Lucy was sent to Cornwall to find out. It was a convenient time to get away. The romance with Johnny had soured. Michael Curnow, a widower, was a pleasant and helpful companion during her investigation.

Author Eric Wright is an accomplished author, better known for his Charlie Salter series.

Baroness Ida "Jack" Troutbeck
Author: Ruth Dudley Edwards

The series featuring Robert Amiss, a rather aimless graduate of the better English schools, began in the Eighties, but was given new life when Baroness Ida Troutbeck, who preferred to be called "Jack" was added to the cast of characters. Robert, a former government employee drifted about, knowing the right people, having a lovely and intelligent fiancée, Rachel, but never finding his niche. His languid nature and his fiancée's frequent overseas postings left Robert vulnerable to the over-powering Jack.

She was a woman of considerable talent who had served as deputy secretary in the Department of Central Planning in Her Majesty's government. At early retirement she became first the bursar, then the Mistress of St. Martha's College, Cambridge. Based upon her achievements she was eventually created a Baroness and served in the House of Lords. These assorted placements gave her the opportunity to ridicule and lampoon government, politics, education, and the British nobility. On a personal level, Jack was rude, domineering, and arrogant. Her politics were conservative, even libertarian. Rules did not apply to her. She drove faster than allowed; smoked cigars where cigarettes were unacceptable, and had sexual liaisons with both genders. Robert became her emissary, her assistant, and perhaps, her stooge. When her participation in the series began, she was in her late fifties/early sixties Among the books which featured Robert before Jack entered the series are: *Corridors of Death*; *St. Valentine's Day Murders*; *English School of Murder* (republished as *The Anglo-Irish Murders*); and *Clubbed to Death*.

Jack enlisted Robert's support during *Matricide at St. Martha's* (HarperCollins, London, 1994) in a battle to determine the future of the College. The use of a major donation was at issue, with militant feminists and traditional scholars fighting to the death. Robert had some difficulty remembering where his loyalties lay. Spurred on by Jack he assisted in identifying a killer and in burying his own guilt.

Jack's admission to the House of Lords in *Ten Lords A-Leaping* (HarperCollins, 1995) came at a propitious moment in English history. Animal activist groups had successfully navigated a bill protecting wildlife through the Commons. In the Lords, there was opposition from the proponents of fox hunting. A series of murders claiming the lives of nineteen members of the House of Lords raised suspicions against agitators. The killers were identified only when a survivor emerged as the real intended victim. The other deaths were designed to confuse the police. Sincere activists had been manipulated to settle a personal grudge.

After venting her spleen on government and academia, Edwards turned her attention to the clergy, specifically those of the Church of England in *Murder in a Cathedral* (HarperCollins, 1996). Baroness Jack, who had limited respect for any institution, convinced Robert to assist the new Bishop, David Elsworthy, now assigned to Westonbury. His clerics were divided between high-church homosexuals and right wing fundamentalists.

Add in lesbian witches and aggressive shamans. Jack stirred the mixture, but three deaths had occurred before the killers' pattern and motives appeared.

In *Publish and Be Murdered* (Poisoned Pen Press, 1999), Robert, a Liberal in his political views, was recruited to manage a right wing journal, *The Wrangler*. Robert's appointment was opposed by the current editor who had the support of the trustees. Jack stepped in to ensure his employment. Robert, in his first full-time position in two years, made a dent in the financial problems of the journal, which were draining the assets of the Papworth Family Trust. When the editor and a trustee died in succession, not only Jack but also Robert's longtime friend, Chief Superintendent James Milton used Robert to develop their case. The Baroness was less active in this one.

These are witty, knowledgeable mysteries with a scandalous touch.

Next book in this series: *Carnage on the Committee* (2003)

Glynis Tryon

Author: Miriam Grace Monfredo

Glynis Tryon was an unconventional female for the pre-Civil War period. She had attended Oberlin College; then, worked as a librarian in Seneca Falls, New York. An attractive woman, she had rejected or at least postponed several marriage proposals by widowed police constable Cullen Stuart.

In *Seneca Falls Inheritance* (St. Martin, 1992), suffragettes converged upon Seneca Falls for a conference where women could issue their own declaration of independence. Glynis' work was interrupted by the death of Rose Walker, a woman searching for her birth parents. The legal rights of a woman to control her own property figured into a motive for murder. Glynis worked with Stuart and his enigmatic Indian deputy, Jacques Sundown.

Glynis' focus turned to the Underground Railway in *The North Star Conspiracy* (St. Martin, 1993). The death of slave catcher Lyle Brogan, and his actress friend Luella, occurred when Cullen had left town for a new job. Glynis helped Niles Peartree, a young friend in love with a mulatto, when he was imprisoned and tried for offenses against the Fugitive Slave Act.

Glynis' feelings for Cullen and Jacques were highlighted in *Blackwater Spirits* (St. Martin, 1995). Murders, tied to the lynching of a young Seneca, were attributed to Sundown. The lynching victim was his half-brother. Cullen was dismayed. Glynis set out to prove that Jacques was innocent. The relationship between Glynis and Cullen did not survive his suspicion that she was in love with Jacques.

Before *Through a Gold Eagle* (Berkley, 1996), Glynis had spent a year in Springfield, Illinois caring for a dying sister-in-law. When she returned to Seneca Falls, she was accompanied by her fashion conscious niece, Emma, and the corpse of a young man killed on the train. Although Cullen had paid marked attention to another woman in her absence, he and Glynis worked together to uncover a counterfeiting ring which subsidized John Brown at Harpers Ferry. The romantic tension between Glynis and Jacques was alleviated when he left Seneca Falls, keeping in touch with her occasionally.

Both Cullen and Jacques taught self-defense to Bronwyn Llyr, Glynis' more adventurous niece and the daughter of her sister Gwen. During *The Stalking Horse* (Berkley, 1998), the self-defense skills came in handy as Bronwyn, then employed by Pinkerton, went undercover in the Confederacy to investigate sabotage to railroads. The plots gradually revealed to Bronwyn were insidious, calling upon her resources and those of new and old friends. Glynis was relegated to the role of chief worrier in this narrative.

The initial involvement of Glynis in the affairs of the Brent family was unrealistic in *Must the Maiden Die* (Berkley, 1999). She befriended Tamar, a mute indentured servant girl accused of murdering her employer, and correctly identified the killer. Niece Bronwyn, still in the Secret Service, worked with Jacques Sundown to cut off arms smuggled to the Confederacy, and with Glynis to locate hidden supplies.

Bronwyn and her sister Kathryn were the primary figures in *Sisters of Cain* (Berkley, 2000) while Glynis appeared only in a ten-page segment and by reference. Bronwyn served as a spy for the Union forces under the supervision of the U.S. Treasury. Kathryn, despite the opposition of Dorothea Dix to her youth, served as a hospital ship nurse under the auspices of the Sanitary Commission. Both the villainous Col. Dorian de Warde and the elusive Jacques Sundown made brief appearances.

Although Glynis had a cameo appearance in *Brothers of Cain* (Berkley, 2001), the emphasis was on her two nieces: Bronwyn Llyr, still a Union spy, and Kathryn, a dedicated nurse. They reappeared in *Children of Cain* (2002), which reputedly is the last of the Civil War trilogy.

The narratives were a reminder of the burdens that women and African-Americans suffered, and their struggle to obtain civil rights. The contributions of white males to both causes were not ignored.

Torrey Tunet

Author: Dicey Deere

Torrey Tunet came from a remarkable background. Her father had been a Romanian explorer, who died as a tourist boat captain off the shores of New Zealand. When she was fourteen, she and a girlfriend stole a "suitcase full of unreported income from the town psychiatrist." She grew up in a small town thirty miles from Boston, but had traveled extensively through her work. Torrey turned her remarkable linguistic skills into a career as a freelance translator through Interpreters International. She was working a Belgian/Hungarian conference in Dublin in the initial narrative, staying at a second rate hotel.

In *The Irish Cottage Murder* (St. Martin, 1999), wealthy Irish-American Desmond Moore offered Torrey a better accommodation in his refurbished Irish castle. He had two objectives in Ireland: (1) to earn a place among the local gentry, and (2) to wreak revenge on the English family who had owned the castle for their ill treatment of his ancestors. His most recent guests included several who had good reason to wish him dead. Unfortunately, when he was murdered the local police considered Torrey a member of that group. Finding a Finnish corpse in the woods and appropriating a valuable piece of jewelry did nothing to help her cause. She and landscaper Luke Willinger, whose family she had injured in the past, exposed Moore's infamy and his killer.

Torrey returned to the Irish countryside in *The Irish Manor House Murder* (St. Martin, 2000) to write a series of multi-lingual books for children. With her own eyes, she saw her friend Rowena Keegan ride her horse roughshod over her grandfather, Dr. Gerald Ashenden. With her own lips Torrey lied to protect Rowena from prosecution. When Ashenden was killed in a subsequent accident, Inspector Egan O'Hare had no doubts as to who was responsible. Torrey and her lover Jasper O'Mara combined their talents to prove him wrong, sifting through decades of deceit that haunted the Ashenden family.

Tales set in Ireland may stretch credulity.

Next book in this series: *The Irish Cairn Murder* (2002)

Jane Turner

Author: Walter Satterthwait

Pinkerton agent, Phil Beaumont narrated the series, set in the 1920s in England and Europe, but Jane Turner played a significant role. She was a tall young Englishwoman, relegated to work as a companion to a difficult older woman, until Beaumont recruited her for the Pinkerton Detective Agency. The narration was interspersed with letters from Jane to her intimate friend Evangeline. She and Evangeline had been fellow students of a Mrs. Applewhite where Jane became proficient in French and German.

In *Escapade* (St. Martin, 1995), Jane had accompanied her employer Marjorie Allardyce to a country estate for a weekend shared by many distinguished guests, including Sir Arthur Conan Doyle and Harry Houdini. Beaumont was present to guard Houdini who had been threatened by a rival escape artist and magician. In a broadly comic treatment, Beaumont and Jane cooperated to roust a ghost, solve the murder of an elderly but licentious Earl, and protect Houdini. Beaumont was so impressed by Jane's help that he suggested to the Pinkerton Detective Agency that she be hired.

Masquerade (St. Martin, 1998) initially concentrated on Beaumont's Parisian assignment to probe the deaths of American Richard Forsythe and his German mistress, Sabine, again in a locked room. The French police had determined the case to be murder/suicide. Richard's mother did not accept that designation, even though his wife and other women of his acquaintance revealed his propensity for self-destructive behavior. Jane was present in France, assigned by the Pinkerton Detective Agency to act as nanny for the children of George, Richard's brother. Among the names dropped here were those of Ernest Hemingway, Gertrude Stein, and again Harry Houdini who helped in "locked door" situations. Working together and becoming personally interested in one another, Jane and Beaumont solved the initial case, but had to leave France hurriedly because Beaumont was wanted for murder. Next stop, Berlin to learn who may have tried to kill Adolf Hitler.

Light and entertaining.

Dr. Samantha "Sam" Turner

Author: Marsha Landreth

Sam Turner had been the second wife of a doctor, who had an adult son, Derek from his first marriage. A doctor herself, she had worked in a San Francisco hospital before her marriage. After her husband's death, she stayed on in Sheridan, Wyoming, fulfilling his dream of running a buffalo/cattle ranch. She was a slight blonde, who shared her home with a 200 pound yellow Labrador Retriever (Boomer), and a cat. Her father was still alive, but suffered from Alzheimer's.

As coroner in *The Holiday Murders* (Walker, 1992) "Sam" noticed the correlation between major holidays and violent deaths in the community. The murder on July 4th confirmed her theory of serial murders, but with an additional complication, this victim was under the Witness Protection Program. Was it a coincidence that Derek arrived in Sheridan to write an article on the buffalo ranch, and returned later for a Christmas visit? After Derek and Samantha became intimate, he left town without explanation.

In *A Clinic for Murder* (Walker, 1993), Derek and Samantha met again at a medical convention in San Diego. Their reunion was prompted by the disclosure of a mutual friend that Samantha was pregnant. When she provided first aid to a dying physician, his last words convinced her to search his hotel room, only to be arrested by the local police. Derek joined his investigative skills with hers as a pathologist, but both became targets for murder. The plot relied heavily on coincidence sending the couple on a honeymoon cruise with most of the suspects.

In *Vial Murders* (Walker, 1994), the series edged closer to science fiction when local deaths by smallpox were connected to a conspiracy to keep the virus alive for scientific research. Samantha and Derek, currently a house-husband and father, did not work together, nor trust one another. They balanced personal and professional loyalties against the lives of local students. The narratives played upon the gender/culture clash as Samantha moved from an urban medical system into a rural macho culture.

Anna Turnipseed

Author: Kirk Mitchell

Anna Turnipseed was an amalgam of races. Her mother had both Modoc Indian and Japanese blood. Her father was full-blooded Modoc. Her line was distinguished in Native American history as descendants of Captain Jack, a great warrior. However, her more recent family relationships were less distinguished. She had been the victim of childhood incest.

After Anna's college degree in sociology with a minor in accounting from the University of California-Berkeley, she entered the FBI Academy. She graduated first in her class. Anna settled in Las Vegas where she owned a small condo, but was frequently assigned to cases on Native American reservations.

There was horrifying violence in *Cry Dance* (Bantam, 1999). The narrative wove the needs and aspirations of Native Americans into the investigation of the death of a government official. Anna and Emmett Parker, a criminal investigator from the Bureau of Indian Affairs, a rival organization, were expected to work together investigating the connections among tribal insurrection, gambling on the reservation, and Jamaican gangsters. A man with every reason to hate Parker used Anna as bait in a trap.

The traumas of Anna's first year as an FBI agent were so serious that in *Spirit Sickness* (Bantam, 2000) she considered resigning. BIA investigator Emmett Parker who loved her, requested her participation in a major investigation, hoping it would restore her sense of competence. A Navajo police officer and his wife had been cruelly murdered. Working together and independently, with Anna taking on major authority, they followed a blood trail to a programmed killer. The complex narrative dealt with youth gangs on the reservation, a renegade Mormon cult, and Navajo traditions as to incest. Anna's own experience of incest personalized her involvement in the case.

Anna and Emmett were dispatched to Oregon to "keep order" and protect bones discovered by a Basque shepherd in *Ancient Ones* (Bantam, 2001). Early estimates touted by eminent archeologist Thaddeus Rankin identified the relics as 14,500 years old and of Caucasian origin. The Native American tribes who occupied the area where the discovery was made sought possession of the bones under federal law and challenged Rankin's characterization of coexisting tribes as cannibals. Science was pitted against tradition. The narrative was chillingly explicit. Emmett's efforts to be patient as Anna overcame her trauma as an incest survivor were indicative of his strong feeling for her.

Next book in this series: *Sky Woman Falling* (2003)

Mary "Ike" Tygart

Author: Polly Whitney

Ike Tygart's ex-husband, "Abby" Abagnarro, narrated the series. Ike existed only as Abby saw her, but he was madly in love and portrayed her with understanding, except for her decision to divorce him after a single infidelity. She was called "Ike" by Abby because of the denim overalls she wore, merchandised by a Midwestern manufacturer, Ike Mason. She had grown up in Missouri, where she earned a graduate degree in journalism from the state university. Over the years Ike had a career as an investigative reporter roaming the globe. She had unmasked a lascivious Minnesota senator who harassed his female staff; had uncovered a terrorist training camp run by Israelis in the desert; and then turned to production of a news program for the All News Network (ANN), winning three Emmys for her skill. Abby, who served as director for Ike's show *Morning Watch*, was a native New

Yorker from a large Italian-American family. His widowed mother, Carole, owned and managed Gypsy's, a restaurant patronized by nearby theatre personnel and patrons. In Abby's repentant eyes, Ike was naive and unforgiving, rooted in Midwestern ideals of marriage. She considered the marriage had ended because the trust on which it had been based was no longer available. This did not mean they never made love. In fact, as Abby knew to his advantage, Ike was "turned on" by danger. She was described as a tiny highly organized blonde who had one blue and one green eye. In happier days they had entered dance contests together, and they continued to do most of their inner city travel on roller skates. Both Ike and Abby were creative and professional, and the background for the narratives was well researched.

The divorce was recent as *Until Death* (St. Martin, 1994) began. Abby was still begging for forgiveness. Connie Candela, the new coanchor on *Morning Watch*, was discovered dead minutes before the show was to begin. Ike and Abby still had to produce a program, but they did so under the eyes of Captain Dennis Fillingeri, who found Ike attractive and Abby suspicious. Ike's expertise in the Mideast and Abby's careful eye for detail led to a spectacular conclusion, but no reconciliation.

By *Until the End of Time* (St. Martin, 1995), Ike had ended a romance with Fillingeri, but she and Abby had to work with him again. A chance attack on Abby tied into a serial killer who murdered homeless men found with their faces painted yellow. The subsequent murder of Dr. Hektor Stefanopolis, a researcher who had appeared on *Morning Watch*, made the connection between Abby's assailant and the serial deaths. Ike and Abby had a wild ride figuring it out.

A shotgun blast during a New York Knicks/Chicago Bulls basketball game at Madison Square Garden began *Until It Hurts* (St. Martin, 1997). Fans and players dropped to avoid injury. "The Big Chill," Archie Thorpe, a major star for the Knicks did not rise. Abby and Ike, who attended the game with her sound technician Church Finnegan, were shocked to learn that Thorpe did not die from the gunshot, but had been stabbed by a sharp object. Abby, who had chased after the shooter, was reluctant to share his insights with unfriendly police detective Dennis Fillingeri. Thorpe's purchase of huge tracks of forest in Brazil, which he intended to clear to raise cattle, had made him no friends among environmentalists. That seemed a weak motive to murder compared with Thorpe's irresponsible romantic life or the impact of his retirement. The method of murder and its delivery were innovative.

These were well-plotted narratives, with clues planted to maintain the reader's interest; however, Ike and Abby never moved beyond their original characterizations.

Amanda Valentine

Author: Rose Beecham, pseudonym for Jennifer Fulton

Amanda Valentine had dual citizenship—American through her mother, and New Zealander through her father. She was eleven when her parents separated, and remained in the custody of her father. Although she had a Ph.D., she became a police officer, first in New York City, then in Wellington, New Zealand. An attractive blonde, Amanda had not totally recovered from the tragic shooting of her female lover on the steps of a police station.

During *Introducing Amanda Valentine* (Naiad, 1992), Amanda juggled an attack on a transvestite informer, financial transgressions in the municipal offices, and a serial murderer, known as the Garbage Dump Killer. She dealt with a seductive television reporter on the personal level. She was successful in her investigations, but became disillusioned, and resigned her position to return to the United States.

The one-year hiatus in the United States ended, Amanda returned to New Zealand in *Second Guess* (Naiad, 1994). Political pressure was applied when the daughter of a prominent Wellington family was found dead in the "dungeon" of a lesbian nightclub.

By *Fair Play* (Naiad, 1995), Amanda was struggling to keep her under-staffed unit functioning while many officers were diverted to deal with political demonstrations. As a result, she took personal charge of the murder of Bruce Petty, a gay Australian who had jumped bail on charges of financial mismanagement. She also involved herself in a case of lesbian rape with no sympathy for the perpetrator. The dialogue in this narrative was cruder and more sexist than in the earlier books.

Tessa Vance

Author: Jennifer Rowe

Tessa's father, Senior Sgt. Doug Vance, was a legend in the police department. His utter devotion to his work unfortunately left little time for family affairs. He was killed in action. Her mother was deeply disappointed when, after Tessa finished her university degree, she entered the Police Academy. She eventually rose to be a senior detective in the homicide squad. In order to please her lover Brett, Tessa asked for a transfer to the district in Sydney closest to the apartment they shared. This was Doug Vance's old stomping ground. His reputation was both a burden and a blessing for her. She was allowed to make the transfer, but was perceived as receiving special treatment. Her reputation was that she was "undisciplined" but intuitive. While in the prior unit, Tessa had testified against Brady Mumm, a cold killer.

Tessa made an inauspicious start at her new precinct in *Suspect* (Ballantine, 1999) published as *Deadline* in Australia. Within days her life was in chaos. Brett, tired of competition from her work, decamped. Brady Mumm was paroled, and Tessa attributed anonymous phone calls and mischief to him. The homicide unit focused on a series of deaths with distinctive touches. Tessa played a substantial role in deducing the pattern of the killer, earning the respect of her new partner, Steve Hayden. It was incomprehensible that neither Tessa nor her superior officers at the prior precinct notified her current Inspector, Malcolm Thorne, of the possible danger to Tessa from Brady Mumm.

The Haven, an estate owned by reclusive Rachel Bryde in *Something Wicked* (Allen & Unwin, 1998; Ballantine, 1999) was the setting for the bizarre death of aging pop star Adam Quinn. Quinn had joined the Bryde household, consisting of Rachel and her three socially isolated daughters, more than four years before. Steve and Tessa were sent from the Sydney police force because there was suspicion of homicide. Their technical skills were supplemented by a canny local constable, but matched against layers of deceit and horror and evil. Rowe added the haunting quality of Daphne du Maurier to a police procedural.

Fran Varaday

Author: Ann Granger

Fran Varaday was a startling contrast to author Ann Granger's other female sleuth, Meredith Mitchell. Where Merry had been a diplomatic official, Fran, a usually unemployed actress, was an outsider. Where Merry tended to be highly organized, Fran was a free spirit. She had been deeply affected by her mother's abandonment. She had attended a good private school at great sacrifice to her father and grandmother Varaday, but was asked to leave because of her behavior and appearance. She wanted desperately to be an actress, but her drama course at the local technical school ended with her father's death and the increasing health problems of her grandmother.

When Gran died, there was no one to care for Fran. She took to the London streets at age sixteen. Over the ensuing years she had a variety of living situations: a commune of squatters, an dangerous apartment arranged by local government officials, and best of all a basement flat arranged by a grateful client. When this ended, she slept in a friend's garage. She acquired Bonnie, (possibly a Jack Russell terrier) by default. Employment was no easier. Low-level jobs came along, but didn't last. Her friend, Ganesh Patel often supplied weekend or part-time work for her through his family's grocery businesses. Friendship was a possibility; a real emotional connection, less likely.

In *Asking for Trouble* (Headline, 1997), the young woman they knew as "Terry" joined the squatters' commune on Jubilee Street but she never bonded. After a summons to evict them all from the building, the group prepared to leave. At that point, they found Terry hanging from the light fixture in her room. Inspector Janice Morgan agreed that this was unlikely to be a suicide. Terry's grandfather, Alistair Monkton paid Fran to research the years that Terry had been a runaway, and why anyone would want her dead. Ganesh reluctantly aided and abetted; then, finally, saved Fran's life.

Even with a basement apartment and a friendly landlady, Daphne Knowles, in *Keeping Bad Company* (Headline, 1997), Fran could not stay out of trouble. A chance encounter with boozy old Alkie Albie Smith involved her in the abduction of a wealthy young woman. The narrative provided lively twists and turns of plot. A former nemesis, Sgt. Wayne Parry, almost became an ally. More alarmingly he became fond of Fran. She saw close relationships as a trap, and was wary of them.

In *Running Scared* (Headline, 1998), problems piled up for Fran at home and at work. Twin nephews wanted Daphne Knowles to deed over her home to them in order to avoid eventual death taxes. Fran was well aware of their distaste for her. A frightened juvenile needed help to return to her country family. She had been "on the street" and was uncertain of her welcome. By now Fran thought of herself as being a part-time enquiry agent. Worst of all, an injured reporter had left damaging evidence in the store managed by Ganesh. When the reporter was murdered, Ganesh and Fran were targeted. They had every right to be scared.

The news that her mother Eva who had abandoned Fran as a small child, was dying came to her via a private investigator in *Risking It All* (Headline, 2001). After years of feeling rejection, Fran had mixed feelings about Eva. Even more so when she visited her at the hospice, only to learn that her mother's dying wish was to know the welfare of a younger daughter, Fran's half-sister, whom Eva had given up for adoption. Rennie Duke, the investigator who had located Fran, was found dead by Fran and Ganesh Patel. Inspector Janice Morgan had dealt with Fran before and wanted more information than Fran was willing to give. Her prospects were looking up as the narrative ended.

Next book in this series: *Watching Out* (2003)

Robin Vaughan

Author: Carolyn Banks

Robin Vaughan was a plump, brown-haired young woman. Her husband Jeet earned a comfortable living as food critic for the Austin *Daily Progress*, allowing her to indulge in her favorite, but expensive, sport of dressage. Her training exercises and competition brought her into the world of the wealthy and socially prominent.

Nika Ballinger, whose enthusiasm for dressage was not matched by her skill, was killed in what seemed to be an accident as *Death by Dressage* (Fawcett, 1993) began. Robin's awareness that Nika had been photographed with a horse not her own and in a habit designed for the highest level of skill dressage prompted her to investigate. A reward in the form of a second horse encouraged Robin to continue her detection.

In *Groomed for Death* (Fawcett, 1995), Robin accompanied Jeet to New York, where he negotiated a book contract. Surprisingly she managed to find horses, dressage, and murder through a casual acquaintance picked up on the city streets. She lied to her husband, and to Flora Benavides, the new friend who was killed in what was perceived as an accident. Accidents did not happen to Robin's acquaintances, so she tied up New York traffic with a frantic gallop down the avenues, and complicated a formal investigation of a sweatshop operation.

Robin visited Mexico in *Murder Well-Bred* (Fawcett, 1995). She parlayed Jeet's assignment to describe Mexican food into a commission to write an article on Mexican horse ranches. Her recollection of a birthmark on a foreign dressage horse led her into danger, and may have contributed to several murders.

The Vaughans return to Austin was short-lived because during *Death on the Diagonal* (Fawcett, 1996) Jeet managed a small town weekly whose deceased editor had been a personal friend. This was expected to be a short-term assignment while a replacement could be found; nevertheless, Robin and her horses moved to Bead, Texas. Her first concern was to find adequate housing and exercise facilities for Plum and Spier. In doing so, she discovered who had killed the former editor.

A Horse to Die For (Fawcett, 1996) found Robin perplexed. The gift horse owned by her dear friend Lola could be a killer or the reincarnation of a dead horse. Either way, someone took Robin's investigation seriously enough to want her out of the way.

Light fare for horse lovers.

Ronnie Ventana

Author: Gloria White

Ronnie Ventana, a former parole agent, became a licensed private detective hoping her Japanese language skills would provide her with work in industrial espionage. Her Mexican father had been a jewel thief; her mother, an American socialite who joined him in his escapades. Ronnie's three-year marriage to Mitch had ended eight years before the narrative began.

During *Murder on the Run* (Dell, 1991), Ronnie witnessed a murder while jogging along San Francisco Bay. While attending a professional meeting, she recognized the killer. Knowing her father's record, Lt. Philly Post of the SFPD had a problem with Ronnie's credibility. The man she had identified was a former investigator for the District Attorney's office. With the help of "Blackie" Coogan, her sixty-five year old retired mentor, she avoided being caught in a dangerous vendetta.

Bink Hanover, a certified public accountant, who had once saved Mitch's life, thought Ronnie could save him from a vengeful woman and three hit men in *Money to Burn* (Dell, 1993). Ronnie knew that Bink was undependable but quickly became so involved in his problems that she needed Mitch, "Blackie" and Lt. Post to put the matter to rights.

Ronnie allowed herself to be set up as a murder suspect in *Charged with Guilt* (Dell, 1995). Her assignment, to test the security of a prominent politician's home, was bogus, and the senator was dead on her arrival. Ronnie not only had to prove her innocence, but protect herself and a developmentally disabled youth from vengeful killers.

The anniversary of the deaths of Ronnie's parents had special meaning for her. As *Sunset and Santiago* (Dell, 1997) began, she returned in the early hours of the morning to the street corner where their accident had occurred. In so doing, she was a witness to the dumping of an unidentified corpse. Young Marina Murieta, who had followed Ronnie, could identify one of those who dropped the body. The police placed no value on Marina's identification, even though the man was found dead later. Ronnie knew that the hostility which city prosecutor Harland P. Harper felt for the Ventana family was part of the problem. She could not understand why her friend, Lt. Philly Post would cooperate with a cover-up.

White had clever plot twists and an engaging character. Her later narratives showed improvement.

Victoire Vernet

Authors: Quinn Fawcett, pseudonym for
Chelsea Yarbro Quinn and Bill Fawcett

Madame Victoire Vernet was a petite young Frenchwoman married to Lucien Jeannot Vernet, a gendarme official attached to the Egyptian based army of Napoleon Bonaparte. Victoire's family was middle class, but the nobility and monarchy had been displaced. She had a private education, encouraged by a mother who had managed the family business in her husband's absence. Victoire had no hesitation about accompanying her husband to Egypt although few reputable women were on the scene of Napoleon's military conquests.

In *Napoleon Must Die* (Avon, 1993), Lucien was held responsible when a golden scepter of symbolic importance to the Egyptians was stolen from booty confiscated by French soldiers. Napoleon decoyed Lucien with a mission, leaving Victoire as a possible accomplice under the care of Marmeluke Roustam Raza. Victoire's determination to discover who stole the scepter and killed the guard convinced Raza of her innocence. Together they provided information that saved Napoleon's life.

Napoleon's safety was at risk again in *Death Wears a Crown* (Avon, 1993). While Lucien traveled to Belgium on business, Victoire carried secret dispatches from the French coast to Paris. Even after her arrival in the capital city, she had to confound French exiles, British patriots, and members of the Imperial staff determined to depose Napoleon. As the narrative ended, Victoire, who was despondent about an earlier miscarriage, was happy to learn that she was pregnant.

Lightweight, but not everyone wants to challenge the intellect in his or her spare time.

Dr. Anne Vernon

Author: Alan Scholefield

Anne Vernon had been raised by her father Henry Vernon, a prosecutor and jurist in the British colonial service in Africa and later an advisor to independent African governments. Her mother, unable to cope with life in Africa, left the family home and returned to England when Anne was a small child. The subsequent contacts between mother and daughter had been rare. Anne returned to England for her medical training, finishing up at the distinguished St. Thomas' facility. She had tentatively accepted a position with a London medical practice, when she learned of her father's illness. During the interval when she was making arrangements for Henry's recuperation and move back to England, the firm rescinded its offer.

There had been alternatives for Anne. By that time, she had met and become pregnant by Paul, a young architect responsible for an addition to the medical facility where she was training. Paul's death in a tragic accident before they could be married left Anne with the joys and difficulties of raising her daughter, Hilary ("Hilly"). The decisions to move to Kingstown, to accept a position in the medical service of the Kingstown Prison, and to purchase a large home jointly with her father, all came together at once. Her other option had been to accept the offer made by her lover, business tycoon Clive Parker, for marriage and a subsidized career in private practice. Clive had been an emotional resource for Anne after Paul's death. He loaned her the money to pay her share of the cost of the Kingstown house. Even with these connections, or perhaps because of them, Anne was unsure that she could make a future with Clive.

Burn Out (Headline, 1994) began with Anne's first days at the prison: her kind welcome by Dr. Tom Melville, head of the Medical Service; the hostility of Jeffrey Jenks, chief of the Nursing Services, and her empathy for former professional tennis player, Jason Newman. An avid tennis player, Anne had played a doubles match against Newman in her early teens, one that convinced her that she had no future in the game. He was in Kingstown on remand, awaiting trial. Anne's professional role was to evaluate his condition for the court, but she needed to know more about him. Henry Vernon became the investigator, meeting with the emotionally disabled members of Jason's family and probing into the background of the alleged victim. This was an absorbing exploration of the impact of one man's obsession on his family, causing his son to be vulnerable to another equally destructive personality.

Haunted by the suicide of a convicted prisoner, later shown to be innocent, Anne and Tom Melville made every effort to safeguard remand prisoner, Mason Chitty in *Buried Treasure* (Headline, 1995). He had pleaded his innocence in the alleged death of Sharon Benson, a young woman with whom he had an affair. The failure to find Sharon's body was not only a flaw in the prosecution's case, but a source of anguish to her mother Lily. While Anne and Henry investigated the Chitty family background, Lily and newfound allies searched for the body. Watchman Malopo, Henry's law clerk and major domo in Africa, joined the Vernon household and added his skills to the search. Another interesting exploration of family dynamics, upper class attitudes to unwed pregnancy, sibling rivalries, and mother-daughter relationships.

Francesca Vierling

Author: Elaine Viets

The marriage of Francesca's parents, thought to be pillars of the church and the suburb of Crestwood, had been a fraud. Both were closet alcoholics who quarreled violently, leaving little time for their daughter. When Francesca was nine, her mother, enraged by her father's infidelity, killed him and shot herself. Her maternal grandparents were older and less wealthy, but they provided her with a stable environment and a sense of being loved.

Little was said of her education but she had been a columnist for the St. Louis *City Gazette* for 15 years when the series began. Francesca enjoyed her job, but was contemptuous of her immediate supervisor Charlie, of Hadley Harris III, the prudish managing editor, and of the sycophants who prospered under this regime. The *Gazette* was heavily beholden to its advertisers, and prided itself on being a clean wholesome publication. Charlie, a notorious letch, failed to live up to these standards. Georgia T. George, the assistant managing editor, was not only the most competent person on staff, but served as a mentor to Francesca. Both realized that the non-resident publisher was unlikely to support the female staff members.

Because of the popularity of her columns, Francesca was allowed considerable leeway. She was the free wheeling columnist on a hidebound newspaper. The *Gazette* had been a vital influence in the community, but the quality of staff had declined over the past decades. She spent more time at places like Uncle Bob's Pancake House than she did at the office. It was there that individuals sought her out with interesting tips for feature stories.

Francesca described herself as "Scrubby Dutch," one of the hardworking Germans who had built St. Louis into a thriving community. The downtown of St. Louis had deteriorated with the relocation of its more prosperous citizens to the suburbs, but Francesca preferred it. The personal rejection she had felt from neighbors and classmates after the tragedy of her parent's deaths left her prejudiced against their conventional lifestyle. She mixed with homosexuals, prostitutes, and minorities without patronizing them, still living in the building that had been her grandparents' home. Francesca was most at home in bars and libraries. Like many other female sleuths, she was attached to her ancient car, a 1986-88 blue Jaguar which she named Ralph. She described herself as a tall blonde in her late thirties. Among her resources were Marlene, the outspoken waitress at Uncle Bob's; Cutup Katie, an assistant medical examiner; and on occasion Detective Matt Mayhew.

Lyle Donnegan, Francesca's long time lover, was an English professor at a local university. He was there for her whenever needed, but she refused to move into his home. When depressed she insisted upon being alone. He offered marriage and security but she was not ready. She had been raised a Catholic but when she considered marriage, spoke of going before a minister, and dodged that question whenever possible.

Backstab (Dell, 1997) mixed a fond description of downtown St. Louis, Missouri and its residents with a mildly tawdry story of murdered transvestites and gay men. Author Eliaine Viets provided great character studies, interesting vignettes that illuminated the eccentricities of the Germanic culture of old St. Louis. Francesca challenged the administration at the *Gazette* to report honestly about conditions that Charlie and Hadley would prefer to ignore.

Viets delivered an engrossing mystery wrapped in an expose of the rich and righteous in *Rubout* (Dell, 1998). Sydney Vander Venter had an extreme reaction to her pending divorce from her powerful and wealthy husband. She took up with the Harley bikers, attending their ball dressed fit to kill. Someone did. Francesca, also present at the gala, went beyond the easy suspects—the motorcyclists. A born and bred Southsider, she focused on residents of Ladue, where the Vander Venters resided. Fortunately she avoided a trip that the killer had planned for her.

Property values had risen due to the rehabilitation of homes on North Dakota Place in *The Pink Flamingo Murders* (Dell, 1999). The ramrod tactics of Caroline, a real estate dealer and the force behind the changes, aroused admiration in some, resentment in others; and finally murder in one. Francesca checked out Caroline's neighbors, treading carefully so as not to rile Charlie at the *Gazette*. Her concentration on the North Dakota murders blinded her to what was happening in her personal life.

Georgia T. George was the only management level employee at the *Gazette* that Francesca could tolerate, or even feel affection towards. So in *Doc in the Box* (Dell, 2000), she made herself available to transport Georgia to her radiology and chemotherapy appointments at Moorton Hospital. Both women were appalled at the callous treatment the radiation therapy staff provided. Someone was even more ticked off. Doctors in the box-like Wellhaven Medical Arts Building, in the hospital clinic, and in their private offices were being shot. There was a great story there, a potential winner. Although nominated, Francesca did not win the McNamara award but came away with a prize.

The series provided good local color: what matters in St. Louis; the traditional foods and drinks; the variance in neighborhoods. If you want the inside story of St. Louis as seen by Viets, these are worth reading.

Francesca took on all of the local powers: the Catholic Church, the police department, the *Gazette*, and city administration. She pointed out their flaws and worked with the "good guys and gals" in the system. She could be compared to Warshawski, except Francesca had a sense of humor. Actually Francesca rarely figured out the killer until she was face to face with him or her wielding a weapon. What's more she admitted this limitation.

Viets has a new series, *The Dead End Job Mysteries* featuring Helen Hawthorne.

Jackie Walsh

Author: Melissa Cleary

Jackie Walsh, a single mother, found all of the excitement she wanted when she added Jake, an Alsatian retired from the police department K-9 corps, to her household. Not only did Jake become a companion for Peter, her ten-year-old son, but he also protected their home in Palmer, Ohio. After her divorce, Jackie had returned to a larger city, where she was employed as a cinematographer in the Communications Department of Rodgers University. During the first three books, a continuing sub-plot was the search for the killer of Jake's owner, retired police officer Matt Dugan.

In *A Tail of Two Murders* (Diamond, 1992), Jackie discovered the corpse of Philip Barger, head of the Communications Department. Jackie's knowledge of intellectual theft helped Lt. Mike MacGowan solve the mystery. He became an important part of her life. MacGowan and Medical Examiner Cosmos Gordon were friends of Dugan and actively seeking his killer.

The internecine war among dog breeders in *Dog Collar Crime* (Diamond, 1993) flared when Basset fancier Mel Sweeten was murdered. MacGowan used Jackie and Jake for access into dogdom, and the case to ingratiate himself with the Walsh family.

Reporter Marcella Jacobs returned to Palmer from a high-powered job in Philadelphia in *Hounded to Death* (Jove, 1993). Her exposé of a local politician became dangerous when Bambi, his mistress, was murdered. Jackie not only identified Bambi's killer, but also solved the murder of Matt Dugan. She and MacGowan carried on a circumspect courtship.

In *Skull and Dog Bones* (Jove, 1994), Ralph Perrin, the potential biographer of a pioneer female director, contacted Jackie shortly before he was found dead. With Jake seriously injured by a burglar, Jackie and Mike visited the West coast where the murder occurred, but a murky ending brought the solution back to Ohio.

The wealthy and stingy Goodwillie family was the source of problems in *First Pedigree Murder* (Berkley, 1994). Jackie pressured the family to donate money for a campus building. Mannheim, the kinder, gentler brother, was murdered on stage during the dedication. The clue to the killer might be a videotape of the ceremony. The narrative, interspersed with extraneous material, used a killer who had made only a minor appearance.

In *Dead and Buried* (Berkley, 1994), who would believe that Merida Green, the murderer Jackie helped to convict, would be paroled after 18 months? Or that she would join up with Jackie in solving the deaths of a Palmer campus cop and Jake's former trainer? An added pet, Maury, son of Jake, was an untrained undisciplined animal that author Melissa Cleary used for comic relief.

Maury played a larger role in *The Maltese Puppy* (Berkley, 1995) during which a former Nobel Prize winner came to the Palmer campus, only to be stabbed in the back.

Marcella Jacobs, Jackie's friend and an investigative reporter, went undercover at the local zoo during *Murder Most Beastly* (Berkley, 1996). She planned to expose shoddy conditions, but a nine-foot tall ostrich savagely attacked Marcella and her escort. Even though Maury saved Marcella, the narrative was beyond salvation. Jackie investigated the death of the keeper who had escorted Marcella and probed a series of illnesses incurred by children who visited the zoo. Justice was achieved only by the intervention of an adult gorilla.

Frances Costello, Jackie's mother, was filling her hours with good deeds as *Old Dogs* (Berkley, 1997) began, which was fine until she involved her daughter. Winnie Swann, the elderly nursing home resident whom Frances visited, had exhausted her funds. She was certain that somewhere in the Swann home money had been secreted to sustain her. Mr. Swann, she declared, had been a bank thief. Incredible, but worth investigating. The "old dogs" were elderly men who had been undisciplined in their youth; one of whom would kill to keep their secret.

And Your Little Dog, Too (Berkley, 1998), the best book of the series, opened as Jackie, after hearing a dog whimpering, was led to the corpse of a homeless woman. Jackie did not accept the police decision to write the death off as exposure and alcohol, and investigated the problems of a powerful, but dysfunctional local family.

Mid-level television stars Lorraine Voss and Kurt Manowski came to Palmer during *In the Dog House* (Berkley, 2000) to perform in a film directed by a young Rodgers College graduate, John McBride., Jackie recommended another media expert, former producer Cameron Clark, to John when the original producer was sidelined. Clark proved to be a disruptive presence on the sets. When he was murdered, McBride, a former student of Jackie's, was suspected. Jackie, who felt responsibility for involving Clark in the film, used her California contacts to learn more about other suspects. Even then, she did not recognize the killer until she was in danger.

The books were at the low end of the sex/violence scale, attractive to those who prefer it that way, but had weak plotting. Some may be annoyed by the unrealistic skills and instincts Cleary ascribed to Jake.

Liz Wareham

Author: Carol Brennan

Liz Wareham was finding it difficult to live alone. She had been divorced twice. Her children were off to college. Her psychiatrist lover had just abandoned her. Tense and lonely, she slept with the lights on, snuggling her two cats. Liz was a shopaholic, mildly dyslexic, and a terrible driver. Enough distinguishing characteristics for a new sleuth.

In *Headhunt* (Carroll & Graf, 1991), Liz had every right to be scared. In her work for The Gentle Group, a public relations firm, she arrived for an early meeting with client King Carter, only to find him stabbed to death. The investigating officer turned out to be former beau Lt. Ike O'Hanlon. When Liz identified the killer, her cleaning woman protected her from serious harm.

In *Full Commission* (Carroll & Graf, 1993), Liz was more subdued, realizing that her interference in the prior case had tragic results. Riding home in a cab early in the morning, she witnessed an encounter between landlord Alfred Stover and a rent control protected tenant. Real estate broker Margaret Rooney feared that a member of her staff was responsible for vicious tricks sabotaging her sales, including murder.

Penelope Warren

Author: Garrison Allen

"Big Mike," Penelope Warren's cat had top billing in the series, but Penelope deserved credit for the investigations. Penelope, who paid her dues in the Marine Corps and the Peace Corps, chose Empty Creek, Arizona as her home and the location of her mystery bookstore, "Mycroft & Company." Big Mike (actually Mycroft) was an Abyssinian alley cat Penelope adopted during her travels. He was totally spoiled, even having his own American Express card.

Penelope did not waste her three college degrees, including a Ph.D. in English Literature. She used them as an assistant professor at the local college. In her spare time, she rode her Arabian filly, Chardonnay, and enjoyed the company of Harris Anderson III a.k.a. Andy, the editor of the local newspaper. Mild mannered Andy had been slow to succumb to Penelope's seductive behavior, but learned fast once he realized what she had in mind; i.e. romantic and fantastic improvisations on love making. Penelope's life was frequently enlivened by visits from her sister, Cassandra (an actress known professionally as Stormy Williams), who enchanted "Dutch" Fowler, the Empty Creek chief of police. Penelope's best female friend was Laney Henders, an author of erotic Westerns.

As *Desert Cat* (Zebra/Kensington 1994) began, Empty Creek was startled by the murder of Louise Fletcher, its most influential citizen. Louise had never been a close friend, but she chose Penelope to identify her attacker, leaving nebulous clues, which finally led to an obvious killer with a weak alibi.

In *Royal Cat* (Kensington, 1995), Penelope was persuaded to serve as "Queen" of the annual Elizabethan Spring Faire, which preoccupied the community every weekend during February and March. Not only did professional vendors and theatrical groups join in the Faire, but the Empty Creek businessmen prospered from the tourists. Penelope's predecessor had been murdered, so her first order of business was to find the killer.

The disappearance of a valuable Arabian stallion and the death of its trainer shortly before the Empty Creek Horse Show galvanized Penelope (and the local police) into action during *Stable Cat* (Kensington, 1996). She had been depressed and conscious of her age. A murder came at just the right time. Penelope's semi-legitimate status allowed her to question the suspects. She researched the lives of the trainer and the owners of the stallion. There were villains galore, and Penelope found them all.

Penelope had never abandoned her loyalty to the Detroit Tigers and Lions sports teams. In *Baseball Cat* (Kensington, 1997), she transferred her interest to the winless Empty Creek farm team. The discovery of the corpse of Peter Adcock, general manager of the Coyotes, in a dugout set Penelope on the trail of his killer. She considered herself an unofficial member of the local police department, interviewed and researched the players, club management and staff, and the denizens of the "Dynamite Lounge."

Dinosaur Cat (Kensington, 1998) had a cluttered cast of characters. The identification of dinosaur bones in desert could be a threat to a major development or a boon to the local economy. Bone hunters from Japan, Israel, and Russia had been attracted to the site, but a subsequent explosion buried the bones under debris. The death of a geology professor made it clear that rival factions were playing for keeps. A family feud and suspicions that a visiting expert had stolen elements of the Dead Sea Scrolls from a Russian museum complicated the investigation. This might be too complex a problem for humans, but the cat, "Big Mike" saved the day.

Penelope learned more about sister Stormy's work life when both had parts in a western movie shot in Empty Creek during *Movie Cat* (Kensington, 1999). Stormy had the more significant role but Penelope and her new alter ego, Elfrida Fallowfield, evened the score by identifying the killer of the movie's director and rescuing five potential victims. The cluttered manuscript added highly sexed screwballs from Los Angeles to the already overcrowded Empty Creek complement.

Penelope's level of involvement in detection was implausible, but the suspects and faithful readers ignored that fact.

Claire Watkins

Author: Mary Logue

Claire Watkins and her daughter Meg moved to northwestern Wisconsin from the Twin Cities in nearby Minnesota after her husband Steve died. He had been killed in a hit and run accident that Claire thought might have been retribution for her investigation into a drug gang, but she had never been able to prove it. She could no longer stay in the Twin Cities without Steve. Claire's younger sister Bridget was married and lived within thirty miles of Fort St. Antoine. Her prior experience as a trained police investigator helped Claire find employment in the sheriff's office in Fort St. Antoine, along the east side of the Mississippi River. Other deputies in the department initially resented her having this top-level position.

Meg, Claire's daughter, had a secret that almost cost her life in *Blood Country* (Walker, 1999). She had seen the redheaded man in a pickup who deliberately ran down her father. "Red" was aware that she was a danger to him. When he appeared in Fort St. Antoine, he tried unsuccessfully to kidnap Meg; then, he did abduct Bridget. Claire traced the strands that led back to Steve's death. She discovered something she did not want to believe. The death of a friendly neighbor gave Claire her first chance to use the skills she had developed as a homicide investigator at the Minneapolis police department. As a bonus, she met pheasant farmer Rich Haggard who filled an empty place in her life and Meg's.

Wracked by nightmares and panic attacks in *Dark Coulee* (Walker, 2000), Claire held back from her growing attachment to Rich Haggard.

Much as she needed his stability and warmth, her first priority at that time was solving the murder of isolated farmer Jed Spitzler. The most likely suspects for Jed's death were well-liked individuals in the community: a local mayor, the sturdy owner of a construction company, and Jed's teenage children. While working her way through her emotional problems with the help of a therapist, Claire reached out to Jed's daughter.

Claire's original motivation in moving out of the Twin Cities had been to get away from violence. In *Glare Ice* (Walker, 2001), she encountered brutality at several levels: the cruelty of a teacher to her daughter Meg, the avariciousness of a caretaker for an elderly woman, and an obsessive relationship that led to the deaths of two kindly gentle men.

A very well written series with an appealing heroine.

Lucy Wayles

Author: Lydia Adamson, pseudonym for Frank King

Lucy Wayles, a retired archivist who had been employed as director of the Urban Natural History Library of the City of New York, was entranced by feathered vertebrates a.k.a. the birds. In fact, she believed that in some previous incarnation, she had been an owl. She had many of the characteristics: wise, curious, and ready to pounce on prey. When she incurred publicity for her imprudent climb on an icy bridge to save a tufted duck, she was unceremoniously deprived of her position as president of the Central Park Bird Watchers. Unfazed, she began her own society, Olmstead's Irregulars. Recruits were few, although her long time suitor Markus Bloch, a researcher in viral genetics, remained loyal.

As *Beware the Tufted Duck* (Signet, 1996) began, Lucy was again at odds with the establishment. The police department had decided that her friend Abraham Lescalles had been murdered by one of the homeless who frequent Central Park. Lucy insisted that the killer was a "birder." Once she selected a primary suspect, Markus had to restrain Lucy from making a citizen's arrest. Just as well, as she had not yet properly researched the victim. When Lucy, a humorless woman, put her mind to a subject she was obsessive.

In *Beware the Butcher Bird* (Signet, 1997), Lucy followed up on the apparent suicide of Jack Wesley, a distinguished ornithological artist. Convinced that Wesley had been murdered, she rallied Olmstead's Irregulars to find his killer. Heedless of the danger to others, particularly Markus, she led them through the urban jungle of New York City. When finally disclosed, the motivation for murder was as obscure as a prehistoric ancestor to birdlife.

There was no improvement in the third narrative, *Beware the Laughing Gull* (Signet, 1998). As members of Lucy's bird group were murdered, jailed, or left town, new birders replaced them, not always copacetic with the original members. When Peter Marin became engaged, no one was too excited. He had never fulfilled any of his prior engagements. This time the ceremony would have been completed had not someone on roller blades shot the bride. Lucy insisted that the Olmstead Irregulars find the killer to clear Peter as a suspect. Aided by birdsong phonograph records the group succeeded in exposing a smuggling racket and identifying a killer.

Lucy was a domineering insensitive heroine whose antics and adventures were narrated by a devoted suitor.

Lydia Adamson is the pseudonym for Frank King. This is his third entry in the Mystery Women series as Adamson. The other two featured veterinarian Deirdre Nightingale and actress Alice Nestleton. As King, he also wrote a shorter series featuring Sally Tepper (covered in *Mystery Women*: Volume 2).

Fiona Wooten "Biggie" Weatherford
Author: Nancy Bell

Biggie Weatherford's husband, Cuthbert had disappeared from her life after the Korean War. Her only son died an alcoholic; his wife, considered their child, young J.R., a burden so she left him behind in Biggie's care. J.R. (age eleven as the series began) was the focus of her life. She was eccentric, as only the extremely wealthy can be. Her behavior, keeping a catfish in the toilet bowl, washing greens in the bathtub, using an open refrigerator as an air conditioner might have labeled her otherwise. Owning about half of Kemp County, Texas protected her from the authorities and public retribution. She drove her car without a license and without concern for the traffic laws. People merely stayed out of her way.

Biggie and her supporting cast of characters were introduced in *Biggie and the Poisoned Politician* (St. Martin, 1996): the loyal tenants who farmed her land and their partly bald daughter who was J.R.'s best pal, the itinerant wannabe author whom she allowed to live above her garage, and her housekeeper/cook who was into voodoo and whose recipes were an extra treat. Biggie, who had a deep interest in family history, would not tolerate the location of a sanitary landfill near her ancestral graveyard. The death of its chief proponent, Mayor Osbert Gribbons, merely deflected her attention temporarily while she found his killer.

During *Biggie and the Mangled Mortician* (St. Martin, 1997), she had several projects in hand: to direct and appear in the local presentation of Gilbert & Sullivan's *H.M.S. Pinafore*, the renovation of the local depot, J.R.'s concern about the appearance of the Wooten Creek Monster, and finally, the murder of Monk Carter, the newly resident mortician. Unsure that the Texas Rangers could handle this matter, Biggie deployed her ex-convict houseman Rosebud to do the field investigations while she set to right other problems besetting the citizens of Job's Crossing.

Biggie and the Fricasseed Fat Man (St. Martin, 1998) divided her attention between the murder of a local businessman and the threat that Jane Culpepper, J.R.'s maternal grandmother would take him back to Montana with her. J.R.'s mother had shown little interest in the boy, but readily transferred her rights to her mother, Janie, whose second husband had recently lost a grandson in an accident. J.R. was on the brink of running away when Biggie solved both problems.

The gift of a swampy land parcel to the James Royce Wooten chapter of the Daughters of the Republic of Texas (Biggie Weatherford, president) brought unexpected consequences in *Biggie and the Meddlesome Mailman* (St. Martin, 1999). The local unit of the right wing Empire of Texas was holding training sessions on the property for anti-government activities. In a parallel plot line, Biggie and J.R. discovered the corpses of two officials, a dangerously inquisitive postal employee and a corrupt state politician. She had to rely on the good will of a teenage boy to save her life, but Biggie was right on target in solving the murders.

Biggie decided that Job's Crossing deserved an historical society equal to that of nearby Quincy, as *Biggie and the Quincy Ghost* (St. Martin, 2001) began. This necessitated overnight stays at the local inn, which prided itself upon having a ghost. It was J.R. who thought he heard a ghost and who discovered the corpse of Annabeth, a pretty young girl who worked at the inn. Biggie and J.R. combined to unearth historical secrets that the local inhabitants would just as soon have left in the past.

Stops just short of being too cute.

Next book in this series: *Biggie and the Devil Diet* (2002)

Molly West

Author: Patricia Tichenor Westfall

Molly West had not been born in Appalachia but moved there fifteen years ago with her husband, Ken. He had an opportunity for a faculty job in sociology at Sycamore State College in southern Ohio. Molly left an excellent position as benefits manager at a bank for a life in the country. The Wests had two children: Amanda, a graphic designer and Todd, who, after a rocky start, had finished college. Their rural life was not what Ken and Molly had planned. He had hoped for a more prestigious university. She had aimed for a bank presidency, but soon Molly was happy in Appalachia, even knowing that she would always be an outlander and eventually Ken (nicknamed Dr. K) came to enjoy the area. More recently she had become associate director of the Tri-County Meal Van Service, delivering to shut-ins plus providing on-site meals at one location. In her fifties, Molly was otherwise undescribed. With an empty nest, Ken and Molly had taken an active role in the Puppy Rescue Association, acting as short-term foster caregivers for abandoned puppies.

One of those to welcome the Wests to the area was Dave Breyers, manager of a local mill, so in *Fowl Play* (St. Martin, 1996), Molly found it difficult to believe that he had killed his former wife. Cathy Breyers had been a shy young woman, less open to making new friends, but Molly discovered that Cathy had a secret life. Molly made good use of her connection with the local sheriff and of the wisdom and courage of Louella Chalmers Benton, an elderly woman to whom she brought food.

During *Mother of the Bride* (St. Martin, 1998), Molly was diverted into investigating the escape of a convict and the presence of bones too new to be of merely historical interest. Amanda and her long time fiancé, Bentley Cottingham, of the Cleveland Cottinghams, decided to make it legal. The wedding was to be in her hometown with multiple bridesmaids from Amanda's high school years. There was one problem: the maid of honor, Bonnie Wheeler Sievers, was the potential target of her escaped convict husband, Luke. Because of connections with Civil War reenactments, the wedding decor would be strictly historical. The complications: gun smuggling, poisoning, and the discovery of bones were more recent.

Virginia West

Author: Patricia Cornwell

See: Judy Hammer, page 262.

Connor Westphal

Author: Penny Warner

At age thirty-seven, Connor Westphal preferred to be called C.W. as befitted her position as the editor of the Flat Skunk weekly newspaper, *Eureka,* published in the Mother Lode country of California. Before moving there Connor had worked for six years on the *San Francisco Chronicle.* Her parents who remained in San Francisco had turned over their rights to her grandparents' small diner and printing press to Connor. She hoped some day to renovate the diner, perhaps providing coffee equal to that she had enjoyed in San Francisco. In the meantime, she lived in the back rooms. She owned a 1957 Chevrolet, which she used for longer trips, but most of her transportation was by her mountain bike. One of Connor's special features was the construction of mystery puzzles that she included in the paper. She was unable to compete with the rival *Mother Lode Monitor* in breaking news, but she did her best.

Connor dealt with her deafness by reading lips plus using both ASL (American Sign Language) and SEE (Seeing Exact English). Her parents had made a conscious effort to maintain Connor within the world of speech. Because she had lost her hearing at age four as a result of meningitis, she had a background as to speech sounds. Her telephone was equipped with TTY, which enabled her to send messages, but her reception had to be translated. Young Jeremiah (Miah) Mercer, son of the local police chief, ran a resale comic/CD/video game business in the former Hotel Penzance where Connor had her office. He worked part-time as Connor's assistant and translator. They exchanged favors as Connor collected "girlie" comics— "Archie and Veronica" and "Lulu." Connor enjoyed Sierra Nevada beer and ate Dove bars for a pickup. She missed the great San Francisco coffee so mixed a cup of cocoa into regular coffee to create her own mocha. Unable to hear an alarm clock, she purchased a shake-awake bed to get her up in the morning.

Connor's personal life was shared with Dan Smith, initially a police officer, then self-employed as an investigator, and with her dog, Casper.

Casper, a Siberian husky, had been trained as a signal dog for the deaf. Her closest female friend was Del Ray Montez, local mortician.

Lacy Penzance, of the illustrious local family, contacted Connor to place an ad seeking her missing sister during *Dead Body Language* (Bantam, 1997). Lacy's murder and the disappearance of hard drinking private investigator Boone Joslin caused Connor to investigate a pair of scams. Her companion, although sometimes he was a suspect, was Dan Smith, Boone's half brother. Connor used her skills, a sense of smell and knowledge of comics, to identify a killer.

Trite but true, the earth moved for Dan and Connor (and everyone else in town) during *Sign of Foul Play* (Bantam, 1998). Two earthquakes and a series of aftershocks hit Flat Skunk. Initially the quake was blamed for the death of soils engineer Cullen Delancey. His body had been found at the site of a building constructed for the *Monitor*, the rival newspaper owned by the Truax family. Connor dug deeper. The corpses piled up. Clues from faulty lip reading and unclear signs led Connor to a crashing finish.

Flat Skunk had old buildings and old secrets to be dealt with in *Right To Remain Silent* (Bantam, 1998). Sparkle Bodie, a wealthy older woman, sought to preserve the town as it had been for her ancestors. Her son, Esken and his wife Sonora preferred to change the town into a tourist attraction. Sparkle was so close to death that she had been taken to the funeral parlor, revived, only to be smothered to death in the hospital. Connor was appalled when Caleb, Sparkle's other son was arrested. Caleb, who had been born deaf, had been treated as developmentally disabled, kept isolated, and never trained to communicate. He needed an advocate and Connor took the job.

Perhaps some new blood in Flat Skunk wouldn't be all bad. The locals seemed addicted to complex marital encounters, confused parentage, and lethal weapons in *A Quiet Undertaking* (Bantam, 2000). Dan Smith involved Connor in paint ball games, but some of their adversaries escalated to more dangerous weapons. Del Ray's mortuary was in serious trouble. Cremains (the residue after cremation), which had been destined for disposal in the ocean, were discovered in a common storage facility. The man responsible had been murdered. Careful readers will note an editing error: a major disclosure was prematurely revealed.

The Mark Twain short story about frog-jumping contests had been seized upon as a draw for tourists by the string of small California towns known as the Mother Lode communities. They had an annual frog-jumping contest as the centerpiece; plus art exhibits, food booths, bake sales, and other money making projects. In *Blind Side* (Perseverance Press, 2001), the Jubilee was marred by the death of the prospective winning frog and its owner. The obvious suspect was Miah Mercer, Connor's assistant at Eureka, who always came in second. Miah and the victim had been rivals for years. Connor followed clues to the local hospital, uncovering a more mercenary motive for multiple murders.

Connor took her interest in Nancy Drew to the heights. An adult, she still collected the books, played an active role when a crime was committed in her area, and took considerable risks. No mention made of her health insurance.

Next book in this series: *Silence is Golden* (2003)

Aunt Dimity Westwood

Author: Nancy Atherton

Those who enjoy fantasy intermixed with romance and enlivened by mystery will relish this series in which a deceased benefactress, Aunt Dimity Westwood, reappeared (through entries in a journal) to advise those whom she loved on earth. Bobby MacLaren, Dimity's fiancé who had been killed during World War II, had left her money, which she used to help the needy through the Westwood Trust. On Dimity's death, Lori Shepherd, the daughter of Dimity's best friend, inherited Dimity's English cottage. Lori's father had also died during World War II, when she was three. She was a librarian, who had worked in a rare book department. When fire seriously damaged the collection and her marriage fell apart, Lori was delighted to move to England.

Aunt Dimity had been a continuing character in the bedtime stories that Lori's mother had told her, but her presence became very real when she took occupancy of the cottage in *Aunt Dimity's Death* (Viking, 1992) and read the 44-year correspondence between Dimity and her mother. Lori had two tasks as a condition of her bequest: to write an introduction to the Aunt Dimity stories as told by the letters, and to uncover and rectify a wrong done by Dimity during the war. The latter quest was accomplished with the help of young Bill Willis, whose Boston law firm handled Dimity's will. They married later.

Lori and Bill played no role in *Aunt Dimity and the Duke* (Viking, 1994) wherein Derek and Emma Harris, caretakers of Dimity's cottage, met and fell in love while solving the problems of a ducal family whose line of descent was in danger.

Lori was in sore straits again as *Aunt Dimity's Good Deed* (Viking, 1996) began. Her husband, Bill Willis, had been devoted during their courtship. On his return to the Boston law practice, he had little time for nurturing their marriage. Her planned second honeymoon faltered when

Bill stayed behind. She went anyway, accompanied by her supportive father-in-law. Willis, Sr. Aunt Dimity's journal led Lori on a merry chase through family history and the English countryside to heal a centuries-old rift.

The tempest brewing in Finch as to who would have occupancy of the schoolhouse in the fall (the Harvest Festival committee headed by Peggy Kitch or the archeology students under the tutelage of Dr. Adrian Culver) came to a happy conclusion in *Aunt Dimity Digs In* (Viking, 1998). Misunderstanding, hidden agendas, and old time resentments gave way to explanations and apologies. Aunt Dimity helped Lori to understand the dynamics of local adults who had not outlived their childhood traumas during World War II.

Lori's poverty in her childhood had meant bleak Christmas holidays, so in *Aunt Dimity's Christmas* (Viking, 1999) she was going all out to make this year's a memorable event. The presence of an unknown tramp in her yard changed all that. With Bill back in the United States on an emergency, Lori and an attractive Catholic priest sought the identity of the ailing man and the circumstances that had brought him to Aunt Dimity's cottage.

Not so much a devil, but a long dead widowed father protecting his daughter to the point of denying her the right to love, was the background for *Aunt Dimity Beats the Devil* (Viking, 2000). Lori went to a border castle where the tragedy of Josian Byrd, his rebellious daughter Claire, and her lover Edward had taken place. Her task was to appraise a library. Claire's ghost invaded Lori's spirit, threatening her marriage. With Aunt Dimity's guidance, Lori played cupid to lovers two generations apart.

A newcomer to Finch, Prunella Hooper had made few friends in the community. Her death as *Aunt Dimity: Detective* (Viking, 2001) opened, had occurred while Bill, Lori and their twins were in the United States visiting his family. On their return, Bill stopped off in London to finish some legal work while Lori and the children went on ahead. Within a short time after her arrival, Lori was scandalizing the locals as she and Nicholas, a handsome male visitor, investigated Prunella's death. There were secrets in Finch. Each suspect pointed a finger at someone else. Lilian Bunting, wife of the vicar and Nicholas' aunt, wanted the truth to come out. Lori seemed to enjoy the attention she was receiving in Bill's absence. She explained to him that she gets carried away when she shares an adventure with someone. Bill took wise precautions to be more adventurous himself.

Very light fare.

Next book in this series: *Aunt Dimity Takes a Holiday* (2003)

Charlotte Sue "Chas" Wheatley

Author: Phyllis Richman

Charlotte Sue Wheatley preferred to be called "Chas." Her personal history had made her mistrustful of men. During her marriage to Chef Ari Boucheron, she had traveled the world. After the divorce, they became friends, joined in their love for their child.

A Parisian romance with aspiring Chef Laurence Levain led to temporary joy, but ended too soon for Chas. A relationship with investigative reporter Dave Zeeger had been kept secret perhaps because she had lost hope that it would provide the commitment she wanted. During the time spent with chefs, Chas studied cooking. She ran a restaurant for a while, but needed a schedule more appropriate to a single mother. Friends encouraged her to try writing again, and to combine that skill with her knowledge of food and restaurants. She became the restaurant critic for the *Washington Examiner,* eventually achieving national syndication. She made her dinner reservations under false names to avoid recognition when possible, and noted not only the service, the quality and portion size of her own food, but also that of other diners. Under editor Bull Stannard, the *Examiner* was striving to establish itself in an area with tough competition from other news media.

Approaching mid-life she lived alone but was in regular contact with her daughter Lily Boucheron, a professional musician. She enjoyed food, reading mysteries, and walking. For her, walking was a way of life. She preferred it to driving around Washington, even through districts that others avoided. She donated her services as a cook to a woman's shelter and a food kitchen at various times. The narrative developed characters from among her coworkers, local chefs, and members of the police department. Two of the characters, both African-Americans, entertainment editor Sherele Travis and detective Homer Jones struck up a romance. As an unofficial investigator, Chas often focused on wrong suspects for a considerable period of time, but persisted even at the risk of personal harm.

In *The Butter Did It* (HarperCollins, 1997), when Chas learned that Laurence Levain was dead, her horror had less to do with his reputation as a great chef than her recollections of their time together in Paris two decades before. That intimacy provided Chas with insights that were in conflict with the official determination that he had died of a heart attack. Dave Zeeger arranged for Chas to share her concerns with epicurean detective Homer Jones. Chas feared learning that the killer was someone for whom she cared deeply.

Murder on the Gravy Train (HarperCollins, 1999) mixed sage advice about what can be learned from a menu with Chas' new assignment. She was to probe ways in which restaurants bilked their customers and tricks used by thieves to cheat restaurants. It became risky business. People were disappearing. Unknown corpses appeared on detective Homer Jones' case list. Chas simplified his task by identifying bodies, matching one bug against another, and finding a mole on the *Examiner* staff. A solicitous waiter saved her life.

The new business reporter, Ringo Laurenge, was an untested ingredient in the *Examiner* newsroom mix during *Who's Afraid of Virginia Ham?* (HarperCollins, 2001). Management was impressed with his high level of production including his ventures into restaurant management, entertainment and the territories of other specialized reporters. His fellow workers considered him a poacher and plagiarist. Chas and her friend Sherele were among the first to recognize Ringo's destructive propensity. When he died after eating Sherele's ham rolls at an *Examiner* buffet, she was arrested. That created a problem for both Chas and detective Homer Jones, who was Sherele's lover.

Richman brought not only her knowledge of food and restaurants to her narrative, but a wicked sense of humor.

Blanche White

Author: Barbara Neely

Blanche White was a heavyset African-American who supported herself in her North Carolina hometown by domestic work. She had candid opinions of her white employers, and no reluctance to trick them. Not all of her opinions were well received; e.g. she believed prostitution should be legalized.

Her habit of writing checks with an insufficient balance in her account put her in court in *Blanche on the Lam* (St. Martin, 1992). She fled the scene after being sentenced to thirty days in jail. Her quick wits made it possible for her to find employment with a wealthy family whose prospective heir needed a friend. Blanche was an excellent cook and a good friend, but never forgot a wrong. She was responsive but not subservient, and had no respect for the police department or the judicial system. Her closest ties were to Ardell, a friend from high school, to her own mother, and to Tafia and Malik, the niece and nephew she was raising. Blanche learned enough to blackmail the family, but she also exposed a killer, and then headed for Boston, Massachusetts.

Blanche's move and some additional money enabled her to send her niece and nephew to excellent schools by *Blanche Among the Talented Tenth* (St. Martin, 1994), but with mixed results. While visiting a New England resort that catered to light-skinned African-Americans, Blanche became aware of prejudice within her own race and its impact on her niece. Not everyone at Amber Cove was unfriendly: distinguished feminist Mattie Harris and handsome pharmacist Robert Stuart sought her company. When an "accidental" death was followed by the suicide of Mattie's godson, Blanche probed the original death. She was enlightened and disillusioned, but with her strength and sense of humor she survived.

Malik's paper on the environment covered the impact of lead poisoning on children, including its potential for causing violent behavior in adolescents. In *Blanche Cleans Up* (Viking, 1998), Blanche took him to local meetings on the topic. She had been filling in as housemaid for prominent white politician Alister Brindle, so her friend Inez could go on vacation. Blanche had no trouble separating the "good guys" from the "bad guys" as she investigated the murder of the attractive young man who was Mrs. Brindle's trainer. She unmasked hypocritical politicians and counseled a pregnant teenager but accepted the help of ex-convicts who had their own kind of justice.

For eight years, Blanche had nurtured her hatred of Dave Palmer who had raped her when she was a servant in his sister's home. In *Blanche Passes Go* (Viking, 2000), she returned to Farleigh, North Carolina to work with her friend Ardell in her catering business. The memories were so strong as to blind Blanche to Palmer's possible involvement in a murder, to haunt her new relationship with a widower, and to cause a death for which she bore some responsibility. The narrative brought insights into the individual and collective responses of African-American women to rape and abuse and a sisterhood of misery. Blanche's past had left her with powerful feelings against white people.

Jane Whitefield

Author: Thomas Perry

Jane Whitefield, a tall dark-skinned woman of partly Native American heritage, had not intended to spend her life breaking the law. It just happened that way, beginning with a young man who needed to leave the country during her sophomore year in college. What began as a single act of kindness developed into a personally rewarding and sometimes profitable business: creating new identities for people who deserved a second chance. She helped battered wives, children who were victims of incest, and those unjustly accused of crimes.

Jane knew little of her blond Irish-American mother who had appeared in New York City at age sixteen, and stayed there for a half-dozen years, but never talked about that time. When she met Henry Whitefield, she changed her life, becoming a model wife and mother in a small New York State town. Jane kept in regular touch with members of her father's Seneca tribe in the United States and Canada, and used them as resources.

Over the years Jane established a network of way stations and document replicators to create new personas for her fugitives. Despite her activities, Jane remained somewhat naïve. In *Vanishing Act* (Random House, 1995), she was vulnerable to John Felker, purportedly an ex-police officer framed for a crime. She gained a valuable ally in her cantankerous neighbor, Jake Reinert.

Dr. Carey McKinnon had been a close friend, although one in whom she never confided her real occupation, but in *Dance for the Dead* (Random, 1996), their relationship became intimate to the point where marriage was a possibility. Before Jane could consider such a step, she had to overcome a devious enemy who threatened the lives of a small boy and a former embezzler. Jane used up aliases, bank accounts, and separate identities that she had built over the years when she became the prey, rather than the rescuer.

Jane had an assignment to complete before she would be free to marry Carey as *Shadow Woman* (Random, 1997) began. Pete Hatcher's charm did not protect him from his employers at a Los Vegas casino when he knew too much about their plans for expansion. Jane's clever ruse to spirit him out of the state and into a new identity fell short, just as she was coming into her new identity as Mrs. Carey McKinnon. She reneged on her promise to Carey, but faced a formidable female adversary who was as dedicated as Jane herself.

Jane's resolve to forego future ventures in relocating threatened individuals lasted one year until Carey asked for her help in *The Face Changers* (Random, 1998). Only his sense of obligation to his mentor, surgeon Richard Dahlman, would justify Carey's placing Jane in danger. He did not realize then that Jane would be competing against a trio from her past. Help came from unlikely places, but Jane had to tread lightly every step of her way to protect Carey's career and their life together.

In *Blood Money* (Random, 2000), Jane found it impossible to reject a frightened young girl pursued by the Mafia. The reappearance of a mob banker with control over twelve million dollars in secret funds complicated the matter. The wall between Jane's past and present became more transparent.

Although credulity may be stretched, these were difficult to put down.

Serena Wilcox

Author: Natalie Buske Thomas

Serena Wilcox was a tiny single woman, past thirty. She had survived the death of her fiancé and the loss of their child by a miscarriage. After a period of adjustment, Serena, who had attended college, entered on a career as a private detective. Unfortunately, her appearance was undistinguished. She lacked a professional wardrobe and training.

Serena made a late entry into *Gene Play* (Independent Spirit, 1998), characterized by short choppy chapters. The plot was ingenious, but the presentation weak. The machinations of an unlicensed doctor, a bigamist, and a cold-hearted con woman were explored. They preyed upon unmarried pregnant women and couples who desperately wanted children. Serena connected the dots along with Karyn, who became her partner, and attorney George Bowmann.

A venal businessman manipulated a commercial system, which allowed an individual to either visualize a prior period in his/her lifetime, or, at considerable expense, to take part in a self-designed "adventure" in *Virtual Memories* (Independent Spirit, 1999). Only the intervention of Serena and Karyn prevented customer Jack Miller from killing a man he had never met. Dan, an employee of Virtual Memories who had been duped by a conniving young woman, helped Serena track a greedy killer and save another life. There were religious overtones to the series, but Serena's justification for ignoring a conflict of interest was weak. She transferred loyalties from one client to another without disclosure.

In *Camp Conviction* (Independent Spirit, 2000), Jack Miller came to Serena with concerns about a "family camp" with questionable practices. Karyn and Dan, now her fiancé, enlisted the help of Dan's eight-year-old nephew to pose as a family attending the camp. After they left, Serena took on a second case: a widowed computer devotee whose efforts to sell property adjacent to the family camp had been thwarted by picketers. They joined forces after Dan, Karyn and the boy had narrow escapes from death. There was improvement in the series as it progressed.

Catherine "Cat" Wilde

Author: Jean Ruryk

Catherine "Cat" Wilde had dealt with multiple tragedies during her sixty-plus years. Her marriage to an unstable alcoholic had ended early. Their daughter and son-in-law were killed in a car crash. Her career as a producer of documentaries for radio and television had ended, and her work as a furniture restorer was all she had for income.

In *Chicken Little Was Right* (St. Martin, 1994), Catherine's most precious possession, the home she had worked so hard to own, was threatened. Her solution was unusual. She robbed a bank, taking a small child and his mother as a hostage. She more or less adopted her hostages. However, a blackmailer, whose demands included assistance in murder, followed her home. Catherine had allies; a pair of gay antique dealers, a former advertising man who ran a gardening business, and a widowed ex-columnist with Mafia connections. She mixed her friends and her personal skills into a scheme to confound her oppressor.

Catherine's sense of loss after daughter Laurie's death never disappeared; in fact, it came back intimately in *Whatever Happened to Jennifer Steele?* (St. Martin, 1996). She recognized in a scabby dirty bag lady, the young girl who had been Laurie's best friend. Catherine fed Jennifer, cleansed her and saw to her medical needs, until the young woman regained her identity; not just as Laurie's friend, but also as a talented actress. With that knowledge came a realization that Jennifer was in danger, and would remain vulnerable until a killer could be identified.

Rena Kundera had a stall at a local flea market that she might lose because of major surgery. In *Next Week Will Be Better* (St. Martin, 1998), Catherine agreed to substitute for her. Her observations of how other vendors handled materials and customers made her suspicious that one might be dealing drugs or selling stolen items, and one might be a killer. Handicapped reporter Mike Melnyk and Catherine's antique hunting friends, Rafe and Charlie helped her find a killer for whom beautiful things had become an obsession.

Catherine was an endearing sleuth who surrounded herself with new elements of family to replace her losses. Of course, one does have to overlook bank robbery and kidnapping. These were low key but emotionally well-grounded narratives.

Kate Wilkinson

Author: Lis Howell

The television business was chancy. Kate Wilkinson had been a full-time employee at LondonVision until her position was made part-time to accommodate a male coworker. She had married Graham when he too worked for LondonVision, but it had not lasted. Graham took a news position in the Middle East. There had been no children. Kate had had an abortion before the marriage, a miscarriage during it, and had no interest in a family. There were so many divergences of opinion between Kate and Rev. John Maple, an Episcopalian priest; yet, they became lovers. She was ardently atheistic, pro-choice, and pro gay rights. His positions were more conservative and more religious. He did not try to influence her beliefs, and hoped she might give him the same tolerance. It had not been easy.

Kate was but one researcher among many for *Your Morning*, a television news show for women as *After the Break* (Hodder & Stoughton, 1995) began. She had been ousted from her London job by Frank Rattle, and was not entirely happy to have him turn up in a supervisory role on *Your Morning*. Robert Pedlar, a researcher for the program had committed suicide before Kate joined the staff. She and other workers suspected that Pedlar had been murdered. Rattle may have been aware of Pedlar's unethical behavior in the production of a documentary on homeless girls but it was not he who killed him. Kate's efforts to identify the killer were assisted by fellow researchers Jenny Sims and Dave Mitchell, and Jenny's sister, a social worker.

In between seasons in the television industry, Kate took on a special assignment in Cumbria, North England during *The Director's Cut* (Hodder & Stoughton, 1996). She accepted the job partly to accommodate her good friend Liz Jones, unaware that Liz was having an affair with erratic producer Andy de Salas. Anticipating a restful and productive interim in the country, Kate came to realize that small, inbred communities had their dark side. The locals were fiercely divided as to land use and new industries. The attitudes were reflected in the film which was designed to showcase what could be accomplished in Northern England. The mysterious death of an elderly tyrant, the emergence of illegal dogfighting in the community, and a series of accidents added to the chaos. Rev. John Maple came to offer his assistance and support.

In *A Job to Die For* (Hodder & Stoughton, 1997), Kate was employed as general manager for a new food and health television channel expected to air in September. Unfortunately, she had some rather unstable associates on the payroll and among the stockholders. One was found dead in the canal near the office warehouse where the television station was located. Another intended to arrange that the new station would never become active. Explicit perverse material and unbelievable characters flawed the narrative.

Elizabeth "Liz" Will

Author: Dorian Yeager

Elizabeth "Liz" Will returned to her hometown Dovekey Beach in Maine, expecting little material success. A blond college graduate now in her thirties, all she wanted was supplies for her watercolors and space for a small art gallery. She was close to having a serious affair with uncommunicative Charles MacKay who headed a research project on a nearby island. Sal, her mother, had moved out of the family home when Liz and her sister Avis were grown to begin a career as a romance novelist. Frank, her dour and obstinate father, continued lobster fishing even as resources diminished.

One way for Liz to earn money was by crewing on Frank's lobster boat. In *Murder Will Out* (St. Martin, 1994), that idea ended in disaster when she recovered the body of town selectman Al Jenness from Frank's lobster pot. Al and Frank had frequently tangled in community affairs, most recently over the legalization of gambling and prostitution on the nearby islands. Liz not only agreed with Al, but also had enjoyed an extra-marital affair with him. Still, she did not believe her father was a killer. With the aid of a lesbian police chief, the family Bible, and a tombstone, Liz made her point.

Summer Will End (St. Martin, 1996) found Liz chafing mentally and physically at the discipline she had set for herself. She rose early in the cold to harvest lobster; then, displayed her artwork to the tourists during the heat of the day. Both lobster and tourist seasons would end soon and she had to make the most of them. Accidents and incidents were felling tourists: heart attacks, shark and rattlesnake appearances, smoke and fire on the ferryboat, food poisonings. Liz was particularly concerned when Eamon, the husband of Elizabeth's high school friend Martha, was at risk. A sad ending.

Charlotte Willett

Author: Margaret Miles

Charlotte Willett was a young widow living in Bracebridge, Massachusetts in 1763. The period covered in the series came after the French Indian war at a time when the first stirrings of resentment against England were surfacing. She had married Aaron Willett, a young Quaker who came to the area to visit, but stayed for love of Charlotte. They farmed together on family land for three years. Then, within a short period of time, both of her parents, her sister Eleanor, and Aaron died from contagious illnesses. Her remaining sibling, brother Jeremy, went to Edinburgh to further his education, leaving Charlotte in charge of the property, which he as the male had inherited. Working with hired hands (her friend Hannah Sloan and members of Hannah's family) and Lem Wainwright who needed a home, Charlotte spent her time lonely but busy. Her only companion at home was an elderly dog, Orpheus, but she was close to her neighbor Richard Longfellow.

Richard, a scientific farmer, was considered rather odd in Bracebridge. He had a glasshouse where he produced new species of plants and kept in touch with scientific discoveries, but he was respected enough to be elected a selectman. Richard had loved Charlotte's sister Eleanor, but she died before they could marry. Charlotte occasionally indulged in ice skating, reading, and spending time with her friends.

Charlotte was content with her good harvest and her friends as *A Wicked Way to Burn* (Bantam, 1998) began. Both she and Richard Longfellow were skeptical of drunken Jack Pennywort's tale of seeing a wealthy merchant disappear in smoke and flames. Mercenary miller Peter Lynch was quick to plant suspicion on Gabriel Fortier, whose family had moved to the area from French Canada. Others hinted at witchcraft. Captain Edmund Montagu, representing the Crown, initially disdained the help of locals like Charlotte and Richard, but came to realize their value. Charlotte was responsible for many of the deductions that solved the mystery.

In *Too Soon for Flowers* (Bantam, 1999), visitors to Bracebridge brought tragedy with them. Dr. Benjamin Tucker came at Richard's request to inoculate volunteers against small pox, which was ravaging New England. Richard's younger half-sister Diana, Phoebe Morris who was engaged to Will Sloan, and Lem Wainwright were among the volunteers. Handsome David Pelham, a visitor from Boston, enlivened Diana's boredom with rural life. Two deaths linked to the inoculations created suspicion among the villagers. Richard, Captain Montagu, and Charlotte shared an investigation.

Singer Gian Carlo Lahte's physical condition was a matter of considerable concern in Bracebridge during *No Rest for the Dove* (Bantam, 2000). He had been castrated as a child to preserve the range of his voice. He visited Richard Longfellow because he was considering moving to the area. When a fellow Italian was murdered nearby, suspicion lodged on Gian Carlo. Additional foreigners followed, creating a web of complicated relationships. The narrative covered the pre-Revolutionary war period with Montagu justifying the Stamp Tax while Richard Longfellow supported the colonist's objections.

An island off the Bracebridge shore was home to two older women and a pack of marauding boars in *Mischief in the Snow* (Bantam, 2001). A cocky young man, Alexander Godwin, who boasted that he had expectations, met the women's everyday needs. His murder followed a quarrel with Lem Wainwright, Charlotte's protégée. She suspected that Lem might be involved in other local skullduggery, but she was certain he was not the killer. Diana, by then married to Captain Montagu, had to reestablish their relationship after the death of their infant son. Richard and Charlotte's friendship gradually took on a more intimate tone.

Kay Williams

Author: William D. Blankenship

Kay Williams had been unfortunate with the men in her life. Her father, an architect whose skills had been diluted by alcohol, died young. She married, and then divorced, a man who was incapable of fidelity. By her thirties, she had parlayed her linguistic skills and her knowledge of antiques into a successful business. Not only did she maintain a shop in Ridgefield, Connecticut, but wealthy collectors hired her to represent them in auctions or to seek out valuable artifacts. This lifestyle kept her insulated from long term relationships and traveling extensively, but she relished it.

The Time of the Cricket (Fine, 1995) found Kay in Tokyo where she sought a sword once owned by the Emperor Meiji. Her negotiations with a local weapons dealer had been successful, but as she completed the transaction, a hired assassin murdered the man. The killer took the sword. Kay barely escaped with her life. However, at this point she had spent her client's money and had no sword in hand. Kay cooperated with Takeo Saji, a rebellious detective, in thwarting the Japanese Mafia. Their romantic affair was short-lived.

Kay returned to the United States from a successful buying trip in Singapore in *The Time of the Wolf* (Fine, 1998). She received a phone call from oil baron, "Billy Boy" Watkins. Watkins, another weapons collector, had learned that Jim Bowie's original knife left at the Alamo, was to be sold by the descendant of a Mexican who had been present at the battle. The weapon attracted the attention of bidders willing to spend millions to gain possession of the knife, including a hired killer. Kay's efforts to get the knife for Watkins, as the killer eliminated the competition, were hampered by the presence of her former husband, Phil. Phil and his more vicious business partner intended to force Kay to subsidize their Caribbean resort venture. A treasury agent, present to monitor possible counterfeit money, was seriously attracted to Kay, but her trickery in securing the knife, left him cold.

Ruth Willmarth

Author: Nancy Means Wright

Ruth Willmarth, in her forties, was at a crossroads. Her divorce from Peter, the man she dropped out of college to marry, was in process. Their older daughter, Sharon was already in her second marriage and had two children. Still at home, she had Emily, a teenager, and Vic, in middle school. Also, she had more than thirty cows to care for on her Branbury, Vermont farm. The cows had literary or theatrical names: "Jane Eyre," "Zelda," and "Dolly Parton."

Ruth was well aware of the economic disparity in the Branbury area. Newcomers, known locally as "flatlanders," fled the cities rejoicing to find lower taxes and land prices, but demanding the level of services which higher taxes could provide. Locals could not afford the luxury of higher land prices or taxes.

There was a lot for Ruth to be angry about in *Mad Season* (St. Martin, 1996). There had been several barn fires in which arson was suspected. Bullies were making Vic miserable, taunting him as a smelly farm boy and physically abusing him. Worst of all, Pete, who had turned his back on Ruth and the farm, wanted to sell the property, which was in joint ownership. Ruth had centered her life on the land since Pete's desertion. Colm Hanna, who had loved and lost Ruth to Pete in high school, became a source of strength. The murder of a neighbor and another unexplained death added to the stress.

What might be deemed instability elsewhere was perceived as merely eccentricity in *Harvest of Bones* (St. Martin, 1998). Ruth's friend, Fay Hubbard was trying to run a bed and breakfast with limited experience. She took in elderly and confused Glenna Flint and her teenage grandniece, Hartley, without any idea of whether or not she would be repaid for their care. When a corpse was discovered on the property, Glenna was certain it was not her husband. Another guest, Kevin who seemed familiar with the area, was seeking his missing wife, Angie. When Angie was found, she was dying, possibly poisoned. Ruth, Colm and a pair of teenagers solved these multi-layered crimes. Ruth did work one thing out. She decided to give Peter the divorce he wanted.

Stan and Moira Earthrowl had purchased a Branbury area orchard, hoping to leave behind the tragic death of their only daughter. In *Poison Apples* (St. Martin, 2000), Ruth and Moira became friends. Emily had summertime employment as a "picker" at the orchard, but most of the workers were Jamaicans. There were more than a few "bad apples" in the neighborhood: a greedy developer who would be satisfied to see the Earthrowls fail; a vengeful employee who coveted the property for himself; and religious cultists who harassed a high school teacher for requiring students to read a controversial novel.

Next book in this series: *Stolen Honey* (2002)

Francesca "Fran" Wilson

Author: Christine Green

Francesca Wilson came to Fowchester shortly after she had been promoted to Detective Sergeant, but under a cloud. In her prior posting at Birmingham, she had turned in her lover, a fellow officer, for abusing a suspect. However necessary that had been for her own conscience, it cost her the support of her coworkers. She had few close ties. Her mother had died and her father had remarried. Her only sister lived in Canada. She was a small woman with dark hair, independent and clever. Superintendent Ringstead assigned Fran to Detective Inspector Connor O'Neill, whose descent into alcoholism after the suicide of his wife put him at risk. Theirs was a difficult pairing. He liked his shots and beer; she was a vegetarian. He was fighting his alcoholism, and needed someone close.

In *Death in the Country* (Bantam, 1995), the discovery of two sets of arms and hands in trash bags set Fran and Connor looking for not one body, but two: one male, one female. Suspects abounded, and most of them were guilty of something. The narrative was engrossing, but made more difficult by confusion as to the names of characters as it progressed.

In *Die in My Dreams* (Bantam, 1995), the improved relationship between Connor and Fran caused Ringstead to warn her not to get too close. When she requested a reassignment, he said no one else would have her. Two murders along the banks of the river close to a popular pub had alarmed the community. Ringstead considered the presence in the community of a recently released woman who had been convicted of murder an obvious solution, but Fran and Connor disagreed. They not only found the killer, but also proved the released convict innocent of the original charges against her.

The death of vicious Denise Parks while immobilized at a beauty parlor in *Fatal Cut* (Severn House, 1999) exposed the lives of her family; i.e. sister, daughter, and mother. The probe went beyond that to the heterosexual and homosexual liaisons of the staff at the beauty shop. Inspector Connor O'Neill's personal interest in Fran had to be shelved temporarily as they sifted through the list of suspects for the one who succumbed to murder.

See page 350 for details of author Christine Green's other series featuring Kate Kinsella.

Lucie D'Arby Wilton

Author: Candace Robb

Owen Archer, a former soldier incapacitated by the loss of an eye, found a new profession as "spy" or investigator for powerful English dignitaries beginning in the 1360s. Among his first suspects was the woman who would become his wife, Lucie D'Arby Wilton, apprentice apothecary to her husband Nicholas. Lucie began life as the daughter of Sir Robert D'Arby and his hostage French wife, Amelie. The older soldier and his young bride had but the one child, disappointingly a daughter. Amelie died while pregnant with another man's child. Lucie was rejected by her father and placed in a convent. He returned to France to serve in the Hundred Years War. Nicholas, master apothecary in York and a friend of Amelie, offered Lucie an alternative to the restrictive life of the convent where she had been treated as the daughter of a promiscuous mother. The calm of their marriage had been broken only by the death of their child, Martin, of the plague.

In *The Apothecary Rose* (St. Martin, 1993), the deaths of an anonymous pilgrim and the nephew of Archer's employer placed Nicholas and Lucie's marriage and their lives in jeopardy. Lucie, denied the rights and luxuries of her birth, was fiercely independent. After Nicholas died she became a master apothecary with Owen as her apprentice. Their love brought marriage, but Owen was frequently called away on missions for John Thoresby, Lord Chancellor and Archbishop. Lucie realized that Owen needed more than the routine life they led in York, but chafed when Owen rejected her involvement in his investigations, particularly where her expertise might be of value.

In *The Lady Chapel* (St. Martin, 1994), the murders of two prominent wool merchants occurred as a result of their political activities, but also through a deep seated need for vengeance for a past wrong. The complex narrative with major historical overtones was enlivened by on-going characters: Brother Wulfstan, in charge of the infirmary at the monastery; young Jasper de Melton, who became a part of the Archer household; Bess Merchet, an outspoken innkeeper who was Lucie's confidante; and Magda Digby, a midwife who operated without the approval of church or state. Lucie had been more suspect than sleuth in the first book, but achieved a supportive status in others.

Lord Chancellor Thoresby and Brother Wulfstan sought Lucie's help in dealing with a hysterical runaway nun in *The Nun's Tale* (St. Martin, 1995). Owen had the active role, roaming the countryside, and dealing with powerful English nobles while Lucie tended victims, and learned the background for their injuries.

Lucie's role in *The King's Bishop* (St. Martin, 1996) was reduced to hand wringing as Owen tried to save a soldier/friend from death. Once Lucie was a mother and had continued responsibilities in her work, it was logical that her participation would be reduced.

Lucie had only a background role in *The Riddle of St. Leonard's* (St. Martin, 1997), during which Bess Merchet assisted Owen. He investigated mysterious deaths among the corrodies (pensioners who had transferred assets to the hospital in exchange for lifetime care).

Lucie appeared only by reference in *A Gift of Sanctuary* (St. Martin, 1998) as her husband and father (with whom she had reconciled) journeyed to Wales in the service of the Duke of Lancaster to appraise the loyalty of the Welsh.

More than distance separated Lucy and Owen in *A Spy for the Redeemer* (Heinemann, 1999). His trip to Wales had been extended when the local Archdeacon pressured him into investigating the death of a gifted stonemason. The separation was difficult for Lucie. The recent death of her father in Wales left a sizeable estate to be managed until her son Hugh reached his majority. Those who offered help to Lucie had agendas of their own: greed, a search for intimacy, or political power.

There were heavy doses of history, essential to understand the motivations of the characters, which may deter some readers. Worth the trouble for a reader with the time and interest.

Next book in this series: *The Cross-Legged Night* (2002 U.K.; 2003 U.S.)

Holly Winter

Author: Susan Conant

The mystery heroine finally went to the dogs. It was about time after cats, cats, and more cats. Holly, a canine fanatic, informed her readers about dog care (no chocolate); responsibility (blame the owner, not the pet for misbehavior); and best breeds (the Malamute). Dogs were so pervasive in the series that even a dedicated dog lover might call "halt." Holly had no trouble recalling dog names and descriptions, but was hazy about the owners. She was a blonde, about thirty, with a veterinarian lover, and a widowed father who bred wolf dogs. Having earned a journalism degree, Holly supported herself by writing a column for a dog magazine, and rented out an apartment building she owned.

During *A New Leash on Death* (Diamond, 1990), Holly and her Malamute, Rowdy, attended obedience training sessions where perfectionist Dr. Frank Stanton was murdered with a leash. With the help of a friendly neighbor policeman, Kevin Dennehy, Holly not only exposed murder, but also dog doping.

Dead and Doggone (Diamond, 1990) moved on to obedience trials. The problems of animals used in experiments, and the disappearance of Buck Winter's wolf dog, vied for attention with a death by dog grooming shears.

By *A Bite of Death* (Diamond, 1991), Holly had added a second dog, Kimi, to her menage. When the previous owner was poisoned, Holly used intimate dog behavior to uncover a deadly relationship.

In *Paws Before Dying* (Diamond, 1991), Holly's ego suffered when her untrained cousin Leah turned out to be a natural dog handler. Holly explored anti-Semitism and child abuse in a dysfunctional suburban family.

During *Gone to the Dogs* (Doubleday, 1992), Holly and her lover Steve Delaney followed the trail of a missing veterinarian, a frigid wife and a dog that need not have died. Holly and Rowdy saved a Vietnam veteran when he confronted the man who had killed a rare Chinook dog.

The series moved into hardcover with *Bloodlines* (Doubleday, 1992). Holly detested pet shops, which sold badly bred dogs. When "Puppy Luv" offered a Malamute pup for sale, she visited the store, only to learn that the owner had been murdered, and the puppy was gone. Holly's primary concern was to rescue the pup, alert the SPCA, and leave Kevin Dennehy and the local police to solve the murder.

Ruffly Speaking (Doubleday, 1994) had the elements of a good plot: an isolated elderly neighbor unable to deal with dogs or children; a deaf female minister; the death of a gay bookstore/restaurant owner; and a precocious child looking for trouble.

As columnist for *Dog's World*, Holly evaluated a summer training camp for dogs and owners in *Black Ribbon* (Doubleday, 1995). Maxene McGuire, the camp proprietor, was thwarted by disloyal staff, resentful guests, and "accidents" designed to ruin the camp's reputation. Eva Spitteler, a constant critic, was killed while using camp equipment without supervision. Rowdy, Holly's Malamute, overcame his instinctive dislike for water in a heroic rescue.

Stud Rites (Doubleday, 1996) explored the rivalries and jealousies among competitors in Malamute dog shows. When murder occurred, it was swathed in canine pedigrees, chilled by frozen semen, and solved by the process of elimination.

Animal Appetite (Doubleday, 1997) forced Holly into the "people" world when she accepted a challenge to write about something besides dogs. Holly researched the life of Hannah Duston, a colonial woman who had been captured by Indians and then escaped after killing most of her captors. Holly conducted a parallel probe into the death of a publisher whose Golden Retriever was proof that he could not have committed suicide. A pleasing variation.

The Barker Street Regulars (Doubleday, 1998) tied a local murder investigation into Sherlock Holmes through several elderly devotees of the British sleuth, including Althea Battlefield, a nursing home resident. Holly and Rowdy had met them when they made their volunteer visits to nursing homes. When Althea's visiting nephew was murdered, the elderly sleuths wanted Holly and Rowdy to assist them in the investigation. Holly suspected that Ceci, Althea's wealthy sister, was being deceived by those who took advantage of her love for her deceased dog.

Holly contracted to write the text for a photographic study of famous dog shows hosted by heiress Geraldine Rockefeller Dodge in *Evil Breeding* (Doubleday, 1999). Her research introduced her to the malfunctioning Motherway family, which had for three generations hidden a nasty secret. The mix of Nazi spies, art thefts, and murder placed a heavy burden on Conant's narrative skills, resulting in an extended last chapter of explanations.

During *Creature Discomforts* (Doubleday, 2000), Holly returned to consciousness on a mountainside in Arcadia National Park, Maine. Amnesiac initially, through Rowdy, Kimi and the contents of her backpack, she returned to an awareness of her name. Only a reenactment of her fall restored her memory and her connection to the death of a chronic complainer. There were two weddings to enliven the narrative but neither was Holly's.

This has been a popular series, even in hardcover.

Next books in this series: *The Wicked Flea* (2002); *The Dogfather* (2003)

Hannah Wolfe

Author: Sarah Dunant

Hannah Wolfe, a Londoner whose politics, lifestyle, and approach to work were unconventional, was anti-establishment all the way. She was single in her mid-thirties, with a three-year college education, which had prepared her for a job working for the European Economic Community. She was too restless to work within the system. Her only sister, Kate, lived a more commonplace existence within marriage and parenthood, sometimes envying

Hannah's adventures. Hannah had tried working as a solo private investigator, but, when the bills mounted up, returned to Frank Comfort's agency where she had learned the business.

In *Birth Marks* (Doubleday, 1992), Augusta Patrick, an elderly spinster hired Hannah to find the young ballet dancer whose education she had sponsored. When Carolyn Hamilton's pregnant corpse was found, Hannah's assignment was changed to finding a killer, who may have been connected to a job Carolyn had taken in Paris, a very intimate assignment.

Frank Comfort had a simple task for Hannah in *Fatlands* (Penzler, 1993): escorting a lonely fourteen-year-old boarding school student to visit her scientist father in London. The assignment blew up, leaving Hannah with guilt, anger, and deep seated suspicions that the girl's father was targeted for murder by animal rights extremists or by his own employer.

Hannah experienced doubts about her sexuality in *Under My Skin* (Scribners, 1995). An undercover assignment at a beauty farm brought her into contact with a lesbian masseuse. She intervened in her sister's marriage, almost with tragic results. These side issues did not prevent her from identifying the prankster who became a killer.

A provocative series.

April Woo

Author: Leslie Glass

April was a second generation Chinese-American whose parents clung to the older traditions. Her mother Sai constantly encouraged April to make a good marriage, or at least to become educated in a field more prestigious than police work. However, for financial reasons, April had foregone full-time college. She took night classes that would lead to a degree. At the time she joined the New York Police Department, only a few detectives were Asians, much less Chinese. These were dark brooding narratives in which her co-protagonist was as likely to be psychiatrist Jason Frank as her police partner, Sgt. Mike Sanchez.

April and Jason worked together in *Burning Time* (Doubleday, 1993), during which his actress/wife Emma was a pivotal character. Her appearance in a sexually oriented art film made Emma a target for mutilation and murder. When Emma disappeared, April was assigned to the case. She saved Emma's life, but was rescued by Sanchez. April turned away from her domineering Chinese boyfriend. She had no physical relationship with Mike, although they were attracted to one another. He was married to an absentee wife dying of leukemia. Any potential romance between Mike and

April moved glacially both because of their mothers' resistance to an inter-racial marriage and the demands of their work schedules.

During *Hanging Time* (Bantam, 1995), Jason's wife Emma found professional advancement and recuperation in California. An aggressive female architect sought Jason's help for her sister's mental illness and possible involvement in the "boutique murders" to which April and Mike were assigned. April prevented a serious injustice at the cost of missing her sergeant's exam.

In *Loving Time* (Bantam, 1996), Mike, now a widower, and April, now a sergeant, were assigned to two possible suicides: a mental patient who had been discharged from psychotherapy fourteen years before, and a therapist who had treated him. If these were not suicides, there were multiple murder suspects: a powerful and seductive psychiatrist with FBI connections, disenchanted spouses, and a violence-prone former nurse.

Rick Liberty had moved beyond his fame as an African-American professional quarterback to becoming a successful businessman in *Judging Time* (Dutton, 1998). He was comfortable with his marriage to an attractive white actress. However when his wife Merritt and his best friend multimillionaire Tor Petersen died within minutes of one another, Liberty became the target of a murder investigation. April, now a sergeant at Midtown North and Mike, a special homicide investigator saw Liberty as only one of several suspects. Physical evidence, once it was properly evaluated, vindicated their uphill battle to prove Liberty innocent. They also reached a closer personal accommodation.

In *Stealing Time* (Dutton, 1999), it took a while for April to tie together two cases: the "suicide" of an alien worker in a sweatshop and the attack on a young Chinese wife and the disappearance of her child. The narrative explored the role of a woman in Chinese society and the workplace abuses of immigrants. April moved closer to Mike and a shared future as she freed herself, at age thirty, from her parent's domination.

April was still trying to cope with a hostile supervisor at work and a disapproving mother. She did not need additional problems. Yet, in *Tracking Time* (Dutton, 2000), she could not refuse to help Jason Frank. Maslow Atkins, whom Frank was training in psychoanalysis, had disappeared in Central Park. This was neither April's case nor her jurisdiction, but she intervened. Suspects included seriously disturbed teenagers whose needs had been ignored by their parents.

April and Mike's romantic plight and their investigations were subordinated to a mixture of explosive characters.

Next books in this series: *The Silent Bride* (2002); *A Killing Gift* (2003)

Susan Donovan Wren

Author: Charlene Weir

Susan Donovan had a tense relationship with her father, Attorney Patrick Donavan. Her mother, who had played violin in the San Francisco symphony orchestra, was more understanding of Susan's goals. In her mid-thirties, Susan was a dedicated San Francisco police officer who had earned a law degree and two commendations for valor. Then she met Dan Wren, the police chief of Hampstead, Kansas. Their marriage was expected to end her professional career. She moved to Kansas, anticipating an uneventful adjustment.

Susan and Dan's honeymoon was short-lived. In *The Winter Widow* (St. Martin, 1992), he was shot in the back while investigating cattle rustlers. Susan intended to return to San Francisco, but not yet. She accepted an interim appointment to Dan's position because she did not intend to leave until his killer had been caught and punished. Susan made some false starts: chasing pigs, releasing a bull from his pen, and foiling her new sister-in-law's plan to sell the family farm. She not only survived with the help of initially hostile deputy Ben Parkhurst, but learned who had killed her husband.

In *Consider the Crows* (St. Martin, 1993), Susan questioned "hippie" Lynnelle Hames in the isolated house she was renting. Lynnelle, who came to town to discover her parentage, was a danger to someone. When she was killed, Susan needed to know who was so vulnerable.

The current generation of the Barrington family had followed their mother into medicine in *Family Practice* (St. Martin, 1995), dominated by the eldest daughter, Dorothy. When Dorothy was murdered, her siblings were the logical suspects. Susan had another concern. The sole possible witness to Dorothy's death was young Jen Bryant, who had been left in Susan's care while her mother was out of town. Susan had to find the killer before another attempt was made on Jen's life.

Susan was the police chief in Hampstead during *Murder Take Two* (St. Martin, 1998); however, when the town was selected as a location by a movie production, her subordinates, Ben Parkhurst and Peter Yancy, were more personally involved. Established movie star Laura Edwards, who believed she was the target of a killer, looked to Ben, her former husband, for protection. Police officer Peter Yancy could not prevent two murders from occurring or separate his own family from involvement in the investigation. Susan came on strong in the resolution of the case, discarding a convenient suspect to identify the killer, and prevent a third murder.

Caley James was exhausted with flu and overwork as *A Cold Christmas* (St. Martin, 2000) began. Her furnace needed repair. She struggled to care for three children, eeking out a living as an organist. Her irresponsible ex-husband Mat rated high on promises; low on performance. The last thing she needed was a dead furnace repairman in her cellar. Susan had only a passing acquaintance with Caley when she handled the investigation, but she reserved her decision as to moving back to San Francisco until the case was closed. She had questions. Why was Caley always tired? What was the connection between Mat James and the victim?

These were well-plotted stories with interesting characters. Author Charlene Weir is an excellent writer, packing more tension into 250 pages than do authors of overblown narratives.

Next book in this series: *Up in Smoke* (2003)

Jolie Wyatt

Author: Barbara Burnett Smith

As the series began, Jolie Wyatt was approaching forty, having just divorced her second husband Matt. After her first husband Steve had deserted her and their infant child, Jolie worked hard to become a successful copywriter in Austin, Texas. A dozen years later, Matt swept her and son, Jeremy, off to Purple Sage, Texas. Jeremy became deeply attached to Matt, but Jolie could not find a life for herself on the ranch or in the nearby small town. Her only close friends were fellow members of a writer's group; her only outlet, writing mystery stories, none of which had ever been published.

In *Writers of the Purple Sage* (St. Martin, 1994), Jolie became a prime suspect when local politician Volney Osler was murdered by a method carefully described in Jolie's manuscript. Who knew about the modus operandi? Only the fellow members of her writing group. Someone who knew Jolie well enough to plant evidence that tied her even closer to the crime. Many in the close-knit community knew she had quarreled with Osler. Matt and Jeremy helped her prove her innocence. Matt and Jolie resumed their relationship and she returned to his ranch, but not as his wife.

As *Dust Devils of the Purple Sage* (St. Martin, 1995) began, Jolie was a news reporter for local station WSGE. She aired the bulletin that young James Jorgenson had escaped from prison with the help of his sister Sharon, and was headed for Purple Sage, armed and dangerous. When Sharon's boyfriend Tim was murdered, James was assumed to be his killer. Jolie's investigation uncovered a bevy of female suspects.

Their non-marital status became a problem for Matt and Jolie during *Celebration in Purple Sage* (St. Martin, 1996). The town's centennial resulted in a host of visitors, including Matt's parents and his former wife, Cecily. Jolie needed her former mother-in-law's knowledge of the community to find the attacker of festival chairman Vera Meece and Sheriff Mac Donelly. With Mac seriously injured, his replacement selected Matt as his number one suspect.

It might have been a mistake for Jolie and Matt to visit Austin in *Mistletoe from Purple Sage* (St. Martin, 1997). She planned to visit old friends, including a former lover, at an office party. Matt looked forward to spending Christmas with his sister Prissy and her family. Jolie hadn't planned on being a suspect in the death of a part-time child-care provider. Still, she solved a crime and saved a child by Christmas morning.

These were light but interesting.

Next book in this series: *Skeletons in Purple Sage* (2002)

Eva Wylie

Author: Liza Cody

Liza Cody, author of the series featuring engaging young private investigator, Anna Lee, introduced Eva Wylie, a dour self-centered female wrestler, who had obsessions rather than relationships.

In *Bucket Nut* (Chatto, 1992; Doubleday, 1993), Eva was determined to find the younger sister, Simone, lost to her during years in foster care. The girl's mother, a drunken prostitute, was unable to care for them both. Eva had few scruples. She lied, stole, bullied, and was a courier for drug dealers. However, on occasion, someone would appeal to Eva's weakness for the underdog—Eleanor Crombie, a drug ridden third-rate young singer, who reminded Eva of her sister. Eva was a pawn of powerful drug interests. For her, survival was success.

What really mattered to Eva was her career as a wrestler, and it was endangered in *Monkey Wrench* (Chatto, 1994; Mysterious Press, 1995). She had worn out her welcome with fight promoters and the men at the gym where she trained. Nevertheless, she promised her friend, Crystal that she would find out who killed her sister Dawn, a prostitute. This, plus her grudging involvement in teaching other prostitutes how to protect themselves on the streets, cost Eva her job and made her an accessory to murder.

In *Musclebound* (Mysterious, 1997), Eva reconnected with her sister. She would do anything to protect Simone. Eva tried to be fair with their irresponsible mother, but her overtures did not produce the affection and loyalty that she sought. Eva discounted Anna Lee's (See Volume 2) offers of employment and the friendship offered by a black wrestler, Keif. She focused on returning to the wrestling ring, but achieved it only by subterfuge.

These were gritty but depressing stories with a heroine to whom it was difficult to relate.

MacLaren Yarbrough

Author: Patricia Houck Sprinkle

MacLaren Yarbrough was a happily married woman, a rarity in mystery series in the Nineties. The Yarbrough family lived in small town Hopemore, Georgia where the couple had owned a hardware store. Unable to compete with the big chain stores, the Yarbroughs switched over to a feed and nursery business. She was described as petite, kept her hair honey brown with the aid of her beautician, and had become plump over the years. Joe Riddley, her husband was devoted to MacLaren. Their two sons Ridd and Walker were grown and married.

Chapters in *When Did We Lose Harriet?* (Zondervan Publishing House, 1997) were alternately narrated by MacLaren and African-American librarian, Josheba Davidson. Young Harriet Lawson felt adrift after the death of the grandmother who had raised her. A placement in her aunt's home was unpleasant. At the end of the school year, she ran away. She had money enough to get to Alabama where she expected to meet the mother who had abandoned her at age two. Her brother's illness prompted Mac-Laren to visit Birmingham, Alabama, and to remain there while he recovered. MacLaren discovered an envelope containing $3,000 in a library book. Her plan to return the money involved her and Josheba in a search for Harriet; then, for her killer.

Thefts of antiques seemed minor compared to the murder and attempted murder that besieged Hopemore in *But Why Shoot the Magistrate?* (Zondervan, 1998). The magistrate in question was Joe Riddley who survived an attack. The target had been MacLaren who was close to discovering the killer of a young nurse who had been too attentive to her patients.

These were cozy, Christian-oriented narratives written by a skilled author.

Next books in this series: *Who Invited the Dead Man?* (2002); *Who Left That Body in the Rain?* (2002); *Who Let That Killer in the House?* (2003)

Magdalena Yoder

Author: Tamar Myers

The Amish with their isolation from modern society formed the background for the Magdalena Yoder series set in Pennsylvania. The Yoder family had relaxed some of the practices of their antecedents, but Magdalena, a tall, well-built woman in her forties, was a faithful adherent of the Amish lifestyle. She had attended the local college earning an associate degree in English, but never graduated. Her younger, and more rebellious sister, Susannah, had scandalized the family by marrying and divorcing a Presbyterian, and then earning a reputation as being promiscuous. Magdalena had remodeled the family home into the prosperous Penn Dutch Inn, which provided Susannah a refuge between her expeditions into the outside world. Magdalena knew her sister's limitations and tolerated them, although she detested Susannah's current beau and eventual husband, the local sheriff, Melvin Stoltzfus. Initially, Magdalena's only romantic interest was an elderly veterinarian who plied her with food and conversation.

Cousin Freni, whose cooking had earned the Inn an enviable reputation, found it difficult to cope with a vegetarian/animal rights convention in *Too Many Cooks Spoil the Broth* (Doubleday, 1994). The group arrived for the opening of deer season, planning to protest hunters. Isolated guest Heather Brown, who merely wanted to be left alone, and young Linda McMahon, a member of the vegetarian group were killed by an obscure poison, hardly a recommendation for the Inn's cuisine.

In *Parsley, Sage, Rosemary, and Crime* (Doubleday, 1995), Magdalena leased the Inn to a film company for background scenes. She was unprepared for internal strife among the dramatic personnel and the unrestrained interest of the locals in becoming extras in the film. Magdalena, not only moved up to a major role after the death of the original scriptwriter, but attracted the interest of Aaron Miller, who had returned to the community to care for his father. The narrative was witty for such a restrained setting, although the plot was fragile.

The death of distant relatives took Magdalena, Susannah, and Freni to Ohio in *No Use Dying Over Spilled Milk* (Doubleday, 1996). Before Yost Yoder's body was in the ground, Magdalena learned that his death might be connected to a cooperative dairy that he and other Amish farmers had established when they became dissatisfied with the local milk purchaser. A stolid Amish farmer like Yost was unlikely to engage in bizarre behavior before his death. Aaron Miller joined Magdalena as soon as the weather and road conditions would allow. He did not arrive in time to rescue her (she had handled the killers herself), but he provided the happy ending with a proposal.

The big wedding day was at hand in *Just Plain Pickled to Death* (Signet, 1997), but one of the gifts included a corpse. Must have been the "something old" because the body had been pickled for twenty years. Sarah Weaver had disappeared long ago, but many of those who might have been responsible for her death would be guests at the wedding. With the Inn filled with non-paying relatives and soon to be in-laws, Magdalena made time to find another body, attend a funeral, and still get married.

Susannah's short-term employment with a paint company ended in disaster. She was back at the Inn as a dependent in *Between a Wok and a Hard Place* (Signet, 1998). Also resident was Aaron's father. The only one missing was Aaron who flew to Minnesota to straighten some things out. After dropping him off at the airport, Magdalena seemed to have struck a body as she passed through town. Not only had the victim died previously, but Melvin Stoltzfus, asked Magdalena to help him solve the murder. She knew the townspeople, including the teenagers who were downtown late at night, and had more information about guests at the Inn. Some were behaving very suspiciously. Magdalena had never had it easy, but this narrative dealt her a cruel blow.

Freni's participation in a cooking contest was assured if she could secure the Penn Dutch Inn for several weeks. In *Eat, Drink and Be Wary* (Signet, 1998), Magdalena agreed to cancel all reservations and accommodate the contestants and judges. Little did she know that one man had been judged already and sentenced to death. There were so many motives for the murder of the CEO of the sponsoring corporation that Magdalena had to be close to death before she selected the appropriate killer.

As if the disaster of her pseudo-marriage to Aaron had not been enough, Magdalena's barn and inn were destroyed by a terrible wind in *Play It Again, Spam* (Signet, 1999). By the time the facility had been restored, the Washington, D.C., New York City and Los Angeles clientele had found a newer favorite. A request for rooms by World War II veterans had a hidden agenda but so did a vicious Nazi criminal living under a false identity.

Magdalena's inn had a houseful of unusual guests in *The Hand that Rocks the Ladle* (Signet, 2000). It couldn't have happened at a more inauspicious time. Barbara Hostetler, Freni's daughter-in-law, delivered her babies, but triplets had been expected, not twins. Not only was Magdalena minus a cook, but she promised Freni to locate the missing infant. Magdalena, no lover of pets, acquired a kitten, which she transported in her bra. Susannah was not the only strange one in the family. Retired cardiologist, Dr. Gabe Rosen, found Magdalena's whimsies attractive.

Magdalena may no longer number the rich and famous among her guests, but in *The Crepes of Wrath* (New American Library, 2001) she had a mixed bag: two African-American psychiatrists; two diminutive retired attorneys; one extremely tall physical education teacher, plus a television star whose wife was a medium. No problem. They all signed into the ALPO (Amish Lifestyle Plan Option), doing their own and some of Magdalena's cleaning to get the full experience. The drug-induced death of Lizzie Mast looked like murder. Even Melvin Stoltfuss knew he couldn't solve the case so he turned it over to Magdalena.

Next books in this series: *Gruel and Unusual Punishment* (2002); *Custard's Last Stand* (2003)

Fanny Zindel

Authors: Serita Stevens and Rayanne Moore

Fanny Zindel, a widowed sixty-five year old grandmother, had worked as an actress and modeled in Chicago department stores in her younger days. She still played tennis, attracted male suitors, and traveled about the world. She narrated, so could make all the wry philosophical statements associated with the role of Jewish mother/grandmother. Fanny was a friendly, warm personality, interested in everyone around her.

In *Red Sea, Dead Sea* (St. Martin, 1991), Fanny journeyed to Israel, not solely as a religious or emotional experience, but to search for her brother. He had disappeared, leaving a reputation as a traitor to the British. When a friend was arrested in the Amsterdam airport for a murder in the men's room using Fanny's crochet scissors, her travel plans were spoiled. Fortunately Fanny's granddaughter Susan joined her, and they were allowed to proceed, carrying highly secret material given to her by an acquaintance.

Fanny would not tolerate an accusation of dishonesty against Susan, so, in *Bagels for Tea* (St. Martin, 1993), she challenged the authorities at her granddaughter's exclusive English boarding school. When both the unpleasant young woman who accused Susan of cheating and the headmistress of the school were murdered, Fanny called on her friend Nathan Weiss and his international contacts to find drug dealers, libidinous teachers, and two killers.

Wilhelmena "Helma" Zukas

Author: Jo Dereske

Helma Zukas fit into the stereotype of a small town (Bellehaven, Washington) librarian. She was described as tiny and trim, precise, and careful as to her appearance. She was attentive to her widowed mother, now resident in a retirement complex, and available for volunteer work such as the local crisis center. Helma, although solitary in her own habits, reached out to the troubled on the crisis line. Once curious, she was persistent in finding answers from her experience on the reference desk. She was a stubborn Lithuanian, born and raised in Michigan. Her best friend was unconventional six-foot tall artist, Ruth Winthrop, with whom she had little in common except affection.

During *Miss Zukas and the Library Murders* (Avon, 1994), a corpse was left in the library. Helma's resistance to computers and her reluctance to have anyone else cull her non-fiction section of the Bellehaven Library enabled her to find the killer. Unwed, but not impervious to the opposite sex, Helma assisted Chief of Police Wayne Gallant who found her attractive.

Compulsive about her responsibilities, Helma could not decline when she was reminded that she had promised to arrange the twentieth reunion of her high school class in *Miss Zukas and the Island Murders* (Avon, 1995). Having prudently invested the class funds, she could underwrite travel and lodging for the entire group at a nearby island resort. Once the group gathered, it was isolated by weather and a killer who had a secret to hide.

Helma was not at all certain that she wanted to be a member of the library team entered in Bellehaven's annual Snow to Surf Run in *Miss Zukas and the Stroke of Death* (Avon, 1995). She treasured memories of her youth, gliding along Michigan lakes in the canoe tailor-made for her by Uncle Tony. Friendship was important to Helma, and particularly her friendship for Ruth. So, against her better judgment, she involved herself in the murder of Joshman Lotz, an ex-convict who had brought misery to others all his life. Ruth had quarreled with Lotz hours before he was killed in the alley adjacent to her home. Burdened with two unsought responsibilities, Helma rose to the occasion.

The inability of Chief of Police Wayne Gallant to shed the trauma of his divorce and pursue a relationship with Helma in *Miss Zukas and the Raven's Dance* (Avon, 1996) made her vulnerable to the attentions of a new admirer. Her professional life was disturbed when her supervisor relocated her in a Native American Culture Center, where she was to complete the work of the deceased cataloger, Stanley Plummer. Plummer was murdered because he had uncovered a secret in the archives. Neatness and organization were significant values for both Plummer and Helma so she was driven to complete his task, even at some risk to herself and a young Native American.

Unable to resist Ruth's blandishments about an adventure on her fortieth birthday in *Out of Circulation* (Avon, 1997), Helma set forth on a three-day hiking trip into the mountains. Helma prepared intensely for the trip and needed all her skills when a treacherous storm found her and Ruth sharing a cabin with a half-dozen wayfarers, including a murderer.

Helma's Aunt Em had been too important in her life to allow the eighty-seven-year-old widow to recuperate in a nursing home. In *Final Notice* (Avon, 1998), she took Em into her home. Em's treasured possessions included memoirs of her ill-spent youth during the prohibition era. What Em wanted to forget, someone else had every intention of finding out.

Because she believed that she had not committed the alleged traffic offense, Helma chose to serve 100 days of court ordered service at the Promise Mission for Homeless men during *Miss Zukas in Death's Shadow* (Avon 1999). The mission was located in a rundown area, but she had no idea that she would be involved in another murder case in which she was among the suspects. The victim, a prominent businessman, was a member of the Library Board with whom Helma had disagreements. Tony, a slow-witted street person, confessed to the killing, but that was not enough to convince Helma that he was guilty. Ruth, who served along side Helma at the Mission, risked her own welfare when Helma came too close to the killer.

Helma did not take her ethical stance as a librarian lightly during *Miss Zukas Shelves the Evidence* (Avon, 2001). She was aware of the mysterious death of Professor Lewis Dixon, the son-in-law of her ex-pugilist neighbor, TNT Stone. Helma refused to divulge the name of the borrower of a book left at the scene of the crime and made it impossible for anyone else to do so. While Helma investigated, Ruth and Helma's mother took care of the ailing Wayne Gallant's children. She needed rescuing, and got it from a man she had always ridiculed. She and Wayne ended up in a promising romantic posture.

For the paperback price, these are treasures.

Author/Character Master List

Although some characters appear in all volumes of a shared series, only those in which a significant role is played will be listed. Books scheduled to appear in the future but not reviewed in this series are marked with the expected date of publication. Unfortunately publication dates can be postponed but every effort was made to get them correct. There are also differences in the date of publication depending on whether the book was published in the United States, Great Britain, Canada, Australia or other country. In the text, I used the date and name of publisher from the copy I reviewed.

Books identified in Hubin, Heising or some equally reliable authority but not available to me for review are listed as NA.

Occasionally titles are changed from one country to another. When possible I provided both titles.

In identifying new publications to be listed but not reviewed, I depended upon book review, magazines such as *Deadly Pleasures*, and newsletters from mystery bookstores. Information gleaned from the publications of Sisters in Crime and Malice Domestic helped me to stay reasonably well informed. Any errors are my own.

Allyn, Doug

Andreae, Christine

Andrews, Donna

Andrews, Sarah

Appel, William

Apostolou, Anna

Arnold, Catherine

Atherton, Nancy

Ayres, Noreen

Bailey, Jo, pseudonym for Joseph Bailey

Buchanan, Edna

Britt Montero. 470
  Contents Under Pressure   *Miami, It's Murder*
  Suitable for Framing   *Act of Betrayal*
  Margin of Error   *Garden of Evil*
  You Only Die Twice   *The Ice Maiden* (2002)

Buckley, Fiona

Ursula Blanchard. 73
  To Shield the Queen a.k.a. *The Robsart Mystery*
  The Doublet Affair   *Queen's Ransom*
  To Ruin a Queen   *Queen of Ambition* (2002)
  Pawn for a Queen (2002)

Buckstaff, Kathryn

Emily Stone. 622
  No One Dies in Branson   *Evil Harmony*

Bugge, Carole

Claire Rawlings. 556
  Who Killed Blanche DuBois? *Who Killed Dorian Gray?*
  Who Killed Mona Lisa?

Burke, Jan

Irene Kelly 339
  Goodnight, Irene   *Sweet Dreams, Irene*
  Dear Irene   *Remember Me, Irene*
  Hocus   *Bones*
  Flight

Cail, Carol a.k.a. Kara Galloway

Maxey Burnell. 97
  Private Lies   *Unsafe Keeping*
  If Two of Them Are Dead *Who Was Sylvia?*

Calloway, Kate

Cassidy James. 309
  1st Impressions   *2nd Fiddle*
  3rd Degree   *4th Down*
  5th Wheel   *6th Sense*
  7th Heaven   *8th Day*

Cannon, Taffy

Nan Robinson 570
  A Pocketful of Karma   *Tangled Roots*
  Class Reunions Are Murder
  Taffy Cannon also completed Rebecca Rothenberg's *The Tumbleweed Murders*

Carlson, P. (Patricia) M. Carlson

Martine "Marty" Hopkins 292
  Gravestone   *Bloodstream*

Daheim, Mary

Emma Lord 389

The Alpine Advocate	*The Alpine Betrayal*
The Alpine Christmas	*The Alpine Decoy*
The Alpine Escape	*The Alpine Fury*
The Alpine Gamble	*The Alpine Hero*
The Alpine Icon	*The Alpine Journey*
The Alpine Kindred	*The Alpine Legacy*
The Alpine Menace	*The Alpine Nemesis*
The Alpine Obituary (2002)	*The Alpine Pursuit* (2003)

Judith McMonigle (Flynn) 442

Just Desserts	*Fowl Prey*
Holy Terrors	*Dune to Death*
Bantam of the Opera	*A Fit of Tempera*
Major Vices	*Murder, My Suite*
Auntie Mayhem	*Nutty As a Fruitcake*
September Mourn	*Wed and Buried*
Snow Place to Die	*Legs Benedict*
Creeps Suzette	*Suture Self*
Silver Scream (2002)	*Hoakus Crocus* (2003)

Dain, Catherine

Freddie O'Neal 505

Lay It on the Line	*Sing a Song of Death*
Walk a Crooked Mile	*Lament for a Dead Cowboy*
Bet Against the House	*The Luck of the Draw*
Dead Man's Hand	

Dalton, Margot

Jackie Kaminsky 336

First Impression	*Second Thoughts*
Third Choice	*Fourth Horseman*

D'Amato, Barbara

Cat Marsala 414

Hardball	*Hard Tack*
Hard Luck	*Hard Women*
Hard Case	*Hard Christmas*
Hard Bargain	*Hard Evidence*
Hard Road	

Suze Figueroa 211

Killer.app	*Good Cop, Bad Cop*
Authorized Personnel Only	

Dams, Jeanne M.

Dorothy Martin 417

The Body in the Transept	*Trouble in the Town Hall*
Holy Terror in the Hebrides a.k.a. *Death in Fingal's Cave*	
Malice in Miniature	*The Victim in Victoria Station*
Killing Cassidy	*To Perish in Penzance*
Sins Out of School (2003)	

Doss, James
  Daisy Perika. 518
    The Shaman Sings   *The Shaman Laughs*
    The Shaman's Bones   *The Shaman's Game*
    The Night Visitor   *Grandmother Spider*
    White Shell Woman (2002)   *Dead Soul* (2003)

Douglas, Carole Nelson
  Irene Adler. 3
    Good Night, Mr. Holmes   *Good Morning, Irene*
    Irene at Large
    Irene's Last Waltz a.k.a. Another Scandal in Bohemia
    Chapel Noir   *Castle Rouge* (2002)
    Femme Fatale (2003)
  Temple Barr & Midnight Louie 36
    Catnap   *Pussyfoot*
    Cat on a Blue Monday   *Cat in a Crimson Haze*
    Cat in a Diamond Dazzle   *Cat With an Emerald Eye*
    Cat in a Flamingo Fedora   *Cat in a Golden Garland*
    Cat on a Hyacinth Hunt   *Cat in an Indigo Mood*
    Cat in a Jeweled Jumpsuit   *Cat in a Kiwi Con*
    Cat in a Leopard Spot   *Cat in a Midnight Choir* (2002)
    Cat in a Neon Nightmare (2003)

Douglas, Lauren Wright
  Allison O'Neil 506
    Death at Lavender Bay   *Swimming Cat Cove*

Drury, Joan M.
  Tyler Jones 333
    The Other Side of Silence   *Silent Words*
    Closed in Silence

Dudley, Karen
  Robyn Devara. 175
    Hoot to Kill   *The Red Heron*
    Macaws of Death (2002)

Duffy, Margaret
  Joanna Mackenzie. 400
    Dressed to Kill   *Prospect of Death*
    Music in the Blood   *A Fine Target*
    A Hanging Matter (2002)

Duffy, Stella
  Saz Martin 419
    Calendar Girl   *Wavewalker*
    Beneath the Blonde   *Fresh Flesh*

Dunant, Sarah
  Hannah Wolfe 710
    Birth Marks   *Fatlands*
    Under My Skin

Goldberg, Leonard
 Dr. Joanna Blalock 72
  Deadly Medicine   *A Deadly Practice*
  Deadly Care   *Deadly Harvest*
  Lethal Measures   *Fatal Care*
  Brainwaves (2002)

Goldstone, Nancy
 Elizabeth Halperin 261
  Mommy and the Murder   *Mommy and the Money*

Gom, Leona
 Vicky Bauer 45
  After-Image   *Double Negative*
  Freeze Frame

Grace, C. L., pseudonym for Paul Harding a.k.a. P. C. Doherty
 Kathryn Swinbrooke 634
  A Shrine of Murders   *The Eye of God*
  The Merchant of Death   *The Book of Shadows*
  Saintly Murders   *A Maze of Murders* (2003)

Granger, Ann, pseudonym for Ann Hulme
 Meredith "Merry" Mitchell 462
  Say It with Poison   *A Season for Murder*
  Cold in the Earth   *Murder Among Us*
  Where Old Bones Lie   *A Fine Place for Death*
  Flowers for His Funeral   *Candle for a Corpse*
  A Touch of Mortality   *A Word After Dying*
  Call the Dead Again   *Beneath These Stones*
  Shades of Murder   *A Restless Evil* (2002)
 Fran Varaday 674
  Asking for Trouble   *Keeping Bad Company*
  Running Scared   *Risking It All*
  Watching Out (2003)

Grant, Anne Underwood
 Sydney Teague 643
  Multiple Listing   *Smoke Screen*
  Cuttings   *Voices in the Sand*

Graves, Sarah
 Jacobia Tiptee. 653
  The Dead Cat Bounce   *Triple Witch*
  Wicked Fix   *Repair to Her Grave*
  Wreck the Halls   *Unhinged* (2003)

Gray, Gallagher, a pseudonym for Katy Munger
 Lil Hubbert 296
  Partners in Crime   *A Cast of Killers*
  Death of a Dream Maker *A Motive for Murder*

Haddad, C. A.

Becky Belski 54
Caught in the Shadows   *Root Canal*

Haddock, Lisa

Carmen Ramirez 551
Edited Out   *Final Cut*

Haffner, Margaret

Catherine Edison 193
A Murder of Crows   *A Killing Frost*

Hager, Jean

Molly Bearpaw 52
Ravenmocker   *The Redbird's Cry*
Seven Black Stones   *The Spirit Caller*

Tess Darcy 167
Blooming Murder   *Dead and Buried*
Death on the Drunkard's Path *The Last Noel*
Weigh Dead   *Bride and Doom*

Haines, Carolyn

Sarah Booth Delaney 174
Them Bones   *Buried Bones*
Splintered Bones (2002)   *Crossed Bones* (2003)

Hall, Parnell

Cora Felton and Sherry Carter. 205, 114
A Clue for the Puzzle Lady   *Last Puzzle and Testament*
Puzzled to Death   *A Puzzle in a Pear Tree* (2002)

Hall, Patricia

Laura Ackroyd. 1
Death by Election   *Dying Fall*
The Dead of Winter   *Perils of the Night*
The Italian Girl   *Dead on Arrival*
Skeleton at the Feast   *Death in Dark Waters* (2002)
Deep Freeze a.k.a. *Deep Waters* (2003)

Hamilton, Lyn

Lara McClintoch 434
The Xibalba Murders   *The Maltese Goddess*
The Moche Warrior   *The Celtic Riddle*
The African Quest   *The Etruscan Chimera* (2002)
The Thai Amulet (2003)

Harper, Karen

Elizabeth I 195
The Poyson Garden   *The Tidal Poole*
The Twylight Tower   *The Queene's Cure* (2002)
The Thorne Maze (2003)   *The Queene's Christmas* (2003)

Harris, Charlaine

Aurora "Roe" Teagarden 642

Real Murders	*A Bone to Pick*
Three Bedrooms, One Corpse	*The Julius House*
Dead Over Heels	*A Fool and His Honey*
Last Scene Alive (2002)	*Poppy Done to Death* (2003)

Lily Bard 28

Shakespeare's Landlord	*Shakespeare's Champion*
Shakespeare's Christmas	*Shakespeare's Trollop*
Shakespeare's Counselor	

Harris, Lee, pseudonym for Syrell Rogovin Leahy

Christine Bennett 55

The Good Friday Murder	*The Yom Kippur Murder*
The Christening Day Murder	*The St. Patrick's Day Murder*
The Christmas Night Murder	*The Thanksgiving Day Murder*
The Passover Murder	*The Valentine's Day Murder*
The New Year's Eve Murder	*The Labor Day Murder*
The Father's Day Murder	*The Mother's Day Murder*
The April Fools' Day Murder	*The Happy Birthday Murder* (2002)

Harrison, Janis

Bretta Solomon 611

Roots of Murder	*Murder Sets Seed*
Lilies That Fester	*A Deadly Bouquet* (2002)

Harstad, Donald

Hester Gorse 241

Eleven Days	*Known Dead*
The Big Thaw	*Code Sixty-One* (2002)
The Heartland Experiment (2003)	*A Long December* (2003)

Hart, Carolyn

Henrietta O'Dwyer Collins 134

Dead Man's Island	*Scandal in Fair Haven*
Death in Lovers' Lane	*Death in Paradise*
Death on the River Walk	*Resort to Murder*

Hart, Ellen, pseudonym for Patricia Boehnhardt

Sophie Greenway 251

This Little Piggy Went to Murder	*For Every Evil*
The Oldest Sin	*Murder in the Air*
Slice and Dice	*Dial M for Meat Loaf*
Death on a Silver Platter (2003)	

Hartzmark, Gini

Kate Millholland 459

Principal Defense	*Final Option*
Bitter Business	*Fatal Reaction*
Rough Track	*Dead Certain*

Hunt, David, pseudonym for William Bayer

Hunter, Fred

Hyde, Eleanor

Iakovou, Tavis and Judy

Isenberg, Jane

Jackson, Hialeah, pseudonym for Polly Whitney

Jackson, Marian J. A., pseudonym for Marian Rogers

Jacobs, Nancy Baker

Jacobs, Jonnie

Jaffe, Jody

Paige, Robin, joint pseudonym for Susan Wittig Albert and William J. Albert

Kathryn "Kate" Ardleigh 14

Death at Bishop's Keep	*Death at Gallows Green*
Death at Daisy's Folly	*Death at Devil's Bridge*
Death at Rottingdean	*Death at Whitechapel*
The Body at Epsom Downs	*Death at Dartmoor* (2002)
Death at Glamis Castle (2003)	

Page, Katherine Hall

Faith Fairchild 200

The Body in the Belfry	*The Body in the Kelp*
The Body in the Boullion	*The Body in the Vestibule*
The Body in the Cast	*The Body in the Basement*
The Body in the Bog	*The Body in the Fjord*
The Body in the Big Apple	*The Body in the Moonlight*
The Body in the Bonfire (2002)	*The Body in the Lighthouse* (2003)

Parker, Barbara

Gail Connor 135

Suspicion of Innocence	*Suspicion of Guilt*
Suspicion of Deceit	*Suspicion of Betrayal*
Suspicion of Malice	*Suspicion of Vengeance*
Suspicion of Madness (2003)	

Parker, Robert B.

Sunny Randall 554

Family Honor	*Perish Twice*
Shrink Rap (2002)	

Patterson, Richard North

Caroline Masters 421

Degree of Guilt	*Eyes of a Child*
The Final Judgment	*Protect and Defend*

Patti, Paul

Gabrielle "Gabe" Amato 9

Silhouettes	*Death Mate*

Pears, Iain

Flavia di Stefano 182

The Raphael Affair	*The Titian Committee*
The Bernini Bust	*The Last Judgement*
Giotto's Hand	*Death and Restoration*
The Immaculate Deception	

Pence, Joanne

Angelina "Angie" Amalfi 7

Something's Cooking	*Too Many Cooks*
Cooking Up Trouble	*Cooking Most Deadly*
Cook's Night Out	*Cooks Overboard*
A Cook in Time	*To Catch a Cook*
Bell, Cook, and Candle (2002)	*If Cooks Could Kill* (2003)
Two Cooks A-Killing (2003)	

Perry, Anne

    Hester Latterly (Monk) 372

        The Face of a Stranger   *A Dangerous Mourning*

        Defend and Betray   *A Sudden Fearful Death*

        The Sins of the Wolf   *Cain His Brother*

        Weighed in the Balance   *The Silent Cry*

        The Twisted Root   *Slaves of Obsession*

        Funeral in Blue   *Death of a Stranger* (2002)

Perry, Thomas

    Jane Whitefield 697

        Vanishing Act   *Dance for the Dead*

        Shadow Woman   *The Face Changers*

        Blood Money

Peterson, Audrey

    Claire Camden 107

        Dartmoor Burial   *Death Too Soon*

        Shroud for a Scholar

Petit, Diane

    Kathryn Bogert. 74

        Goodbye, Charli   *Goodbye, Charli-Take Two*

        Goodbye, Charli-Third Time Lucky   *Goodbye, Charli-Fourth Edition*

Phillips, Clyde

    Jane Candiotti 109

        Fall From Grace   *Blindsided*

        Sacrifice (2003)

Pincus, Elizabeth

    Nell Fury 228

        The Two-Bit Tango   *The Solitary Twist*

        The Hangdog Hustle

Plante, Pele, pseudonym for Patricia Planette

    Cynthia Cheney "C. C." Scott 584

        Getting Away with Murder   *Dirty Money*

Pomidor, Bill

    Dr. Calista "Cal" Marley 413

        Murder by Prescription   *The Anatomy of Murder*

        Skeletons in the Closet   *Ten Little Medicine Men*

        Mind Over Murder

Powell, Deborah

    Hollis Carpenter 112

        Bayou City Secrets   *Houston Town*

Proulx, Suzanne

    Victoria Lucci. 393

        Bad Blood   *Bad Luck*

        Bad Medicine   *Declared Dead* (2002)

Robb, J. D., pseudonym for romance novelist Nora Roberts

Naked in Death	*Glory in Death*
Immortal in Death	*Rapture in Death*
Ceremony in Death	*Vengeance in Death*
Holiday in Death	*Conspiracy in Death*
Loyalty in Death	*Judgment in Death*
Witness in Death	*Betrayal in Death*
Seduction in Death	*Purity in Death* (2002)
Reunion in Death (2002)	*Portrait in Death* (2003)
Imitation in Death (2003)	

Roberts, Gillian

Time and Trouble	*Whatever Doesn't Kill You*

Roberts, Lillian M.

Riding for a Fall	*The Hand That Feeds You*
Almost Human	

Roberts, Lora

Murder in a Nice Neighborhood	*Murder Mile High*
Murder in the Marketplace	*Murder Bone by Bone*
Murder Crops Up	*Murder Follows Money*

Robinson, Leah Ruth

First Cut	*Unnatural Causes*
Blood Run	

Robitaille, Julie

Jinx	*Iced*

Roe, C. F.

A Nasty Bit of Murder a.k.a. *The Lumsden Baby*
A Fiery Hint of Murder a.k.a. *Death by Fire*
A Classy Touch of Murder a.k.a. *Bad Blood*
A Bonny Case of Murder a.k.a. *Deadly Partnership*
A Torrid Piece of Murder a.k.a. *Fatal Fever*
A Relative Cause of Murder a.k.a. *Death in the Family*
A Hidden Cause of Murder
A Tangled Knot of Murder

Rogers, Chris

Bitch Factor	*Rage Factor*
Chill Factor	

Walker, Mary Willis

   The Red Scream   *Under the Beetle's Cellar*
   All the Dead Lie Down

Walker, Robert W.

   Killer Instinct   *Fatal Instinct*
   Primal Instinct   *Pure Instinct*
   Darkest Instinct   *Extreme Instinct*
   Blind Instinct   *Unnatural Instinct* (2002)
   Bitter Instinct (2003)   *Grave Instinct* (2003)
   Cutting Edge   *Double Edge*
   Cold Edge

Wallingford, Lee

   Cold Tracks   *Clear Cut Murder*

Walsh, Jill Paton

   The Wyndham Case   *A Piece of Justice*
(NB: Walsh has also continued the Dorothy L. Sayer series on Lord Peter
Wimsey and Harriet Vane covered in Volume I)

Warner, Penny

   Dead Body Language   *Sign of Foul Play*
   Right to Remain Silent   *A Quiet Undertaking*
   Blind Side   *Silence is Golden* (2003)

Waterhouse, Jane

   Graven Images   *Shadow Walk*
   Dead Letter

Weber, Janice

   Frost the Fiddler   *Hot Ticket*

Weir, Charlene

   The Winter Widow   *Consider the Crows*
   Family Practice   *Murder Take Two*
   A Cold Christmas   *Up in Smoke* (2003)

Welch, Pat

   Murder by the Book   *Still Waters*
   A Proper Burial   *Open House*
   Smoke and Mirrors   *Fallen From Grace*
   Snake Eyes   *Moving Targets*

Wilson, Barbara Jaye

Brenda Midnight 455
> *Death Brims Over*
> *Death Flips Its Lid*
> *A Hatful of Homicide*

> *Accessory to Murder*
> *Capped Off*
> *Murder and the Mad Hatter*

Wilson, Karen Ann

Samantha Holt 290
> *Eight Dogs Flying*
> *Beware Sleeping Dogs*

> *Copy Cat Crimes*
> *Circle of Wolves*

Wiltse, David

Karen Crist (Becker) 150
> *Close to the Bone*
> *Into the Fire*
> *Blown Away*

> *The Edge of Sleep*
> *Bone Deep*

Wishnia, k.j.a.

Filomena "Fil" Buscarsela 99
> *23 Shades of Black*
> *The Glass Factory*
> *Blood Lake* (2002)

> *Soft Money*
> *Red House*

Wolzien, Valerie

Josie Pigeon 527
> *Shore to Die*
> *Deck the Halls with Murder*
> *Murder in the Forecast*

> *Permit for Murder*
> *This Old Murder*
> *A Fashionable Murder* (2003)

Woods, Paula L.

Charlotte Justice 335
> *Inner City Blues*
> *Dirty Laundry* (2003)

> *Stormy Weather*

Woods, Sherryl

Molly De Witt 178
> *Hot Property*
> *Hot Money*

> *Hot Secrets*
> *Hot Schemes*

Woods, Stuart

Holly Barker 29
> *Orchid Beach*
> *Blood Orchid* (2002)

> *Orchid Blues*

Woodward, Ann

Lady Aoi 11
> *The Exile Way*

> *Of Death and Black Rivers*

Woodworth, Deborah

Sister Rose Callahan 104
> *Death of a Winter Shaker*
> *Sins of a Shaker Summer*
> *Killing Gifts*

> *A Deadly Shaker Spring*
> *A Simple Shaker Murder*
> *Dancing Dead* (2002)

Index of Characters – Volumes 1, 2, 3

1 refers to Volume I, 2 refers to Volume II, and 3 refers to Volume III of the series

1 refers to Volume I, 2 refers to Volume II, and 3 refers to Volume III of the series

1 refers to Volume I, 2 refers to Volume II, and 3 refers to Volume III of the series

1 refers to Volume I, 2 refers to Volume II, and 3 refers to Volume III of the series

1 refers to Volume I, 2 refers to Volume II, and 3 refers to Volume III of the series

1 refers to Volume I, 2 refers to Volume II, and 3 refers to Volume III of the series

1 refers to Volume I, 2 refers to Volume II, and 3 refers to Volume III of the series

1 refers to Volume I, 2 refers to Volume II, and 3 refers to Volume III of the series

1 refers to Volume I, 2 refers to Volume II, and 3 refers to Volume III of the series

1 refers to Volume I, 2 refers to Volume II, and 3 refers to Volume III of the series

1 refers to Volume I, 2 refers to Volume II, and 3 refers to Volume III of the series

1 refers to Volume I, 2 refers to Volume II, and 3 refers to Volume III of the series

1 refers to Volume I, 2 refers to Volume II, and 3 refers to Volume III of the series

Book Titles Index

All titles were taken from my personal book reviews or from advance notices of future books and were rechecked for accuracy with recognized authorities such as Hubin, Heising, Twentieth Century Crime and Mystery Writers, and with newsletters by mystery book stores. Any errors are my own. Those titles marked with an asterisk (*) which are not reviewed are followed by a date. They are to be published soon but at a later date than this volume covers.

Title of Book	Author	Character
#		
12 Drummers Drumming	Diana Deverell	Casey Collins
1-900-DEAD	Tony Fennelly	Margo Fortier
1st Impressions	Kate Calloway	Cassidy James
23 Shades of Black	k.j.a. Wishnia	Filomena "Fil" Buscarsela
2nd Fiddle	Kate Calloway	Cassidy James
3rd Degree	Kate Calloway	Cassidy James
4th Down	Kate Calloway	Cassidy James
5th Wheel	Kate Calloway	Cassidy James
6th Sense	Kate Calloway	Cassidy James
7th Heaven	Kate Calloway	Cassidy James
77th Street Requiem	Wendy Hornsby	Maggie MacGowen
82 Desire	Julie Smith	Skip Langdon
8th Day	Kate Calloway	Cassidy James
A		
Above the Law	Patricia D. Benke	Judith Thornton
Absent Friends	Gillian Linscott	Nell Bray
Absolution by Murder	Peter Tremayne	Sister Fidelma
Accessory to Murder	Barbara Jaye Wilson	Brenda Midnight
An Accidental Shroud	Marjorie Eccles	Abigail Moon
Acid Bath	Nancy Herndon	Elena Jarvis
Acquired Motives	Sarah Lovett	Dr. Sylvia Strange
Act of Betrayal	Edna Buchanan	Britt Montero
Act of Mercy	Peter Tremayne	Sister Fidelma
Acts of Malice	Perri O'Shaughnessy	Nina Reilly
Add One Dead Critic	Cathie John	Kate Cavanaugh
Adjusted to Death	Jaqueline Girdner	Kate Jasper
Affirmative Reaction	Aileen Schumacher	Tory Travers
The African Quest	Lyn Hamilton	Lara McClintoch
After the Break	Lis Howell	Kate Wilkinson
After-Image	Leona Gom	Vicky Bauer
Agatha Raisin and the Case of the Curious Curate (2003)	M. C. Beaton	Agatha Raisin
Agatha Raisin and the Day the Floods Came (2002)	M. C. Beaton	Agatha Raisin
Agatha Raisin and the Fairies of Fryfam	M. C. Beaton	Agatha Raisin
Agatha Raisin and the Haunted House (2003)	M. C. Beaton	Agatha Raisin

Title of Book	Author	Character
Agatha Raisin and the Love from Hell	M. C. Beaton	Agatha Raisin
Agatha Raisin and the Murderous Marriage	M. C. Beaton	Agatha Raisin
Agatha Raisin and the Potted Gardener	M. C. Beaton	Agatha Raisin
Agatha Raisin and the Quiche of Death	M. C. Beaton	Agatha Raisin
Agatha Raisin and the Terrible Tourist	M. C. Beaton	Agatha Raisin
Agatha Raisin and the Vicious Vet	M. C. Beaton	Agatha Raisin
Agatha Raisin and the Walkers of Dembley	M. C. Beaton	Agatha Raisin
Agatha Raisin and the Wellspring of Death	M. C. Beaton	Agatha Raisin
Agatha Raisin and the Witch of Wyckhadden	M. C. Beaton	Agatha Raisin
Agatha Raisin and the Wizard of Evesham	M. C. Beaton	Agatha Raisin
Ah, Sweet Mystery	Celestine Sibley	Kate Mulcay a.k.a. Katy Kincaid
An Air That Kills	Andrew Taylor	Jill Francis
Airtight Case	Beverly Connor	Lindsay Chamberlain
Akin to Death	Carroll Lachnit	Hannah Barlow
aka Jane	Maureen Tan	Jane Nichols
Alibi for an Actress	Gillian B. Farrell	Annie McGrogan
All My Enemies	Barry Maitland	Sgt. Kathy Kolla
All My Suspects	Louise Shaffer	Angie DaVito
All Shall Be Well	Deborah Crombie	Gemma James
All That Remains	Patricia D. Cornwell	Dr. Kay Scarpetta
All the Dead Lie Down	Mary Willis Walker	Molly Cates
All the Old Men	Carol Caverly	Thea Barlow
The Alligator's Farewell	Hialeah Jackson	Annabelle Hardy-Maratos
Almost Human	Lillian M. Roberts	Dr. Andi Pauling
Along the Journey River	Carole LaFavor	Renee LaRoche
The Alpine Advocate	Mary Daheim	Emma Lord
The Alpine Betrayal	Mary Daheim	Emma Lord
The Alpine Christmas	Mary Daheim	Emma Lord
The Alpine Decoy	Mary Daheim	Emma Lord
The Alpine Escape	Mary Daheim	Emma Lord
The Alpine Fury	Mary Daheim	Emma Lord
The Alpine Gamble	Mary Daheim	Emma Lord
The Alpine Hero	Mary Daheim	Emma Lord
The Alpine Icon	Mary Daheim	Emma Lord
The Alpine Journey	Mary Daheim	Emma Lord
The Alpine Kindred	Mary Daheim	Emma Lord
The Alpine Legacy	Mary Daheim	Emma Lord
The Alpine Menace	Mary Daheim	Emma Lord
The Alpine Nemesis	Mary Daheim	Emma Lord
The Alpine Obituary (2002)	Mary Daheim	Emma Lord
The Alpine Pursuit (2003)	Mary Daheim	Emma Lord
Amateur Night	K. K. Beck	Jane da Silva
The Anatomy of Murder	Bill Pomidor	Dr. Calista "Cal" Marley
Ancient Ones	Kirk Mitchell	Anna Turnipseed
And Justice There Is None (2002)	Deborah Crombie	Gemma James
And None Shall Sleep	Priscilla Masters	Joanna Piercy

Title of Book	Author	Character
And Your Little Dog, Too	Melissa Cleary	Jackie Walsh
Angel at Troublesome Creek	Mignon F. Ballard	Augusta Goodnight
Angel of Death	Rochelle Majer Krich	Jessica Drake
An Angel to Die For	Mignon F. Ballard	Augusta Goodnight
Angel Trumpet	Ann McMillan	Narcissa Powers, Judah Daniel
The Angel Whispered Danger (2003)	Mignon F. Ballard	Augusta Goodnight
Angel's Bidding	Sharon Gwyn Short	Patricia Delaney
Animal Appetite	Susan Conant	Holly Winter
Animal Instincts	Eleanor Hyde	Lydia Miller
Another Scandal in Bohemia a.k.a. *Irene's Last Waltz*	Carole Nelson Douglas	Irene Adler
Anything Goes	Jill Churchill	Lily Brewster
The Apothecary Rose	Candace M. Robb	Lucie D'Arby Wilton
Appointed to Die	Kate Charles	Lucy Kingsley
The April Fools' Day Murder	Lee Harris	Christine Bennett
Aquarius Descending	Martha C. Lawrence	Dr. Elizabeth Chase
The Arabian Pearl	Marian J. A. Jackson	Abigail Danforth
Arkansas Traveler	Earlene Fowler	Albenia "Benni" Harper
Artist Unknown	Jeanne McCafferty	Dr. Mackenzie Griffin
As Crime Goes By	Diane K. Shah	Paris Chandler
Ashes of Aries	Martha C. Lawrence	Dr. Elizabeth Chase
Asking for Trouble	Ann Granger	Fran Varaday
At Large	Lynne Murray	Josephine Fuller
At Point Blank	Virginia Stem Owens	Beth Marie Cartwright
Atlanta Graves	Ruth Birmingham	Sunny Childs
Aunt Dimity and the Duke	Nancy Atherton	Dimity Westwood, Lori Shepherd
Aunt Dimity Beats the Devil	Nancy Atherton	Dimity Westwood, Lori Shepherd
Aunt Dimity Digs In	Nancy Atherton	Dimity Westwood, Lori Shepherd
Aunt Dimity Takes a Holiday (2003)	Nancy Atherton	Dimity Westwood, Lori Shepherd
Aunt Dimity: Detective	Nancy Atherton	Dimity Westwood, Lori Shepherd
Aunt Dimity's Christmas	Nancy Atherton	Dimity Westwood, Lori Shepherd
Aunt Dimity's Death	Nancy Atherton	Dimity Westwood, Lori Shepherd
Aunt Dimity's Good Deed	Nancy Atherton	Dimity Westwood, Lori Shepherd
Auntie Mayhem	Mary Daheim	Judith McMonigle (Flynn)
Authorized Personnel Only	Barbara D'Amato	Suze Figueroa
The Axeman's Jazz	Julie Smith	Skip Langdon

B

Title of Book	Author	Character
Babel (2002)	Barry Maitland	Sgt. Kathy Kolla
Baby, It's Cold	Jaye Maiman	Robin Miller
Back to School Murder	Leslie Meier	Lucy Stone
Backstab	Elaine Viets	Francesca Vierling
Backtrack	Carol Dawber	Liz Gresham
Bad Blood	Suzanne Proulx	Victoria Lucci
Bad Blood a.k.a. *A Classy Touch of Murder*	C. F. Roe	Dr. Jean Montrose
A Bad Hair Day	Sophie Dunbar	Claire Claiborne Jenner
Bad Intent	Wendy Hornsby	Maggie MacGowen
Bad Luck	Suzanne Proulx	Victoria Lucci
Bad Manners	Marne Davis Kellogg	Lilly Bennett
Bad Medicine	Suzanne Proulx	Victoria Lucci
Bad Medicine	Aimee and David Thurlo	Ella Clah
Bad Moon Rising	Barbara Johnson	Colleen Fitzgerald

Title of Book	Author	Character
Bad News Travels Fast	Gar Anthony Haywood	Dottie Loudermilk
Bad to the Bone	Katy Munger	Casey Jones
Bad Vibes	Joyce Holms	Fizz Fitzgerald
The Bad Witness (2002)	Laura Van Wormer	Sally Harrington
Bagels for Tea	Serita Stevens, Rayanne Moore	Fanny Zindel
Bagged	Jo Bailey	Jan Gallagher
Bait	C. J. Songer	"Meg" Gillis
The Ballad of Frankie Silver	Sharyn McCrumb	Nora Bonesteel
Baltimore Blues	Laura Lippman	Tess Monaghan
Bantam of the Opera	Mary Daheim	Judith McMonigle (Flynn)
The Barker Street Regulars	Susan Conant	Holly Winter
Barking	Liz Evans	Grace Smith
Baroque and Desperate	Tamar Myers	Abigail "Abby" Timberlake
Baseball Cat	Garrison Allen	Penelope Warren
The Bastard's Tale (2003)	Margaret Frazer	Sister Frevisse
Bayou City Secrets	Deborah Powell	Hollis Carpenter
The Beach Affair	Barbara Johnson	Colleen Fitzgerald
Beacon Street Mourning	Dianne Day	Caroline "Fremont" Jones
Beaned in Boston	Gail E. Farrelly	Lisa King
The Beastly Bloodline (2003)	Patricia Guiver	Delilah Doolittle
Beat a Rotten Egg to the Punch	Cathie John	Kate Cavanaugh
Beat Up a Cookie	Denise Dietz	Ellie Bernstein
The Beekeeper's Apprentice	Laurie R. King	Mary Russell (Holmes)
A Beer at a Bawdy House	David J. Walker	Kirsten
Behind Eclaire's Doors	Sophie Dunbar	Claire Claiborne Jenner
Bell, Cook, and Candle (2002)	Joanne Pence	Angelina "Angie" Amalfi
Beneath the Ashes	Sue Henry	Jessie Arnold
Beneath the Blonde	Stella Duffy	Saz Martin
Beneath These Stones	Ann Granger	Merry Mitchell
The Bernini Bust	Iain Pears	Flavia di Stefano
The Beryllium Murder	Camille Minichino	Gloria Lamerino
The Best Defense	Sarah Gregory	Sharon Hays
The Best Defense	Kate Wilhelm	Barbara Holloway
Best in Show (2003)	Laurien Berenson	Melanie Travis
The Best Revenge (2003)	Stephen White	Lauren Crowder
Bet Against the House	Catherine Dain	Freddie O'Neal
Betrayal in Death	J. D. Robb	Lt. Eve Dallas
Betrayed in Cornwall	Jane Bolitho	Rose Trevelyan
A Better Class of Sleuth	Joyce Christmas	Elizabeth Anne "Betty" Trenka
Better Off Dead	Katy Munger	Casey Jones
Better Than Sex	Susan Holtzer	Anneke Haagen
Better to Rest (2002)	Dana Stabenow	Wyanet "Wy" Chouinard
Between a Wok and a Hard Place	Tamar Myers	Magdalena Yoder
Beware Sleeping Dogs	Karen Ann Wilson	Samantha Holt
Beware Taurus	Linda Mather	Jo Hughes
Beware the Butcher Bird	Lydia Adamson	Lucy Wayles
Beware the Laughing Gull	Lydia Adamson	Lucy Wayles
Beware the Tufted Duck	Lydia Adamson	Lucy Wayles
Beyond Ice, Beyond Death	Thomas McCall	Nora Callum
The Big Thaw	Donald Harstad	Hester Gorse
Biggie and the Devil Diet (2002)	Nancy Bell	Biggie Weatherford
Biggie and the Fricasseed Fat Man	Nancy Bell	Biggie Weatherford
Biggie and the Mangled Mortician	Nancy Bell	Biggie Weatherford
Biggie and the Meddlesome Mailman	Nancy Bell	Biggie Weatherford

Title of Book	Author	Character
Biggie and the Poisoned Politician	Nancy Bell	Biggie Weatherford
Biggie and the Quincy Ghost	Nancy Bell	Biggie Weatherford
Bird Brained	Jessica Speart	Rachel Porter
Birth Marks	Sarah Dunant	Hannah Wolfe
Birthday Party	Marne Davis Kellogg	Lilly Bennett
Birthday Party Murder (2002)	Leslie Meier	Lucy Stone
The Bishop's Tale	Margaret Frazer	Sister Frevisse
Bitch Factor	Chris Rogers	Dixie Flannigan
A Bite of Death	Susan Conant	Holly Winter
Bitter Business	Gini Hartzmark	Kate Millholland
Bitter End	Joyce Holms	Fizz Fitzgerald
A Bitter Feast	S. J. Rozan	Lydia Chin
Bitter Herbs	Natasha Cooper	Willow King
Bitter Instinct (2003)	Robert W. Walker	Dr. Jessica Coran
Bitter Sugar	Carolina Garcia-Aguilera	Guadalupe "Lupe" Solano
Bitter Sweets	G. A. McKevett	Savannah Reid
The Black Cat Caper	Georgette Livingston	Dr. Jennifer Gray
Black Delta Night	Jessica Speart	Rachel Porter
Black Diamond	Susan Holtzer	Anneke Haagen
Black Diamonds (2002)	Jon Land	Danielle Barnea
Black Notice	Patricia D. Cornwell	Dr. Kay Scarpetta
Black Ribbon	Susan Conant	Holly Winter
Black Rubber Dress	Lauren Henderson	Sam Jones
Black Salamander	Marilyn Todd	Claudia Seferius
Black Water	Doug Allyn	Michelle "Mitch" Mitchell
Blackening Song	Aimee and David Thurlo	Ella Clah
Blackwater Spirits	Miriam Monfredo	Glynis Tryon
Blanche Among the Talented Tenth	Barbara Neely	Blanche White
Blanche Cleans Up	Barbara Neely	Blanche White
Blanche on the Lam	Barbara Neely	Blanche White
Blanche Passes Go	Barbara Neely	Blanche White
Bleeding Dodger Blue	Crabbe Evers	Petronella "Petey" Biggers
Bleeding Heart	Mary Freeman	Rachel O'Connor
Bleeding Maize and Blue	Susan Holtzer	Anneke Haagen
A Bleeding of Innocents	Jo Bannister	Liz Graham
A Blessed Death	Carroll Lachnit	Hannah Barlow
Blind Bloodhound Justice	Virginia Lanier	Jo Beth Sidden
Blind Descent	Nevada Barr	Anna Pigeon
Blind Instinct	Robert W. Walker	Dr. Jessica Coran
Blind Justice	William Bernhardt	Christina McCall
Blind Side	Penny Warner	Connor Westphal
Blind Spot	Judy Mercer	Ariel Gold
Blindsided	Clyde Phillips	Jane Candiotti
Blood and Rubles	Stuart Kaminsky	Elena Timafeyeva
Blood Country	Mary Logue	Claire Watkins
Blood Lake (2002)	k.j.a. Wishnia	Filomena "Fil" Buscarsela
Blood Lies	Marianne Macdonald	Dido Hoare
Blood Lure	Nevada Barr	Anna Pigeon
Blood Money	Rochelle Majer Krich	Jessica Drake
Blood Money	Thomas Perry	Jane Whitefield
Blood of an Aries	Linda Mather	Jo Hughes
Blood Orchid (2002)	Stuart Woods	Holly Barker
Blood Red Roses	Margaret Lawrence	Hannah Trevor
Blood Relations (2003)	Rett MacPherson	"Torie" O'Shea
Blood Run	Leah Ruth Robinson	Dr. Evelyn Sutcliffe

Title of Book	Author	Character
Blood Tracks	Karen Rose Cercone	Helen Sorby
Blood Trance	R. D. Zimmerman	Maddy Phillips
Blood Will Tell	Terris McMahon Grimes	Theresa Galloway
Blood Will Tell	Dana Stabenow	Kate Shugak
Blood Work	Fay Zachary	Dr. Liz Broward
Bloodlines	Susan Conant	Holly Winter
Bloodroot	Susan Wittig Albert	China Bayles
Bloodstream	P. M. Carlson	Martine "Marty" Hopkins
Bloody Bonsai	Peter Abresch	Dodee Swisher
Bloody Roses	Natasha Cooper	Willow King
Bloody Secrets	Carolina Garcia-Aguilera	Guadalupe "Lupe" Solano
Bloody Shame	Carolina Garcia-Aguilera	Guadalupe "Lupe" Solano
Bloody Waters	Carolina Garcia-Aguilera	Guadalupe "Lupe" Solano
Blooming Murder	Jean Hager	Tess Darcy
Blow Fly (2003)	Patricia D. Cornwell	Dr. Kay Scarpetta
Blowing Smoke	Barbara Block	Robin Light
Blown Away	David Wiltse	Karen Crist (Becker)
Blue	Abigail Padgett	Emily "Blue" McCarron
Blue Blood	Pamela Thomas-Graham	Nikki Chase
Blue Genes	Val McDermid	Kate Brannigan
Blue Plate Special	Ruth Birmingham	Sunny Childs
Blue Poppy	Skye Kathleen Moody	Venus Diamond
Blue Widows (2003)	Jon Land	Danielle Barnea
Blue Wolf	Lise McClendon	Alix Thorssen
The Bluejay Shaman	Lise McClendon	Alix Thorssen
The Body at Epsom Downs	Robin Paige	Kathryn "Kate" Ardleigh
Body English	Linda Mariz	Laura Ireland
The Body Farm	Patricia D. Cornwell	Dr. Kay Scarpetta
The Body in the Basement	Katherine Hall Page	Faith Fairchild
The Body in the Belfry	Katherine Hall Page	Faith Fairchild
The Body in the Big Apple	Katherine Hall Page	Faith Fairchild
The Body in the Bog	Katherine Hall Page	Faith Fairchild
The Body in the Bonfire (2002)	Katherine Hall Page	Faith Fairchild
The Body in the Boullion	Katherine Hall Page	Faith Fairchild
The Body in the Cast	Katherine Hall Page	Faith Fairchild
The Body in the Fjord	Katherine Hall Page	Faith Fairchild
The Body in the Kelp	Katherine Hall Page	Faith Fairchild
The Body in the Lighthouse (2003)	Katherine Hall Page	Faith Fairchild
The Body in the Moonlight	Katherine Hall Page	Faith Fairchild
The Body in the Transept	Jeanne M. Dams	Dorothy Martin
The Body in the Vestibule	Katherine Hall Page	Faith Fairchild
Body of Evidence	Patricia D. Cornwell	Dr. Kay Scarpetta
Body of Lies (2002)	Iris Johansen	Eve Duncan
A Body to Die For	Valerie Frankel	Wanda Mallory
Body Wave (2002)	Nancy J. Cohen	Marla Shore
The Bohemian Murders	Dianne Day	Caroline "Fremont" Jones
Bonded for Murder	Bruce Most	Ruby Dark
The Bone Collector	Jeffrey Wilds Deaver	Amelia Sachs
Bone Dancing (2002)	Jonathan Gash	Dr. Clare Burtonall
Bone Deep	David Wiltse	Karen Crist (Becker)
Bone Hunter	Sarah Andrews	Emily "Em" Hansen
Bone of Contention (2002)	Roberta Gellis	Magdalene la Bâtarde
A Bone to Pick	Charlaine Harris	Aurora "Roe" Teagarden
The Bone Vault (2003)	Linda Fairstein	Alexandra Cooper
Bones	Jan Burke	Irene Kelly

Title of Book	Author	Character
Bones to Pick (2002)	Suzanne North	Phoebe Fairfax
A Bonny Case of Murder a.k.a. *Deadly Partnership*	C. F. Roe	Dr. Jean Montrose
Book of Light (2003)	Michelle Blake	Rev. Lily Connor
Book of Moons	Rosemary Edghill	Karen Hightower a.k.a. Bast
The Book of Shadows	C. L. Grace	Kathryn Swinbrooke
Bootlegger's Daughter	Margaret Maron	Deborah Knott
Border Prey	Jessica Speart	Rachel Porter
The Boric Acid Murder (2002)	Camille Minichino	Gloria Lamerino
The Bowl of Night	Rosemary Edghill	Karen Hightower a.k.a. Bast
The Boy's Tale	Margaret Frazer	Sister Frevisse
A Brace of Bloodhounds	Virginia Lanier	Jo Beth Sidden
Brainwaves (2002)	Leonard Goldberg	Joanna Blalock
Breach of Promise	Perri O'Shaughnessy	Nina Reilly
Bread on Arrival	Lou Jane Temple	Heaven Lee
Breakaway	Laura Crum	Dr. Gail McCarthy
Breaking Point	Martina Navratilova, Liz Nickles	Jordan Myles
Breakup	Dana Stabenow	Kate Shugak
Bride and Doom	Jean Hager	Tess Darcy
The Bride's Kimono	Sujata Massey	Rei Shimura
A Bright Flamingo Shroud	Meg O'Brien	Jessica "Jesse" James
Broken Lines	Jo Bannister	Liz Graham
Broken Star	Lizbie Brown	Elizabeth Blair
Brotherly Love	Randye Lordon	Sydney Sloane
Brothers of Cain	Miriam Monfredo	Glynis Tryon
Bucket Nut	Liza Cody	Eva Wylie
The Bulrush Murders	Rebecca Rothenberg	Claire Sharples
Buried Bones	Carolyn Haines	Sarah Booth Delaney
Buried in Cornwall	Jane Bolitho	Rose Trevelyan
Buried Treasure	Alan Scholefield	Dr. Anne Vernon
Burn Out	Alan Scholefield	Dr. Anne Vernon
The Burning Bride	Margaret Lawrence	Hannah Trevor
Burning Time	Leslie Glass	April Woo
Bury Him Darkly	Roger Ormerod	Phillipa Lowe
Bury the Bishop	Kate Gallison	Mother Lavinia Grey
Burying Ariel	Gail Bowen	Joanne "Jo" Kilbourn
But for the Grace	Patricia Brooks	Molly Piper
Butchers Hill	Laura Lippman	Tess Monaghan
The Butter Did It	Phyllis Richman	Chas Wheatley
Buttons and Foes (2002)	Dolores Johnson	Mandy Dyer
By Evil Means	Sandra West Prowell	Phoebe Seigel

C

Cabin Fever	Carol Schmidt	Laney Samms
Cadaver	Mary Kittredge	Edwina Crusoe
Cain His Brother	Anne Perry	Hester Latterly (Monk)
Calendar Girl	Stella Duffy	Saz Martin
Call the Dead Again	Ann Granger	Merry Mitchell
Camp Conviction	Natalie Buske Thomas	Serena Wilcox
Cancellation by Death	Dorian Yeager	Victoria "Vic" Bowering
Candle for a Corpse	Ann Granger	Merry Mitchell
Capitol Offense	Tony Gibbs	Diana Speed
Capitol Offense	Barbara Mikulski, Marylouise Oates	Sen. Eleanor Gorzack

Title of Book	Author	Character
Capitol Scandal	Sarah Gregory	Sharon Hays
Capitol Venture	Barbara Mikulski Marylouise Oates	Sen. Eleanor Gorzack
Capped Off	Barbara Jaye Wilson	Brenda Midnight
Carcass Trade	Noreen Ayres	Smokey Brandon
Carnage on the Committee (2003)	Ruth Dudley Edwards	Baroness "Jack" Troutbeck
Carve a Witness to Shreds	Cathie John	Kate Cavanaugh
Casanova Crimes	Nancy Herndon	Elena Jarvis
The Case of the Good-for-Nothing Girlfriend	Mabel Maney	Cherry Aimless, Nancy Clue
The Case of the Murdered Muckraker (2003)	Carola Dunn	Daisy Dalrymple
The Case of the Not-So-Nice Nurse	Mabel Maney	Cherry Aimless, Nancy Clue
The Case of the Orphaned Bassoonist	Barbara Wilson	Cassandra Reilly
A Cast of Killers	Gallagher Gray	Lil Hubbert
Castle Rouge (2002)	Carole Nelson Douglas	Irene Adler
The Catalyst a.k.a. The Strange Attractor	Desmond Cory	Dr. Kate Coyle
A Cat By Any Other Name	Lydia Adamson	Alice Nestleton
A Cat in a Chorus Line	Lydia Adamson	Alice Nestleton
Cat in a Crimson Haze	Carole Nelson Douglas	Temple Barr & Midnight Louie
Cat in a Diamond Dazzle	Carole Nelson Douglas	Temple Barr & Midnight Louie
Cat in a Flamingo Fedora	Carole Nelson Douglas	Temple Barr & Midnight Louie
A Cat in a Glass House	Lydia Adamson	Alice Nestleton
Cat in a Golden Garland	Carole Nelson Douglas	Temple Barr & Midnight Louie
Cat in a Jeweled Jumpsuit	Carole Nelson Douglas	Temple Barr & Midnight Louie
Cat in a Kiwi Con	Carole Nelson Douglas	Temple Barr & Midnight Louie
Cat in a Leopard Spot	Carole Nelson Douglas	Temple Barr & Midnight Louie
Cat in a Midnight Choir (2002)	Carole Nelson Douglas	Temple Barr & Midnight Louie
Cat in a Neon Nightmare (2003)	Carole Nelson Douglas	Temple Barr & Midnight Louie
Cat in an Indigo Mood	Carole Nelson Douglas	Temple Barr & Midnight Louie
A Cat in Fine Style	Lydia Adamson	Alice Nestleton
A Cat in the Manger	Lydia Adamson	Alice Nestleton
A Cat in the Wings	Lydia Adamson	Alice Nestleton
A Cat in Wolf's Clothing	Lydia Adamson	Alice Nestleton
A Cat Named Brat (2002)	Lydia Adamson	Alice Nestleton
A Cat of a Different Color	Lydia Adamson	Alice Nestleton
A Cat of One's Own	Lydia Adamson	Alice Nestleton
A Cat on a Beach Blanket	Lydia Adamson	Alice Nestleton
Cat on a Blue Monday	Carole Nelson Douglas	Temple Barr & Midnight Louie
Cat on a Hyacinth Hunt	Carole Nelson Douglas	Temple Barr & Midnight Louie
A Cat on a Winning Streak	Lydia Adamson	Alice Nestleton
A Cat on Jingle Bell Rock	Lydia Adamson	Alice Nestleton
A Cat on Stage Left	Lydia Adamson	Alice Nestleton
A Cat on the Bus (2002)	Lydia Adamson	Alice Nestleton
A Cat on the Cutting Edge	Lydia Adamson	Alice Nestleton
Cat on the Scent	Rita Mae Brown	Mary "Harry" Haristeen & Mrs. Murphy
A Cat Under the Mistletoe	Lydia Adamson	Alice Nestleton
A Cat With a Fiddle	Lydia Adamson	Alice Nestleton
Cat With an Emerald Eye	Carole Nelson Douglas	Temple Barr & Midnight Louie
A Cat With No Clue	Lydia Adamson	Alice Nestleton
A Cat With No Regrets	Lydia Adamson	Alice Nestleton
A Cat With the Blues	Lydia Adamson	Alice Nestleton

Title of Book	Author	Character
The Christmas Garden Affair (2002)	Ann Ripley	Louise Eldridge
The Christmas Night Murder	Lee Harris	Christine Bennett
Chutes and Adders	Barbara Block	Robin Light
Circle of Wolves	Karen Ann Wilson	Samantha Holt
Circles of Confusion	April Henry	Claire Montrose
A Citizen of the Country	Sarah Smith	Perdita Halley
Civil Blood	Ann McMillan	Narcissa Powers, Judah Daniel
Class Action	Catherine Arnold	Karen Perry-Mondori
Class Reunions Are Murder	Taffy Cannon	Nan Robinson
A Classy Touch of Murder a.k.a. *Bad Blood*	C. F. Roe	Dr. Jean Montrose
Claws and Effect	Rita Mae Brown	Mary "Harry" Haristeen & Mrs. Murphy
Clean Break	Val McDermid	Kate Brannigan
Clear and Convincing Proof (2003)	Kate Wilhelm	Barbara Holloway
Clear Cut Murder	Lee Wallingford	Ginny Trask
Clearwater	Catherine Ennis	Dr. Bernadette "Bernie" Hebert
Clerical Errors	D. M. Greenwood	Rev. Theodora Braithwaite
The Clerk's Tale (2002)	Margaret Frazer	Sister Frevisse
A Clinic for Murder	Marsha Landreth	Dr. Samantha Turner
Close to the Bone	David Wiltse	Karen Crist (Becker)
Close to You	Mary Jane Clark	Eliza Blake
Closed in Silence	Joan M. Drury	Tyler Jones
Closing Stages	Eileen Dewhurst	Phyllida Moon
Closing Statement	Tierney McClellan	Schuyler Ridgway
Club Twelve	Amanda Kyle Williams	Madison McGuire
A Clue for the Puzzle Lady	Parnell Hall	Cora Felton & Sherry Carter
Coal Bones	Karen Rose Cercone	Helen Sorby
Coastal Disturbance (2003)	Jessica Speart	Rachel Porter
Code Sixty-One (2002)	Donald Harstad	Hester Gorse
Coffee To Die For	Linda French	Teodora "Teddy" Morelli
Coffin Corner	Megan Mallory Rust	Taylor Morgan
The Coffin Dancer	Jeffrey Wilds Deaver	Amelia Sachs
Cold and Pure and Very Dead	Joanne Dobson	Karen Pelletier
Cold Blood	Lynda La Plante	Lorraine Page
Cold Call	Diane G. Pugh	Iris Thorne
Cold Case	Stephen White	Lauren Crowder
A Cold Christmas	Charlene Weir	Susan Donavan Wren
Cold Company (2002)	Sue Henry	Jessie Arnold
A Cold Day for Murder	Dana Stabenow	Kate Shugak
Cold Edge	Robert W. Walker	Meredyth "Mere" Sanger
Cold Feet	Kerry Tucker	Libby Kincaid
Cold Front	Kathleen Taylor	Tory Bauer
The Cold Hard Fax	Leslie O'Kane	Molly Masters
Cold Heart	Lynda La Plante	Lorraine Page
The Cold Heart of Capricorn	Martha C. Lawrence	Dr. Elizabeth Chase
Cold Hit	Linda Fairstein	Alexandra Cooper
Cold in the Earth	Ann Granger	Merry Mitchell
Cold Iron	Melisa Michaels	Rosie Lavine
Cold Justice (2002)	Jonnie Jacobs	Kali O'Brien
Cold Shoulder	Lynda La Plante	Lorraine Page
Cold Smoked	K. K. Beck	Jane da Silva
Cold Tracks	Lee Wallingford	Ginny Trask
Cold Trail (2002)	Ruth Birmingham	Sunny Childs

Title of Book	Author	Character
Crystal Mountain Veils	Kieran York	Royce Madison
Cuckoo	Alex Keegan	Caz Flood
The Cuckoo Clock	Michele Bailey	Matilda Haycastle
The Curious Cape Cod Skull	Marie Lee	Marguerite Smith
Curl Up and Die	Christine T. Jorgensen	Stella the Stargazer a.k.a. Jane Smith
Curly Smoke	Susan Holtzer	Anneke Haagen
Cursed in the Blood	Sharan Newman	Catherine Le Vendeur
Curtsey	Marne Davis Kellogg	Lilly Bennett
Custard's Last Stand (2003)	Tamar Myers	Magdalena Yoder
Cut and Dry	Jo Dereske	Ruby Crane
Cut to: Murder	Denise Osborne	Queenie Davilov
Cutter	Laura Crum	Dr. Gail McCarthy
Cutting Edge	Robert W. Walker	Meredyth "Mere" Sanger
Cuttings	Anne Underwood Grant	Sydney Teague
Cyberkiss	Sally Chapman	Julie Blake

D

Damsel in Distress	Carola Dunn	Daisy Dalrymple
Dance for the Dead	Thomas Perry	Jane Whitefield
A Dance in Deep Water	Doug Allyn	Michelle "Mitch" Mitchell
Dancing Dead (2002)	Deborah Woodworth	Sister Rose Callahan
Dancing in the Dark	Sharon Zukowski	Blaine Stewart
The Dandelion Murders	Rebecca Rothenberg	Claire Sharples
Danger in High Places	Sharon Gilligan	Alix Nicholson
Danger! Cross Currents	Sharon Gilligan	Alix Nicholson
Dangerous Attachments	Sarah Lovett	Dr. Sylvia Strange
A Dangerous Mourning	Anne Perry	Hester Latterly (Monk)
Dantes' Inferno	Sarah Lovett	Dr. Sylvia Strange
The Daphne Decisions	Meg O'Brien	Jessica "Jesse" James
Dark Alchemy (2003)	Sarah Lovett	Dr. Sylvia Strange
A Dark and Sinful Death	Alison Joseph	Sister Agnes Bourdillon
Dark Coulee	Mary Logue	Claire Watkins
Dark Horse (2002)	Marilyn Todd	Claudia Seferius
Dark Justice	William Bernhardt	Christina McCall
Dark Moon Crossing (2002)	Sylvia Nobel	Kendall O'Dell
A Darker Shade of Crimson	Pamela Thomas-Graham	Nikki Chase
Darkest Instinct	Robert W. Walker	Dr. Jessica Coran
Darkness Take My Hand	Dennis Lehane	Angela Gennaro
Dartmoor Burial	Audrey Peterson	Claire Camden
A Dash of Death	Claudia Bishop	Sarah "Quill" Quilliam
Date with a Dead Doctor	Toni Brill	Midge Cohen
Date with a Plummeting Publisher	Toni Brill	Midge Cohen
Date with the Perfect Dead Man	Annie Griffin	Hannah Malloy, Kiki Goldstein
Dating Can Be Deadly	Victoria Pade	Jimi Plain
Days of Crime and Roses	Kate Morgan	Dewey James
Dead Ahead	Ruby Horansky	Nikki Trakos
Dead Ahead	Bridget McKenna	Caley Burke
Dead Air	Rochelle Majer Krich	Jessica Drake
Dead and Blonde	Jean Marcy	Meg Darcy
Dead and Buried	Melissa Cleary	Jackie Walsh
Dead and Buried	Jean Hager	Tess Darcy
Dead and Doggone	Susan Conant	Holly Winter
Dead As Dead Can Be	Ann Crowleigh	Clare & Mirinda Cliveley
Dead Beat	Val McDermid	Kate Brannigan
Dead Beat and Deadly	Margaret Chittenden	Charlie Plato

Title of Book	Author	Character
Deadly Bond	Christine Green	Kate Kinsella
A Deadly Bouquet (2002)	Janis Harrison	Bretta Solomon
Deadly Care	Leonard Goldberg	Dr. Joanna Blalock
Deadly Deception	Gilbert Morris	Danielle "Dani" Ross
Deadly Deceptions	Ruth Ruby Moen	Kathleen O'Shaughnessy
Deadly Decisions	Kathy Reichs	Dr. Temperance Brennan
The Deadly Dog-Bone	Georgette Livingston	Dr. Jennifer Gray
Deadly Echo (2002)	Christine Green	Kate Kinsella
Deadly Errand	Christine Green	Kate Kinsella
Deadly Gamble	Connie Shelton	Charlie Parker
Deadly Harvest	Leonard Goldberg	Dr. Joanna Blalock
Deadly Harvest	Ellen Rawlings	Rachel Crowne
Deadly Justice	William Bernhardt	Christina McCall
Deadly Legacy	Betty Rowlands	Melissa Craig
Deadly Medicine	Leonard Goldberg	Dr. Joanna Blalock
Deadly Nightshade	Mary Freeman	Rachel O'Connor
Deadly Partners	Christine Green	Kate Kinsella
Deadly Partnership a.k.a. *A Bonny Case of Murder*	C. F. Roe	Dr. Jean Montrose
A Deadly Pâté	Ruthe Furie	Fran Tremaine Kirk
A Deadly Practice	Leonard Goldberg	Dr. Joanna Blalock
Deadly Practice	Christine Green	Kate Kinsella
Deadly Reunion	Jackie Manthorne	Harriet Hubbley
Deadly Rx	Renee B. Horowitz	Ruthie Kantor Morris
Deadly Safari	Karin McQuillan	Jazz Jasper
Deadly Sanctuary	Sylvia Nobel	Kendall O'Dell
A Deadly Shaker Spring	Deborah Woodworth	Sister Rose Callahan
Deadroll	Greg Moody	Cheryl Crane
Dear Irene	Jan Burke	Irene Kelly
Death and Faxes	Leslie O'Kane	Molly Masters
Death and Restoration	Iain Pears	Flavia di Stefano
Death and the Delinquent	B. J. Oliphant	Shirley McClintock
Death and the Oxford Box	Veronica Stallwood	Kate Ivory
Death at Bishop's Keep	Robin Paige	Kathryn "Kate" Ardleigh
Death at Buckingham Palace	C. C. Benison	Jane Bee, Queen Elizabeth II
Death at Daisy's Folly	Robin Paige	Kathryn "Kate" Ardleigh
Death at Dartmoor (2002)	Robin Paige	Kathryn "Kate" Ardleigh
Death at Dearley Manor	Betty Rowlands	Sukey Reynolds
Death at Devil's Bridge	Robin Paige	Kathryn "Kate" Ardleigh
Death at Face Value	Joyce Christmas	Elizabeth Anne "Betty" Trenka
Death at Gallows Green	Robin Paige	Kathryn "Kate" Ardleigh
Death at Glamis Castle (2003)	Robin Paige	Kathryn "Kate" Ardleigh
Death at High Tide	Beth Sherman	Anne Hardaway
Death at Lavender Bay	Lauren Wright Douglas	Allison O'Neil
Death at Montpelier a.k.a. *Murder, She Meowed*	Rita Mae Brown	Mary "Harry" Haristeen & Mrs. Murphy
Death at Rottingdean	Robin Paige	Kathryn "Kate" Ardleigh
Death at Sandringham House	C. C. Benison	Jane Bee, Queen Elizabeth II
Death at the Spring Plant Sale (2003)	Ann Ripley	Louise Eldridge
Death at the Wheel	Kate Flora	Thea Kozak
Death at Wentwater Court	Carola Dunn	Daisy Dalrymple
Death at Whitechapel	Robin Paige	Kathryn "Kate" Ardleigh
Death at Windsor Castle	C. C. Benison	Jane Bee, Queen Elizabeth II
Death Brims Over	Barbara Jaye Wilson	Brenda Midnight

Title of Book	Author	Character
Death by Chocolate (2003)	G. A. McKevett	Savannah Reid
Death by Dressage	Carolyn Banks	Robin Vaughan
Death by Election	Patricia Hall	Laura Ackroyd
Death by Fire a.k.a.	C. F. Roe	Dr. Jean Montrose
A Fiery Hint of Murder		
Death by Rhubarb	Lou Jane Temple	Heaven Lee
Death by the Riverside	J. M. Redmann	Michelle "Micky" Knight
Death Comes As Epiphany	Sharan Newman	Catherine Le Vendeur
Death Comes for the Critic	Noreen Wald	Jake O'Hara
Death Crosses the Border	Janice Steinberg	Margo Simon
Death Dines Out	Claudia Bishop	Sarah "Quill" Quilliam
Death Down Home	Eve K. Sandstrom	Nicky Titus
Death du Jour	Kathy Reichs	Dr. Temperance Brennan
Death Echo	Kerry Tucker	Libby Kincaid
Death Flips Its Lid	Barbara Jaye Wilson	Brenda Midnight
Death Hits the Fan	Jaqueline Girdner	Kate Jasper
Death in a City of Mystics	Janice Steinberg	Margo Simon
Death in a Cold Hard Light	Francine Mathews	Merry Folger
Death in a Funhouse Mirror	Kate Flora	Thea Kozak
Death in a Hot Flash	Jane Isenberg	Bel Barrett
Death in a Mood Indigo	Francine Mathews	Merry Folger
Death in Bloodhound Red	Virginia Lanier	Jo Beth Sidden
Death in Dark Waters (2002)	Patricia Hall	Laura Ackroyd
Death in Fingal's Cave a.k.a.	Jeanne M. Dams	Dorothy Martin
Holy Terror in the Hebrides		
Death in Good Company	Gretchen Sprague	Martha Patterson
Death in Lacquer Red	Jeanne M. Dams	Hilda Johansson
Death in Lovers' Lane	Carolyn Hart	Henrietta O'Dwyer Collins
Death in Paradise	Carolyn Hart	Henrietta O'Dwyer Collins
Death in Rough Water	Francine Mathews	Merry Folger
Death in Still Waters	Barbara Lee	Eve Elliott
Death in Store	Jennifer Rowe	Verity "Birdie" Birdwood
Death in the Country	Christine Green	Francesca "Fran" Wilson
Death in the Family a.k.a.	C. F. Roe	Dr. Jean Montrose
A Relative Cause of Murder		
Death in the Off-Season	Francine Mathews	Merry Folger
Death Is Semisweet (2002)	Lou Jane Temple	Heaven Lee
Death Is Sweet	Susan B. Kelly	Alison Hope
Death Is the Issue	Janet Harward	Josephine Blake
Death Mate	Paul Patti	Gabrielle "Gabe" Amato
Death Never Takes a Holiday	Noreen Wald	Jake O'Hara
Death of a Damn Yankee	Toni L. P. Kelner	Laura Fleming
Death of a D.J.	Jane Rubino	Cat Austen
Death of a Dream Maker	Gallagher Gray	Lil Hubbert
Death of a Dustbunny	Christine T. Jorgensen	Stella the Stargazer a.k.a. Jane Smith
Death of a Garden Pest	Ann Ripley	Louise Eldridge
Death of a Healing Woman	Allana Martin	Texana Jones
The Death of a Much-Travelled Woman	Barbara Wilson	Cassandra Reilly
Death of a Myth Maker	Allana Martin	Texana Jones
Death of a Postmodernist	Janice Steinberg	Margo Simon
Death of a PTA Goddess (2002)	Leslie O'Kane	Molly Masters
Death of a Russian Priest	Stuart Kaminsky	Elena Timafeyeva
Death of a Saint Maker	Allana Martin	Texana Jones
Death of a Stranger (2002)	Anne Perry	Hester Latterly (Monk)

Title of Book	Author	Character
Death of a Sunday Writer	Eric Wright	Lucy Trimble (Brenner)
Death of a Winter Shaker	Deborah Woodworth	Sister Rose Callahan
A Death of Distinction	Marjorie Eccles	Abigail Moon
Death of the Last Villista	Allana Martin	Texana Jones
Death of the Office Witch	Marlys Millhiser	Charlie Greene
Death of the River Master (2003)	Allana Martin	Texana Jones
Death on a Silver Platter	Ellen Hart	Sophie Greenway
Death on the Cliff Walk	Mary Kruger	Brooke Cassidy (Devlin)
Death on the Diagonal	Carolyn Banks	Robin Vaughan
Death on the Drunkard's Path	Jean Hager	Tess Darcy
Death on the River Walk	Carolyn Hart	Henrietta O'Dwyer Collins
Death on the Rocks	Eric Wright	Lucy Trimble (Brenner)
Death Pays the Rose Rent	Valerie S. Malmont	Tori Miracle
Death Qualified	Kate Wilhelm	Barbara Holloway
Death Row (2003)	William Bernhardt	Christina McCall
Death Served Up Cold	B. J. Oliphant	Shirley McClintock
Death Takes a Hand a.k.a. *Take-Out Double*	Susan Moody	Cassandra "Cassie" Swann
Death Takes Passage	Sue Henry	Jessie Arnold
Death Too Soon	Audrey Peterson	Claire Camden
Death Train to Boston	Dianne Day	Caroline "Fremont" Jones
Death Trance	R. D. Zimmerman	Maddy Phillips
Death Trap (2003)	Sue Henry	Jessie Arnold
Death Walker	Aimee and David Thurlo	Ella Clah
The Death We Share	Sharon Gwyn Short	Patricia Delaney
Death Wears a Crown	Quinn Fawcett	Victoire Vernet
Death With Honors	Ron Nessen, Johanna Neuman	Jane Day
Death with Reservations	Kate Kingsbury	Cecily Sinclair
Death, Bones, and Stately Homes (2003)	Valerie S. Malmont	Tori Miracle
Death, Guns, and Sticky Buns	Valerie S. Malmont	Tori Miracle
Death, Lies, and Apple Pies	Valerie S. Malmont	Tori Miracle
Death, Snow, and Mistletoe	Valerie S. Malmont	Tori Miracle
Death's a Beach	Beth Sherman	Anne Hardaway
Death's a Beach	Winona Sullivan	Sr. Cecille Buddenbrooks
Death's Autograph	Marianne Macdonald	Dido Hoare
Death's Domain	Alex Matthews	Cassidy McCabe
Deathday Party	Paula Carter	Jane Ferguson, Hillary Scarborough
Death-Fires Dance	Janice Steinberg	Margo Simon
Deaths of Jocasta	J. M. Redmann	Michelle "Micky" Knight
The Debt Collector	Lynn S. Hightower	Sonora Blair
Deck the Halls	Carol Higgins Clark, Mary Higgins Clark	Regan Reilly
Deck the Halls with Murder	Valerie Wolzien	Josie Pigeon
Decked	Carol Higgins Clark	Regan Reilly
Declared Dead (2002)	Suzanne Proulx	Victoria Lucci
Deep Freeze a.k.a. *Deep Waters* (2003)	Patricia Hall	Laura Ackroyd
Deep South	Nevada Barr	Anna Pigeon
Deep Valley Malice	Kirk Mitchell	Dee Laguerre
Deep Water	Sally Gunning	Connie Bartholomew
Deep Waters a.k.a. *Deep Freeze* (2003)	Patricia Hall	Laura Ackroyd
Defend and Betray	Anne Perry	Hester Latterly (Monk)
Defense for the Devil	Kate Wilhelm	Barbara Holloway

Title of Book	Author	Character
Do Or Die	Grace F. Edwards	Mali Anderson
Do You Want to Know a Secret?	Mary Jane Clark	Eliza Blake
The Dobie Paradox	Desmond Cory	Dr. Kate Coyle
Doc in the Box	Elaine Viets	Francesca Vierling
Dog Collar Crime	Melissa Cleary	Jackie Walsh
Dog Eat Dog	Laurien Berenson	Melanie Travis
The Dog Named Elvis Caper	Georgette Livingston	Dr. Jennifer Gray
The Dog Who Bit a Policeman	Stuart Kaminsky	Elena Timafeyeva
The Dog Who Knew Too Much	Carol Lea Benjamin	Rachel Kaminsky Alexander
The Dogfather (2003)	Susan Conant	Holly Winter
Dogtown	Mercedes Lambert	Whitney Logan
The Dollmaker's Daughters	Abigail Padgett	Barbara "Bo" Bradley
Done Wrong	Eleanor Taylor Bland	Marti MacAlister
Don't Blame the Snake	Tony Fennelly	Margo Fortier
Don't Cry for Me, Hot Pastrami	Sharon Kahn	Ruby Rothman
Don't Drink the Water	Susan Rogers Cooper	E. J. Pugh
Don't Forget to Die	Margaret Chittenden	Charlie Plato
Don't Mess with Mrs. In-Between	Liz Evans	Grace Smith
Don't Turn Your Back on the Ocean	Janet Dawson	Jeri Howard
Doomsday Flight	Ed Stewart	Beth Seibelli
Double Act	Eileen Dewhurst	Phyllida Moon
Double Cross	Barbara Taylor McCafferty, Beverly Taylor Herald	Bert & Nan Tatum
Double Date	Barbara Taylor McCafferty, Beverly Taylor Herald	Bert & Nan Tatum
Double Dealer	Barbara Taylor McCafferty, Beverly Taylor Herald	Bert & Nan Tatum
Double Edge	Robert W. Walker	Meredyth "Mere" Sanger
Double Espresso	Anthony Bruno	Loretta Kovacs
Double Exposure	Barbara Taylor McCafferty, Beverly Taylor Herald	Bert & Nan Tatum
Double Murder	Barbara Taylor McCafferty, Beverly Taylor Herald	Bert & Nan Tatum
Double Negative	Leona Gom	Vicky Bauer
Double Take	Judy Mercer	Ariel Gold
Double Take Out	Tracey Richardson	Stevie Houston
Double Vision	Annie Ross	Bel Carson
Double Wedding Ring	Lizbie Brown	Elizabeth Blair
Doubled in Spades	Susan Moody	Cassandra "Cassie" Swann
The Doublet Affair	Fiona Buckley	Ursula Blanchard
The Down Home Heifer Heist	Eve K. Sandstrom	Nicky Titus
Down Home Murder	Toni L. P. Kelner	Laura Fleming
Downsized to Death	Joyce Christmas	Elizabeth Anne "Betty" Trenka
Dr. Nightingale Chases Three Pigs	Lydia Adamson	Dr. Deirdre "Didi" Nightingale
Dr. Nightingale Comes Home	Lydia Adamson	Dr. Deirdre "Didi" Nightingale
Dr. Nightingale Enters the Bear Cave	Lydia Adamson	Dr. Deirdre "Didi" Nightingale
Dr. Nightingale Follows a Canine Clue	Lydia Adamson	Dr. Deirdre "Didi" Nightingale
Dr. Nightingale Goes the Distance	Lydia Adamson	Dr. Deirdre "Didi" Nightingale
Dr. Nightingale Goes to the Dogs	Lydia Adamson	Dr. Deirdre "Didi" Nightingale
Dr. Nightingale Meets Puss in Boots	Lydia Adamson	Dr. Deirdre "Didi" Nightingale
Dr. Nightingale Races the Outlaw Colt	Lydia Adamson	Dr. Deirdre "Didi" Nightingale
Dr. Nightingale Rides the Elephant	Lydia Adamson	Dr. Deirdre "Didi" Nightingale

Title of Book	Author	Character
Dr. Nightingale Rides to the Hounds	Lydia Adamson	Dr. Deirdre "Didi" Nightingale
Dr. Nightingale Seeks Greener Pastures	Lydia Adamson	Dr. Deirdre "Didi" Nightingale
Dr. Nightingale Traps the Missing Lynx	Lydia Adamson	Dr. Deirdre "Didi" Nightingale
Drag Strip	Nancy Bartholomew	Sierra Lavotini
Dragon Bones (2003)	Lisa See	Liu Hulan
Dreadful Lies	Michele Bailey	Matilda Haycastle
Dream Boat (2002)	Marilyn Todd	Claudia Seferius
The Dream Stalker	Margaret Coel	Vicky Holden
Dreaming of the Bones	Deborah Crombie	Gemma James
A Dress to Die For	Dolores Johnson	Mandy Dyer
Dressed to Die	Beverly Connor	Lindsay Chamberlain
Dressed to Kill	Margaret Duffy	Joanna Mackenzie
Drift Away	Kerry Tucker	Libby Kincaid
A Drink Before the War	Dennis Lehane	Angela Gennaro
A Drink of Deadly Wine	Kate Charles	Lucy Kingsley
The Drowning Pool a.k.a. *Fruiting Bodies*	Natasha Cooper	Willow King
Drumsticks	Charlotte Carter	Nanette Hayes
Due Process	Catherine Arnold	Karen Perry-Mondori
Dummy Hand	Susan Moody	Cassandra "Cassie" Swann
Dune to Death	Mary Daheim	Judith McMonigle (Flynn)
Duped by Derivatives	Gail E. Farrelly	Lisa King
Dust Devils of the Purple Sage	Barbara Burnett Smith	Jolie Wyatt
Dying Breath	Sarah J. Mason	Sergeant Stone
Dying By Degrees	Judith Cutler	Sophie Rivers
Dying By The Book	Judith Cutler	Sophie Rivers
Dying Cheek to Cheek	Diane K. Shah	Paris Chandler
Dying Fall	Judith Cutler	Sophie Rivers
Dying Fall	Patricia Hall	Laura Ackroyd
Dying for a Clue	Judy Fitzwater	Jennifer Marsh
Dying for Chocolate	Diane Mott Davidson	Goldy Bear (Schulz)
Dying For Millions	Judith Cutler	Sophie Rivers
Dying For Power	Judith Cutler	Sophie Rivers
Dying in Discord (2002)	Judith Cutler	Sophie Rivers
The Dying Light	Alison Joseph	Sister Agnes Bourdillon
Dying On Principle	Judith Cutler	Sophie Rivers
Dying Room Only	Kate Kingsbury	Cecily Sinclair
Dying to Be Murdered	Judy Fitzwater	Jennifer Marsh
Dying to Deceive (2003)	Judith Cutler	Sophie Rivers
Dying to Get Even	Judy Fitzwater	Jennifer Marsh
Dying to Get Her Man (2002)	Judy Fitzwater	Jennifer Marsh
Dying to Get Published	Judy Fitzwater	Jennifer Marsh
Dying to Help	Penny Kline	Dr. Anna McColl
Dying to Remember	Judy Fitzwater	Jennifer Marsh
Dying To Score	Judith Cutler	Sophie Rivers
Dying to See You	Margaret Chittenden	Charlie Plato
Dying to Sing	Margaret Chittenden	Charlie Plato
Dying To Write	Judith Cutler	Sophie Rivers
Dynamite Pass	J. F. Trainor	Angela "Angie" Biwaban

E

The Eagle Catcher	Margaret Coel	Vicky Holden
Eagles Die Too	Meg O'Brien	Jessica "Jesse" James
Earth Has No Sorrow	Michelle Blake	Rev. Lily Connor

Title of Book	Author	Character
Earthwork	Carol Dawber	Liz Gresham
Easeful Death (2002)	Eileen Dewhurst	Phyllida Moon
Easier to Kill	Valerie Wilson Wesley	Tamara Hayle
East of Niece	Randye Lordon	Sydney Sloane
An Easy Day for a Lady a.k.a. *Widow's Peak*	Gillian Linscott	Nell Bray
Eat, Drink, and Be Buried	Kate Kingsbury	Cecily Sinclair
Eat, Drink, and Be Wary	Tamar Myers	Magdalena Yoder
Echoes of Death	Janet Harward	Josephine Blake
The Edge of Sleep	David Wiltse	Karen Crist (Becker)
Edited Out	Lisa Haddock	Carmen Ramirez
An Educated Death	Kate Flora	Thea Kozak
Eight Dogs Flying	Karen Ann Wilson	Samantha Holt
Elective Murder	Janet McGiffin	Dr. Maxene St. Clair
Electric City	K. K. Beck	Jane da Silva
Elementary, Mrs. Hudson	Sydney Hosier	Emma Hudson
Elephants' Graveyard	Karin McQuillan	Jazz Jasper
Eleven Days	Donald Harstad	Hester Gorse
Embroidering Shrouds	Priscilla Masters	Joanna Piercy
Emergency Murder	Janet McGiffin	Dr. Maxene St. Clair
Emperor Norton's Ghost	Dianne Day	Caroline "Fremont" Jones
The Empty Chair	Jeffrey Wilds Deaver	Amelia Sachs
The End of an Altruist	Margaret Logan	Olivia Chapman
The End of April	Penny Sumner	Victoria Cross
The End of Emerald Woods	David J. Walker	Kirsten
Endangered Species	Nevada Barr	Anna Pigeon
Endangered Species	Barbara Block	Robin Light
Endangering Innocents (2003)	Priscilla Masters	Joanna Piercy
Ending in Tears	Penny Kline	Dr. Anna McColl
Enemy Way	Aimee and David Thurlo	Ella Clah
Engineered for Murder	Aileen Schumacher	Tory Travers
Enter Dying (2002)	Noreen Wald	Jake O'Hara
Erased	Jo Bailey	Jan Gallagher
Escapade	Walter Satterthwait	Jane Turner
Estate of Mind	Tamar Myers	Abigail "Abby" Timberlake
The Etruscan Chimera (2002)	Lyn Hamilton	Lara McClintock
Every Breath You Take	Michelle Spring	Laura Principal
Every Crooked Nanny	Kathy Hogan Trocheck	Julia "Callahan" Garrity
Every Deadly Sin	D. M. Greenwood	Rev. Theodora Braithwaite
Everything You Have Is Mine	Sandra Scoppetone	Lauren Laurano
Everywhere That Mary Went	Lisa Scottoline	Mary DiNunzio
Eviction by Death	Dorian Yeager	Victoria "Vic" Bowering
Evidence of Guilt	Jonnie Jacobs	Kali O'Brien
Evil Angels Among Them	Kate Charles	Lucy Kingsley
Evil Breeding	Susan Conant	Holly Winter
Evil Dead Center	Carole LaFavor	Renee LaRoche
Evil Harmony	Kathryn Buckstaff	Emily Stone
Exhaustive Enquiries	Betty Rowlands	Melissa Craig
Exile	Denise Mina	Maureen O'Donnell
The Exile Way	Ann Woodward	Lady Aoi
Existing Solutions	Jennifer L. Jordan	Kristin Ashe
Exit Wounds (2003)	J. A. Jance	Joanna Brady
Exposé	Laura Van Wormer	Sally Harrington
Extreme Instinct	Robert W. Walker	Dr. Jessica Coran
Extreme Justice	William Bernhardt	Christina McCall

Title of Book	Author	Character
Father Forgive Me	Randye Lordon	Sydney Sloane
The Father's Day Murder	Lee Harris	Christine Bennett
Father's Day Murder (2003)	Leslie Meier	Lucy Stone
Fatlands	Sarah Dunant	Hannah Wolfe
Fault Line	Natasha Cooper	Trish Maguire
Fault Line (2002)	Sarah Andrews	Emily "Em" Hansen
Fault Lines	Anna Salter	Dr. Michael Stone
Fax Me a Bagel	Sharon Kahn	Ruby Rothman
The Fax of Life	Leslie O'Kane	Molly Masters
Fear in Fenway	Crabbe Evers	Petronella "Petey" Biggers
Feeling Bad	Penny Kline	Dr. Anna McColl
Femme Fatale (2003)	Carole Nelson Douglas	Irene Adler
A Fiery Hint of Murder a.k.a. *Death by Fire*	C. F. Roe	Dr. Jean Montrose
File Under: Arson	Sarah Lacey	Leah Hunter
File Under: Deceased	Sarah Lacey	Leah Hunter
File Under: Jeopardy	Sarah Lacey	Leah Hunter
File Under: Missing	Sarah Lacey	Leah Hunter
Film Strip	Nancy Bartholomew	Sierra Lavotini
Final Arrangements	Donna Huston Murray	Ginger Barnes
Final Closing	Barbara Lee	Eve Elliott
The Final Curtain	Gilbert Morris	Danielle "Dani" Ross
Final Cut	Lisa Haddock	Carmen Ramirez
Final Design	Noreen Gilpatrick	Kate MacLean
Final Jeopardy	Linda Fairstein	Alexandra Cooper
The Final Judgment	Richard North Patterson	Caroline Masters
Final Notice	Jo Dereske	Wilhelmena "Helma" Zukas
Final Option	Gini Hartzmark	Kate Millholland
Final Rest	Mary Morell	Lucia Ramos
Final Session	Mary Morell	Lucia Ramos
Final Take	Jackie Manthorne	Harriet Hubbley
Finales and Overtures	Jeanne McCafferty	Dr. Mackenzie Griffin
A Fine and Bitter Snow (2002)	Dana Stabenow	Kate Shugak
A Fine Place for Death	Ann Granger	Merry Mitchell
A Fine Target	Margaret Duffy	Joanna Mackenzie
A Finer End	Deborah Crombie	Gemma James
Finishing Touch	Betty Rowlands	Melissa Craig
Fire and Fog	Dianne Day	Caroline "Fremont" Jones
Fire and Ice	Dana Stabenow	Wyanet "Wy" Chouinard
Fire Cracker	Shirley Kennett	P. J. Gray
Fire Water	Sally Gunning	Connie Bartholomew
Firestorm	Nevada Barr	Anna Pigeon
First Cut	Leah Ruth Robinson	Dr. Evelyn Sutcliffe
First Impression	Margot Dalton	Jackie Kaminsky
First Pedigree Murder	Melissa Cleary	Jackie Walsh
A Fit of Tempera	Mary Daheim	Judith McMonigle (Flynn)
Five Alarm Fire	D. B. Borton	Catherine "Cat" Caliban
Five Dead Men	Emer Gillespie	Karen McDade
Flashback (2003)	Nevada Barr	Anna Pigeon
Flashpoint	Lynn S. Hightower	Sonora Blair
Fleeced	Carol Higgins Clark	Regan Reilly
Flight	Jan Burke	Irene Kelly
Flight of the Serpent	Val Davis	Nicolette "Nick" Scott
Flight of the Stone Angel a.k.a. *Stone Angel*	Carol O'Connell	Sgt. Kathleen Mallory

G

Title of Book	Author	Character
Garden of Evil	Edna Buchanan	Britt Montero
The Garden Tour Affair	Ann Ripley	Louise Eldridge
Garden View (2002)	Mary Freeman	Rachel O'Connor
Garnethill	Denise Mina	Maureen O'Donnell
Gator Aide	Jessica Speart	Rachel Porter
Gaudi Afternoon	Barbara Wilson	Cassandra Reilly
Gemini Doublecross	Linda Mather	Jo Hughes
Gene Play	Natalie Buske Thomas	Serena Wilcox
Getting Away with Murder	Pele Plante	Cynthia Cheney "C. C." Scott
The Ghost and Mrs. Jeffries	Emily Brightwell	Hepzibah Jeffries
A Ghost in the Closet	Mabel Maney	Cherry Aimless, Nancy Clue
Ghost Motel	Jackie Manthorne	Harriet Hubbley
Ghost of a Chance	Helen Chappell	Hollis Ball
Ghost Walk	Marianne Macdonald	Dido Hoare
The Ghost Walker	Margaret Coel	Vicky Holden
Ghostwriter	Noreen Wald	Jake O'Hara
A Gift of Sanctuary	Candace M. Robb	Lucie D'Arby Wilton
Gilt By Association	Tamar Myers	Abigail "Abby" Timberlake
Gin Lane	James Brady	Lady Alix Dunraven
Giotto's Hand	Iain Pears	Flavia di Stefano
Give My Secrets Back	Kate Allen	Alison Kaine
Give the Dog a Bone (2002)	Leslie O'Kane	Allie Babcock
Given the Crime	Margaret Barrett, Charles Dennis	Susan Given
Given the Evidence	Margaret Barrett, Charles Dennis	Susan Given
Giving Up the Ghost	Helen Chappell	Hollis Ball
Glare Ice	Mary Logue	Claire Watkins
The Glass Ceiling	Anabel Donald	Alex Tanner
The Glass Coffin (2002)	Gail Bowen	Joanne "Jo" Kilbourn
The Glass Factory	k.j.a. Wishnia	Filomena "Fil" Buscarsela
Glory in Death	J. D. Robb	Lt. Eve Dallas
Go Close Against the Enemy	Tavis and Judy Iakovou	Julia Lambros
Go Not Gently	Cath Staincliffe	Sal Kilkenny
The Goddess Affair	Lillian O'Donnell	Gwen Ramadge
Going Nowhere Fast	Gar Anthony Haywood	Dottie Loudermilk
Golden Eggs and Other Deadly Things	Nancy Tesler	Carrie Carlin
Gone Quiet	Eleanor Taylor Bland	Marti MacAlister
Gone to the Dogs	Susan Conant	Holly Winter
Gone, Baby, Gone	Dennis Lehane	Angela Gennaro
Good Cop, Bad Cop	Barbara D'Amato	Suze Figueroa
The Good Daughter	Wendi Lee	Angela Matelli
The Good Friday Murder	Lee Harris	Christine Bennett
Good Morning, Irene	Carole Nelson Douglas	Irene Adler
Good Night, Mr. Holmes	Carole Nelson Douglas	Irene Adler
Goodbye, Charli	Diane Petit	Kathryn Bogert
Goodbye, Charli-Fourth Edition	Diane Petit	Kathryn Bogert
Goodbye, Charli-Take Two	Diane Petit	Kathryn Bogert
Goodbye, Charli-Third Time Lucky	Diane Petit	Kathryn Bogert
Goodnight, Irene	Jan Burke	Irene Kelly
Goose in the Pond	Earlene Fowler	Albenia "Benni" Harper
Governing Bodies	Anne Wilson	Sara Kingsley
The Governor	Lynda La Plante	Helen Hewitt
Governor II	Lynda La Plante	Helen Hewitt

Title of Book	Author	Character
Hard Luck	Barbara D'Amato	Cat Marsala
Hard Road	Barbara D'Amato	Cat Marsala
Hard Tack	Barbara D'Amato	Cat Marsala
Hard Women	Barbara D'Amato	Cat Marsala
Hardball	Barbara D'Amato	Cat Marsala
Hardwired	Sally Chapman	Julie Blake
Hare Today, Gone Tomorrow	Meg O'Brien	Jessica "Jesse" James
Harm's Way	Stephen White	Lauren Crowder
Harvest of Bones	Nancy Means Wright	Ruth Willmarth
Harvest of Murder	Ann Ripley	Louise Eldridge
Hasty Retreat	Kate Gallison	Mother Lavinia Grey
A Hatful of Homicide	Barbara Jaye Wilson	Brenda Midnight
The Haunted Abbot (2002)	Peter Tremayne	Sister Fidelma
A Haunting Refrain	Patricia H. Rushford	Helen Bradley
Havana Heat	Carolina Garcia-Aguilera	Guadalupe "Lupe" Solano
Hayburner (2003)	Laura Crum	Dr. Gail McCarthy
Haycastle's Cricket	Michele Bailey	Matilda Haycastle
He Who Dies	Wendi Lee	Angela Matelli
Headhunt	Carol Brennan	Liz Wareham
The Healing of Holly-Jean	Irene Lin-Chandler	Holly-Jean Ho
Healthy, Wealthy, and Dead	Suzanne North	Phoebe Fairfax
Heart and Bones	Margaret Lawrence	Hannah Trevor
The Heart Shaped Box	April Henry	Claire Montrose
Heart Trouble	Kathy Hogan Trocheck	Julia "Callahan" Garrity
The Heartland Experiment (2003)	Donald Harstad	Hester Gorse
Heavenly Vices	D. M. Greenwood	Rev. Theodora Braithwaite
Heir Condition	Tierney McClellan	Schuyler Ridgway
Held Accountable	Karen Hanson Stuyck	Liz James
The Helium Murder	Camille Minichino	Gloria Lamerino
A Hell of a Dog	Carol Lea Benjamin	Rachel Kaminsky Alexander
Help Line	Faye Sultan, Teresa Kennedy	Portia McTeague
Hemlock at Vespers (ss)	Peter Tremayne	Sister Fidelma
Hen's Teeth	Manda Scott	Dr. Kellen Stewart
Here Lies a Hidden Scorpion	Tavis and Judy Iakovou	Julia Lambros
Here's to the Newly Dead	B. J. Oliphant	Shirley McClintock
Heresy (2002)	Sharan Newman	Catherine Le Vendeur
Hickory, Dickory, Stalk	Susan Rogers Cooper	E. J. Pugh
A Hidden Cause of Murder	C. F. Roe	Dr. Jean Montrose
Hidden Power (2002)	Judith Cutler	Kate Power
High Country Murder	J. F. Trainor	Angela "Angie" Biwaban
High Desert Malice	Kirk Mitchell	Dee Laguerre
High Five	Janet Evanovich	Stephanie Plum
Higher Authority	Stephen White	Lauren Crowder
The Hippie in the Wall	Tony Fennelly	Margo Fortier
The Hireling's Tale	Jo Bannister	Liz Graham
The Historical Society Murder Mystery	Graham Landrum	Harriet Bushrow, Helen Delaporte
Hoakus Crocus (2003)	Mary Daheim	Judith McMonigle (Flynn)
Hocus	Jan Burke	Irene Kelly
Hold the Cream Cheese, Kill the Lox (2002)	Sharon Kahn	Ruby Rothman
Holiday in Death	J. D. Robb	Lt. Eve Dallas
The Holiday Murders	Marsha Landreth	Dr. Samantha Turner
Holy Terror in the Hebrides a.k.a. *Death in Fingal's Cave*	Jeanne M. Dams	Dorothy Martin

Title of Book	Author	Character
Holy Terrors	Mary Daheim	Judith McMonigle (Flynn)
Holy Terrors	D. M. Greenwood	Rev. Theodora Braithwaite
Home Again, Home Again	Susan Rogers Cooper	E. J. Pugh
Home Sweet Homicide	Kate Morgan	Dewey James
Homemade Sin	Kathy Hogan Trocheck	Julia "Callahan" Garrity
Hometown Heroes	Susanna Hofmann McShea	Mildred Bennett, Irene Purdy
Homicide and Old Lace	Dolores Johnson	Mandy Dyer
The Homicide Report	Eve K. Sandstrom	Nell Matthews
Honeymoons Can Be Murder	Connie Shelton	Charlie Parker
The Hoodoo Man	Judith Smith-Levin	Starletta Duvall
Hoofprints	Laura Crum	Dr. Gail McCarthy
Hook	C. J. Songer	"Meg" Gillis
Hoot to Kill	Karen Dudley	Robyn Devara
Hope Against Hope	Susan B. Kelly	Alison Hope
Hope Will Answer	Susan B. Kelly	Alison Hope
A Hopeless Case	K. K. Beck	Jane da Silva
Hornet's Nest	Patricia D. Cornwell	Judy Hammer
Horse of a Different Killer	Jody Jaffe	Natalie Gold
A Horse to Die For	Carolyn Banks	Robin Vaughan
Hot and Bothered (2003)	Jane Isenberg	Bel Bickoff Barrett
Hot Dog (2002)	Laurien Berenson	Melanie Travis
Hot Fudge	Anthony Bruno	Loretta Kovacs
Hot Money	Sherryl Woods	Molly De Witt
Hot Potato (2003)	Joyce Holms	Fizz Fitzgerald
Hot Property	Sherryl Woods	Molly De Witt
Hot Schemes	Sherryl Woods	Molly De Witt
Hot Secrets	Sherryl Woods	Molly De Witt
Hot Six	Janet Evanovich	Stephanie Plum
Hot Ticket	Janice Weber	Leslie Frost
Hot Water	Sally Gunning	Connie Bartholomew
The Hotel South Dakota	Kathleen Taylor	Tory Bauer
Hounded to Death	Melissa Cleary	Jackie Walsh
The Hour of Our Death	Alison Joseph	Sister Agnes Bourdillon
The Hour of the Knife	Sharon Zukowski	Blaine Stewart
Hour of the Tigress	Irene Lin-Chandler	Holly-Jean Ho
House of Blues	Julie Smith	Skip Langdon
House of Cards	Kay Hooper	Lane Montana
The House on Bloodhound Lane	Virginia Lanier	Jo Beth Sidden
The House That Ate the Hamptons	James Brady	Lady Alix Dunraven
Houston Town	Deborah Powell	Hollis Carpenter
Hung in the Balance	Roger Ormerod	Phillipa Lowe
Hung Up to Die	Dolores Johnson	Mandy Dyer
Hunter's Moon	Dana Stabenow	Kate Shugak
Hunting Game	Nancy Herndon	Elena Jarvis
Hunting Season (2002)	Nevada Barr	Anna Pigeon
Hush Puppy	Laurien Berenson	Melanie Travis
The Hydrogen Murder	Camille Minichino	Gloria Lamerino

I

I Left My Heart	Jaye Maiman	Robin Miller
I Will Survive	Miriam Ann Moore	Marti Hirsch
I, Claudia	Marilyn Todd	Claudia Seferius
I'll Be Leaving You Always	Sandra Scoppetone	Lauren Laurano
The Ice	Louis Charbonneau	Kathy McNeely
The Ice Maiden (2002)	Edna Buchanan	Britt Montero

Title of Book	Author	Character
Ice Water	Sally Gunning	Connie Bartholomew
Iced	Carol Higgins Clark	Regan Reilly
Iced	Julie Robitaille	Kathleen "Kit" Powell
Icewater Mansions	Doug Allyn	Michelle "Mitch" Mitchell
Icing Ivy (2002)	Evan Marshall	Jane Stuart
The Icing on the Corpse	Mary Jane Maffini	Camilla McPhee
Identity Unknown	Frances Ferguson	Jane Perry
Idol Bones	D. M. Greenwood	Theodora Braithwaite
If Cooks Could Kill (2003)	Joanne Pence	Angelina "Angie" Amalfi
If I Should Die	Grace F. Edwards	Mali Anderson
If Looks Could Kill	Ruthe Furie	Fran Tremaine Kirk
If Two of Them Are Dead	Carol Cail	Maxey Burnell
Ill Wind	Nevada Barr	Anna Pigeon
Imitation in Death	J. D. Robb	Lt. Eve Dallas
The Immaculate Deception	Iain Pears	Flavia di Stefano
Immaculate Reception	Jerrilyn Farmer	Madelyn Bean
Immortal in Death	J. D. Robb	Lt. Eve Dallas
Imperfect Justice	Catherine Arnold	Karen Perry-Mondori
The Impertinent Miss Bancroft	Karla Hocker	Sophy Bancroft
Impolite Society	Cynthia Smith	Emma Rhodes
In a Strange City	Laura Lippman	Tess Monaghan
In at the Deep End	Anabel Donald	Alex Tanner
In Big Trouble	Laura Lippman	Tess Monaghan
In Colt Blood	Jody Jaffe	Natalie Gold
In Memory of Murder	Janet Harward	Josephine Blake
In Murder We Trust	Eleanor Hyde	Lydia Miller
In Plain Sight	Barbara Block	Robin Light
In Self Defense	Sarah Gregory	Sharon Hays
Intent to Harm (2003)	Jonnie Jacobs	Kali O'Brien
In the Dark	Carol Brennan	Emily Silver
In the Dog House	Melissa Cleary	Jackie Walsh
In the Game	Nikki Baker	Virginia Kelly
In the Midnight Hour	Michelle Spring	Laura Principal
In the Midnight Hour	Peg Tyre	Kate Murray
In the Still of the Night	Jill Churchill	Lily Brewster
In Your Face	Scarlett Thomas	Lily Pascale
An Inconsiderate Death	Betty Rowlands	Sukey Reynolds
The Incorrigible Sophia	Karla Hocker	Sophy Bancroft
Indigo Dying (2003)	Susan Wittig Albert	China Bayles
Inner City Blues	Paula L. Woods	Charlotte Justice
The Inspector and Mrs. Jeffries	Emily Brightwell	Hepzibah Jeffries
The Interior	Lisa See	Liu Hulan
The Intersection of Law and Desire	J. M. Redmann	Michelle "Micky" Knight
Interview with Mattie	Shelley Singer	Barrett Lake
Into the Fire	David Wiltse	Karen Crist (Becker)
Introducing Amanda Valentine	Rose Beecham	Amanda Valentine
Invasion of Privacy	Perri O'Shaughnessy	Nina Reilly
Irene at Large	Carole Nelson Douglas	Irene Adler
Irene's Last Waltz a.k.a. Another Scandal in Bohemia	Carole Nelson Douglas	Irene Adler
The Irish Cairn Murder (2002)	Dicey Deere	Torrey Tunet
Irish Chain	Earlene Fowler	Albenia "Benni" Harper
The Irish Cottage Murder	Dicey Deere	Torrey Tunet

Title of Book	Author	Character
Killer Instinct	Martina Navratilova, Liz Nickles	Jordan Myles
Killer Instinct	Robert W. Walker	Dr. Jessica Coran
Killer Market	Margaret Maron	Deborah Knott
Killer Pancake	Diane Mott Davidson	Goldy Bear (Schulz)
Killer Wedding	Jerrilyn Farmer	Madelyn Bean
Killer Whale	Elizabeth Quinn	Dr. Lauren Maxwell
Killer.app	Barbara D'Amato	Suze Figueroa
A Killing at the Track	Janet Dawson	Jeri Howard
Killing Cassidy	Jeanne M. Dams	Dorothy Martin
Killing Cousins (2002)	Rett MacPherson	"Torie" O'Shea
Killing Critics	Carol O'Connell	Sgt. Kathleen Mallory
A Killing Frost	Margaret Haffner	Catherine Edison
The Killing Game	Iris Johansen	Eve Duncan
A Killing Gift (2003)	Leslie Glass	April Woo
Killing Gifts	Deborah Woodworth	Sister Rose Callahan
Killing Grounds	Dana Stabenow	Kate Shugak
A Killing in Real Estate	Tierney McClellan	Schuyler Ridgway
Killing Me Softly	Marjorie Eccles	Abigail Moon
The Killing of Monday Brown	Sandra West Prowell	Phoebe Seigel
Killing Raven (2003)	Margaret Coel	Vicky Holden
A Killing Season (2002)	Jessica Speart	Rachel Porter
A Killing Spring	Gail Bowen	Joanne "Jo" Kilbourn
Killing Thyme	Peter Abresch	Dodee Swisher
The Kindness of Strangers	Julie Smith	Skip Langdon
Kindred Crimes	Janet Dawson	Jeri Howard
King of Hearts	Susan Moody	Cassandra "Cassie" Swann
The King's Bishop	Candace M. Robb	Lucie D'Arby Wilton
Kingfisher	Alex Keegan	Caz Flood
Kissed a Sad Goodbye	Deborah Crombie	Gemma James
Knight and Day	Ron Nessen, Johanna Neuman	Jane Day
The Knowledge of Water	Sarah Smith	Perdita Halley
Known Dead	Donald Harstad	Hester Gorse

L

Title of Book	Author	Character
The Labor Day Murder	Lee Harris	Christine Bennett
The Lady Chapel	Candace M. Robb	Lucie D'Arby Wilton
Lady Vanishes	Carol Lea Benjamin	Rachel Kaminsky Alexander
Ladybug, Ladybug	Susanna Hofmann McShea	Mildred Bennett, Irene Purdy
Lamb to the Slaughter	Elizabeth Quinn	Dr. Lauren Maxwell
Lamb to the Slaughter	Jennifer Rowe	Verity "Birdie" Birdwood
Lament for a Dead Cowboy	Catherine Dain	Freddie O'Neal
Larceny and Old Lace	Tamar Myers	Abigail "Abby" Timberlake
Large Target	Lynne Murray	Josephine Fuller
Larger Than Death	Lynne Murray	Josephine Fuller
Larkspur	Sheila Simonson	Lark Dailey (Dodge)
The Last Blue Plate Special	Abigail Padgett	Emily "Blue" McCarron
Last Dance	Miriam Ann Moore	Marti Hirsch
The Last Judgement	Iain Pears	Flavia di Stefano
The Last Lover	Laura Van Wormer	Sally Harrington
The Last Manly Man	Sparkle Hayter	Robin Hudson
The Last Noel	Jean Hager	Tess Darcy
The Last of Her Lies	Jean Taylor	Maggie Garrett
The Last Place (2002)	Laura Lippman	Tess Monaghan
The Last Precinct	Patricia D. Cornwell	Dr. Kay Scarpetta
Last Puzzle and Testament	Parnell Hall	Cora Felton & Sherry Carter

Title of Book	Author	Character
The Lumsden Baby a.k.a. *A Nasty Bit of Murder*	C. F. Roe	Dr. Jean Montrose
A Lying Silence	Laura Coburn	Kate Harrod

M

Title of Book	Author	Character
The "M" Word	Jane Isenberg	Bel Barrett
Macaws of Death	Karen Dudley	Robyn Devara
Mad as the Dickens	Toni L. P. Kelner	Laura Fleming
Mad Season	Nancy Means Wright	Ruth Willmarth
The Magician's Tale	David Hunt	Kay Farrow
Maid to Murder	Kate Kingsbury	Cecily Sinclair
The Maiden's Tale	Margaret Frazer	Sister Frevisse
Mail-Order Murder a.k.a. *Mistletoe Murder*	Leslie Meier	Lucy Stone
The Main Corpse	Diane Mott Davidson	Goldy Bear (Schulz)
The Main Line Is Murder	Donna Huston Murray	Ginger Barnes
Major Vices	Mary Daheim	Judith McMonigle (Flynn)
The Makeover Murders	Jennifer Rowe	Verity "Birdie" Birdwood
Malarkey	Sheila Simonson	Lark Dailey (Dodge)
The Malcontenta	Barry Maitland	Sgt. Kathy Kolla
Malice in Miniature	Jeanne M. Dams	Dorothy Martin
Malice Poetic	Betty Rowlands	Melissa Craig
Malice Prepense	Kate Wilhelm	Barbara Holloway
The Malignant Heart	Celestine Sibley	Kate Mulcay a.k.a. Katy Kincaid
Mallory's Oracle	Carol O'Connell	Sgt. Kathleen Mallory
The Maltese Goddess	Lyn Hamilton	Lara McClintoch
Maltese Manuscript (2003)	Joanne Dobson	Karen Pelletier
The Maltese Puppy	Melissa Cleary	Jackie Walsh
Mama Cracks a Mask of Innocence	Nora DeLoach	Candi & Simone Covington
Mama Pursues Murderous Shadows	Nora DeLoach	Candi & Simone Covington
Mama Saves a Victim	Nora DeLoach	Candi & Simone Covington
Mama Solves a Murder	Nora DeLoach	Candi & Simone Covington
Mama Stalks the Past	Nora DeLoach	Candi & Simone Covington
Mama Stands Accused	Nora DeLoach	Candi & Simone Covington
Mama Traps a Killer	Nora DeLoach	Candi & Simone Covington
Man Eater	Marilyn Todd	Claudia Seferius
The Man in the Window	Betty Rowlands	Melissa Craig
The Man Who Cast Two Shadows	Carol O'Connell	Sgt. Kathleen Mallory
Mandarin Plaid	S. J. Rozan	Lydia Chin
Manner of Death	Stephen White	Lauren Crowder
Maquette for Murder	Gretchen Sprague	Martha Patterson
Margin of Error	Edna Buchanan	Britt Montero
Marigolds for Mourning	Audrey Stallsmith	Regan Culver
Marinade for Murder	Claudia Bishop	Sarah "Quill" Quilliam
Mariner's Compass	Earlene Fowler	Albenia "Benni" Harper
The Marx Sisters	Barry Maitland	Sgt. Kathy Kolla
The Mask of Zeus	Desmond Cory	Dr. Kate Coyle
Masquerade	Walter Satterthwait	Jane Turner
Masterpiece of Murder	Mary Kruger	Brooke Cassidy (Devlin)
Matricide at St. Martha's	Ruth Dudley Edwards	Baroness "Jack" Troutbeck
A Maze of Murders (2003)	C. L. Grace	Kathryn Swinbrooke
Meadowlark	Sheila Simonson	Lark Dailey (Dodge)
Mean Woman Blues (2003)	Julie Smith	Skip Langdon
Medusa (2003)	Skye Kathleen Moody	Venus Diamond
Memories Can Be Murder	Connie Shelton	Charlie Parker
Memory Can Be Murder	Elizabeth Daniels Squire	Peaches Dann

Title of Book	Author	Character
The Moor	Laurie R. King	Mary Russell (Holmes)
Morality for Beautiful Girls	Alexander McCall Smith	Precious Ramotswe
A Mortal Bane	Roberta Gellis	Magdalene la Bâtarde
The Mortal Sickness	Andrew Taylor	Jill Francis
Mortal Spoils	D. M. Greenwood	Theodora Braithwaite
Most Baffling, Mrs. Hudson	Sydney Hosier	Emma Hudson
A Most Deadly Retirement	John Miles	Laura Michaels
Most Likely to Die	Jaqueline Girdner	Kate Jasper
Mother May I	Randye Lordon	Sydney Sloane
Mother Nature	Sarah Andrews	Emily "Em" Hansen
Mother of the Bride	Patricia Tichenor Westphal	Molly West
The Mother Tongue	Teri Holbrook	Gale Grayson
The Mother's Day Murder	Lee Harris	Christine Bennett
Motion to Dismiss	Jonnie Jacobs	Kali O'Brien
Motion to Suppress	Perri O'Shaughnessy	Nina Reilly
A Motive for Murder	Gallagher Gray	Lil Hubbert
Mourn Not Your Dead	Deborah Crombie	Gemma James
Mourning Shift	Kathleen Taylor	Tory Bauer
Move to Strike	Perri O'Shaughnessy	Nina Reilly
Movie Cat	Garrison Allen	Penelope Warren
Moving Image	Annie Ross	Bel Carson
Moving Targets	Pat Welch	Helen Black
Mr. Big	Joyce Holms	Fizz Fitzgerald
Mrs. Jeffries and the Missing Alibi	Emily Brightwell	Hepzipah Jeffries
Mrs. Jeffries Dusts for Clues	Emily Brightwell	Hepzipah Jeffries
Mrs. Jeffries on the Ball	Emily Brightwell	Hepzipah Jeffries
Mrs. Jeffries on the Trail	Emily Brightwell	Hepzipah Jeffries
Mrs. Jeffries Pinches the Post	Emily Brightwell	Hepzipah Jeffries
Mrs. Jeffries Plays the Cook	Emily Brightwell	Hepzipah Jeffries
Mrs. Jeffries Pleads Her Case (2003)	Emily Brightwell	Hepzipah Jeffries
Mrs. Jeffries Questions the Answer	Emily Brightwell	Hepzipah Jeffries
Mrs. Jeffries Reveals Her Art	Emily Brightwell	Hepzipah Jeffries
Mrs. Jeffries Rocks the Boat	Emily Brightwell	Hepzipah Jeffries
Mrs. Jeffries Stands Corrected	Emily Brightwell	Hepzipah Jeffries
Mrs. Jeffries Takes Stock	Emily Brightwell	Hepzipah Jeffries
Mrs. Jeffries Takes the Cake	Emily Brightwell	Hepzipah Jeffries
Mrs. Jeffries Takes the Stage	Emily Brightwell	Hepzipah Jeffries
Mrs. Jeffries Weeds the Plot	Emily Brightwell	Hepzipah Jeffries
Muddy Water	Sally Gunning	Connie Bartholomew
Mudlark	Sheila Simonson	Lark Dailey (Dodge)
Mulch	Ann Ripley	Louise Eldridge
Multiple Listing	Anne Underwood Grant	Sydney Teague
A Multitude of Sins	Virginia Stem Owens	Beth Marie Cartwright
Mumbo Gumbo (2003)	Jerrilyn Farmer	Madelyn Bean
The Mummy Beads	Dawn Stewardson	Marina Haines
The Mummy Case	Dawn Stewardson	Marina Haines
The Mummy's Ransom (2002)	Fred Hunter	Emily Charters
Murder Among Friends	Jonnie Jacobs	Kate Austen
Murder Among Neighbors	Jonnie Jacobs	Kate Austen
Murder Among Strangers	Jonnie Jacobs	Kate Austen
Murder Among the Angels	Stefanie Matteson	Charlotte Graham
Murder Among Us	Ann Granger	Merry Mitchell
Murder Among Us	Jonnie Jacobs	Kate Austen
Murder and a Muse	Gillian B. Farrell	Annie McGrogan
Murder and the Mad Hatter	Barbara Jaye Wilson	Brenda Midnight

Title of Book	Author	Character
Murder in the Sentier (2002)	Cara Black	Aimee Leduc
Murder in the Shadows	Ellen Godfrey	Janet Barkin
A Murder in Thebes	Anna Apostolou	Miriam Bartimaeus
Murder in Vegas	Steve Allen	Jayne Meadows
Murder in Wrigley Field	Crabbe Evers	Petronella "Petey" Biggers
Murder Is Germane	Karen Saum	Brigid Donovan
Murder Is Material	Karen Saum	Brigid Donovan
Murder Is Relative	Karen Saum	Brigid Donovan
The Murder Lover	Ellen Rawlings	Rachel Crowne
Murder Makes Waves	Anne George	The Tate Sisters
Murder Me Now	Annette Meyers	Olivia Brown
Murder Mile High	Lora Roberts	Liz Sullivan
Murder Most Beastly	Melissa Cleary	Jackie Walsh
Murder Most Fowl	Kate Morgan	Dewey James
Murder Most Grizzly	Elizabeth Quinn	Dr. Lauren Maxwell
Murder Most Mellow	Jaqueline Girdner	Kate Jasper
A Murder of Crows	Margaret Haffner	Catherine Edison
Murder Offscreen	Denise Osborne	Queenie Davilov
Murder on a Bad Hair Day	Anne George	The Tate Sisters
Murder on a Girl's Night Out	Anne George	The Tate Sisters
Murder on an Astral Plane	Jaqueline Girdner	Kate Jasper
Murder on Astor Place	Victoria Thompson	Sarah Decker Brandt
Murder on Gramercy Park	Victoria Thompson	Sarah Decker Brandt
Murder on High	Stefanie Matteson	Charlotte Graham
Murder on Mulberry Bend (2003)	Victoria Thompson	Sarah Decker Brandt
Murder on St. Mark's Place	Victoria Thompson	Sarah Decker Brandt
Murder on the Atlantic	Steve Allen	Jayne Meadows
Murder on the Barbary Coast	Kate Bryan	Magdalena "Maggie" Maguire
Murder on the Cliff	Stefanie Matteson	Charlotte Graham
Murder on the Flying Scotsman	Carola Dunn	Daisy Dalrymple
Murder on the Gravy Train	Phyllis Richman	Chas Wheatley
Murder on the Iditarod Trail	Sue Henry	Jessie Arnold
Murder on the Loose	Ellen Godfrey	Janet Barkin
Murder on the Lovers' Bridge	Ellen Godfrey	Janet Barkin
Murder on the Run	Gloria White	Ronnie Ventana
Murder on the Silk Road	Stefanie Matteson	Charlotte Graham
Murder on the Trans-Siberian Express	Stuart Kaminsky	Elena Timafeyeva
Murder on the Yukon Quest	Sue Henry	Jessie Arnold
Murder on Washington Square (2002)	Victoria Thompson	Sarah Decker Brandt
Murder on Wheels	Valerie Frankel	Wanda Mallory
Murder One	William Bernhardt	Christina McCall
Murder Runs in the Family	Anne George	The Tate Sisters
Murder Sets Seed	Janis Harrison	Bretta Solomon
Murder Shoots the Bull	Anne George	The Tate Sisters
Murder Take Two	Charlene Weir	Susan Donavan Wren
Murder Takes Two	Bernie Lee	Pat Pratt
Murder Under the Palms	Stefanie Matteson	Charlotte Graham
Murder Well-Bred	Carolyn Banks	Robin Vaughan
Murder Well-Done	Claudia Bishop	Sarah "Quill" Quilliam
Murder Will Out	Dorian Yeager	Elizabeth "Liz" Will
Murder with Peacocks	Donna Andrews	Meg Langslow
Murder with Puffins	Donna Andrews	Meg Langslow
Murder Without Reservation	Bernie Lee	Pat Pratt

Title of Book	Author	Character
No Human Involved	Barbara Seranella	Munch Mancini
No Laughing Matter (2003)	Betty Rowlands	Melissa Craig
No Love Lost	Eileen Dewhurst	Phyllida Moon
No Man Standing (2002)	Barbara Seranella	Munch Mancini
No Offense Intended	Barbara Seranella	Munch Mancini
No One Dies in Branson	Kathryn Buckstaff	Emily Stone
No Rest for the Dove	Margaret Miles	Charlotte Willett
No Time for an Everyday Woman	Wanda Wardell Morrone	Lorelei Muldoon
No Time to Die	Grace F. Edwards	Mali Anderson
Nothing Gold Can Stay	Dana Stabenow	Wyanet "Wy" Chouinard
The Novice's Tale	Margaret Frazer	Sister Frevisse
Now I Lay Me Down to Sleep	Patricia H. Rushford	Helen Bradley
Now This	Nancy Star	May Morrison
Now May You Weep (2003)	Deborah Crombie	Gemma Jones
Now You See Her	Eileen Dewhurst	Phyllida Moon
The Nun's Tale	Candace M. Robb	Lucie D'Arby Wilton
Nutty As a Fruitcake	Mary Daheim	Judith McMonigle (Flynn)

O

O Jerusalem	Laurie R. King	Mary Russell (Holmes)
Obstruction of Justice	Perri O'Shaughnessy	Nina Reilly
Occasion of Revenge	Marcia Talley	Hannah Ives
Of Death and Black Rivers	Ann Woodward	Lady Aoi
Officer of the Court	Lelia Kelly	Laura Chastain
Old Black Magic	Jaye Maiman	Robin Miller
Old Dogs	Melissa Cleary	Jackie Walsh
The Old School Dies	Kate Morgan	Dewey James
The Oldest Sin	Ellen Hart	Sophie Greenway
Once Bitten	Laurien Berenson	Melanie Travis
One Dead Tory	Stephen Cook	Judy Best
One for the Money	D. B. Borton	Catherine "Cat" Caliban
One for the Money	Janet Evanovich	Stephanie Plum
One Must Wait	Penny Mickelbury	Carole Ann Gibson
One Too Many (NA)	Melissa Chan	Francesca Miles
One, Two, What did Daddy Do?	Susan Rogers Cooper	E. J. Pugh
Only in the Ashes	Maxine O'Callaghan	Dr. Anne Menlo
Only One Way Out	Ruth Ruby Moen	Kathleen O'Shaughnessy
Open House	Pat Welch	Helen Black
Ophelia O. and the Antenatal Mysteries	Tanya Jones	Ophelia O (Meredith)
Ophelia O. and the Mortgage Bandits	Tanya Jones	Ophelia O (Meredith)
Orchid Beach	Stuart Woods	Holly Barker
Orchid Blues	Stuart Woods	Holly Barker
auto*Osprey Reef*	Victoria McKernan	Chicago Nordejoong
The Other Side of Silence	Joan M. Drury	Tyler Jones
Our Lady of Darkness	Peter Tremayne	Sister Fidelma
Out of Circulation	Jo Dereske	Wilhelmena "Helma" Zukas
Out of Hormone's Way (2002)	Jane Isenberg	Bel Barrett
Out of the Dark (2002)	Natasha Cooper	Trish Maguire
Out of Time	Katy Munger	Casey Jones
Outlaw Mountain	J. A. Jance	Joanna Brady
The Outlaw's Tale	Margaret Frazer	Sister Frevisse
Outside Chance	Louisa Dixon	Laura Owen
Ovation by Death	Dorian Yeager	Victoria "Vic" Bowering
Over the Edge	Betty Rowlands	Melissa Craig

Title of Book	Author	Character
Pink Balloons and Other Deadly Things	Nancy Tesler	Carrie Carlin
The Pink Flamingo Murders	Elaine Viets	Francesca Vierling
The Pink Rabbit Caper	Georgette Livingston	Dr. Jennifer Gray
Pisces Rising	Martha C. Lawrence	Dr. Elizabeth Chase
A Plague of Kinfolks	Celestine Sibley	Kate Mulcay a.k.a. Katy Kincaid
Play Dead	Leslie O'Kane	Allie Babcock
Play It Again, Spam	Tamar Myers	Magdalena Yoder
Play with Fire	Dana Stabenow	Kate Shugak
Playing Dead	Lindsay Maracotta	Lucy Freers
Plot Twist	Jane Rubino	Cat Austen
A Pocketful of Karma	Taffy Cannon	Nan Robinson
Point Deception	Victoria McKernan	Chicago Nordejoong
Point No-Point	David Willis McCullough	Rev. Ziza Todd
Point of Origin	Patricia D. Cornwell	Dr. Kay Scarpetta
Poison Apples	Nancy Means Wright	Ruth Willmarth
Poison Flowers	Natasha Cooper	Willow King
A Poison in the Blood	Fay Zachary	Dr. Liz Broward
Popped (2003)	Carol Higgins Clark	Regan Reilly
Poppy Done to Death (2003)	Charlaine Harris	Aurora "Roe" Teagarden
Portrait in Death (2003)	J. D. Robb	Lt. Eve Dallas
Possessions	Kaye Davis	Maris Middleton
Postmortem	Patricia D. Cornwell	Dr. Kay Scarpetta
The Potbellied Pig Caper	Georgette Livingston	Dr. Jennifer Gray
Power Games	Judith Cutler	Kate Power
Power in the Blood	E. L. Wyrick	Tammi Randall
Power On Her Own	Judith Cutler	Kate Power
The Poyson Garden	Karen Harper	Queen Elizabeth I
Practice to Deceive	Janet L. Smith	Annie MacPherson
Pray For Us Sinners	Philip Luber	Veronica Pace
Prayers for Rain	Dennis Lehane	Angela Gennaro
The Precocious Parrot Caper	Georgette Livingston	Dr. Jennifer Gray
Prelude to Death	Sharon Zukowski	Blaine Stewart
Prescription for Death	Janet McGiffin	Dr. Maxene St. Clair
Presence of Mind	Fred Hunter	Emily Charters
Press Corpse	Ron Nessen, Johanna Neuman	Jane Day
Presumption of Death (2003)	Perri O'Shaughnessy	Nina Reilly
Presumption of Guilt	Lelia Kelly	Laura Chastain
Pretty Boy	Lauren Henderson	Sam Jones
Prey Dancing	Jonathan Gash	Dr. Clare Burtonall
Prey to All	Natasha Cooper	Trish Maguire
Primal Instinct	Robert W. Walker	Dr. Jessica Coran
Primary Justice	William Bernhardt	Christina McCall
Prime Cut	Diane Mott Davidson	Goldy Bear (Schulz)
Prime Suspect	Lynda La Plante	Jane Tennison
Prime Suspect 2	Lynda La Plante	Jane Tennison
Prime Suspect 3	Lynda La Plante	Jane Tennison
Prime Time for Murder	Valerie Frankel	Wanda Mallory
The Primrose Convention	Jo Bannister	Primrose "Rosie" Holland
The Primrose Switchback	Jo Bannister	Primrose "Rosie" Holland
Principal Defense	Gini Hartzmark	Kate Millholland
The Prioress' Tale	Margaret Frazer	Sister Frevisse
Prison Blues (2002)	Anna Salter	Dr. Michael Stone
Private Lies	Carol Cail	Maxey Burnell
Private Practices	Stephen White	Lauren Crowder

Title of Book	Author	Character
Privileged Information	Stephen White	Lauren Crowder
Profile	C. J. Koehler	Margaret Loftus
The Program	Stephen White	Lauren Crowder
A Proper Burial	Pat Welch	Helen Black
Prospect of Death	Margaret Duffy	Joanna Mackenzie
Protect and Defend	Richard North Patterson	Caroline Masters
The Providence File	Amanda Kyle Williams	Madison McGuire
Public Trust	Sarah Gregory	Sharon Hays
Publish and Be Murdered	Ruth Dudley Edwards	Baroness "Jack" Troutbeck
Pulse	Echo Heron	Adele Monsarrat
The Pumpkin Shell Wife	Susanna Hofmann McShea	Mildred Bennett, Irene Purdy
The Punjat's Ruby	Marian J. A. Jackson	Abigail Danforth
Pure Instinct	Robert W. Walker	Dr. Jessica Coran
Purity in Death (2002)	J. D. Robb	Lt. Eve Dallas
Pushover	Diane G. Pugh	Iris Thorne
Pussyfoot	Carole Nelson Douglas	Temple Barr & Midnight Louie
A Puzzle in a Pear Tree (2002)	Parnell Hall	Cora Felton & Sherry Carter
Puzzled to Death	Parnell Hall	Cora Felton & Sherry Carter

Q

Quaker Indictment	Irene Allen	Elizabeth Elliot
Quaker Silence	Irene Allen	Elizabeth Elliot
Quaker Testimony	Irene Allen	Elizabeth Elliot
Quaker Witness	Irene Allen	Elizabeth Elliot
The Quality of Mercy	Gilbert Morris	Danielle "Dani" Ross
Queen of Ambition (2002)	Fiona Buckley	Ursula Blanchard
Queen's Ransom	Fiona Buckley	Ursula Blanchard
The Queene's Cure (2002)	Karen Harper	Queen Elizabeth I
The Queene's Christmas (2003)	Karen Harper	Queen Elizabeth I
A Question of Preference	J. Dayne Lamb	Teal Stewart
Questionable Behavior	J. Dayne Lamb	Teal Stewart
Questionable Remains	Beverly Connor	Lindsay Chamberlain
The Quick and the Dead	Alison Joseph	Sister Agnes Bourdillon
A Quiet Undertaking	Penny Warner	Connor Westphal
Quieter Than Sleep	Joanne Dobson	Karen Pelletier

R

Race with Death	Gilbert Morris	Danielle "Dani" Ross
Rage Factor	Chris Rogers	Dixie Flannigan
The Raggedy Man	Lillian O'Donnell	Gwen Ramadge
Rain Dance	Skye Kathleen Moody	Venus Diamond
The Rampant Reaper (2002)	Marlys Millhiser	Charlie Greene
Ransom at Sea (2003)	Fred Hunter	Emily Charters
Ransom at the Opera	Fred Hunter	Emily Charters
Ransom for a Holiday	Fred Hunter	Emily Charters
Ransom for a Killing	Fred Hunter	Emily Charters
Ransom for an Angel	Fred Hunter	Emily Charters
Ransom for Our Sins	Fred Hunter	Emily Charters
Ransom Unpaid	Fred Hunter	Emily Charters
The Raphael Affair	Iain Pears	Flavia di Stefano
Rapture in Death	J. D. Robb	Lt. Eve Dallas
Rare Earth	Cecil Dawkins	Ginevra Prettifield
Rattle His Bones	Carola Dunn	Daisy Dalrymple
Rattlesnake Crossing	J. A. Jance	Joanna Brady
The Raven and the Nightingale	Joanne Dobson	Karen Pelletier
Ravenmocker	Jean Hager	Molly Bearpaw

Title of Book	Author	Character
Raw Data	Sally Chapman	Julie Blake
Razorbill	Alex Keegan	Caz Flood
Real Murders	Charlaine Harris	Aurora "Roe" Teagarden
Reckless Eyeballin'	Judith Smith-Levin	Starletta Duvall
A Record of Death	Kate Bryan	Magdalena "Maggie" Maguire
Recycled	Jo Bailey	Jan Gallagher
Red Beans and Vice (2002)	Lou Jane Temple	Heaven Lee
The Red Heron	Karen Dudley	Robyn Devara
Red House	k.j.a. Wishnia	Filomena "Fil" Buscarsela
Red Line	Megan Mallory Rust	Taylor Morgan
Red Mesa	Aimee and David Thurlo	Ella Clah
The Red Scream	Mary Willis Walker	Molly Cates
Red Sea, Dead Sea	Serita Stevens, Rayanne Moore	Fanny Zindel
Red Sky in Mourning	Patricia H. Rushford	Helen Bradley
Red Trance	R. D. Zimmerman	Maddy Phillips
Red Wine Goes with Murder	Paula Carter	Jane Ferguson, Hillary Scarborough
Red, White, and Blue Murder	Jeanne M. Dams	Hilda Johansson
The Redbird's Cry	Jean Hager	Molly Bearpaw
Redneck Riviera	Sophie Dunbar	Claire Claiborne Jenner
The Reeve's Tale	Margaret Frazer	Sister Frevisse
Reflecting the Sky	S. J. Rozan	Lydia Chin
A Relative Cause of Murder a.k.a. *Death in the Family*	C. F. Roe	Dr. Jean Montrose
Remember Me, Irene	Jan Burke	Irene Kelly
Remember the Alibi	Elizabeth Daniels Squire	Peaches Dann
Remembrance of Murders Past	Noreen Wald	Jake O'Hara
Remote Control	Stephen White	Lauren Crowder
Repair to Her Grave	Sarah Graves	Jacobia Tiptee
Requiem for a Mezzo	Carola Dunn	Daisy Dalrymple
Resolution (2002)	Denise Mina	Maureen O'Donnell
Resort to Murder	Carolyn Hart	Henrietta O'Dwyer Collins
Rest in Pieces	Rita Mae Brown	Mary "Harry" Haristeen & Mrs. Murphy
A Restless Evil (2002)	Ann Granger	Merry Mitchell
The Return of the Spanish Lady	Val Davis	Nicolette "Nick" Scott
Return to the Kill	Ruth Ruby Moen	Kathleen O'Shaughnessy
Reunion in Death (2002)	J. D. Robb	Lt. Eve Dallas
Reunions Can Be Murder (2003)	Connie Shelton	Charlie Parker
Revenge at the Rodeo	Gilbert Morris	Danielle "Dani" Ross
Revenge of the Barbecue Queens	Lou Jane Temple	Heaven Lee
Revenge of the Cootie Girls	Sparkle Hayter	Robin Hudson
Revenge of the Wrought-Iron Flamingos	Donna Andrews	Meg Langslow
Rhode Island Red	Charlotte Carter	Nanette Hayes
The Riddle of St. Leonards	Candace M. Robb	Lucie D'Arby Wilton
Riding for a Fall	Lillian M. Roberts	Dr. Andi Pauling
Right to Remain Silent	Penny Warner	Connor Westphal
Rigor Mortis	Mary Kittredge	Edwina Crusoe
Ring for Tomb Service	Kate Kingsbury	Cecily Sinclair
Risking It All	Ann Granger	Fran Varaday
River Quay	Janet McClellan	Tru North
Road Kill	Marianne Macdonald	Dido Hoare
Robin (NA)	Alex Keegan	Caz Flood
The Robsart Mystery a.k.a. *To Shield the Queen*	Fiona Buckley	Ursula Blanchard

Title of Book	Author	Character
The School Board Murders	Leslie O'Kane	Molly Masters
School of Hard Knocks	Donna Huston Murray	Ginger Barnes
A Score to Settle	Donna Huston Murray	Ginger Barnes
Scream in Silence	Eleanor Taylor Bland	Marti MacAlister
Sea of Troubles	Janet L. Smith	Annie MacPherson
The Search	Melanie McAllester	Elizabeth "Tenny" Mendoza
Searching for Sara	Shelley Singer	Barrett Lake
A Season for Murder	Ann Granger	Merry Mitchell
Second Guess	Rose Beecham	Amanda Valentine
Second Thoughts	Margot Dalton	Jackie Kaminsky
Secret's Shadow	Alex Matthews	Cassidy McCabe
Seduction in Death	J. D. Robb	Lt. Eve Dallas
See No Evil	Eleanor Taylor Bland	Marti MacAlister
Seeing Is Deceiving	Sarah J. Mason	Sergeant Stone
Seeing Is Deceiving	Suzanne North	Phoebe Fairfax
Seneca Falls Inheritance	Miriam Monfredo	Glynis Tryon
The Sensational Music Club Mystery	Graham Landrum	Harriet Bushrow, Helen Delaporte
A Sensitive Kind of Murder (2002)	Jaqueline Girdner	Kate Jasper
September Mourn	Mary Daheim	Judith McMonigle (Flynn)
The Servant's Tale	Margaret Frazer	Sister Frevisse
Service for Two	Kate Kingsbury	Cecily Sinclair
Settlement Day	Rebecca Tinsley	Charlotte Carter
Seven Black Stones	Jean Hager	Molly Bearpaw
Seven Sisters	Earlene Fowler	Albenia "Benni" Harper
Seven Up	Janet Evanovich	Stephanie Plum
Sew Easy to Kill	Sarah J. Mason	Sergeant Stone
Sex and Salmonella	Kathleen Taylor	Tory Bauer
Shades of Murder	Ann Granger	Merry Mitchell
The Shadow Dancer (2002)	Margaret Coel	Vicky Holden
Shadow of An Angel (2002)	Mignon F. Ballard	Augusta Goodnight
Shadow of Death	Noreen Gilpatrick	Kate MacLean
Shadow of Doubt	Jonnie Jacobs	Kali O'Brien
Shadow of the Child	Maxine O'Callaghan	Dr. Anne Menlo
Shadow Queen	Tony Gibbs	Diana Speed
Shadow Walk	Jane Waterhouse	Garner Quinn
Shadow Woman	Thomas Perry	Jane Whitefield
Shadows of Sin	Rochelle Majer Krich	Jessica Drake
Shakespeare's Champion	Charlaine Harris	Lily Bard
Shakespeare's Christmas	Charlaine Harris	Lily Bard
Shakespeare's Counselor	Charlaine Harris	Lily Bard
Shakespeare's Landlord	Charlaine Harris	Lily Bard
Shakespeare's Trollop	Charlaine Harris	Lily Bard
The Shaman Laughs	James Doss	Daisy Perika
The Shaman Sings	James Doss	Daisy Perika
The Shaman's Bones	James Doss	Daisy Perika
The Shaman's Game	James Doss	Daisy Perika
A Share in Death	Deborah Crombie	Gemma James
Sharks, Jellyfish and Other Deadly Things	Nancy Tesler	Carrie Carlin
Shattered Rhythms	Phyllis Knight	Lil Ritchie
She Walks These Hills	Sharyn McCrumb	Nora Bonesteel
Shell Game	Carol O'Connell	Sgt. Kathleen Mallory
Shiny Water	Anna Salter	Dr. Michael Stone
Shivaree	Sophie Dunbar	Claire Claiborne Jenner

Title of Book	Author	Character
Skylark	Sheila Simonson	Lark Dailey (Dodge)
Sky Woman Falling (2003)	Kirk Mitchell	Anna Turnipseed
A Slash of Scarlet	Nancy Baker Jacobs	Devon MacDonald
Slaves of Obsession	Anne Perry	Hester Latterly (Monk)
A Slay at the Races	Kate Morgan	Dewey James
Sleeping Lady	Sue Henry	Jessie Arnold
Slice and Dice	Ellen Hart	Sophie Greenway
Slickrock	Laura Crum	Dr. Gail McCarthy
Slippery Slopes and Other Deadly Things (2003)	Nancy Tesler	Carrie Carlin
Slow Burn	Eleanor Taylor Bland	Marti MacAlister
Slow Dancing with the Angel of Death	Helen Chappell	Hollis Ball
Slow Dissolve	Della Borton	Gilda Liberty
Slow Dollar (2002)	Margaret Maron	Deborah Knott
Slow Squeeze	Diane G. Pugh	Iris Thorne
A Small Target	Christine Andreae	Lee Squires
Small Towns Can Be Murder	Connie Shelton	Charlie Parker
Smiling at Death	Betty Rowlands	Melissa Craig
Smoke and Mirrors	Pat Welch	Helen Black
Smoke in the Wind	Peter Tremayne	Sister Fidelma
Smoke Screen	Anne Underwood Grant	Sydney Teague
Smoke Screen	Marianne Macdonald	Dido Hoare
The Smoking Gun	Eve K. Sandstrom	Nell Matthews
Snagged	Carol Higgins Clark	Regan Reilly
Snake Dance	Linda Mariz	Laura Ireland
Snake Eyes	Pat Welch	Helen Black
Snapped in Cornwall	Jane Bolitho	Rose Trevelyan
The Snares of Death	Kate Charles	Lucy Kingsley
Snow Place to Die	Mary Daheim	Judith McMonigle (Flynn)
So Dear to Wicked Men	Tavis and Judy Iakovou	Julia Lambros
So Faux, So Good	Tamar Myers	Abigail "Abby" Timberlake
So Sure of Death	Dana Stabenow	Wyanet "Wy" Chouinard
Soft Money	k.j.a. Wishnia	Filomena "Fil" Buscarsela
The Solitary Twist	Elizabeth Pincus	Nell Fury
Somebody Else's Child	Terris McMahon Grimes	Theresa Galloway
Someone to Watch	Jaye Maiman	Robin Miller
Someone to Watch Over Me	Jill Churchill	Lily Brewster
Something to Kill For	Susan Holtzer	Anneke Haagen
Something Wicked	Jennifer Rowe	Tessa Vance
Something's Cooking	Joanne Pence	Angelina "Angie" Amalfi
Son of a Gun (2003)	Randye Lordon	Sydney Sloane
The Songcatcher	Sharyn McCrumb	Nora Bonesteel
Soultown	Mercedes Lambert	Whitney Logan
Sound of Murder	Patricia and Clayton Matthews	Casey Farrel
Sounds Easy	Carol Dawber	Liz Gresham
Sour Grapes	G. A. McKevett	Savannah Reid
Southern Cross	Patricia D. Cornwell	Judy Hammer
Southern Discomfort	Margaret Maron	Deborah Knott
Speak Daggers to Her	Rosemary Edghill	Karen Hightower a.k.a. Bast
Speak Ill of the Dead	Mary Jane Maffini	Camilla McPhee
A Species of Revenge	Marjorie Eccles	Abigail Moon
Spider in the Sink	Celestine Sibley	Kate Mulcay a.k.a. Katy Kincaid
The Spider's Web	Peter Tremayne	Sister Fidelma
The Spirit Caller	Jean Hager	Molly Bearpaw

Title of Book	Author	Character
Suffer Little Children	Peter Tremayne	Sister Fidelma
The Suffocating Night	Andrew Taylor	Jill Francis
Sugar and Spite	G. A. McKevett	Savannah Reid
The Sugar House	Laura Lippman	Tess Monaghan
Suitable for Framing	Edna Buchanan	Britt Montero
Summer Will End	Dorian Yeager	Elizabeth "Liz" Will
The Sunken Treaure	Marian J. A. Jackson	Abigail Danforth
Sunset and Santiago	Gloria White	Ronnie Ventana
A Sunset Touch	Marjorie Eccles	Abigail Moon
Sunshine and Shadow (2003)	Earlene Fowler	Albenia "Benni" Harper
The Superintendent's Daughter	Marjorie Eccles	Abigail Moon
A Superior Death	Nevada Barr	Anna Pigeon
Suspect a.k.a. *Deadline*	Jennifer Rowe	Tessa Vance
Suspicion of Betrayal	Barbara Parker	Gail Connor
Suspicion of Deceit	Barbara Parker	Gail Connor
Suspicion of Guilt	Barbara Parker	Gail Connor
Suspicion of Innocence	Barbara Parker	Gail Connor
Suspicion of Madness (2003)	Barbara Parker	Gail Connor
Suspicion of Malice	Barbara Parker	Gail Connor
Suspicion of Vengeance	Barbara Parker	Gail Connor
Suture Self	Mary Daheim	Judith McMonigle (Flynn)
Sweet Cherry Wine	Carol Schmidt	Laney Samms
Sweet Dreams, Irene	Jan Burke	Irene Kelly
Sweet Georgia	Ruth Birmingham	Sunny Childs
Sweet Sixteen	Michael Molloy	Sarah Keane
Swimming Cat Cove	Lauren Wright Douglas	Allison O'Neil
Switching the Odds	Phyllis Knight	Lil Ritchie
Sympathy for the Devil	Jerrilyn Farmer	Madelyn Bean
T		
The Tail of the Tip-Off (2003)	Rita Mae Brown	Mary "Harry" Haristeen & Mrs. Murphy
A Tail of Two Murders	Melissa Cleary	Jackie Walsh
Take a Number	Janet Dawson	Jeri Howard
Taken by Storm	Linda Kay Silva	Delta Stevens
Taken to the Cleaners	Dolores Johnson	Mandy Dyer
Take-Out Double a.k.a. *Death Takes a Hand*	Susan Moody	Cassandra "Cassie" Swann
Takes One to Know One	Kate Allen	Alison Kaine
Talked to Death	Louise Shaffer	Angie DaVito
Talking Rain	Linda French	Teodora "Teddy" Morelli
Tall, Dead, and Handsome	Annie Griffin	Hannah Malloy, Kiki Goldstein
A Tangled Knot of Murder	C. F. Roe	Dr. Jean Montrose
Tangled Roots	Taffy Cannon	Nan Robinson
Target for Murder	J. F. Trainor	Angela "Angie" Biwaban
Tarnished Icon	Stuart Kaminsky	Elena Timafeyeva
A Taste for Burning	Jo Bannister	Liz Graham
A Taste for Murder	Claudia Bishop	Sarah "Quill" Quilliam
Taste of Evil	Patricia and Clayton Matthews	Casey Farrel
The Tears of the Giraffe	Alexander McCall Smith	Precious Ramotswe
Tea-Totally Dead	Jaqueline Girdner	Kate Jasper
The Teddy Bear Murders	Janet Harward	Josephine Blake
Tell Me What You Like	Kate Allen	Alison Kaine
Tell No Tales	Eleanor Taylor Bland	Marti MacAlister
Telling Lies	Wendy Hornsby	Maggie MacGowen
The Telltale Turkey Caper	Georgette Livingston	Dr. Jennifer Gray

Title of Book	Author	Character
To Shield the Queen a.k.a. *The Robsart Mystery*	Fiona Buckley	Ursula Blanchard
To the Nines (2003)	Janet Evanovich	Stephanie Plum
To Wear the White Cloak	Sharan Newman	Catherine Le Vendeur
A Toast Before Dying	Grace F. Edwards	Mali Anderson
Tombstone Courage	J. A. Jance	Joanna Brady
A Ton of Trouble (2002)	Lynne Murray	Josephine Fuller
Too Many Blondes	Lauren Henderson	Sam Jones
Too Many Cooks	Joanne Pence	Angelina "Angie" Amalfi
Too Many Cooks Spoil the Broth	Tamar Myers	Magdalena Yoder
Too Rich	Melissa Chan	Francesca Miles
Too Soon For Flowers	Margaret Miles	Charlotte Willett
A Torrid Piece of Murder a.k.a. *Fatal Fever*	C. F. Roe	Dr. Jean Montrose
Tortoise Soup	Jessica Speart	Rachel Porter
The Total Zone	Martina Navratilova, Liz Nickles	Jordan Myles
Touch Me Not	Betty Rowlands	Sukey Reynolds
A Touch of Mortality	Ann Granger	Merry Mitchell
Touch of Terror	Patricia and Clayton Matthews	Casey Farrel
A Touch of the Grape	Claudia Bishop	Sarah "Quill" Quilliam
Tough Cookie	Diane Mott Davidson	Goldy Bear (Schulz)
Towers of Silence (2002)	Cath Staincliffe	Sal Kilkenny
Track of the Cat	Nevada Barr	Anna Pigeon
Track of the Scorpion	Val Davis	Nicolette "Nick" Scott
Tracking Bear (2003)	Aimee and David Thurlo	Ella Clah
Tracking Time	Leslie Glass	April Woo
Trail of Murder	Christine Andreae	Lee Squires
Tramp	Marne Davis Kellogg	Lilly Bennett
Trial and Retribution	Lynda La Plante	Pat North
Trial and Retribution II	Lynda La Plante	Pat North
Trial and Retribution III	Lynda La Plante	Pat North
Trial and Retribution IV	Lynda La Plante	Pat North
Trial and Retribution V	Lynda La Plante	Pat North
Trick of Light a.k.a. *Trick Shot*	David Hunt	Kay Farrow
Trick or Treat Murder	Leslie Meier	Lucy Stone
Triple Witch	Sarah Graves	Jacobia Tiptee
Tropical Storm	Linda Kay Silva	Delta Stevens
Trouble Becomes Her	Laura Van Wormer	Sally Harrington
Trouble in the Town Hall	Jeanne M. Dams	Dorothy Martin
Trouble in Transylvania	Barbara Wilson	Cassandra Reilly
Trouble Looking for a Place to Happen	Toni L. P. Kelner	Laura Fleming
The Trouble with a Bad Fit	Trella Crespi	Simona Griffo
The Trouble with a Hot Summer	Trella Crespi	Simona Griffo
The Trouble with a Small Raise	Trella Crespi	Simona Griffo
The Trouble with Going Home	Trella Crespi	Simona Griffo
The Trouble with Moonlighting	Trella Crespi	Simona Griffo
The Trouble with Thin Ice	Trella Crespi	Simona Griffo
The Trouble with Too Much Sun	Trella Crespi	Simona Griffo
Troubled Water	Sally Gunning	Connie Bartholomew
Trunk Show	Alison Glen	Charlotte Sams
Truth or Dare	Anne Wilson	Sara Kingsley
The Tumbleweed Murders	Rebecca Rothenberg, Taffy Cannon	Claire Sharples

Title of Book	Author	Character
Until the Final Verdict (2002)	Christine McGuire	Kathryn Mackay
Until We Meet Again	Christine McGuire	Kathryn Mackay
Untimely Graves	Marjorie Eccles	Abigail Moon
Unwanted Company	Barbara Seranella	Munch Mancini
Up in Smoke (2003)	Charlene Weir	Susan Donavan Wren
Up Jumps the Devil	Margaret Maron	Deborah Knott
Up Next	Nancy Star	May Morrison
Used to Kill	Lillian O'Donnell	Gwen Ramadge

V

Vacations Can Be Murder	Connie Shelton	Charlie Parker
Valentine Murder	Leslie Meier	Lucy Stone
The Valentine's Day Murder	Lee Harris	Christine Bennett
Valley of the Shadow	Peter Tremayne	Sister Fidelma
The Vanished Child	Sarah Smith	Perdita Halley
The Vanished Man (2003)	Jeffrey Wilds Deaver	Amelia Sachs
Vanishing Act	Barbara Block	Robin Light
Vanishing Act	Thomas Perry	Jane Whitefield
A Veiled Antiquity	Rett MacPherson	"Torie" O'Shea
Vendetta Defense (2002)	Lisa Scottoline	"Bennie" Rosato Law Firm
Vendetta's Victim	Alex Matthews	Cassidy McCabe
Vengeance in Death	J. D. Robb	Lt. Eve Dallas
Verdict in Blood	Gail Bowen	Joanne "Jo" Kilbourn
The Verdict on Winter	Eileen Dewhurst	Phyllida Moon
A Very Eligible Corpse	Annie Griffin	Hannah Malloy, Kiki Goldstein
Vial Murders	Marsha Landreth	Dr. Samantha Turner
The Victim in Victoria Station	Jeanne M. Dams	Dorothy Martin
A Vintage Murder	Janet L. Smith	Annie MacPherson
The Violence Beat	Eve K. Sandstrom	Nell Matthews
Virgin Territory	Marilyn Todd	Claudia Seferius
Virtual Memories	Natalie Buske Thomas	Serena Wilcox
Virtual Stranger	Emer Gillespie	Karen McDade
Vision of Death	Patricia and Clayton Matthews	Casey Farrel
Visions of Sugarplums (2002)	Janet Evanovich	Stephanie Plum
Voices in the Sand	Anne Underwood Grant	Sydney Teague
A Vow of Adoration	Veronica Black	Sister Joan
A Vow of Chastity	Veronica Black	Sister Joan
A Vow of Compassion	Veronica Black	Sister Joan
A Vow of Devotion	Veronica Black	Sister Joan
A Vow of Fidelity	Veronica Black	Sister Joan
A Vow of Obedience	Veronica Black	Sister Joan
A Vow of Penance	Veronica Black	Sister Joan
A Vow of Poverty	Veronica Black	Sister Joan
A Vow of Sanctity	Veronica Black	Sister Joan
A Vow of Silence	Veronica Black	Sister Joan
Vulture	Alex Keegan	Caz Flood

W

Wait for the Dark	Ann Crowleigh	Clare & Mirinda Cliveley
Wake of the Hornet	Val Davis	Nicolette "Nick" Scott
Wake Up to Murder	Steve Allen	Jayne Meadows
Walk a Crooked Mile	Catherine Dain	Freddie O'Neal
Walk in the Darkness	Jon Land	Danielle Barnea
Walking Dead Man	Mary Kittredge	Edwina Crusoe
The Walls of Jericho	Jon Land	Danielle Barnea
The Wandering Arm	Sharan Newman	Catherine Le Vendeur

Title of Book	Author	Character
A Wicked Way to Burn	Margaret Miles	Charlotte Willett
A Wide and Capable Revenge	Thomas McCall	Nora Callum
Widowmaker	William Appel	Kate Berman
Widows' Watch	Nancy Herndon	Elena Jarvis
Widow's Peak a.k.a. *An Easy Day for a Lady*	Gillian Linscott	Nell Bray
A Wild Justice	Alex Keegan	Caz Flood
Wildcrafters	Skye Kathleen Moody	Venus Diamond
Will Power	Judith Cutler	Kate Power
Winding Up the Serpent	Priscilla Masters	Joanna Piercy
Windy City Dying (2002)	Eleanor Taylor Bland	Marti MacAlister
Winter and Night (2002)	S. J. Rozan	Lydia Chin
The Winter Garden Mystery	Carola Dunn	Daisy Dalrymple
The Winter Widow	Charlene Weir	Susan Donavan Wren
The Winter Women Murders	David Kaufelt	Wyn Lewis
The Wire in the Blood	Val McDermid	Carol Jordan
Wish You Were Here	Rita Mae Brown	Mary "Harry" Haristeen & Mrs. Murphy
Witches' Bane	Susan Wittig Albert	China Bayles
With Child	Laurie R. King	Kate Martinelli a.k.a K. C.
With Deadly Intent	Louise Hendrickson	Dr. Amy Prescott
With Intent to Kill	Frances Ferguson	Jane Perry
Witness for the Defense	Jonnie Jacobs	Kali O'Brien
Witness in Death	J. D. Robb	Lt. Eve Dallas
Witness to Evil	Janet Dawson	Jeri Howard
A Wolf in Death's Clothing	Elizabeth Quinn	Dr. Lauren Maxwell
Wolf Whistle	Marilyn Todd	Claudia Seferius
The Woman Who Found Grace (2003)	B. Reece Johnson	Cordelia Morgan
The Woman Who Knew Too Much	B. Reece Johnson	Cordelia Morgan
The Woman Who Rode to the Moon	B. Reece Johnson	Cordelia Morgan
A Word After Dying	Ann Granger	Merry Mitchell
A World the Color of Salt	Noreen Ayres	Smokey Brandon
Worse Than Death	Jean Bedford	Anna Southwood
A Wreath for My Sister	Priscilla Masters	Joanna Piercy
A Wreath for the Bride	Lillian O'Donnell	Gwen Ramadge
Wreck the Halls	Sarah Graves	Jacobia Tiptee
Writ of Execution	Perri O'Shaughnessy	Nina Reilly
Writers of the Purple Sage	Barbara Burnett Smith	Jolie Wyatt
The Wrong Dog	Carol Lea Benjamin	Rachel Kaminsky Alexander
Wrongful Death	Catherine Arnold	Karen Perry-Mondori
The Wyndham Case	Jill Paton Walsh	Imogen Quy

X

The Xibalba Murders	Lyn Hamilton	Lara McClintoch

Y

The Year 2000 Killers	Wanda Wardell Morrone	Lorelei Muldoon
The Yom Kippur Murder	Lee Harris	Christine Bennett
You Bet Your Life	Christine T. Jorgensen	Stella the Stargazer a.k.a. Jane Smith
You Only Die Twice	Edna Buchanan	Britt Montero

Z

Zen Attitude	Sujata Massey	Rei Shimura

Mystery Women Chronology
1860-1999

Year in which female character made first published appearance in a novel or collection of short stories. The chronological listing of female sleuths refers to first significant appearance. An asterisk (*) indicates that the character made at least three appearances in books that are clearly mysteries and that were published before December 31, 2001. © Indicates copyright date, used when publication date was unavailable. U.K. indicates the date was published in the United Kingdom; U.S. indicates the date of publication in the United States; CAN indicates the date of publication in Canada; AUS indicates the date of publication in Australia.

Volume 1

1861:	Mrs. Paschal
1864:	Mrs. G.
1875:	Valeria Woodville
1884:	Madeline Payne
1894:	Loveday Brooke
1895:	Caroline "Cad" Mettie
1897:	Amelia Butterworth*; Dorcas Dene
1898:	Hagar Stanley
1899:	Lois Cayley; Madame Katherine Koluchy
1900:	Dora Myrl*; Hilda Wade
1903:	Madame Sara
1905:	Mary J. "Polly" Burton; Henrietta Van Raffles

1906:   Frances Baird

1910:   Lady Molly Robertson-Kirk

1911:   Letitia "Tish" Carberry

1912:   Judith Lee

1913:   Constance Dunlap ©; Ruth Fielding*

1914:   Madelyn Mack; Mercedes Quero*

1915:   Molly Morganthau*; Violet Strange

1917:   Millicent Newberry*; Evelyn Temple; Olga von Kopf

1922:   Prudence "Tuppence" Beresford*

1923:   Rosie Bright; Sylvia Shale

1924:   Fidelity Dove

1925:   Eileen "Bundle" Brent; Sophie Lang; Blue Jean Billy Race;
           Madame Rosika Storey*

1926:   Juliet Jackson*

1927:   Meg Garret*; Leslie Maughan (U.S.); Jane Ollerby

1928:   Angela Bredon; Lynn MacDonald*

1929:   Dame Adela Beatrice Lestrange Bradley*; Four Square Jane;
           Sarah Keate*; Maud Silver* (U.S.)

1930:   Nancy Drew*; Ellen Gilchrist Soames; Gwynn Leith Keats;
           Gail McGurk*; Jane Marple*; Kate Marsh*; Polack Annie;
           Harriet Vane*; Louisa Woolfe*; Daphne Wrayne*

1931:   Fah Lo Suee*; Solange Fontaine; Prudence Whitby ;
           Hildegarde Withers*

1932:   Hilda Adams*; Avis Bryden*; Angeline Tredennick; Mrs.
           Caywood "Julia" Weston

1933:   Amanda Fitton Campion; Lizzie Collins*; Olga
           Knaresbrook; Della Street; Mrs. Elizabeth Warrender*

1934:   Nora Charles; Clarice Claremont; Susan Dare; Peggy
           Fairfield; Anne Layton; Ariadne Oliver*; Alice Penny;
           Matilda Townsend*

1935:   Jane Amanda Edwards*; Penny Mercer*; Matilda Perks; Palmyra Pym*

1936:   Iris Pattison Duluth*; Baroness Clara Linz (U.S.); Anne Holt McNeill*; Dr. Joan Marvin; Georgia Cavendish Strangeways; Ethel Thomas*

1937:   Adelaide Adams; Theolinda "Dol" Bonner; Carey Brent*; Patricia "Pat" Preston Cordry*; Grace Latham*; Anne "Davvie" Davenport McLean*; Daisy Jane Mott; Lucy Mott (U.S.); Tamara Valeshoff

1938:   Agatha Troy Alleyn; Mary Carner*; Kay Cornish*; Valerie Dundas; Coco Hastings; Carole Trevor; Lace White*

1939:   Hilea Bailey*; Janet "Janie" Allen Barron*; Bertha Cool*; Helene Brand Justus*; Sue MacVeigh*; Emma Marsh*; Rachel and Jennifer Murdoch*; Anne Seymour Webb; Susan Yates*

1940:   Ethel Abbott; Amanda and Lutie Beagle; Margot Blair*; Jane Carberry*; Elsie Mae Hunt*; Pamela "Pam" North*; Miss Mabie Otis*; Katherine "Peter" Piper*; Haila Rogers Troy*; Sister Ursula; Agatha Welch

1941:   Jean Holly Abbott*; Eleanora Burke; Gypsy Rose Lee; Sarah O'Brien; Andrea Reid Ramsay; Hannah Van Doren*; Kitty McLeod Whitney*

1942:   Arabella "Arab" Blake*; Louise "Liz" Boykin Parrott*; Grace Pomeroy

1943:   Christine Andersen; Georgine Wyeth McKinnon; Doris "Dodo" Trent and Nell Witter*

1944:   Kit Marsden Acton*; Judy Ashbane; Maria Black*; Lorna Donahue; Vicky Gaines; Lady Lapin Hastings*; Abbie Harris*; Bessie Petty and Beulah Pond*

1945:   Nora Hughes Blaine; Amy Brewster*; Dr. Mary Finney*; Jenny Gillette Lewis*; Katherine Forrester Vigneras

1946:   Elizabeth; Eve MacWilliams; Maggie Slone; Tessie Venable

1947:   Hortense Clinton*; Gale Gallagher; Suzanne "Suzy" Marshall; Lucy Pym; Terry Terence*; Julia Tyler*

1948:   Jane Hamish Brown*; Eve Gill*

1949:   Miriam Birdseye* and Natasha Nevkorina*; Emily Murdoch Bryce*; Janice Cameron and Lily Wu*; Marka de Lancey*

1950:   Sumuru*; Ma Tellford*; Hilda Trenton

1951:   Petunia Best; Liane "Lee" Craufurd*; Shirley Leighton Harper*; Laura Scudamore, The Sinister Widow*; Ginger Tintagel; Sarah Vanessa*

1952:   Ann McIntosh*

1953:   Nell Bartlett; Norma "Nicky" Lee*

1954:   Sally Dean; Sally Strang*

1955:   Miss Flora Hogg*; Mavis Seidlitz*; English translations of Souer Angele*

1956:   Eileen Burke*; Sally Merton Heldar*; Marion Kerrison; Julia Probyn*; Daye Smith*

1957:   Mrs. Annie Norris*; Honey West*

1958:   Mother Paul*; Elizabeth "Liz" Doane

1959:   Arabella Frant; Madame Maigret; Kate Starte; Marla Trent

1960:   Forsythia Brown*; Kate Harris; Emmy Tibbett* (U.S.)

1962:   Myra Savage (U.S.)

1963:   Hillary Brand*; June Beattie Grant

1964:   Telzey Amberdon*; Maxene Dangerfield*; Charmian Daniels*(U.S.); Kate Fansler*; Mary Morgan Kelly*; Sue Carstairs Maddox; Selena Mead

1965:   Modesty Blaise*; Jane Boardman; Amanda Curzon*; Emma Greaves*; Anna Zordan*

1966:   Sibyl Sue Blue; Mrs Elma Craggs (U.S.); Lee Crosley*; April Dancer*; Emily Pollifax*; Effie Schlupe*

1967:   Madame Dominique Aubry (U.S.); Felicia Dawlish; Eve Drum*; Julia Homberg*; Freya Matthews; Emma Peel*; Sylvia Plotkin*; Regina; Charity Ross; Paola Smith; Lucilla Edith Cavell Teatime*

1968:   Julie Barnes of Mod Squad*; Angel Brown*; Bernarda "Bunty" Felse* (U.S.) Dominique Frayne; Tracy Larrimore*; Amanda Nightingale*; Stevie O'Dowda; Christie Opara*; Miss Emily Seeton*; Dr. Grace Severance*; Katy Touchfeather

1969:   Lisa Clark*; Gail Rogers Mitchell; Jennifer Norrington* (U.K.); Claudine St. Cyr*; Kate Theobald*

1970:   Tessa Crichton* (U.K.); Kiss Darling*; Millicent Hetherege; Hon. Constance Morrison-Burke*; Deirdre O'Connor; Sheila Roath; Charity Tucker*

1971:   Cherry Delight*; Donna Bella*; Cynthia Godwin; Lucy Ramsdale*; Helga Rolfe*(U.K.); Kitty Telefair*

1972:   Lucy Beck*; Arlette Van Der Valk Davidson*; Laurie Grant*; Cordelia Gray (U.K.); Jacqueline Kirby*; Octavia "Tavy" Martin (U.S.); Norah Mulcahaney*; Hilary Quayle*

1973:   Vicky Bliss*; Thea Crawford; Helen Blye Horowitz*; Cleopatra Jones; Melinda Pink*; Baroness Penelope St. John-Orsini*

1974:   Shauna Bishop*; Vera Castang; Catherine Alexander Douglas*; Rosa Epton* (U.S.); Ann Fielding Hales; Susan Silverman*; Kate Weatherly*

1975:   Pepper Anderson*; Claire Reynolds Atwell*; Helen Bullock*; Constance Cobble; Amelia Peabody Emerson*; Angela Harpe*; Ms Squad; Dr. Nora North*; Molly Owens*; Minnie Santangelo; Bea Wentworth*

1976:   Jannine Austin*; Edwina Charles* (U.K.); Julie Hayes*; Hannah Land; Natasha O'Brien; Lexey Jane Pelazoni; Anna Peters*; Rebecca Rosenthal; Jaime Sommers (The Bionic Woman); Morgan Studevant

1977:   Mici Anhalt*; Jana Blake; Charlie's Angels*; Betty Crighton Jones*; Sharon McCone*; Jemima Shore*; Persis Willum*

1978:   Marilyn Ambers*; Kay Barth*; Tory Baxter*; Margaret Binton*; Dulcie Bligh; Darby Castle; Virginia Freer*; Helen Keremos*; Hildy Pace*; Maxine Reynolds*; Delia Riordan*; Sarah Saber; Helen Marsh Shandy; Terry Spring*

1979:   Adrienne Bishop; Janna Brill*; Cody* (U.K.); Maggie Courtney*; Charlotte Eliot; Margo Franklin*; Carol Gates*; Alison B. Gordon*; Kate Graham; Anna Jugedinski*; Sarah Kelling*; Valerie Lambert*; Ann Lang; Pauline Lyons*; Megan Marshall; Charlotte Ellison Pitt*; Maggie Rome*; Penelope Spring*; Julia Sullivan; Nell Willard

Volume 2

1980:   T. T. Baldwin*; Juliet Bravo* a.k.a. Jean Darblay; Ginny Fistoulari*; Karen Kovacs*; Clarissa Lovelace*; Joan Stock*; Amy Tupper; Alicia Von Helsing; Janet Wadman (Rhys)*; Delilah West*

1981:   Cathy McVeigh Carter*; Sr. Mary Theresa "Emtee" Dempsey*; Fiona Fitzgerald*; Davina Graham* (U.S.); Lt. Sigrid Harald*; Dittany Henbit; Viera Kolarova; Julia Larmore, Selena Jardine, and perhaps Hilary Tamar*; Anna Lee* (U.S.); Jill Smith*; Lizzie Thomas* (U.S.); Lettie Winterbottom*

1982:   Charity Day; Sarah Deane*; Maggie Elliott*; Sgt. Carollee Fleetwood; Tamara Hoyland* (U.S.); Helen Markham; Kinsey Millhone*; Eugenia Potter*; Rebecca Schwartz*; Nila Wade*; V. I. Warshawski*

1983:   Mona Moore Dunbar; Norma Gold*; Jennifer Grey*; Judy Hill*; Roz Howard*; Cass Jameson*; Kyra Keaton; Elena Olivarez*; Julie Tendler Oliver; Jocelyn O'Roarke*; Bridget O'Toole*; Dolly Rawlins (U.K.); Fiona Kimber-Hutchinson Samson* (U.S.); Harriet Unwin*; Rosie Vicente*; Elizabeth Lamb Worthington*

1984:   Gillian Adams*; Lauren Adler; Rev. Claire Aldington*; Sarah Cable*; Jenny Cain*; Agnes Carmichael* (U.S.); Iris Cooper*; Kate Delafield*; Vejay Haskell*; Rachel Hennings; Sgt. Hilary Lloyd (U.S.); Elizabeth MacPherson*; Dr. Tina May*; Patience "Pay" McKenna*; Mary Frances "M. F" Mulrooney; Pam Nilsen*; Sr. Mary Helen O'Connor and Kate Murphy*; Amelia Trowbridge Patton (U.S.); Andrea Perkins*; Deb Ralston*; Clio Rees (Marsh)*; Eleanor Roosevelt*; Abigail "Sandy" Sanderson*; Ellie Simon (Haskell)*; Ms Michael Tree*

1985: Liz Archer a.k.a. Angel Eyes*; Kate Baeier* (U.S.); Susan Bright*; Sabina Carpenter; Liz Connors*; Serendipity "Sarah" Dahlquist; Donna Miro and Lorna Doria; Geraldine Farrar; Jessica Fletcher*; Fiora Flynn*; Paula Glenning*; Glad Gold; Ellie Gordon*; Celia Grant* (U.S.); Marion Larch*; Isabel Macintosh*; Stoner McTavish*; Michelle Merrill*; Cassandra Mitchell*; Rain Morgan*; Theresa "Terri" Morrison; J. D. Mulroy; Rita Gardella O'Dea; Deirdre O'Hara* (CAN); Celia Prentisse; Maggie Ryan*; Rachel Sabin; Lucy Shannon; Gertrude Stein and Alice B. Toklas; Kate Trevorne; Alexandra "Alex" Winter; Matilda Worthing*

1986: Jane Britland; Rosie Caesare; Sarah Calloway*; Doran Fairweather*; Theresa Fortunato; Cynthia Frost; Judith Hayes (U.S.); Calista Jacobs*; Gwen Jones*; Rina Lazarus (Decker)*; Denise Lemoyne; Claire Malloy*; Tish McWhinny*; Susan Melville*; Debbie Miles*; Kate Miskin; Ella Nidech; Molly Palmer-Jones*; Molly Rafferty*; Joan Spencer*; Joanna Stark*; Penny Wananwake* (U.S.)

1987: Finny Aletter; Jane Bailey*; Maggie Bennett*; Mavis Bignell* (U.S.); Dr. Marissa Blumenthal; Carlotta Carlyle*; Marlene Ciampi (Karp)*; Lisa Davis; A. J. Egan; Lindsay Gordon*; Lonia Guiu (U.S.); Meg Halloran*; Arly Hanks*; Jennifer Heath*; Nikki Holden; Bonnie Indermill*; Willa Jansson*; Charlotte Kent*; Raina Lambert*; Annie Laurance (Darling)*; Constance Leidl*; Daisy Marlow; Alvira Meehan*; Melita Pargeter* (U.S.); Amanda Pepper*; Caitlin Reese*; Countess Aline Griffith Romanones*; Quin St. James*; Sara Spooner; Dee Street* (U.K.); Dixie Flannigan Struthers*; Kate Byrd Teague; Anna Tyree*; Dee Vaughn*; Emma Victor*; Jane Winfield (Hall)*

1988: Samantha Adams*; Carol Ashton*; Angela Benbow and Caledonia Wingate*; Kori Price Brichter*; Sydney Bryant*; Angel Cantini; Laura Di Palma*; Trixie Dolan and Evangeline Sinclair* (U.S.); Lydia Fairchild*; Kit Franklyn*; Ingrid Langley Gilliard* (U.S.); Rachel Gold*; Neil Hamel*; Barbara Havers*; Susan Henshaw; Sara Joslyn; Meg Lacey; Loretta Lawson* (U.S.); Kate Maddox*; Daphne Matthews*; Georgia Lee Maxwell; Nina McFall*; Mom*; Karen Orr; Claire Parker* (U.S.); Marvia Plum*; Lady Margaret Priam*;

Catherine Sayler*; Aline Scott*; Hana Shaner; Veronica Sheffield; Veronica Slate*; Sabina Swift; Tina Tamiko; Ann Tate; Sally Tepper; Sheila Travis*; Jane Tregar; Claudia Valentine* (AUS.); Gillian Verdean*; Evelyn Wade

1989:   Beth Austin*; Margaret Barlow*; Bertha Barstow; Martha "Moz" Brant*; Rhea Buerklin; Emma Chizzit*; Kat Colorado*; Katharine Craig; Sandrine Casette Curry*; Dr. Janet Eldine (U.S.); Nina Fischman*; Phryne Fisher* (AUS); Anne Fitzhugh; Sgt. Molly Flanagan; Sarah Fortune*; Clara Dawson Gamadge*; Peg Goodenough; Blanche Hampton*; Kate Henry* (U.S.); Lady Jane Hildreth* (U.S.); Maggie Hill and Claire Conrad; Zee Madeiras Jackson; Harriet Jeffries*; Jane Jeffry*; Helena Justina*; Jennifer Terry Kaine*; Mavis Lashley*; Jane Lawless*; Darina Lisle* (U.K.); LuEllen*; Sheila Malory*; Dawn Markey; Chris Martin* (U.K.); Jennie McKay*; Rosie Monaghan (AUS); Cassie Newton; Rita Noonan; Abby Novack (McKenzie)*; Lee Ofsted*; Peggy O'Neill*; Kieran O'Shaughnessy*; Carrie Porter; Georgina Powers* (U.K.); Anabel Reed (Smith)*; Amanda Roberts*; Rune*; Vonna Saucier; Emma Shaw (U.S.); Lisa Thomas (AUS); Diane Tregarde*; Helen West; Leslie Wetzon and Xenia Smith*; Johanna "Jo" Wilder; Grace Willis; Francesca Wilson* (U.S.); Miriam Winchester

Volume 3

Whether or not a character has made three or more significant appearances, as shown by an asterisk, is based upon information through June 2003 and is subjective in nature.

1990:   Irene Adler*; Gabrielle "Gabe" Amato; Connie Bartholomew*; Goldy Bear (Schulz)*; Mildred Bennett*; Helen Black*; Claire Breslinsky*; Paris Chandler; Edwina Crusoe*; Lark Dailey (Dodge)*; Abigail Danforth*; Poppy Dillworth*; Flavia Di Stefano*; Brigid Donovan*; Faith Sibley Fairchild*; Charlotte Graham*; Mary Minor "Harry" Haristeen*; Alison Hope*; Jerusha "Jeri" Howard*; Dewey James*; Jessica "Jesse" James*; Jazz Jasper*; Sister Joan*; Joanne "Jo" Kilbourn* (CAN); Willow King*; Michelle "Micky" Knight*; Skip Langdon*; Hester Latterly*; Lavinia London; Philipa Lowe*

(U.K.); Annie MacPherson*; Cat Marsala*; Shirley McClintock*; Madison McGuire*; Jayne Meadows*; Alice Nestleton*; Chicago Nordejoong*; Patricia "Pat" Pratt*; Gwen Ramadge*; Lucia Ramos; Cassandra Reilly*; Dr. Kay Scarpetta*; Aurora "Roe" Teagarden*; Nicky Titus*; Nikki Trakos; Holly Winter*

1991: Jessie Arnold*; Sophia "Sophy" Bancroft; Kate Berman; Petronella "Petey" Biggers ; Verity "Birdie" Birdwood*; Julie Blake*; Rev. Theodora Braithwaite*; Nell Bray*; Hollis Carpenter; Midge Cohen; Dr. Kate Coyle*; Melissa Craig*; Lauren Crowder*; Jan Gallagher*; Simona Griffo*; Dr. Bernadette "Bernie" Hebert; Barbara Holloway*; Lil Hubbert*; Kate Jasper*; Virginia Kelly*; Libby Kincaid*; Amanda Knight; Lauren Laurano*; Whitney Logan; Devon MacDonald*; Wanda Mallory*; Judith McMonigle (Flynn)*; Kathy McNeely; Francesca Miles*; Robin Miller*; Meredith "Merry" Mitchell*; Lane Montana; Dr. Jean Montrose* (U.K.); Kate Mulcay (one earlier book in 1958 as Kate Kincaid)*; Kathleen "Kit" Powell; Danielle "Dani" Ross*; Cynthia Chenery "C.C." Scott; Claire Sharples*; Anna Southwood* (AUS); Delta Stevens*; Blaine Stewart*; Lucy Stone*; Jane Tennison*; Rev. Ziza Todd; Ginny Trask; Ronnie Ventana*; Liz Wareham; Fanny Zindel

1992: Kristin Ashe; Temple Barr*; China Bayles*; Molly Bearpaw*; Becky Belski; Christine Bennett*; Eleanor "Ellie" Bernstein; Judy Best*; Elizabeth Blair*; Joanna Blalock*; Nora Bonesteel*; Victoria "Vic" Bowering*; Smokey Brandon*; Harriet Bushrow*; Rosalie Cairns*; Claire Camden*; Beth Marie Cartwright; Dr. Jessica Coran*; Karen Crist*; Victoria Cross; Jane da Silva*; Molly DeWitt*; Catherine Edison; Elizabeth Elliot*; Casey Farrel*; Sister Frevisse*; Leslie Frost; Nell Fury*; Julia "Callahan" Garrity*; Charlie Greene*; Liz Gresham*; Leah Hunter*; Laura Ireland; Sarah Keane; Lucy Kingsley*; Kate Kinsella* (U.S.); Deborah Knott*; Emma Lord*; Marti MacAlister*; Maggie MacGowen*; Caroline Masters*; Christine McCall*; Annie McGrogan; Laura Michaels*; Kate Millholland*; Britt Montero*; Freddie O'Neal*; Maddy Phillips*; E. J. (Eloise Janine) Pugh*; Agatha Raisin*; Regan Reilly*; Lil Ritchie; Maxene St.

Clair*; Charlotte Sams; Kate Shugak*; Diana Speed; Lee
Squires*; Elena Timofeyeva*; Glynis Tryon*; Samantha
Turner*; Amanda Valentine*; Jackie Walsh*; Dimity
Westwood and Lori Shepherd*; Blanche White*; Hannah
Wolfe*; Susan Donavan Wren*; Eve Wylie* (U.K.)

1993: Laura Ackroyd*; Cherry Aimless and Nancy Clue*; Angelina
"Angie" Amalfi*; Angela Biwaban *; Barbara "Bo" Bradley*;
Joanna Brady*; Kate Brannigan*; Sr. Cecile Buddenbrooks*;
Caley Burke*; Maxey Burnell*; Catherine "Cat" Caliban*;
Nora Callum*; Clare and Mirinda Cliveley; Henrietta
"Henrie" O'Dwyer Collins*; Nancy Cook; Mary DiNunzio;
Jessica Drake*; Kay Engels; Laura Fleming*; Insp. Liz
Graham*; Amanda Hazard*; Martine "Marty" Hopkins*;
Kate Ivory*; Gemma James*; Hepzibah Jeffries*; Claire
Claiborne Jenner*; Tyler Jones*; Alison Kaine*; Irene Kelly*;
"Kimmey" Kruse; Barrett Lake*; Catherine LeVendeur*;
Wynsome "Wyn" Lewis*; Kathryn Mackay*; Kate MacLean*;
Royce Madison*; Kate Martinelli*; Dr. Lauren Maxwell*; Dr.
Anna McColl* (U.K.); Alix Nicholson; Kathleen
O'Shaughnessy;* Jane Perry*; Anna Pigeon*; Dr. Amy
Prescott*; Gin Prettifield; Imogen Quy; Nan Robinson*;
Laney Samms*; Beth Seibelli (Cole)*; Phoebe Siegel*; Cecily
Sinclair*; Sydney Sloane*; Teal Stewart*; Sergeant Stone*;
Kathryn Swinbrooke*; Alex Tanner*; Iris Thorne*; Elizabeth
Anne "Betty" Trenka*; Robin Vaughan*; Madame Victoire
Vernet; Lucie D'Arby Wilton (Archer)*(U.S.); April Woo*

1994: Kathryn "Kate" Ardleigh*; Cat Austen*; Kate Austen*;
Johnnie Baker; Thea Barlow*; Liz Broward; Charlotte
Carter; Brooke Cassidy (Devlin)*; Molly Cates*; Olivia
Chapman; Emily Charters*; Lydia Chin*; Gail Connor*;
Candi and Simone Covington*; Fey Croaker*; Daisy
Dalrymple*; Peaches Dann*; Tess Darcy*; Queenie Davilov;
Angie DaVito; Patricia Delaney*; Louise Eldridge*; Queen
Elizabeth I*; Lynn Evans; Phoebe Fairfax* (CAN); Caz
Flood* (U.K.); Merry Folger*; Margo Fortier*; Jill Francis*;
Angela Gennaro*; Sophie Greenway*; Mackenzie "Mac"
Griffin*; Anneke Haagen (Genesko)*; Marina Haines; Emily
"Em" Hansen*; Benni Harper*; Matilda Haycastle*; Tamara
Hayle*; Karen Hightower a.k.a. Bast*; Samantha Holt*;

Harriet Hubbley* (CAN); Robin Hudson*; Jo Hughes*
(U.S.); Sal Kilkenny* (U.K.); Sgt. Kathy Kolla* (U.K.);
Thea Kozak*; Robin Light*; Margaret Loftus; Dottie
Loudermilk; Joanna Mackenzie*; Lt. Gianna "Anna"
Maglione; Kathleen Mallory*; Saz Martin*; Angela Matelli*;
Dr. Gail McCarthy*; Nuala Anne McGrail*; Elizabeth
"Tenny" Mendoza; Tori Miracle*; Kate Murray; Jordan
Myles*; Dr. Deirdre "Didi" Nightingale*; Veronica Pace*;
Lorraine Page* (U.K.); Daisy Perika*; Stephanie Plum*;
Laura Principal*(U.K.); Sarah "Quill" Quilliam*; Carmen
Ramirez; Tammi Randall*; Mary Russell (Holmes)*; Desiree
"Dez" Shapiro*; Emily Silver; Jane Smith a.k.a. Stella the
Stargazer*; Emily Stone*; Liz Sullivan*; Cassandra "Cassie"
Swann* (U.S.); Alix Thorssen*; Mary "Ike" Tygart*; Dr.
Anne Vernon; Penelope Warren*; Catherine "Cat" Wilde*;
Elizabeth "Liz" Will; Jolie Wyatt*; Magdalena Yoder*;
Wilhelmena "Helma" Zukas*

1995:   Hannah Barlow*; Ginger Barnes*; Lilly Bennett*; Sonora
Blair*; Bel Carson*; Dr. Elizabeth Chase*; Ella Clah*;
Cheryl Crane*; Lt. Eve Dallas*; Jane Day*; Eve Elliott*;
Colleen Fitzgerald; Maggie Garrett; Ariel Gold*; Natalie
Gold*; Jennifer Gray*; Gale Grayson*; Mother Lavinia
Grey*; Elizabeth Halperin; Kate Harrod*; Sharon Hays*;
Helen Hewitt (U.K.); Holly-Jean Ho*; Vicky Holden*; Liz
James*; Elena Jarvis*; Caroline "Fremont" Jones*; Sam
(Samantha) Jones*; Carol Jordan*; Lisa King; Sara Kingsley;
Fran Tremaine Kirk*; Dee Laguerre; Dr. Calista "Cal" Marley*;
Dorothy Martin*; Ophelia O. Meredith; Lydia Miller; Michelle
"Mitch" Mitchell*; Phyllida Moon*; Charlotte "Charlie"
Parker*; Joanna Piercy*; Garner Quinn*; Savannah Reid*; Nina
Reilly*; Schuyler Ridgway*; Sophie Rivers*; Claudia Seferius*;
Jo Beth Sidden*; Margo Simon*; Marguerite Smith*; Dr. Sylvia
Strange*; Judith Thornton*; Melanie Travis*; Jane Turner; Jane
Whitefield*; Kate Wilkinson*; Kay Williams ; Francesca
"Fran" Wilson* (U.S.)

1996:   Rachel Kaminsky Alexander*; Margit Andersson; Lady Aoi;
Jane Austen*; Hollis Ball*; Lily Bard*; Tory Bauer*; Vicky
Bauer*; Jane Bee*; Josephine Blake*; Sister Agnes Bourdillon*;
Lucy Trimble Brenner; Lindsay Chamberlain*; Alexandra

Cooper*; Ruby Crane*; Ruby Dark*; Venus Diamond*; Starletta Duvall*; Sister Fidelma*; Suze Figueroa*; Fizz Fitzgerald*; Lucy Freers; Sen. Theresa Galloway*; Eleanor "Norie" Gorzack; P. J. Gray*; Perdita Halley*; Beth Hartley*; Dido Hoare*; Patricia Anne Hollowell and Mary Alice Crane a.k.a. The Tate Sisters*; Emma Hudson*; Cassidy James*; Texana Jones*; Julia Lambros*; Renee LaRoche; Heaven Lee*; Lt. Tory Lennox; Molly Masters*; Cassidy McCabe*; Dr. Anne Menlo; Abigail Moon*; Kali O'Brien*; Allison O'Neil; Dr. Andi Pauling*; Karen Perry-Mondori*; Josie Pigeon*; Caro Radcliffe; Emma Rhodes*; Benedetta "Bennie" Rosato*; Nicolette "Nick" Scott*; Barbara Simons; Guadalupe "Lupe" Solano* (U.K.); Bert and Nan Tatum*; Abby Timberlake*; Hannah Trevor*; Lucy Wayles*; Fiona Wooten "Biggie" Weatherford*; Molly West; Ruth Willmarth*

1997:   Mali Anderson*; Lady Susanna Appleton*; Kate Banning*; Danielle Barnea*; Miriam Bartimaeus; Alma Bashears; Ursula Blanchard*; Kathryn Bogert*; Helen Bradley*; Dr. Temperance "Tempe" Brennan*; Dr. Clare Burtonall*; Filomena "Fil" Buscarsela*; Sister Rose Callahan*; Letty Campbell*; Carrie Carlin*; Kate Cavanaugh*; Rachel Crowne; Meg Darcy*; Delilah Doolittle*; Mandy Dyer*; Kay Farrow; Josephine "Jo" Fuller*; Judy Hammer*; Nanette Hayes*; Marti Hirsch*; Primrose Holland; Stevie Houston*; Liu Hulan*; Casey Jones*; Jackie Kaminsky*; Loretta Kovacs*; Gloria Lamerino*; Rosie Lavine; Munch Mancini*; Nell Matthews*; Dr. Haley McAlister; Lara McClintoch*; Sutton McPhee*; Maris Middleton*; Brenda Midnight*; Tess Monaghan*; Ruthie Kantor Morris; Lorelei Muldoon; Jane Nichols; Pat North* Tru North*; "Torie" O'Shea*; Martha Patterson; Karen Pelletier*; Charlie Plato*; Rachel Porter*; Maggy Renard; "Sukey" Reynolds*; Amelia Sachs*; Meredyth "Mere" Sanger*; Rei Shimura*; Grace Smith*; Helen Sorby*; Dr. Michael Stone*; Dr. Evelyn Sutcliffe* (first book in a different form was published in 1988); Tory Travers*; Rose Trevelyan*; Tessa Vance; Fran Varaday*; Francesca Vierling*; Connor Westphal*; "Chas" Wheatley*; MacLaren Yarbrough

1998:   Billie August and Emma Howe; Allida "Allie" Babcock*;
        Holly Barker; Janet O'Hara Barkin*; Madeline Bean*; Eliza
        Blake; Jane Candiotti; Caroline Canfield; Nikki Chase;
        Laura Chastain*; Sunny Childs*; Wyanet "Wy" Chouinard*;
        Kathryn "Casey" Collins; Regan Culver*; Robyn Devara
        (CAN); Eve Duncan; Lady Alix Dunraven*; Dixie Flannigan*;
        Carole Ann Gibson*; "Meg" Gillis; Susan Given; Hester
        Gorse*; Ann Hardaway*; Honey Huckleberry*; Kirsten;*
        Sierra Lavotini*; Magdalena "Maggie" Maguire*; Trish
        Maguire*; Hannah Malloy and Kiki Goldstein*; Jennifer
        Marsh*; Emily "Blue" McCarron; Karen McDade; Portia
        McTeague; Adele Monsarrat*; Kellie Montgomery*; Teddy
        Morelli*; Cordelia Morgan; Taylor Morgan; May Morrison;
        Kendall O'Dell; Maureen O'Donnell; Laura Owen; Lily
        Pascale; Molly Piper; Kate Power* (U.K.); Narcissa Powers
        and Judah Daniel*; Precious Ramotswe*; Ruby Rothman*;
        Dodee Swisher* ; Sydney Teague*; Jacobia Tiptree*; Serena
        Wilcox*; Charlotte Willett*

1999:   Bel Bickoff Barrett*; Sarah Decker Brandt*; Lily Brewster*;
        Olivia Brown; Rev. Lily Connor; Sarah Booth Delaney;
        Betsy Devonshire*; Cora Felton and Sherry Carter*; Jane
        Ferguson and Hillary Scarborough*; Augusta Goodnight*;
        Annabelle Hardy-Maratos; Sally Harrington*; Hannah Ives*;
        Hilda Johansson*; Charlotte Justice; Leigh Koslow*;
        Magdalene la Batarde*; Meg Langslow*; Aimee Leduc; Gilda
        Liberty*; Victoria "Vicky" Lucci*; Camilla McPhee; Claire
        Montrose*; Rachel O'Connor*; Jake O'Hara*; Jimi Plain;
        "Sunny" Randall; Claire Rawlings*; Marla Shore*; Bretta
        Solomon*; Jane Stuart*; Torrey Tunet; Anna Turnipseed*;
        Tessa Vance; Claire Watkins*

About the Author

Colleen A. Barnett was born in Green Bay, Wisconsin, the daughter of a trial attorney and his wife. She earned bachelor's and master's degrees in Political Science from the University of Wisconsin in Madison. She remained at home to raise a family of seven children after her marriage to attorney John Barnett, but returned to work when her youngest child was in grade school.

Colleen has since worked as a volunteer coordinator and social work supervisor for a county department of Social Services. She took early retirement from Social Services, to re-enter the University of Wisconsin Law School where she received her law degree cum laude.

Later she was employed as an attorney and mediator, and as a lecturer in Political Science at the University of Wisconsin Center-Richland. She is currently retired and working on Volume 3 of *Mystery Women*.

Over the years, Colleen has built a personal library of over 4,000 volumes, concentrating her collection on mysteries featuring women sleuths. She is a member of Sisters in Crime.

To receive a free catalog of other Poisoned Pen Press titles, please contact us in one of the following ways:

Phone: 1-800-421-3976
Facsimile: 1-480-949-1707
Email: info@poisonedpenpress.com
Website: www.poisonedpenpress.com

Poisoned Pen Press
6962 E. First Ave. Ste 103
Scottsdale, AZ 85251